American Foreign Policy

American Foreign Policy

A History / to 1914

THIRD EDITION

Thomas G. Paterson
University of Connecticut

J. Garry Clifford
University of Connecticut

Kenneth J. Hagan
United States Naval Academy

D. C. HEATH AND COMPANY
Lexington, Massachusetts   Toronto

Cover: *Armistice Day, 1918* by Gifford Beal (Indiana University Art Museum)

Published simultaneously in Canada.

Printed in the United States of America.

International Standard Book Number: 0-669-12664-0

Library of Congress Catalog Card Number: 87-81183

6 7 8 9 0

For

COLIN GRAHAM PATERSON

CAROL DAVIDGE

VERA LOW HAGAN

Preface

As scholars we are proud that *American Foreign Policy* represents some of our best research and writing, gratified that our colleagues in the United States and abroad have appreciated its up-to-date scholarship, and pleased that students have found it both challenging and entertaining. The opportunity to offer a third edition meant that we could improve the two volumes based upon users' and reviewers' critical suggestions, our own ongoing research, and the latest historical literature, and bring the story forward to the present.

Writing a survey book is necessarily a learning experience, for the authors must read and synthesize the prolific work of fellow scholars. We have brought our own research in primary sources and our own interpretations to this synthesis, but the scholarship of our friends and colleagues in diplomatic history has proven indispensable. We have cited their contributions in our extensive footnotes and in the bibliographic sections, and we gratefully acknowledge their contribution to this third edition and the earlier two.

We have designed this book to include the tools needed to study American diplomatic history. The illustrations, many of them rare and unusual prints selected from depositories in the United States, Great Britain, and elsewhere, have been closely integrated with the text. Their captions elaborate material in the text and offer additional material. The book also includes maps, charts, and graphs to render the historical record precise and complete. Each chapter presents a listing of the Presidents and Secretaries of State, with their terms of office, and the Appendix adds the Chairmen of the Senate Foreign Relations Committee, the Secretaries of Defense, and Assistants to the President for National Security Affairs. The footnotes and "Further Reading" sections, reflecting recent scholarship, will assist the curious in further exploration, as will the General Bibliography and its lists of reference works, documents, bibliographies, and overviews of relations with specific countries and regions and of subjects such as "intelligence," "nuclear arms race," "President," and "propaganda."

For continuity, thoroughness, and thematic unity, we have treated in each chapter such basic points as the comparative influence of ideology, economics, and strategy, the importance of personalities and styles, domestic politics, bureaucratic and executive-legislative competition, criticisms of and alternatives to American foreign policy, definitions of the national interest, historical "lessons," measurements of American power, and the impact of American interventions on other cultures. We emphasize the theme of expansionism. "People" are central to history as both actors and victims. Thus we have incorporated a good deal of biography in the diplomatic story and have liberally quoted participants and scholars, letting them speak for themselves. Each chapter opens with a "diplomatic crossroad," a significant event that helps illustrate the chief characteristics and issues of the era. The opening episode is then placed in its large historical context and the main themes and characters of the period are discussed. Chronological and topical sections follow next. Each chapter closes with a discussion of the legacy of the period—the lessons each generation bequeathed to the next generation of Americans.

Thomas G. Paterson initiated this project and coordinated its development. He wrote most of Chapters 5, 6, 8, 9, 10, 12, 13, 14, 15, and 16, and shared in writing Chapters 4 and 11. J. Garry Clifford wrote most of Chapters 1, 2, and 3 and shared in writing chapter 11. Kenneth J. Hagan wrote most of Chapter 7 and shared in writing Chapter 4. In all three editions, the authors criticized one another's work, interchanged suggestions and ideas frequently, and worked as a team to ensure a unified book.

In this third edition we have completely revised Chapters 5 and 16. In all other chapters we have incorporated new research and interpretations. New maps, charts, illustrations, and captions appear throughout. The "Further Reading" sections, Appendix, and General Bibliography have been revised and updated. We have also increased our coverage of the nuclear arms race, United States relations with Canada and Africa, and the impact of nineteenth-century United States expansion on Native Americans.

The People's Republic of China in the late 1970s adopted a new system for rendering Chinese phonetic characters into the Roman alphabet. Called the Pinyin method, it replaced the Wade-Giles technique, which had long been used in English. The United Nations, United States Board of Geographic Names, *National Geographic, Foreign Affairs,* and many other newspapers and journals shifted to the new Pinyin system, and, accordingly, we have also. Many changes are minor and pose no problem: Mao Tse-tung, for example, has become Mao Zedong and Shan-tung has become Shandong. But when we first use a possibly confusing Pinyin spelling, we have put the Wade-Giles spelling in parenthesis—for example, Jiang Jieshi (Chiang Kai-shek) or Beijing (Peking). Some names deeply rooted in English usage, such as Canton, have not been changed.

Many people have assisted us in preparing this third edition. We acknowledge with sincere thanks the reviews and comments provided by Richard Bradford, Kinley J. Brauer, John Coogan, Reginald Horsman, Thomas M. Leonard, John Offner, David M. Pletcher, Stephen G. Rabe, William W. Stueck, Jr., Duane Tananbaum, and Jonathan G. Utley. We also appreciate the recommendations of Melville T. Kennedy, Jr., Salvatore Prisco, Michael Roskin, and Elbert B. Smith. We thank Lisa Ferriere, Roberta Lusa, and Diedra Gosline for typing, and Barney J. Rickman, III, Ann Balcolm, and David Sheinen for research and suggestions.

We are also pleased to recognize again the assistance we received during the preparation of the first and second editions. We thank Robert Beisner, R. Christian Berg, Kinley J. Brauer, Paul Goodwin, Alan Henrikson, Gregg Herken, George Herring, Michael Hunt, Burton Kaufman, Thomas Lairson, Lester D. Langley, Dennis Merrill, Jean-Donald Miller, Stephen Rabe, Thomas G. Smith, Mark Stoler, Ralph E. Weber, Edmund S. Wehrle, Joan Hoff Wilson, and Thomas Zoumaras for reading all or parts of the manuscript and improving it. For other assistance in the first and second editions, we thank Richard Baker, Richard Dean Burns, Carol Davidge, Mark Del Vecchio, Justus Doenecke, Xavier Franco, James Gormly, Eric Hafter, Edythe and Richard Izard, Chen Jian, Leith Johnson, Burton I. Kaufman, Herman Mast, Robert McMahon, R. Kent Newmyer, Holly I. Paterson, Wayne Repeta, Anna Lou Smethurst, George Turner, Sol Woolman, and Li Yan. We continue to appreciate the valuable, if not always respectful, comments of the midshipmen at the U.S. Naval Academy.

We welcome comments on *American Foreign Policy* from both students and instructors.

T.G.P.

J.G.C.

K.J.H.

Contents

Chapter **1** **An Independent American Foreign Policy: The Beginnings to 1789**

Diplomatic Crossroad: Jay, Franklin, and Adams and Independent
  Negotiations, 1782 3
Reaching for Independence: Principle and Reality 6
The French Connection 12
Cutting Diplomatic Teeth in Europe 17
Peace Without Propriety: The Treaty of Paris 20
Awkward Diplomacy under the Articles of Confederation 24
The New Constitution and the Legacy of the Founding Fathers . . 30
Further Reading for the Period to 1789 34
Notes to Chapter 1 35

Chapter **2** **Independence and Expansion in a World at War, 1789–1815**

Diplomatic Crossroad: The *Chesapeake* Affair, 1807 39
Europe's Wars, America's Crises 42
Commerce, Politics, and Diplomacy: Jay's Treaty 46
Pinckney's Treaty, France, and Washington's Farewell 49
The XYZ Affair and the Quasi-War with France 52
The Louisiana Purchase and Empire for Liberty 58
Blockades and Impressment: The Perils of Neutral Trade, 1803–1807 . . 62
"Peaceable Coercions" and the Coming of the War of 1812 65
War for Sovereignty by Land and Sea 69
Wartime Diplomacy and the Peace of Ghent 72
Europe's Wars and American Independence, 1789–1815: The Legacy . . 75
Further Reading for the Period 1789–1815 77
Notes to Chapter 2 78

Chapter **3** **Making Way for Continental Expansion, 1815–1848**

Diplomatic Crossroad: Mexican-American War on the Rio Grande, 1846   81
Manifest Destiny or Manifest Design: The Roots of Expansionism   84
Commercial Empire on the Pacific   89
Nibbling and Swallowing Florida   91
The Monroe Doctrine Clears the Way   94
Anglo-American Accommodations and Tensions   99
Contest over Oregon   103
Taking Texas   105
Wartime Diplomacy and the Peace   109
The Lessons and Costs of Continental Expansion, 1815–1848   113
Further Reading for the Period 1815–1848   117
Notes to Chapter 3   118

Chapter **4** **Sputtering Expansionism, Sectionalism, and Civil War Diplomacy, 1848–1865**

Diplomatic Crossroad: Commodore Perry's "Opening" of Japan, 1853–
  1854   121
Sectionalism and Sputtering Expansionism   124
The South's Dream of Empire: Filibustering and Slave Expansion   128
Cuba by Hook or by Crook   132
Nudging the British out of Central America   135
1861: Year of Crises   138
"Lookers On" Across the Atlantic   143
"A Power of the First Class": The Expansionist Revival   146
Further Reading for the Period 1848–1865   148
Notes to Chapter 4   149

Chapter **5** **Global Rivalry, Regional Power, 1865–1895**

Diplomatic Crossroad: The Foiled Grab of Santo Domingo, 1869–1870   153
Expansionism, Imperialism, and Nationalism   156
Economic Expansion and Foreign Policy   158
Toward Command of the Seas: Naval Expansion   161
Secretary William H. Seward Eyes the Future   163
North American Rivals: Great Britain, Canada, and the United States   166

Contending with Asia: China, Japan, and Korea 168
Pacific Prizes: Hawaii and Samoa 172
Probing the "Dark Continent": Americans in Africa 175
Regional Power: The United States in Latin America 178
Further Reading for the Period 1865–1895 182
Notes to Chapter 5 183

Chapter **6** **Imperialist Thrust, 1895–1900**

Diplomatic Crossroad: The Venezuelan Crisis, 1895 187
American Foreign Policy After Venezuela 191
The Making of American Foreign Policy in the 1890s 194
The Cuban Revolution and the United States, 1895–1897 195
The Road to War: McKinley's Diplomacy, 1897–1898 197
Why War: Exploiting Opportunity 200
The Spanish-American-Cuban-Filipino War 203
Peace and Empire: The Debate in the United States 205
Asian Challenges: The Philippine Insurrection and the Open Door in China 207
Toward World Power, 1895–1900 212
Further Reading for the Period 1895–1900 213
Notes to Chapter 6 214

Chapter **7** **Managing and Extending the American Empire, 1900–1914**

Diplomatic Crossroad: Taking Panama, 1903 217
The Conservative Shapers of the American Empire 223
The Cuban Protectorate 226
Policing the Caribbean: Venezuela, the Dominican Republic, and the Roosevelt Corollary 229
The Quest for Stability in Haiti and Nicaragua 231
Meddling in Mexico 233
The Open Door and Dollar Diplomacy in East Asia 239
The Anglo-American Rapprochement 244
American Foreign Policy on the Eve of the "Great War" 248
Further Reading for the Period 1900–1914 252
Notes to Chapter 7 254

Appendix

Makers of American Foreign Policy   i

General Bibliography

Reference Works   v
Documents (Collections and Series)   vi
Bibliographies   vi
Overviews of Relations with Countries and Regions   vii
Overviews of Subjects   x

Index
                                                                                                xv

Maps and Graphs

The United States After the Treaty of Paris, 1783   25
American Naval Battles, 1798–1815   57
Looking West, 1803–1807   60
The War with Mexico   82
United States Territorial Expansion   111
The Asian Frontier   125
The Southern Perspective on Expansion   129
United States Trade Expansion, 1865–1914   158
The Colonization of Africa, Turn of the Century   177
The Great Powers in Asia, 1900   210
Panama Canal Zone   220
United States Interventions in the Caribbean   232

American Foreign Policy

French Snuffbox. Benjamin Franklin's reputation as a representative of frontier America is captured in a contemporary French snuffbox. In this compliment the revered gentleman from Pennsylvania joins two other philosophers, Rousseau and Voltaire. (The Metropolitan Museum of Art, Gift of William H. Huntington, 1883. All rights reserved.)

An Independent American Foreign Policy: The Beginnings to 1789

DIPLOMATIC CROSSROAD:
JAY, FRANKLIN, AND ADAMS AND INDEPENDENT NEGOTIATIONS, 1782

Two disgruntled Americans rode the same carriage from Versailles to the Parisian suburb of Passy on the afternoon of August 10, 1782. John Jay and Benjamin Franklin had just spent a frustrating two hours with the French Foreign Minister, the Comte de Vergennes. These American peace commissioners, seeking to end the Revolutionary War for independence waged since 1775, had asked for French advice on two troublesome problems that had arisen in their concurrent negotiations with British and Spanish representatives. Since the Continental Congress had instructed them to make no decisions without the knowledge and counsel of the French, Jay and Franklin had asked Vergennes whether or not the United States should insist on explicit recognition of independence from England *prior* to a final peace treaty with the "mother country," and whether the western boundary of the new American nation should be the Mississippi River. On both points Vergennes and his secretary, Gerard de Rayneval, made suggestions that seemed to deny American interests. Do not worry about technicalities, Vergennes advised. If independence were made an article of the final treaty, as the British were proposing, Americans should not make a fuss about formal titles during the negotiation. Regarding the western boundary, according to Jay, Vergennes and Rayneval made it clear that "we [Americans] claimed more than we had a right to," and that Spain and England had valid claims to territory east of the Mississippi.[1]

Jay and Franklin wondered why their French ally was giving such negative advice. Jay was particularly suspicious, telling his older colleague that Vergennes was plotting to delay negotiations with England so that Spain, having captured West Florida, could acquire the whole Gulf Coast and additional territory to the north. Franklin agreed that Spain wanted to "coop us up within the Allegheny Mountains," but he did not think that the French were deliberately sacrificing American interests in order to gratify Spain.[2] The discussion than became extremely animated, and when the carriage reached Passy, Franklin invited Jay inside his apartment to continue their conversation. "Have we any reason to doubt the good faith of the King of France?" inquired Franklin. "We can depend on the French," Jay rejoined, "only to see that we are separated from England, but it is not in their interest that we should become a great and formidable people, and therefore they will not help us to become so." Franklin asked on whom the United States should rely. "We have no rational dependence except on God and ourselves," Jay solemnly answered. The Pennsylvanian shot back: "Would you deliberately break Congress' instructions?" "Unless we violate these instructions the dignity of Congress will be in the dust," Jay asserted. The seventy-five-year-old Franklin pressed further: "Then you are prepared to break our instructions if you intend to take an independence course now." Jay stood up. "*If* the instructions conflict with America's honor and dignity I would break them—like this!" The dignified New Yorker threw his long clay pipe hard into Franklin's fireplace. It shattered.[3]

Nothing that occurred in the diplomacy of the next several weeks elevated John Jay's opinion of Europeans in general, or of Frenchmen and Spaniards in particular. In early September, after further discussions about a suitable western boundary, Rayneval gave Jay a memorandum of "personal ideas" to expedite peace negotiations with England as well as a boundary settlement with Spain. Again, arguing from historical precedent, Rayneval urged the Americans not to press for the Mississippi. Jay, despite Rayneval's "personal" disclaimers, correctly assumed that the memorandum also reflected Vergennes' sentiments. A few days later Rayneval disappeared from Paris, having been dispatched on a secret mission to London. Jay was immediately suspicious. Paris was buzzing with rumors. Even the usually unflappable Franklin became worried. Perhaps Rayneval's mission was designed to bring the same arguments to the British that he was making to the Americans; perhaps France sought the role of arbiter in North America, supported British claims north of the Ohio River, and wanted to give Spain full control over the Mississippi. The next day Jay received from a British agent in Paris an intercepted French dispatch, in cipher, which urged a strong stand against American claims to the Newfoundland fisheries. Franklin cautiously pointed out that this dispatch, sent by a French envoy in America, did not necessarily reflect the views of Vergennes or King Louis XVI. It was enough for Jay, however. On September 11, without first informing Franklin, Jay boldly sent his own secret emissary to London with the proposal that secret and separate negotiations for peace begin at once. The British jumped at the chance to split the Franco-American alliance. When he learned what his younger colleague had done, Franklin protested. But he went along.

By the time the third American peace commissioner arrived in Paris, private talks with the British had gone on for several weeks. John Adams had just successfully negotiated a commercial treaty with the Dutch. He had been in Paris earlier in the war and did not like the French; nor did he like Dr. Franklin, whom he thought too cozy with the French. The cantankerous New Englander found it difficult to trust anyone, but he immediately found a kindred spirit in Jay, who apprised him of the state of the negotiations. He warned Jay that Franklin was hopelessly subservient to Vergennes. Like Jay, Adams thought that Vergennes opposed American expansion and kept "his hand under our chin to prevent us from drowning, but not to lift our heads out of the water."[4] Adams dallied for four days before making a courtesy call on Franklin. Once at Passy, Adams immediately launched into a lecture. Everything Jay had done was correct. Jay was right in his suspicions toward Vergennes. Jay was right to insist on prior independence, access to the fisheries, and extensive western boundaries. Adams waxed enthusiastic about the decision to ignore Vergennes and negotiate separately with the British on these issues. To do otherwise would be leaving "the lamb to the custody of the wolf."[5] His conscience unburdened, Adams returned to his apartment in the Hotel du Roi.

Franklin hardly replied to Adams' outburst. Suffering from the gout, the old philosopher listened patiently and tolerantly to the person he later described as "always an honest man, often a wise one, but sometimes, and in some things, absolutely out of his senses."[6] Franklin agreed that the United States should remain firm on both the fisheries and the Mississippi boundary. Access to the Newfoundland fishing grounds was vital to New England's economy, while the "Father of Waters" stood as an indispensable highway for trans-Allegheny commerce. "A Neighbor might as well ask me to sell my Street Door," he had said to Jay regarding the Mississippi.[7] What bothered Franklin was the failure to consult Vergennes. French loans had kept America solvent through six long years of war, and French ships and troops had contributed mightily to the decisive victory at Yorktown in 1781. Franklin valued the French alliance. "If we were to break our faith with this nation," he wrote, "England would again trample on us and every other nation despise us."[8] Unlike his younger colleagues, Franklin was not convinced that the French were dealing with Spain and England behind American backs. Nevertheless, Franklin realized the importance of a united front in negotiations. Always a pragmatist, he had written in his *Autobiography*: "So convenient a thing it is to be a *reasonable creature*, since it enables one to find or make a reason for everything one has a mind to do."[9] Franklin decided to be reasonable. The next day, October 30, just prior to meeting with the British commissioners, he startled John Jay: "I am of your opinion, and will go with these gentlemen in the business without consulting this court."[10]

Franklin remained true to his word, and on November 30, 1782, England and the United States signed a "preliminary treaty" of peace. The terms, enumerated in a comprehensive treaty some ten months later, guaranteed American independence and provided generous boundaries. It was, in the words of historian Samuel Flagg Bemis, "the greatest victory in the annals of American diplomacy."[11]

The American decision to negotiate separately in 1782 was as symbolic as it was successful. By going to war with England, the colonies had sought to win their independence, enlarge their commerce, and expand their territorial domain. Patriot leaders hoped to attain these goals without getting entangled in European politics. One motive for independence was the desire to escape the constant wars and dynastic intrigues that characterized eighteenth-century Europe. But victory required help. France became America's ally in 1778, and in the next two years Spain and the Netherlands also joined the war against England. The war for American independence hence became part of a world war. The entanglements Americans hoped to avoid inevitably followed. At the critical moment in the peace negotiations, Jay and Adams rightly suspected that their French ally, although committed to American independence, did not share the expansive American vision of that independence. The two commissioners thereupon persuaded Franklin to pursue an *independent* course, take advantage of European rivalries, and extract a generous treaty from the British. In Adams' eyes especially, these American diplomats were

John Adams (1735–1826). Native of Braintree (Quincy), Massachusetts, graduate of Harvard, Boston lawyer, colonial rebel, and diplomat, Adams helped negotiate the treaty of peace with England. Introspective, analytical, and courageous, Adams became President in 1797. (The Metropolitan Museum of Art, Purchase, 1960. Harris Brisbane Dick Fund. All rights reserved.)

6

"Blessed Are the Peacemakers." In this critical British cartoon of 1783 a Spaniard and Frenchman lead George III by the neck while Lord Shelburne carries the "Preliminaries of Peace." The procession is commanded by an American wielding a whip and tugging a sulking, boorish Dutchman. (British Museum)

Blessed are the PEACE MAKERS

maintaining American honor by breaking instructions which French diplomats had forced on a pliant Congress. It was an ironic moment. Americans said they pursued independence and empire not merely for selfish motives, but also for a more civilized mode of international relations, free from the monarchical double-dealing of European power politics. "We are fighting for the dignity and happiness of human nature," Franklin had stated rather grandly in 1777.[12] To gain their ends, however, Franklin, Jay, and Adams employed the same Machiavellian tactics that they despised in Europeans.

REACHING FOR INDEPENDENCE: PRINCIPLE AND REALITY

The United States could not have won independence from England without assistance from France. This was the inescapable fact of early American diplomacy. However much the patriots of 1776 wanted to isolate themselves from the wars and diplomatic maneuverings of Europe, European events provided them with the opportunity for national liberation.

The century-old rivalry between France and England for pre-eminence in Europe and control of North America provided the immediate backdrop for the American Revolution. Four wars fought between 1688 and 1763 were European in origin, but had profound consequences in the New World. The most recent war, 1756–1763, called the Seven Years War in Europe and the French and Indian War in America, had ensured the virtual elimination of French power from North America. By the Treaty of Paris (1763) the defeated French ceded Canada and the Ohio Valley to the British and relinquished Louisiana to the Spanish. Spain, in turn, gave up the Floridas to England. For the most part colonial leaders cheered the victorious British war for empire. Benjamin Franklin, then a colonial agent in England, urged removal of the French from Canada. "I have long been of opinion," he wrote in 1760, "that the foundations of the future grandeur and stability of the British empire lay in America. . . . All the country from the St. Lawrence to the Mississippi will be in another century filled with British people."[13] A youthful John Adams similarly predicted that with the defeat of "the turbulent Gallicks, our people according to the exactest computations, will in another century become more numerous than England itself."[14]

The euphoria was short-lived. As soon as the French and Indian War ended, London began to tighten the machinery of empire. A standing army of 10,000 men was sent to America for imperial defense. To pay for its upkeep, and to help defray the costs of the recent war with France, Parliament levied new taxes on the colonies. Old mercantile regulations forbidding direct American trade with foreign ports in the West Indies were now enforced. The Treaty of Ft. Stanwix in 1768 fixed the Ohio as the boundary for Indian lands and effectively curtailed American settlements west of the Alleghenies. The colonials retaliated with petitions, economic boycotts, and sporadic outbreaks of violence. Parliament responded with more taxes. The Tea Act of 1773 led to the Boston Tea Party, which, in turn, triggered the Coercive Acts. Galling to expansionist Americans, the Quebec Act of 1774 made the Ohio Valley an integral part of Canada. Armed resistance exploded at Lexington and Concord in the spring of 1775, followed by battles around Boston. Then came an abortive American invasion of Quebec in December, 1775. By this time John Adams and Benjamin Franklin were urging ties with the same "turbulent Gallicks" they had hoped to destroy twenty years before.

As American leaders moved cautiously toward independence, the emerging republican ideology, which embraced the "rights of Englishmen" and the principles of representative government, also contained the roots of an independent foreign policy. Historical lessons seemed to point toward independence. "I have but one lamp by which my feet are guided," said Patrick Henry in 1775, "and that is by the lamp of experience. I know of no way of judging the future but by the past."[15] Benjamin Franklin asked the central question: "Have not all Mankind in all Ages had the Right of deserting their Native Country? . . . Did not the Saxons desert their Native Country when they came to Britain?"[16] More specifically, Americans looked to their colonial past. As British mercantile restrictions tightened in the 1760s, colonial leaders began to argue that the imperial connection with England was one-sided, and that Americans were constantly embroiled in England's wars against their will. Attacks by the French and Indians along the northern frontier usually had their origins in European quarrels, yet Americans nevertheless had to pay taxes, raise armies, and fight and die. Britain did not always seem to appreciate colonial sacrifices. The most telling example occurred in 1745 when New Englanders, through good luck and enormous exertion, captured the strategic French fortress of Louisbourg on Cape Breton Island. In the European peace treaty three years later, however, the British handed back Louisbourg in exchange for French conquests in India. Americans had no wish to be pawns in England's colonial wars. Franklin probably exaggerated when he told Parliament in 1766 that the Americans had been in "perfect peace with both French and Indians" and that the recent conflict had been "really a British war."[17] He was nonetheless expressing what one scholar has called "a deep-seated feeling of escape from Europe and a strong tendency, encouraged by European diplomacy, to avoid becoming entangled in European conflict, whenever it was to their interest to do so."[18]

Americans advocating independence also found arguments in recent British history. Many of the same English Whig writers whom Americans quoted in defense of "no taxation without representation" had also taken part in a great debate over the direction of British foreign policy during the first half of the eighteenth century. These Whigs had criticized British involvement in continental European wars. Since the European balance of power was always unstable, they argued that continental entanglements might improve the German territorial interests of the House of Hanover but certainly not those of England. There was suspicion of England's German kings. "This great, this powerful, this formidable kingdom, is considered only as a province to a despicable electorate [Hanover]," William Pitt complained in 1743.[19] England's true interests, these Whigs never ceased to point out, lay in expanding its commerce and empire. Political alliances were taboo; they have not "produced any advantage to us."[20] One pamphleteer posited a general rule in 1744: "A Prince or State ought to avoid all Treaties, except such as tend towards Commerce or Manufactures. . . . All other Alliances may be look'd upon as so many Incumbrances."[21] The similarity between these arguments for British isolation from Europe and the later American rationale for independence is striking. American leaders were quite aware of the British debate. Benjamin Franklin, as a colonial agent in London in the pre-Revolutionary period, knew many of the Whig critics intimately. Merchants, lawyers, and plantation owners visited England or studied in England. In their desire to avoid British wars and British taxes, it was not surprising that Revolutionary leaders would appropriate British precepts.

Another source of American thinking on independence and foreign policy came in the writings of the French *philosophes.* As sons of the Enlightenment and spokesmen for the rising bourgeoisie, the *philosophes* launched an attack on all diplomatic and political practices that thwarted the proper rule of reason in international affairs. Traditional diplomacy was synonymous with double-dealing, they argued, "an obscure art which hides itself in the folds of deceit, which fears to let itself be seen and believes it can succeed only in the darkness of mystery."[22] Like the English Whigs, the *philosophes* emphasized commercial expansion over standard power politics. Political barriers were artificial; commerce tied the "family of nations" together with "threads of silk."[23] Trade should be as free as possible, unfettered by mercantile restrictions. Some *philosophes* hoped that enlightened princes could transform international relations; more radical writers like Condorcet wanted to take diplomacy out of the hands of princes and remove all obstacles to a direct expression of the popular will. "Alliances," wrote Condorcet, "are only means by which the rulers of states precipitate the people into wars from which they benefit either by covering up their mistakes or by carrying out their plots against freedom."[24] Diplomacy should be as simple as possible, consisting largely of commercial interchange between individual persons rather than governments. Such views impressed some Americans. Although historian James H. Hutson has shown that the *philosophes* were never as widely read or quoted in America as the English Whigs, their ideas provided Revolutionary leaders with a humanitarian credo as they sought to win independence and an empire from the British crown. Like John Winthrop's Puritans, they would not merely be benefiting themselves, but also erecting a model for the rest of the world. John Adams was quite sincere when he told Vergennes in 1781 that "the dignity of North America does not consist in diplomatic ceremonials. . . . [It] consists solely in reason, justice, truth, the rights of mankind, and the interests of the nations of Europe."[25]

The movement for an independent foreign policy reached its climax with the convocation of the Second Continental Congress, following Lexington and Concord, in the summer of 1775. "We are between the hawk and the buzzard," said delegate Robert Livingston of New York, and "we puzzle ourselves between the commercial and warlike opposition."[26] Some Americans who still wanted to remain within the British Empire held out hope that continued commercial opposition—no imports, no exports—would force Parliament and the King to negotiate. More radical delegates wanted to continue the war and declare independence. Benjamin Franklin proposed "articles of confederation" that would give Congress full power to make war and peace. John Adams called for construction of an American navy. Other advocates of independence urged the opening of American ports to foreign trade, arguing that only with protection from foreign navies could American merchant ships reach European ports. With their British market no longer available, the thirteen colonies needed commerce to survive. Foreign trade required foreign assistance. This argument for independence, made repeatedly behind the closed doors of Congress, finally became public on January 10, 1776, with the appearance of Thomas Paine's pamphlet *Common Sense*.

Tom Paine was an English Quaker who had come to America in 1774. While in England he had drunk deeply at the well of Whig dissent, and once in Philadelphia he became friends with the faction of Congress aspiring to independence. Their arguments were summarized in Paine's pamphlet. Opposing further petitions to the King, urging construction of a navy and the immediate formation of a confederation, emphasizing the need for foreign assistance, and calling for the opening of American ports to the rest of the world, Paine's celebrated call for independence also spelled out the benefits of an independent foreign policy. Not only was reconciliation with England no longer possible, it was undesirable as well. As Paine put it with some exaggeration, there was not "a single advantage that this continent can reap by being connected with Great Britain." On the contrary, "France and Spain never were, nor perhaps ever will be, our enemies as Americans, but as Our being subjects of Great Britain." For Paine and his American friends, "Our plan is commerce, and that, well attended to, will secure us the Peace and friendship of all Europe; because it is in the interest of all Europe to have America as a free port. . . . As Europe is our market for trade, we ought to form no partial connection with any part of it. It is the true interest of America to steer clear of European contentions."[27] As soon as independence was declared, he predicted, Europe would compete for America's commercial favors. America would benefit, and so would the rest of the world. Of course, part of what Paine wrote was more nonsense than "common sense," particularly his playing down of privileges that Americans enjoyed as part of the British Empire. Americans would miss British naval protection, British credit, and easy access to the British West Indies after independence. The pamphlet was effective propaganda nonetheless. More than 300,000 copies of *Common Sense* were sold, the equivalent of one copy for every ten persons living in the thirteen colonies in 1776. "For a long time," concluded historian Felix Gilbert, "every utterance on foreign policy [in the United States] starts from Paine's words and echoes his thoughts."[28]

Paine emphasized the attraction of American commerce and assumed that a foreign nation would assist America to protect that trade. With the abortive invasion of Canada in the winter of 1775–76 and the arrival of British reinforcements, it became obvious that some foreign help was necessary for survival. Congress opened American ports in April, 1776, but Paine's logic seemed irrefutable: no foreign power would openly aid the American rebels until independence was a declared fact. Virginia's Richard Henry Lee, on June 6, offered a resolution: "These United Colonies are, and of right ought to be, free and independent States."[29] Lee echoed Paine's thoughts. "No State in Europe," he explained to Patrick Henry, "will either Treat or Trade with us so long as we consider ourselves Subjects of G.B. . . . It is not choice . . . but necessity that calls for Independence, as the only means by which foreign Alliances can be obtained."[30] Thomas Jefferson wrote the Declaration of Independence and Congress endorsed it on July 4, 1776.

The next step was to secure foreign support. Congress designated a committee to prepare a "model treaty" to be presented to the French court. The committee's so-called "Plan of 1776," which Congress debated in August, would also serve as the basis for alliances with other countries. A final, amended version then accompanied Benjamin Franklin to France when he was named American minister at the end of the year. John Adams was the principal author of the Model Treaty. Like Paine, the lawyer from Braintree eschewed political entanglements. "I am not for soliciting any political connection, or military assistance, or indeed naval, from France," he told a friend. "I wish for nothing but commerce, a mere marine treaty with them."[31] Adams' imprint on the Model Treaty was obvious, for it was almost

Thomas Paine (1737–1809). This working-class Englishman found his way to Philadelphia in 1774, where he took a job as a journalist and became caught up in the excitement of the independence movement. He wrote the anti-British *Common Sense* in 1776, a "best-seller" in its day. The irascible Paine joined the Continental Army and later participated in the French Revolution. (National Gallery of Art)

purely a treaty of commerce and navigation, which would permit American ships free entry into French ports while French military supplies entered American ports in ever increasing quantities. Included also were elaborate rules protecting neutral commerce in wartime. The Model Treaty suggested that the United States and France grant the nationals of each country the same "Rights, Liberties, Privileges, Immunities and Exemptions" in trade, but that if "his most Christian Majesty shall not consent" to such a novel idea, then the American commissioners should try to obtain a most-favored-nation clause, whereby American merchants would receive the same commercial benefits enjoyed by other nations.[32]

The only political obligation in the Model Treaty came in Article VIII, which stipulated that America would not aid England in any conflict between Britain and France. Some of his closest friends in Congress, Adams later recalled, "thought there was not sufficient temptation to France to join us. They moved for cessions and concessions, which implied warranties and political alliance that I had studiously avoided."[33] The New Englander argued strenuously for the original wording; like most Americans in 1776, he feared that France, if offered political inducements, might demand Canada and access to the Newfoundland fisheries, both of which the new republic sought for itself. Even a motion to offer France concessions in the West Indies was defeated in Congress. Although their expectations proved somewhat naive, Adams and his colleagues were convinced that the ending of England's monopoly over North American commerce, accomplished through American independence, would by itself suffice to gain French support.

The neutral rights provisions of the Model Treaty deserve special attention. Although these commercial articles would not apply to the war against England, in which the United States was already a belligerent, they formed the basis of what later became America's historic policy of "freedom of the seas." Lifted almost word for word from earlier treaties involving powers with small navies, these commercial clauses guaranteed the principles of "free ships, free goods" (that is, the neutral flag protected noncontraband cargoes from capture), the freedom of neutrals to trade in noncontraband between ports of belligerents, a restricted and narrowly defined list of contraband materials exempting naval stores and food-stuffs from seizure, and a generally liberal treatment of neutral shipping. Such principles of neutral rights were becoming increasingly accepted in the late eighteenth century, particularly among enlightened publicists and countries lacking large navies. Although England had accepted liberal provisions in a few individual treaties, British statesmen were understandably reluctant to endorse them as international law. In a war against an inferior naval power, the British believed that the enemy would allow neutral shipping to carry its commerce, thus protecting its own vulnerable vessels from capture. Moreover, if neutrals were permitted to supply an enemy nation freely, especially with naval stores, it would not be long before Britain's maritime supremacy would be undermined. Americans, on the other hand, looking ahead to independence, envisaged future European wars and hoped, in the absence of political entanglements, to expand their commerce at such times. France, in the event of a naval war against the more powerful British, would benefit from American neutrality. Americans could fatten their pocketbooks and at the same time serve mankind by supporting more civilized rules of warfare.

The Model Treaty, then, introduced the main themes of early American foreign policy. It set forth the ideal of commercial expansion and political isolation, or, as

Thomas Jefferson later put it: "Peace, commerce, and honest friendship with all nations, entangling alliances with none."[34] By specifically binding France against acquiring Canada, it also projected a continental domain for America beyond the thirteen coastal settlements. But did the Model Treaty project goals that could be achieved? Historian Walter LaFeber has pointed out a central dilemma of early American diplomacy, namely, "a longing for landed and/or commercial expansion without having to make the requisite political commitments."[35] To Benjamin Franklin fell the mission to determine whether Adams' "mere marine treaty" was sufficient to secure French assistance.

THE FRENCH CONNECTION

Patriot leaders did not err in thinking that France would aid American independence. Indeed, in the years following the humiliating peace of 1763, when France had been stripped of its empire, the compelling motive of French foreign policy was *revanche*. The French foreign minister in the 1760s, the Duc de Choiseul, smacked his lips at England's colonial troubles. "There will come in time a revolution in America," he told the French King, "which will put England into a state of weakness where she will no longer be a terror in Europe. . . . The very extent of English possessions in America will bring about their separation from England."[36] Americans knew of this intense French preoccupation. "All Europe is attentive to the dispute," Benjamin Franklin wrote from London in 1770, "and I . . . have a satisfaction in seeing that our part is taken everywhere."[37] Aside from strengthening the Bourbon Family Compact with Spain and sending secret observers to North America, France made no overt moves to intervene before Choiseul left office in 1770.

The decision to succor the Americans fell to Choiseul's successor, Charles Gravier, the Comte de Vergennes. Suave, polished, outwardly unemotional, Vergennes looked every inch the model of a successful diplomat of the ancien régime. In actuality, there was a streak of impetuosity in him (he had risked his diplomatic career by carrying on a secret liaison with a Franco-Turkish widow and then marrying her against the wishes of the French court), and when the American colonies began their armed rebellion, he adopted the motto *Aut nunc aut nunquam* ("now or never").[38] A perfect scheme for aiding the insurrectionaries short of war presented itself early in 1776 in the person of Pierre Augustin Caron de Beaumarchais. The adventurous author of the *Barber of Seville* proposed to set up a dummy trading company, Rodrigue Hortalez and Company, to be headed by himself, through which munitions and other military supplies could be clandestinely shipped to the American colonies. The French court (and perhaps the Spanish as well) could provide secret financing. Vergennes jumped at Beaumarchais' idea and set about persuading a reluctant Louis XVI. In a remarkable memorandum, Vergennes listed the advantages that would accrue to France from American independence:[39]

> First, it will diminish the power of England, and increase in proportion that of France. Second, it will cause irreparable loss to English trade, while it will considerably extend ours. Third, it presents to us as very probable the recovery of a part of the possessions which the English have taken from us in America, such as the fisheries of Newfoundland. . . . We do not speak of Canada.

The Comte de Vergennes (1717–1787). Charles Gravier, the Comte de Vergennes and the French foreign minister under Louis XVI, sought to delay formal war with England until the French navy was better prepared. Then he thought he could rearrange the balance of power. According to the historian Jonathan Dull, Vergennes "did not want to crush Britain; he merely wished to teach her some humility." (Library of Congress)

Beaumarchais (1732–1799). This man of intrigue aided the American rebels through a dummy company that put the Franco-American relationship on a path to alliance. Ironically, Beaumarchais later became a go-between in the embittered XYZ affair of 1797–1798, which eventually led to the formal ending of that alliance. (New York Public Library)

By May of 1776, before any American agent reached France and even before the Declaration of Independence, Paris took the plunge. One million livres (about $200,000) was secretly transferred from the French Treasury to Beaumarchais' "company." Charles III of Spain made a similar grant, and the first shipments of muskets, cannon, powder, tents, and clothing soon began to cross the Atlantic. By the time of Franklin's arrival in December, 1776, then, French assistance was an established fact. Whether this assistance could be converted into recognition and a formal treaty remained to be determined.

Franklin took Paris by storm. Plainly dressed and wearing a comfortable fur cap, the seventy-year-old philosopher was already well known to Frenchmen. *Poor Richard's Almanac,* with its catchy aphorisms, had run through several French editions, and Franklin's electrical experiments and philosophical writings had earned him honored membership in the French Academy. Parisians expected Franklin to be the personification of Rousseau's natural man, and he did not disappoint them. Disarmingly modest, soft-spoken, attentive to the ladies of the court, Franklin won friends everywhere. The British Ambassador, Lord Stormont, immediately recognized that he was "a very dangerous engine" and might soon win open French support.[40] Vergennes warmed to him. Franklin's kindly features were soon appearing on medals and snuffbox covers. The ladies of the French court adopted a *coiffure à la Franklin* in imitation of his omnipresent fur cap, and no social affair could be a success without his presence. Not without hyperbole, John Adams noted that the old Philadelphian was "so fond of the fair sex that one was not enough for him, but he must have one on each side, and all the ladies both old and young were ready to eat him up."[41] Franklin explained the intricacies of physics to Queen Marie Antoinette, played chess with the Duchesse de Bourbon, and even proposed marriage to the wealthy Madame Helvetius. The lady in question avoided Franklin's entangling alliance, but her "careless, jaunty air" and the fact that she kissed the "Good Doctor" in public scandalized Abigail Adams. "I was highly disgusted and never wish for an acquaintance with any ladies of this cast," she wrote.[42] It was, withal, a popular triumph unmatched by an American abroad. Thomas Jefferson did not exaggerate when, on becoming minister to France in 1784, he said that he was merely succeeding Franklin, for no one could replace him.

Social popularity did not ensure diplomatic success, however. Vergennes might have recognized American independence prior to Franklin's arrival had not the successful British military campaign in New York in the summer of 1776 made the French court cautious. Recognition meant war with England, and the French were reluctant to proceed without Spanish assistance. Spain was dragging its feet. Although French loans and supplies continued through 1776 and 1777, Vergennes avoided any formal commitment until there was a sure sign of American military success. Then came Saratoga on October 17, 1777, a battle in which 90 percent of American arms and ammunition had come from French merchants. The defeat of "Gentleman Johnny" Burgoyne's troops in the forests of northern New York helped persuade England to send out peace feelers, with terms offering less than complete independence. Franklin was not averse to using the threat of reconciliation with England as a lever on Vergennes. A French diplomat asked Franklin what action was necessary to prevent Congress from coming to an agreement with England short of "full and absolute independence."[43] Franklin replied: "The immediate conclusion of a treaty of commerce and alliance would induce the

Benjamin Franklin (1706–1790) at the Court of France. The elderly philosopher-journalist-humorist-politician-diplomat fascinated the snobbish courts of France. He seems to have spent as much time on wooing the French privileged classes to the American cause as he did rallying mass public opinion in France. (Courtesy of Kenneth M. Newman, Old Print Shop, New York City)

Deputies to close their ears to any proposal which should not have as its basis entire liberty and independence, both political and commercial."[44] And so, on February 6, 1778, Vergennes and Franklin affixed their signatures to two pacts. The first, a treaty of amity and commerce, gave the United States most-favored-nation privileges (which meant that any commercial favors granted by France to other countries would also be enjoyed by America). The two nations also agreed on a definition of contraband and neutral rights that followed the articles of the Model Treaty.

The second pact, however, was a treaty of alliance, and it contained political commitments that departed from John Adams' original plan. Instead of the meager promise not to aid England if France entered the war for independence, Franklin had to agree not to make peace with the British without first obtaining French consent. Vergennes made a similar promise. Although Franklin managed to retain the prohibition against French territorial gains on the North American continent, the United States agreed to recognize any French conquests in the Caribbean and to guarantee "from the present time and forever" all French possessions in America and any others that might be obtained at the peace table. France paid an equivalent price. According to Article II, "The essential and direct End of the present defensive alliance is to maintain effectually the liberty, Sovereignty, and independence absolute and unlimited of the said United States, as well in matters of Gouvernement as of commerce." Vergennes also guaranteed "from the present time and forever" American "Possessions, and the additions or conquests that their Confederation may obtain during the war, from any of the Dominions now or heretofore possessed by Great Britain in North America."[45] While France made no specific commitment to help the Americans conquer Canada, Vergennes stood ready to guarantee whatever boundaries Franklin and his colleagues could wrest from England.

The French alliance seemed to constitute the kind of political entanglement that Thomas Paine and John Adams had warned against. Certainly the stipulation prohibiting any peace without French consent, as well as the guarantee of territories, "entangled" American interests in the foreign policies of another power. Congress had retreated considerably from the principles of 1776, having instructed Franklin to seek an alliance with Spain in which the United States would assist Spain in conquering Florida and declare war against Portugal in return for diplomatic recognition and outright military assistance. Such a treaty did not materialize, but the instructions indicated the extent to which Congress, after two years without a major victory, was willing to compromise its ideals for military help against Britain. Both Paine and Adams accepted the French alliance, Paine so enthusiastically that he became for a few years a paid propagandist for the French. Adams, after some initial hesitation, was soon calling the treaty "a rock upon which we may safely build."[46] The treaty did fulfill the most important of Adams' original expectations—that the political and economic independence of the United States from England would be too great a prize for France to pass up. French and American interests coincided on the issue of independence. The French dreaded "the United British Empire" so much that they could not possibly "let slip the opportunity of striking one pistol at least" from "an enemy who constantly threatened them with two."[47] Where French interests diverged was on the extent of American independence. Notwithstanding vows of self-denial regarding Canada, Vergennes had no wish to replace Britain with a great American empire that might eventually chase the French and the Spanish, as well as the English, out of the New World. "[T]hey would not stop here," he said in 1775, "but would in process of time advance to the Southern Continent of America and either subdue the inhabitants or carry them along with them, and in the end not leave a foot of that Hemisphere in the possession of any European power."[48] The French made a commitment to American independence, not expansion.

The French commitment was tested at the very beginning of the alliance. When the Elector Maximilian of Bavaria died, on December 30, 1777, Joseph II of Austria promptly occupied and annexed that German principality. Frederick the Great of Prussia virtuously went to war on behalf of Bavarian independence. Austria urged France, allied to Austria since 1756, to join the War of Bavarian Succession against Prussia. The Austrian Netherlands would be France's reward, the same Flanders that Louis XIV had coveted and for which French soldiers would die again in the twentieth century. Vergennes was not tempted. A war for Flanders would require peace with England just when the opportunity for revenge was greatest. Toward Austria, therefore, Vergennes slyly assumed the role of benevolent mediator, hoping to keep Europe quiet in order to concentrate on the maritime war against England. This mediation of the *Kartoffelkrieg* ("Potato War"), so-called because the starving soldiers of Austria and Prussia spent the winter of 1778–79 eating frozen potatoes, was successfully accomplished in 1779. Ironically enough, Emperor Joseph was not at all pleased with French interference, and when the opportunity

King George III (1738–1820). He ruled England from 1760 to 1820, progressively going insane. In 1787, for example, he alighted from his carriage in Windsor Park and addressed an oak tree as the King of Prussia. Although against leniency toward the rebellious Americans, his close relationship with Lord Shelburne led to the latter's appointment as Prime Minister and, consequently, to a generous peace settlement. (Courtesy of Her Majesty the Queen. Copyright reserved.)

presented itself in the summer of 1781, he returned the French favor and offered to mediate between Britain and France. Russia also joined in the mediation offer. Since it came at a low point in the military struggle in America, Vergennes might have been forced to accept Austro-Russian mediation (the terms of which would *not* have recognized American independence) in 1781 had not English King George III stubbornly resisted any solution short of complete submission by the American colonies. The point is clear: France, whatever the entanglements and temptations of the European continent, was bent on humiliating England. In Vergennes' steadfast opinion, the best way to accomplish that goal was to back American independence. By the end of the war in 1783 France had expended some 48 million livres (9.6 million dollars) in behalf of American independence.

CUTTING DIPLOMATIC TEETH IN EUROPE

Except for the successful alliance with France, there was something comic, even unseemly, about the futile search for treaties in European courts. Franklin himself had argued that "a virgin state should preserve the virgin character, and not go about suitoring after alliances, but wait with decent dignity for the application of others."[49] Congress, needing money and hoping for military assistance, ruled otherwise. Thus did American diplomats scurry to Berlin, Madrid, Vienna, St. Petersburg, Amsterdam, and other capitals in quest of alliances that never quite materialized. Frederick the Great had intimated that Prussia would recognize American independence if France did, but when William Lee arrived in Berlin, Frederick told his chief minister: "Put him off with compliments."[50] It was difficult for Americans to understand European hesitation. Fear of revolutionary principles, the danger of British retaliation, trading opportunities, and territorial ambitions closer to home—all made the European monarchies reluctant to challenge Britain, their jealousy toward British power notwithstanding. What America needed, John Adams concluded, was the shift by one neutral to belligerency. "Without it, all may nibble and piddle and dribble and fribble, waste a long time, immense treasures, and much human blood, and they must come to it at last."[51]

The Dutch were a case in point. With institutions of representative government firmly entrenched in the Dutch Estates General, one might have expected the Netherlands to be the first to recognize American independence. Not so. The burghers of Amsterdam were more interested in making money. Until Britain declared war on the United Provinces, in December, 1780, the Dutch busied themselves by carrying naval stores from the Baltic to France, as well as using their West Indian island of St. Eustatius as an entrepôt for contraband trade with the Americans. These activities, plus a willingness to join Catherine the Great's League of Armed Neutrality in the year 1780, led to war with England, but the Dutch steadfastly refused to sign a treaty with the United States until October, 1782, by which time the war was virtually over. John Adams, who negotiated the treaty of amity and commerce (following the "Plan of 1776"), could agree with a foreign visitor's assessment of Holland as "a land, where the demon of gold, crowned with tobacco, sat on a throne of cheese."[52] It should be noted, however, that while the Dutch treaty came too late to be of any military assistance in the war, Adams was also able to negotiate a loan of 5,000,000 guilders in June, 1782, from a consortium of Amsterdam bankers. This was the first of a series of Dutch loans, totaling some

9,000,000 guilders ($3,600,000), which served to sustain American credit through the 1780s.

American efforts to join the Armed Neutrality of 1780 marked another episode in futile diplomacy. Organized by Catherine II of Russia, the Armed Neutrality also included Denmark, Sweden, Austria, Prussia, Portugal, and the Kingdom of the Two Sicilies. Its purpose was ostensibly to enforce liberal provisions of neutral rights ("free ships, free goods," no paper blockades, narrow definition of contraband) in trading with belligerents. Never very effective (Catherine herself called it *cette nullité armée* [armed nullity]), the league seemed to hold out some hope for the American cause.[53] Because the Armed Neutrality's principles so closely resembled the "Plan of 1776," Congress immediately adopted its rules by resolution and commissioned a plenipotentiary to St. Petersburg to gain formal adherence to the league by treaty. It was an impossible mission. Aside from the obvious incongruity of a belligerent nation attempting to join an alliance of neutrals, it should have been obvious that Catherine, while no enemy of American independence, would not risk war with England by granting recognition prematurely. Her real purpose was to divert British attention while preparing to seize the Crimea from Ottoman Turkey. American envoy Francis Dana of Massachusetts spent two long years in the Russian capital without ever being received officially. Indeed, formal relations with Russia did not begin until 1809, when Catherine's grandson, Tsar Alexander I, received as American minister John Quincy Adams, who as a fourteen-year-old had been Dana's secretary during the abortive wartime mission.

There was another ironic epilogue. Once peace negotiations in Paris had established American independence in 1783, the Dutch government urged the United States to join the Armed Neutrality through a formal treaty with the Netherlands. At this point, however, with the war all but over, Congress reconsidered. In a resolution on June 12, 1783, Congress admitted that "the liberal principles on which the said confederacy was established, are conceived to be in general favourable to the interests of nations, and particularly to those of the United States," but there could be no formal treaty. The reason? "The true interest of these [United] states requires that they should be as little as possible entangled in the politics and controversies of European nations."[54] Thus, however much Americans desired freedom of trade for reasons of both profit and principle, they did not want to resort to political entanglements to achieve such an objective. The dilemma would have to be faced again and again.

The most frustrating diplomacy of all was with Spain. Despite previous financial support for the embattled colonials, and notwithstanding the outwardly close alliance with France (the Bourbon Family Compact), the government of Charles III was in no hurry to take up arms against England—especially if Spain's principal objective, reclamation of Gibraltar, could be obtained by other means. Moreover, in view of its own extensive colonial empire in the Americas, Spain was understandably less eager than France to encourage overseas revolutions. Not only might colonial rebellion prove to be a contagious disease, but a powerful American republic could threaten Spanish possessions as effectively as an expanding British Empire. Spanish Foreign Minister Count Floridablanca therefore hemmed and hawed, playing a double game by dickering with both France and England in the hope of regaining Gibraltar. Only by the Treaty of Aranjuez, signed on April 12, 1779, did Spain agree on war with England, and even then the alliance was with France, not with the United States. One article held enormous importance for

American diplomacy. Because of Madrid's obsession with Gibraltar, France agreed to keep on fighting until that rocky symbol of Spanish pride was wrested from the British. It will be remembered that, according to the terms of the Franco-American alliance of 1778, the United States and France had pledged not to make a separate peace and to continue the war until England recognized American independence. Now France was promising to fight until Gibraltar fell. In this curious, devious fashion, without being a party to the treaty or even being consulted, the Americans found their independence, in historian Samuel Flagg Bemis' memorable phrase, "chained by European diplomacy to the Rock of Gibraltar."[55] And because the terms of Aranjuez remained secret, American diplomats could only guess at these new political entanglements.

Congress sent John Jay to Madrid in September, 1779 to obtain a formal alliance. The handsome, thirty-four-year-old New Yorker of Huguenot descent did not have an easy time of it. Not once during his two-and-a-half-year stay was Jay officially received by the Spanish court. With Jay's mail opened and read and spies snooping everywhere, "only the lice in Spanish inns gave him a warm welcome," according to historian Esmond Wright."[56] Only rarely would Floridablanca deign to communicate with the American diplomat. Even more galling, Jay ran out of money and was forced to ask the Spanish for funds. There was also the personal tragedy of his infant daughter's dying shortly after Jay and his wife Sarah arrived in Madrid. The Spanish count did give Jay some $175,000, but only to keep the American dangling while he secretly negotiated with a British agent, Richard Cumberland, in the hope that Britain would accept outside mediation and cede Gibraltar. Fortunately for American diplomacy, George III remained as stubborn about Gibraltar as he did about American independence, and the Cumberland talks collapsed.

At one point in the summer of 1781 Jay received instructions from Congress that permitted him to give up the American demand for navigation of the Mississippi, if only Spain would recognize American independence and make an alliance. Such instructions reflected the dangerous military situation in the autumn of 1780, following the British capture of Charleston and successful invasion of the South. While personally believing it "better for America to have no treaty with Spain than to purchase one on such servile terms," Jay obediently sought an interview with the Spanish foreign minister.[57] After several weeks an audience was granted. The American made his proposal: a treaty relinquishing navigation rights on the Mississippi south of 31° north latitude, a Spanish guarantee to the United States of "all their respective territories," and an American guarantee to the Spanish King of "all his dominions in America."[58] Floridablanca refused. Had he accepted, the navigation of the "Father of Waters" and the boundary of West Florida—both destined to be troublesome issues in Spanish-American diplomacy—would have been settled to Spain's advantage. As it was, Floridablanca preferred to gamble, to put off that evil day of recognition. Already Spanish troops from New Orleans had occupied West Florida, and possibly they could claim more territory between the Mississippi and the Alleghenies. Rebuffed, Jay withdrew the concession on Mississippi navigation. He explained to Congress that if Spain refused to make an alliance during the war, the United States should be prepared to reassert its Mississippi claims in any final peace treaty. Congress endorsed his actions. Jay, by now, was furious with the Spaniards. "This government has little money, less wisdom, no credit, nor any right to it," he grumbled.[59] Moreover, he had begun to suspect, from conversations with the French ambassador in Madrid, that the French were encouraging Spain in its trans-Appalachian territorial ambitions. Indeed, by the end of his sojourn in Spain, John Jay had become, in historian Lawrence Kaplan's words, "an almost xenophobic American."[60] Jay's suspicious attitude was to have a decisive effect on the peace negotiations of 1782.

PEACE WITHOUT PROPRIETY: THE TREATY OF PARIS

The event that precipitated serious peace negotiations was the surrender of Lord Cornwallis' army at Yorktown on October 19, 1781. General Washington's French lieutenant, the Marquis de Lafayette, wrote home: "The play is over. . . . the fifth act has just ended."[61] George III stubbornly tried to fight on, but the burgeoning public debt and war weariness finally caused the ministry of Lord North to fall early in 1782. The King reluctantly accepted a new ministry under the Marquess of Rockingham, committed to a restoration of peace, but undecided as to what the terms should be.

The English sent an agent to Paris in April, 1782, to sound out Benjamin Franklin. The emissary, Richard Oswald, seemed a curious choice, his chief qualifications being a previous friendship with Franklin and first-hand knowledge of America, derived in part from the slave trade. Franklin sized up Oswald quickly. After introducing the British envoy to Vergennes and saying that the United States would make no separate peace without French concurrence, Franklin privately hinted to Oswald that reconciliation was possible if England granted complete independence and generous boundaries. Franklin even mentioned Canada. The American did not demand Canada, for England might find such a stipulation "humiliating." A voluntary cession, however, would have "an excellent effect . . . [on] the mind of the [American] people in general."[62] Oswald was struck by the suggestion and promised to try to persuade his superiors in London. "We parted exceedingly good friends," Franklin wrote in his journal.[63]

Peace talks stalled for the next several weeks, as the British were preoccupied by another Cabinet crisis. Not until Rockingham's death and Lord Shelburne's succession as Prime Minister on July 1 were the British able to agree on a

"**The American Rattlesnake.**" Coiled around the armies of Burgoyne and Cornwallis, the American snake gloats over triumph in 1782:

> Britons within the Yankeean Plains,
> Mind how ye March & Trench,
> The Serpent in the Congress reigns,
> As well as in the French.

(Library of Congress)

Cod Fishing, Newfoundland. In the land of the cod—New England—fishing, curing, and drying the fish was central to the economy. John Adams represented his native region well when he made sure that the treaty of peace preserved an American stake in Newfoundland waters, but the issue constantly disturbed American diplomacy thereafter. (Map Division, New York Public Library, Astor, Lenox and Tilden Foundations)

negotiating position, and even then Shelburne had to proceed cautiously for fear of offending his prickly sovereign. It was during this interval that Franklin summoned his fellow peace commissioners, Jay and Adams, to Paris. Jay, delighted to escape Madrid, arrived by the end of June. Adams continued commercial negotiations in the Netherlands and did not reach the French capital until October 26. In view of the subsequent American decision to disregard Congress's instructions and negotiate separately and secretly with the British, it should be noted that Franklin, in his initial conversation with Oswald, had intimated the possibility of a separate peace. The elderly American never told Vergennes of his suggestions concerning Canada. More trusting of the French than his younger colleagues (and more appreciative of the need for French assistance), Franklin nevertheless always placed American interests first. Whether in matters of the heart or in diplomatic relations, the philosopher from Philadelphia knew when to break the rules.

The success of the separate negotiations, which began in October and ended on November 30, owed much to the conciliatory attitude of Shelburne. An intuitive believer in natural rights and *"liberté du commerce"* through his friendship with French *philosophes*, the Prime Minister wanted very much to wean the United States away from the alliance with France. The peace terms were thus exceedingly generous; as Vergennes later put it: "The English buy the peace more than they make it."[64] Not only was the United States granted complete independence, but also the new nation's extensive boundaries (the Great Lakes and St. Lawrence River to the north, Mississippi River to the west, 31° line across Florida to the south) far surpassed what Americans had won on the battlefield. Any chance of obtaining Canadian territory was probably foreclosed by eleventh-hour British naval victories in the Caribbean and the failure of a combined French-Spanish siege of Gibraltar in September, 1782. With the issues of independence and boundaries easily settled, the most heated dispute occurred over the lesser articles of the treaty. The fisheries question caused much wrangling. The British commissioners argued that access to the fishing grounds off the Grand Banks of Newfoundland, as well as the right to dry and cure fish on Canadian shores, should be limited to citizens of the British Empire. The Americans disagreed. New England, where codfish was king and not George III, had a stubborn spokesman in John Adams. The Americans finally won their point, although the treaty ambiguously granted the "liberty" to fish, not the "right," thus perpetuating a controversy over which succeeding generations of diplomats (and succeeding generations of Adamses) would battle for more than a century.

Sharpest disagreement came over the twin issues of Loyalists and pre-Revolutionary debts. The British, quite understandably, sought generous treatment for the thousands of colonials who had been driven into exile for their loyalty to the Crown. The British negotiators wanted restitution of confiscated property, or at least compensation. The Americans remained adamant, especially Franklin, whose own son William, the former royal governor of New Jersey, had deserted to the British cause. Even the moderate Jay spoke of Loyalists as having "the most dishonourable of human motives" and urged that "every American must set his face and steel his heart" against them.[65] As to the debts, which consisted of some five million pounds owed by Americans (mostly Southern planters) to British merchants, there was a natural reluctance to repay obligations contracted prior to 1775. After considerable argument, Adams found an acceptable compromise. Vowing that he had "no Notion of cheating any Body," the redoubtable New Englander persuaded his colleagues to accept a formula whereby British creditors would "meet with no lawful impediment" in collecting their lawfully incurred debts.[66] This particular clause was instrumental in gaining the support of the British commercial classes for what was an otherwise unpopular treaty; as Adams put it, American concession on the debts prevented the British merchants "from making common Cause with the Refugees [Tories]."[67] The British, for their part, accepted an article in the treaty which forbade all further persecution of Loyalists and "earnestly recommended" to the states that properties seized during the war be restored. Because Congress could not dictate to the states under the Articles of Confederation, both the British and American commissioners understood that the "earnest recommendations" might not be followed.

The preliminary peace terms, because they obtained so much, were received enthusiastically in America. There were some worries that the independent negotiations might strain relations with France. Congress's Secretary for Foreign Affairs, Robert Livingston, informed the commissioners that "it gives me pain that the character for candor and felicity to its engagements which should always characterize a great people should have been impeached thereby."[68] As for Vergennes, the French foreign minister gave no rebuke to the Americans for failing to consult, saying only that they had "managed well."[69] Then, after two weeks of silence, Vergennes wrote plaintively to Franklin: "You are wise and discreet, sir; you perfectly understand what is due to propriety; you have all your life performed your duties. I pray to you to consider how you propose to fulfill those which are due to the [French] King?"[70] Franklin thereupon delivered one of the most beguiling replies in the history of diplomacy. He admitted that the American commissioners had been indiscreet—guilty of a lack of *bienséance* (propriety)—in not keeping the French fully informed, but he hoped that this indiscretion would not harm the alliance. "The English, I just now learn," he told Vergennes, "flatter themselves they have already divided us." Franklin added that he hoped the British would find themselves "totally mistaken."[71] The Frenchman said nothing more. In fact, he even agreed to an additional loan of some 6,000,000 livres, which Franklin had requested.

The mild French response was not difficult to explain. Vergennes, with Paris and Versailles honeycombed with spies, knew all along about the secret negotiations, even if the final terms seem to have startled him. He did not protest because he understood that England was indeed trying to break up the Franco-American alliance. Franklin's hint verified this. Moreover, the separate American peace offered Vergennes a way out of a sticky tangle with Spain. He could now tell the stubborn Spaniards that Gibraltar was no longer a practicable objective with the Americans effectively out of the war. To Vergennes the fact of American independence was more important than Gibraltar, and although he would have preferred a treaty that left the United States more dependent on France, he was not displeased with what Jay, Adams, and Franklin had accomplished. In Lawrence Kaplan's phrase, "even if Vergennes was serving his country first, he served America well."[72]

Peace negotiations between England and France, as well as England and Spain, took several months. The final Treaty of Paris was not signed until September 3,

"The General P--s, or Peace." The peace signed, Britain, the Netherlands, the United States, Spain, and France have put down their arms. Who would have thought, read this English cartoon of 1783, "that they'd so soon come to a general P---?" (Library of Congress)

1783. Except for some complications regarding Florida (Spain received the Floridas from England in the final treaty), the terms were precisely those of the preliminary treaty between England and the United States. America's diplomats had performed well in overcoming political entanglements and exploiting European rivalries. "Undisciplined marines as we were," said John Adams, "we were better tacticians than we imagined."[73] The more restrained assessment of historian Jonathan Dull is that American success "depended on a heavy dose of foreign help and abundant good luck" and "the moral of the American Revolution thus may be the unpredictability, the expense, and the danger of war."[74] To obtain both independence and empire, most would agree, was an impressive achievement.

AWKWARD DIPLOMACY UNDER THE ARTICLES OF CONFEDERATION

Americans were in an exuberant, expansive mood in 1783. "We have the experience of the whole world before our eyes," wrote Noah Webster in the preface to his famous speller. "It is the business of Americans to select the wisdom of all nations . . . [and] to add superior dignity to this infant Empire and to human nature."[75] Nearly half the national territory, some 220 million acres of wilderness, lay across the Appalachian chain, and the flood of emigrants westward, fleeing from heavy taxes to lower ones, from poorer to better lands, was inexorable. More than one hundred thousand Americans settled in Kentucky and Tennessee alone in the years between 1775 and 1790. As Jay put it in 1785, "a rage for emigrating to the western country prevails . . . and the seeds of a great people are daily planting beyond the mountains."[76] Peace also brought trading opportunities. Foreign ships could now enter American ports without fear of British retaliation. Americans could regain British markets for their agricultural exports, trade directly with other European countries, and develop as extensive and free a trade as possible with the rest of the world. One Massachusetts newspaper gave optimistic thanks "to the supreme ruler of the universe by whose beneficence our commerce is freed from those shackles it used to be cramped with, and bids fair to extend to every part of the globe, without passing through the medium of England, that rotten island."[77] The broad Atlantic would serve as both a highway of commerce and a barrier against European predators.

The optimism of 1783 was only partly fulfilled. Trade expanded rapidly in the years after the Revolution. Approximately 72,000 tons of shipping cleared America's busiest port, Philadelphia, in the year 1789, compared to an average of 45,000 tons in 1770-1772. Boston's tonnage increased from 42,506 in 1772 to 55,000 in 1788. Clearances in Maryland and Virginia doubled in volume over the figures from 1769. Tobacco exports brought a favorable balance of more than a million dollars a year in trade with France during the 1780s. By 1788 the Netherlands was importing more than four million dollars annually of tobacco, rice, and naval stores from the United States. Merchants were enterprising in gaining new markets. The *Empress of China,* the first American ship to trade with the Far East, set sail from New York in February, 1784, and reached Canton some six months later. The cargo was ginseng, which the Chinese believed would restore sexual potency to the aged. Another pioneering vessel, the *Columbia,* left Boston in 1787, wintered on the Pacific coast of North America near Vancouver Island, and traded metal trinkets to the Indians for otter furs. The *Columbia* then voyaged to China, exchanged the furs for tea, and returned to Boston—the first American ship to circumnavigate the

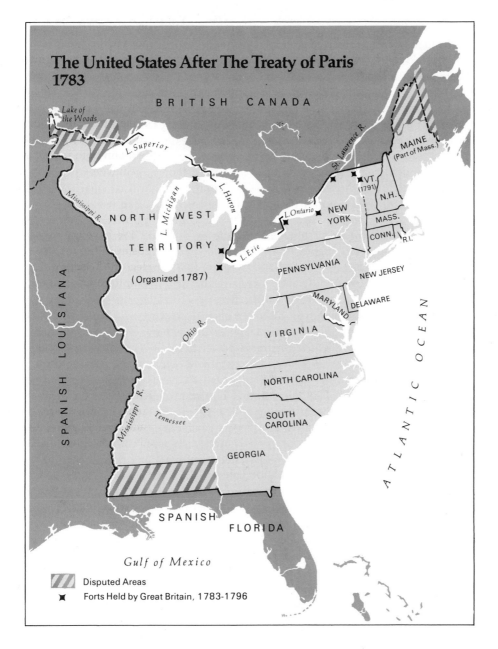

The United States After The Treaty of Paris 1783

globe. Other ships soon followed. Thus began a curiously complicated trade, which often included a stop at the Hawaiian (or Sandwich) Islands to pick up sandalwood for Chinese consumers; the trade brought profits to New England merchants for more than thirty years. On her second voyage, in 1792, the *Columbia* entered the mouth of the river named after her and thus helped establish the American claim to Oregon.

Despite the expansion of trade, the instant prosperity that many Americans expected in 1783 did not materialize. Part of the problem was the dual economic adjustment that the United States had to make—the changeover from a wartime to peacetime economy, and from a favored position within the British Empire to independent status in a world dominated by mercantilist restrictions. Because of commercial habits and British credit facilities, the bulk of American trade continued to be with England. In 1790, the earliest year for which full statistics are available, nearly half of all American exports went to England, while 90 percent of American imports originated in England. Fully three-fourths of America's foreign trade remained with the former mother country. Contrary to Paine's *Common Sense,* however, independence brought an end to privileges that had been part of the imperial connection. New England was particularly hard hit when American ships were prohibited from trading with the British West Indies. Even with smuggling, the exports of Massachusetts in 1786 totaled only one-fourth of what they had been in 1774. Moreover, because each of the thirteen states had its own customs service and tariff schedules, American diplomats could not threaten commercial retaliation against England. "It would be idle to think of making commercial regulations on our part," George Washington complained. "One State passes a prohibitory law respecting some article, another State opens wide the avenue for its admission. One Assembly makes a system; another Assembly unmakes it."[78]

Indeed, as peacetime problems multiplied, structural weaknesses under the Articles of Confederation loomed as a major obstacle to successful diplomacy. Not only did the sovereignty of the individual states prevent any uniform commercial policy, but states' rights thwarted national power in other respects as well. Congress had raised a Continental Army and constructed a small Navy during the war, but in peace these "implied" powers collapsed; all naval vessels were sold or scrapped by the end of 1784, and the Army dwindled to a mere regiment. Congress remained nominally in charge of foreign policy. Yet during the war this large body had proven itself so faction-ridden and devoid of responsibility that it had given the French foreign minister veto power over American peace commissioners, and thus, in the words of one scholar, "eliminated itself from any prominent role in foreign affairs for the remainder of the Revolution."[79] The legislative body took a forward step in 1784 by creating a Department of Foreign Affairs and selecting John Jay as secretary. Although Congress retained the basic powers of foreign policy—the right to make war and peace, to send and receive ambassadors, to make treaties and alliances—it lacked the power to enforce its diplomacy. Individual states violated the 1783 peace treaty with impunity. Diplomacy became an awkward, frustrating affair.

Relations with England quickly deteriorated after 1783. In the first flush of peace it had looked like the United States might actually conclude a favorable commercial treaty with the British. Lord Shelburne's grand scheme of rapprochement would have continued the benefits Americans had enjoyed under the Crown, including free access of American goods and ships to British and West Indian ports, and during the negotiations British Commissioner David Hartley had spoken about a common citizenship for the two countries. But Shelburne was soon forced from office for having given the Americans too much, and his successors (even the liberal William Pitt, who became Prime Minister in 1784) found commercial reciprocity with the United States a political impossibility. Mercantilist thinking was still powerful in England. Pamphleteers like the Earl of Sheffield argued that the United States, if allowed to resume the privileges of the British Empire without any of the responsibilities, would eventually outstrip Britain in shipping, trade, and the production of manufactured goods. A restrictive policy, however would allow England to increase its carrying trade, particularly in the

West Indies, where colonial shipping had long predominated. Canada and Ireland could serve as alternative sources of provisions for the West Indian planters. Such mercantilist precepts became institutionalized in a series of orders in council, according to which American raw materials and foodstuffs, but not manufactures, were permitted to enter the British home islands aboard American vessels, while Canada and the West Indies remained closed to American shipping. Such restrictions, it was believed, would not hurt British exports to America. As Sheffield prophetically observed: "At least four-fifths of the importations from Europe into the American States were at all times made upon credit; and undoubtedly the States are in greater want of credit at this time than at former periods. It can be had only in Great Britain."[80] As for possible commercial retaliation, the British scoffed at the likelihood that all thirteen "dis-united" states could agree on a uniform set of tariff schedules. "Pish! . . . What can Americans do?" boasted one Briton. "They have neither government nor power. Great Britain could shut up all their ports. . . ."[81]

The British refusal to evacuate the northwest forts was another serious irritant. These fortified posts, which ranged from Dutchman's Point on Lake Champlain to Michilimackinac on Lake Michigan, strategically controlled the frontier, including the fur trade and Indian tribes between the Great Lakes and the Ohio River. The Six Nations of the Iroquois in the northeast, the Shawnees and Algonquins in the northwest, and the Creeks and Muskogeans in the southeast remained the majority in the region, despite an influx of white settlers. The Indians had not been represented in the peace negotiations in Paris, and their claims to lands above and below the Ohio were still valid. Partly to placate the Indians and partly to protect Loyalists who had fled to the frontier, the British did not lower the Union Jack from the forts, despite their promise in Article II of the peace treaty to relinquish them with "all convenient speed." Retention of the posts was later justified on the grounds that Americans themselves had violated the treaty by their failure to repay debts to British creditors and by the shabby treatment accorded Loyalists. The British adopted a "wait-and-see" policy in the west, holding the forts, encouraging the Indians, but avoiding overt provocation of the Americans by refusing Indian requests for troops to guarantee Indian territory. American shipping was thus effectively excluded from the Great Lakes after 1783, and settlements were confined largely to Kentucky and Tennessee.

At the time of Shays' Rebellion in 1786, British officials in Canada, thinking that the United States might soon break up, entered into secret talks with separatist leaders in Vermont, luring them with special trade privileges along the Champlain–St. Lawrence water route. If the breakup did occur, Vermont could easily be attached to Canada, along with the lightly populated territories north of the Ohio. There were further complaints about slaves the British had carried off at the end of the war, as well as a controversy over the Maine–New Brunswick boundary. Americans could only watch, helpless. With no army, no navy, no executive, no power to control the national commerce, the United States under the Articles of Confederation could do little to force British respect for the 1783 peace treaty. As historian Julian P. Boyd has argued, British policies "may well have contributed more to the convoking and to the success of the Federal Convention of 1787 than many who sat in that august body."[82]

The thankless task of enduring humiliation fell to John Adams, who became the first American minister to the Court of St. James's in 1785. King George scarcely concealed his contempt for the young republic, and his ministers were similarly uncordial. When Adams protested the failure of the British to send their own minister to the United States, he was asked whether there should be one envoy or thirteen. "This people cannot look me in the face," Adams wrote. "There is conscious guilt and shame in their countenances when they look at me. They feel they have behaved ill and that I am sensible of it."[83] The New Englander could make no dent in British policy toward trade or toward the forts. The author of the Model Treaty saw the impossibility of free trade. "If we cannot obtain reciprocal liberality," he wrote in 1785, "we must adopt reciprocal prohibitions, exclusions, monopolies, and imposts."[84] British complacency irritated Adams. "If an angel from heaven," he noted sarcastically, "should declare to this nation that our states will unite, retaliate, prohibit, or trade with France, they would not believe it."[85] Indeed, if there was one message that Adams repeated to Congress in dispatch after dispatch during his three frustrating years in England, it was the necessity of giving Congress the power to regulate commerce; otherwise the British would not negotiate. As late as February, 1788, when the new federal Constitution was on the verge of adoption, Adams assured John Jay "that as soon as there shall be one [a national government], the British court will vouchsafe to treat with it."[86]

Diplomacy with Spain after 1783 fared little better. Just as the British refused to evacuate the Ohio Valley after the war, the Spanish tried to retain control over the Southwest. Part of the problem stemmed from ambiguities in the peace treaty. According to Article VII of the Anglo-American treaty, the United States was guaranteed free navigation of the Mississippi "from its source to the ocean" and the northern boundary of Florida was set at 31 degrees. Yet Spain had not agreed to either stipulation. British Florida prior to the war had extended northward to the Yazoo River, and Madrid had no intention of yielding territory or encouraging American settlement by guaranteeing free navigation. Spanish troops continued to hold Natchez on the Mississippi. Like the British north of the Ohio, Spain made alliances with the Creeks and other Indian tribes, and there were occasional attempts to bribe frontier leaders, like General James Wilkinson, into a secessionist connection with the Spanish Crown. The most threatening move came in 1784 when Spain closed the mouth of the Mississippi to American commerce. Westerners exploded in violent protest, for control over the Mississippi meant the difference between a subsistence economy or one of agrarian expansion. George Washington, who visited the frontier territories that summer, reported: "the western settlers . . . stand as it were upon a pivot; the touch of a feather would turn them any way."[87]

Less powerful than the British and unprepared for a war on the frontier, the Spanish preferred to negotiate. Don Diego de Gardoqui arrived in New York in 1785, a crafty, charming envoy, whose instructions were to obtain an American surrender on the Mississippi by dangling trade concessions in Spain and the Canary Islands. Gardoqui also brought a Spanish offer to intercede with the Sultan of Morocco, whose pirates were seizing American merchantmen in the Mediterranean. Since such a treaty would obviously benefit the commercial Northeast at the expense of southern expansionists and western farmers, the Spanish envoy worked hard at flattering Secretary Jay and the other easterners. Gardoqui had a large expense account, and he used it. He gave splendid dinners with the best wines, acquired Spanish jackasses for General Washington, and squired Mrs. Jay to one festivity after another. "I am acting the gallant and accompanying Madame [Jay] to the official entertainments and dances," he reported, "because she likes it and I will do everything which appeals to me for the King's best interest."[88] Jay took the gilded bait. At one point in 1786 he asked Congress for permission to negotiate a treaty whereby the United States would relinquish the *use* of the Mississippi River for twenty-five or thirty years while reserving the *right* to navigate until a time when American power would be sufficient to force Spanish concessions.

Jay's request sparked heated debate in Congress. Dividing geographically, seven northern delegations voted to make the necessary concession, while the five southern delegations stood unanimously opposed. Although negotiations with Gardoqui continued into 1787, it was obvious to Jay that he could never obtain the minimum of nine states necessary to approve a treaty under the Articles. He told Congress that it must decide "either to wage war with Spain or settle all differences by treaty on the best terms available."[89] Congress did neither. Spain resumed its intrigues with western leaders, and in 1788 the Mississippi was temporarily reopened to American shipping after the payment of special duties. A definitive treaty did not come until 1795. The most immediate consequence of the Jay-Gardoqui conversations was to accentuate the political alliance between the South and West and to ensure a clause in the new Constitution that retained a two-thirds majority for senatorial approval of treaties.

Relations with France were equally frustrating. Since the alliance of 1778 contained a mutual guarantee of territories, one might have expected the French to support American claims in the West. France did nothing, however, holding true to Vergennes' view that a United States of limited territorial strength would remain a weak and dependent French client. Thomas Jefferson, who succeeded Franklin as minister to France in 1784, did what he could. He genuinely liked the French and continued the tradition of the cultivated citizen of the world so well set by his predecessor. Jefferson hoped that France could replace England as America's principal trading partner, and he worked very hard to convert the French to liberal commercial theories. Except for the opening of a limited number of French West Indian ports in 1784 and the negotiation of a consular treaty four years later, he ran into the same kind of mercantilist restrictions John Adams faced in England. Whenever Jefferson pressed for commercial concessions, he was usually reminded of the outstanding Revolutionary debt of 35 million livres. The inability of Congress to retaliate distressed Jefferson. He momentarily thought of abandoning commerce and diplomacy and having the United States "stand, with respect to Europe, precisely on the footing of China."[90] Given political and economic realities in America, however, Jefferson understood that such rigid isolation was impossible, so he advocated constitutional reform. "My primary object in the formation of treaties," he wrote in 1785, "is to take the commerce of the states out of the hands of the states, and to place it under the superintendence of Congress, so far as the imperfect provisions of our constitution will admit, and until the states by new compact make them more perfect."[91]

Another impetus to constitutional reform grew out of the dreary record of dealings with the Barbary pirates in the 1780s. The rulers of the North African states—Algiers, Tunis, Tripoli, and Morocco—had transformed piracy into a national industry. By capturing merchantmen, holding sailors and cargoes for ransom, extorting protection money from nations willing to pay, the petty sultans nearly drove American shipping out of the Mediterranean. Through a fortuitous set of circumstances, the United States was able to negotiate a satisfactory treaty with Morocco in 1787, at the bargain price of only $10,000, but other negotiations proved fruitless. The young republic had neither the revenue to pay for protection nor the armed force to coerce the North African pirates. Thomas Jefferson asked for a "fleet of one hundred and fifty guns" to wipe out the pirates, but no steps were taken toward constructing a navy.[92] Americans faced humiliation and tight pocketbooks. For John Jay such awkward diplomacy was a blessing in disguise: "The more we are ill-treated abroad the more we shall unite and consolidate at home."[93]

THE NEW CONSTITUTION AND THE LEGACY OF THE FOUNDING FATHERS

It was amidst this troubled international setting that fifty-five delegates attended the Federal Convention in Philadelphia from May to September, 1787. Although economic woes and Shays' Rebellion in Massachusetts provided the immediate impetus for reform, the "Founding Fathers" had foreign policy in mind too. When Edmund Randolph introduced the Virginia plan to the convention, he cited the need for a stronger foreign policy first among his arguments for increasing federal power. The federal Constitution, approved by the Philadelphia assembly and ratified by the states over the next two years, eliminated most of the weaknesses that had plagued diplomacy under the Articles of Confederation. A central government consisting of an executive, a bicameral legislature, and a judiciary—all designed to balance one another—replaced the weak confederation of sovereign states. Responsibility for negotiations rested with the President, who would make treaties "by and with the advice and consent of the Senate . . . provided two-thirds of the Senators present concur." The impunity with which the individual states had violated the 1783 treaty with England was responsible for Benjamin Franklin's proposal that treaties shall be "the Supreme Law of the land . . . any thing in the Constitution or laws of any State to the contrary notwithstanding."[94] Southerners, remembering the Jay-Gardoqui negotiations, were wary of giving Congress too much power over commerce. Nevertheless, in return for a constitutional prohibition against taxes on exports and a twenty-year moratorium on interference with the slave trade, southern delegates granted Congress the right to regulate imports by a simple majority. The option was open now for commercial retaliation against England. The Constitution also provided for a standing army and navy, thus freeing national defense from dependence on requisitions from the various states. In every respect the United States had strengthened itself. "Tis done!" Benjamin Rush of Pennsylvania exclaimed. "We have become a nation. . . . We are no longer the scoff of our enemies."[95]

An interesting discussion at Philadelphia, particularly in view of subsequent developments, concerned the warmaking power. The early drafts of the Constitution granted Congress the power to "make" war. Delegates soon perceived, however, that both houses might lack sufficient knowledge and unity to act quickly in the event of attack. Congress might not even be in session. When it was suggested that the President be responsible, the evil memories of Julius Caesar and George III intruded. As delegate Elbridge Gerry of Massachusetts put it, he "never expected to hear in a republic a motion to empower the Executive alone to declare war."[96] Virginia's George Mason, in a telling phrase, was for "clogging rather than facilitating war; but for facilitating peace." Fearful of executive tyranny, but not wanting to leave the country defenseless, Gerry and James Madison of Virginia proposed a compromise whereby Congress retained the power to "declare" war, while the President, as Commander-in-Chief, would still be able to "repel sudden attacks."[97] Since Congress was granted authority to raise and support armies and navies, call out the militia, make rules and regulations for all the armed forces, and control all policy functions associated with national defense, it seems evident that the Philadelphia delegates intended the executive to be subordinate.

The size of the federal republic also aroused debate at Philadelphia. According to classic political theory, particularly the writings of Montesquieu, republics stood the best chance of survival if territorial limits remained small. If the theory were accurate, a real disparity existed between the thirteen coastal states and the vast trans-Allegheny expanse stretching to the Mississippi. It took the thirty-five-year-old Virginia lawyer James Madison to articulate the philosophy of a growing republican empire. Not only did Madison draft much of the handiwork at Philadelphia, he also (along with John Jay and Alexander Hamilton) wrote the *Federalist Papers,* which were so influential in the campaign for ratification of the new Constitution in 1787–1788. According to Madison, the greatest threat to a republic arose when a majority faction tyrannized others. Since such factions derived more from economic differences than from territorial size, expansionism benefited a republic. As Madison argued in *Federalist 10,* once you "extend the sphere" of government, "you take in a greater variety of parties and interests; you make it less probable that a majority . . . will have a common motive to invade the right of other citizens; or, if such a common motive exists, it will be more difficult for all who feel it to discover their own strength and to act in unison with each other."[98] Although Madison's republican theories may not have necessitated continual expansion to ensure survival, the man who later as secretary of state presided over the huge Louisiana Purchase in 1803 welcomed westward expansion from the outset. Most delegates at Philadelphia did.

It was no coincidence that Congress's last official measure under the Articles of Confederation during the same summer of 1787 dealt with this very issue of westward expansion. With a bare quorum of eight states represented, the dying Congress enacted the Northwest Ordinance of 1787, which set up guidelines for governing the territories of the Old Northwest until they were ready for statehood. Its terms called for Congress to appoint a governor, secretary, and three judges, who would govern until the population of a territory reached 5,000, at which time the settlers would elect a legislature. The territorial legislature would then rule in conjunction with a council of five selected by the governor and by Congress. The governor retained veto power. As soon as the population grew to 60,000, inhabitants could write a constitution and apply for statehood on terms of equality with the original thirteen. Slavery was forbidden. The Founding Fathers at Philadelphia took cognizance of the new law, and stipulated, according to Article IV, Section 3 of the new Constitution, that "Congress shall have Power to dispose of and make all needful Rules and Regulations respecting the territory or other property belonging to the United States." A blueprint for an American colonial system was thus laid down. The same process that led to statehood for Ohio, Indiana, Michigan, Illinois, and Wisconsin continued into the twentieth century, including the admission of Hawaii and Alaska as states in the 1950s.

When George Washington took the oath of office as President on the balcony of Federal Hall in New York on April 30, 1789, he could look optimistically at the international prospects of the federal republic. Not only could Washington employ the new diplomatic tools fashioned at Philadelphia, but he and his countrymen could also make good use of the foreign policy experiences of the past thirteen

John Jay (1745–1829). This dignified New Yorker, a graduate of King's College (now Columbia University), became an indefatigable diplomat during the Revolution and the early years of independence. As one of the three main peace commissioners in 1782 and the negotiator of Jay's Treaty with England in 1794, Jay might well be called the founding father of American foreign policy. (National Portrait Gallery, Smithsonian Institution, Washington, D.C.)

years. Indeed, if the American Revolution and its aftermath produced nothing else, it provided the United States with a remarkable reservoir of leaders who were sophisticated in world affairs. Diplomats like Jefferson, Jay, and Adams were soon contributing their expertise to the new Administration. Washington himself, as his wartime collaboration with the French attested, understood the intricacies of alliance politics, as did his wartime aide, Alexander Hamilton. Other "demigods" at the Philadelphia convention—Gouverneur Morris, Edmund Randolph, Rufus King, James Madison, to name but a few—would occupy important diplomatic posts in the new government.[99] Because intellectual and political leaders were often the same men in this era, and because domestic, economic, and foreign policies were inextricably related, the Revolutionary generation gave rise to a foreign policy elite of exceptional skills.

The diplomatic goals of independence and expansion were both practical and idealistic. Adams' Model Treaty in 1776 had projected a vision whereby American commerce would be open to the entire world, thus diminishing one of the major causes of war and increasing American profits. Independence and extensive boundaries would protect a republican experiment which, in turn, could serve as a countervailing model for a world of monarchies. The Mississippi River, it seems, even had divine sanction. John Jay told the Spanish in 1780 that "Americans, almost to a man, believed that God Almighty had made that river a highway for the people of the upper country to go to the sea by."[100] For some the vision was even more expansive. The American geographer Jedidiah Morse wrote in 1789: "It is well known that empire has been travelling from east to west. Probably her last and broadest seat will be America. . . . We cannot but anticipate the period, as not far distant, when the AMERICAN EMPIRE will comprehend millions of souls, west of the Mississippi."[101] Of course, before Americans could move beyond the Mississippi, the boundaries of 1783 had to be made secure.

Americans wanted to obtain independence and empire without resort to European-style power politics. The attractions of American commerce proved insufficient to bring automatic aid and recognition; so Franklin in 1778 negotiated the alliance with France. The American preference for commercial treaties instead of political alliances did not diminish after 1778, however, and the commercial and neutral rights provisions of the Model Treaty remained essential to American diplomacy. Commercial treaties in the 1780s with Sweden, Prussia, and the Netherlands followed those principles. Minister to France Thomas Jefferson, in historian Merrill Peterson's estimation, thought of himself as undertaking "nothing less than a diplomatic mission to convert all Europe to the commercial principles of the American Revolution."[102] Probably more than most Americans of his generation, Jefferson retained this faith in the efficacy of commercial power as a substitute for military power. Americans believed, however, that the emphasis on commerce did not exalt profits over principles. As Jefferson's friend James Monroe later wrote: "People in Europe suppose us to be merchants, occupied exclusively with pepper and ginger. They are much deceived. . . . The immense majority of our citizens . . . are . . . controlled by principles of honor and dignity."[103]

Nevertheless, the United States had been forced to compromise principle—to make the alliance with France to win independence. The value of the French alliance was obvious. Without Comte de Rochambeau's army and Admiral de Grasse's fleet, Washington could not possibly have forced Cornwallis' surrender in 1781. French loans of some 35 million livres had kept an impecunious Congress solvent during the war. To be sure, Vergennes wanted to limit American boundaries; French agents in Philadelphia used their influence with Congress to hamstring American diplomats abroad; and as late as 1787 the French chargé d'affaires predicted that America would break up and urged his government to plan the seizure of New York or Rhode Island before the British could act. Still, the French alliance had secured American independence, and the treaty remained valid in 1789, including the provision guaranteeing French possessions in the New World. Most Americans, according to historian William Stinchcombe, "assumed that the alliance would officially end with the arrival of the definitive treaty of peace."[104] Not so.

The status of the French alliance notwithstanding, the eschewing of foreign entanglements remained a cardinal American tenet in the 1780s. "The more attention we pay to our resources and the less we rely on others," wrote Connecticut's Roger Sherman, "the more surely shall we provide for our own honor and success and retrieve that balance between the contending European powers."[105] George Mason echoed these sentiments: "I wish America would put her trust in God and herself, and have as little to do with the politics of Europe as possible."[106]

American diplomats abroad simply did not trust European countries. Europe had its own set of interests, America another. Even a Francophile like Jefferson could write: "Our interest calls for a perfect equality in our conduct towards [England and France]; but no preferences any where."[107] John Adams concurred. "My system," he wrote in 1785, "is a very simple one; let us preserve the friendship of France, Holland, and Spain, if we can, and in case of a war between France and England, let us preserve our neutrality, if possible. In order to preserve our friendship with France and Holland and Spain, it will be useful for us to avoid a war with England."[108] So wary were American leaders of foreign entanglements, they could contemplate political alliances only in the event of attack.

Americans, in short, sought fulfillment of their diplomatic goals without war or foreign allies. The federal Constitution strengthened national power. With an abundant federal revenue came stronger national credit. A flourishing foreign commerce and the power to regulate that commerce, it was hoped, provided an important diplomatic lever. American military power was insignificant. Europeans who visited America in the 1780s analyzed American speech patterns, described the flora and fauna, admired the landscape, but said little of military matters. The United States with its 3.5 million population seemed a slight threat to 15 million British or 25 million French. The traditional Anglo-Saxon fear of standing armies, and the expense of naval construction, made Americans, even under the Constitution, slow to build a defense establishment. Even Hamilton, the most military-minded member of Washington's government, predicted that it would be fifty years before the United States developed military forces sufficient to tip the balance between competing European powers or between the Old World and the New. Without military power or a foreign ally, the United States might find it difficult to maintain its independence, claim its boundaries, and expand its commerce. No one could foresee that the French Revolution would break out within a few months of Washington's inauguration, thus provoking a series of European wars that carried diplomatic consequences for the United States and a serious testing of the young republic's strength, patience, and foreign policy principles.

FURTHER READING FOR THE PERIOD TO 1789

For the colonial background to American diplomacy, see Felix Gilbert, *The Beginnings of American Diplomacy: To the Farewell Address* (1965); Lawrence S. Kaplan, *Colonies into Nation* (1972); Walter LaFeber, "Foreign Policies of a New Nation," in William A. Williams, ed., *From Colony to Empire* (1972); Max Savelle, *The Origins of American Diplomacy: The International History of Anglo-America, 1492–1763* (1967); Geoffrey Symcox, ed., *War, Diplomacy, and Imperialism, 1618–1763* (1973); and Richard W. Van Alstyne, *The Rising American Empire* (1960).

The diplomacy of the Revolutionary era is treated in Samuel Flagg Bemis, *The Diplomacy of the American Revolution* (1957); Ronald Hoffman and Peter J. Albert, eds., *Diplomacy and Revolution: The French-American Alliance of 1778* (1981) and *Peace and the Peacemakers: The Treaty of 1783* (1986); Jonathan R. Dull, *A Diplomatic History of the American Revolution* (1985); Reginald Horsman, *The Diplomacy of the New Republic, 1776–1815* (1985); Lawrence S. Kaplan, ed., *The American Revolution and "A Candid World"* (1977); Isabel de Madariaga, *Britain, Russia, and the Armed Neutrality of 1780* (1962); Richard B. Morris, *The Peacemakers* (1965); Orville T. Murphy, *Charles Gravier, Comte de Vergennes* (1982); J. W. S. Nordholt, *The Dutch Republic and American Independence* (1986); William Stinchcombe, *The American Revolution and the French Alliance* (1969); U.S. Library of Congress, *Impact of the American Revolution Abroad* (1976); and Richard W. Van Alstyne, *Empire and Independence* (1965). See also essays on the 1783 peace in *International History Review* (August, 1983).

Foreign policy under the Articles of Confederation is recounted in Arthur B. Darling, *Our Rising Empire* (1940); Merrill Jensen, *The New Nation* (1950); Daniel G. Lang, *Foreign Policy in the Early Republic* (1985); Frederick W. Marks, *Independence on Trial: Foreign Affairs and the Making of the Constitution* (1986); Jack N. Rakove, *The Beginnings of National Politics* (1979); Charles R. Ritcheson, *Aftermath of Revolution: British Policy toward the United States, 1783–1795* (1969); Abraham Sofaer, *War, Foreign Affairs and Constitutional Power—Vol. I, The Origins* (1976); and J. Leitch Wright, *Britain and the American Frontier, 1783–1815* (1975).

For studies of individuals see Jonathan R. Dull, *Franklin the Diplomat* (1982); Eric Foner, *Tom Paine and Revolutionary America* (1976); James H. Hutson, *John Adams and the Diplomacy of the American Revolution* (1980); Lawrence S. Kaplan, *Jefferson and France* (1963); essays on Franklin, Hamilton, and Jefferson in Frank Merli and Theodore A. Wilson, eds., *Makers of American Diplomacy* (1974); Dumas Malone, *Jefferson and the Ordeal of Liberty* (1962); Frank Monoghan, *John Jay* (1935); Page Smith, *John Adams* (1962); Gerald Stourzh, *Benjamin Franklin and American Foreign Policy* (1969); and Esmond Wright, *Franklin of Philadelphia* (1986).

See also the General Bibliography and the following notes.

NOTES TO CHAPTER 1

1. Quoted in Richard B. Morris, *The Peacemakers: The Great Powers and American Independence* (New York: Harper and Row, 1965), p. 307.
2. Quoted in Francis Wharton, ed., *The Revolutionary Diplomatic Correspondence of the United States* (Washington: Government Printing Office, 1889; 6 vols.), V, 657.
3. Quoted in Morris, *Peacemakers*, pp. 309–310.
4. Quoted in Bradford Perkins, "The Peace of Paris: Patterns and Legacies," in Ronald Hoffman and Peter J. Albert, eds., *Peace and the Peacemakers: The Treaty of 1783* (Charlottesville: University Press of Virginia, 1986), p. 206.
5. Quoted in Morris, *Peacemakers*, p. 357.
6. Quoted in Albert H. Smyth, ed., *The Writings of Benjamin Franklin* (New York: Macmillan, 1905–1907; 10 vols.), IX, 62.
7. Quoted in Jonathan R. Dull, *A Diplomatic History of the American Revolution* (New Haven: Yale University Press, 1985), p. 147.
8. Quoted in Wharton, ed., *Revolutionary Diplomatic Correspondence*, VI, 169.
9. Quoted in Richard B. Morris, *Seven Who Shaped Our Destiny* (New York: Harper and Row, 1973), p. 9.
10. Quoted in L. H. Butterfield, ed., *Diary and Autobiography of John Adams* (Cambridge: Harvard University Press, 1961; 4 vols.), III, 82.
11. Samuel Flagg Bemis, *The Diplomacy of the American Revolution* (Bloomington, Ind.: Indiana University Press, 1957), p. 256.
12. Quoted in Paul A. Varg, *Foreign Policies of the Founding Fathers* (Baltimore: Penguin Books, 1970), p. 3.
13. Quoted in Richard Van Alstyne, *The Rising American Empire* (Chicago: Quadrangle Books, 1965), p. 26.
14. Quoted in Richard Van Alstyne, *Empire and Independence: The International History of the American Revolution* (New York: John Wiley & Sons, 1965), p. 1.
15. Quoted in H. Trevor Colbourn, *The Lamp of Experience: Whig History and the Intellectual Origins of the American Revolution* (Chapel Hill: University of North Carolina Press, 1965), Frontispiece.
16. Quoted *ibid.*, p. 129.

17. Quoted in Gerald Stourzh, *Benjamin Franklin and American Foreign Policy* (Chicago: University of Chicago Press, 1969; 2nd ed.), p. 92.
18. Max Savelle, "Colonial Origins of American Diplomatic Principles," *Pacific Historical Review*, III (1934), 337.
19. Quoted in Felix Gilbert, *The Beginnings of American Diplomacy: To the Farewell Address* (New York: Harper Torchbook, 1965), p. 25.
20. Quoted *ibid.*, p. 28.
21. *Ibid.*
22. Quoted *ibid.*, p. 61.
23. Quoted *ibid.*, p. 57.
24. Quoted *ibid.*, p. 65.
25. Quoted in Jan W. Schulte Nordhott, *The Dutch Republic and American Independence* (Chapel Hill: University of North Carolina Press, 1982), p. 190.
26. Worthington C. Ford, ed., *Journals of the Continental Congress* (Washington: Government Printing Office, 1904–37; 34 vols.), III, 484.
27. Thomas Paine, *Common Sense* (New York: Wiley, 1942), pp. 26–32.
28. Gilbert, *Beginnings of American Diplomacy*, p. 43.
29. Ford, ed., *Journals of the Continental Congress*, V, 425.
30. Quoted in Van Alstyne, *Empire and Independence*, p. 106.
31. Edmund C. Burnett, ed., *Letters of Members of the Continental Congress* (Washington: Carnegie Institution, 1921–36; 8 vols.), I, 502.
32. Ford, ed., *Journals of the Continental Congress*, V, 768–769.
33. Charles Francis Adams, ed., *The Works of John Adams* (Boston: Little, Brown, 1850–1865; 10 vols.), X, 269.
34. James D. Richardson, ed., *A Compilation of the Messages and Papers of the Presidents 1789–1897* (Washington: Government Printing Office, 1897–1900; 9 vols.), I, 323.
35. Walter LaFeber, "Foreign Policies of a New Nation: Franklin, Madison, and the 'Dream of a New Land to Fulfill with People in Self-Control,' 1750–1804," in William A. Williams, ed., *From Colony to Empire* (New York: Wiley, 1972), p. 19.

36. Quoted in Claude H. Van Tyne, "French Aid Before the Alliance of 1778," *American Historical Review*, XXXI (October, 1925), 27.

37. Quoted in Van Alstyne, *Empire and Independence*, p. 43.

38. Quoted in Morris, *Peacemakers*, p. 113.

39. Quoted in Bemis, *Diplomacy of the American Revolution*, p. 27.

40. Quoted in Van Alstyne, *Empire and Independence*, p. 116.

41. Quoted *ibid.*, p. 163.

42. Quoted in Claude-Anne Lopez, *Mon Cher Papa: Franklin and the Ladies of Paris* (New Haven: Yale University Press, 1966), pp. 257–258.

43. Quoted in Stourzh, *Franklin and Foreign Policy*, p. 139.

44. *Ibid.*, p. 140.

45. Gilbert Chinard, ed., *The Treaties of 1778 and Allied Documents* (Baltimore: The Johns Hopkins Press, 1928), pp. 51–55.

46. Wharton, ed., *Revolutionary Diplomatic Correspondence*, II, 676.

47. John Adams quoted in James H. Hutson, "Early American Diplomacy: A Reappraisal," in Lawrence S. Kaplan, ed., *The American Revolution and "A Candid World"* (Kent, Ohio: Kent State University Press, 1977), pp. 56–57.

48. Quoted in Van Alstyne, *Empire and Independence*, p. 93n.

49. Quoted in Elmer Bendiner, *The Virgin Diplomats* (New York: Knopf, 1976), p. 63.

50. Quoted in P. L. Haworth, "Frederick the Great and the American Revolution," *American Historical Review*, IX (April, 1904), 468.

51. Wharton, ed., *Revolutionary Diplomatic Correspondence*, V, 415.

52. Quoted in Morris, *Peacemakers*, p. 200.

53. Quoted in Isabel de Madariaga, *Britain, Russia, and the Armed Neutrality of 1780* (New Haven: Yale University Press, 1962), p. 255.

54. Ford, ed., *Journals of the Continental Congress*, XXIV, 394.

55. Samuel Flagg Bemis, *A Diplomatic History of the United States* (New York: Holt, Rinehart and Winston, 1965; 5th ed.), p. 34.

56. Esmond Wright, "The British Objectives, 1780–1783," in Hoffman and Albert, *Peace and the Peacemakers*, p. 6.

57. Quoted in Frank Monaghan, *John Jay* (Indianapolis: Bobbs-Merrill, 1935), p. 136.

58. Quoted in Morris, *Peacemakers*, p. 242.

59. Quoted *ibid.*, p. 243.

60. Lawrence S. Kaplan, *Colonies into Nation: American Diplomacy, 1763–1801* (New York: Macmillan, 1972), p. 135.

61. Quoted in Louis Gottschalk, *LaFayette and the Close of the American Revolution* (Chicago: University of Chicago Press, 1942), p. 331.

62. Quoted in Morris, *Peacemakers*, p. 263.

63. Quoted in Carl Van Doren, *Benjamin Franklin* (New York: The Viking Press, 1938), p. 671.

64. Quoted in Morris, *Peacemakers*, p. 383.

65. H. P. Johnston, ed., *Correspondence and Public Papers of John Jay* (New York: G. P. Putnam's Sons, 1890–93; 4 vols.), II, 344.

66. Quoted in Mary Beth Norton, *The British-Americans: The Loyalist Exiles in England, 1774–1789* (Boston: Little, Brown, 1972), pp. 175–176.

67. Quoted *ibid.*, p. 176.

68. Quoted in Kaplan, *Colonies into Nation*, p. 143.

69. Quoted in Van Doren, *Benjamin Franklin*, p. 695.

70. Wharton, ed., *Revolutionary Diplomatic Correspondence*, VI, 140.

71. Quoted in David Schoenbrun, *Triumph in Paris: The Exploits of Benjamin Franklin* (New York: Harper and Row, 1976), p. 383.

72. Kaplan, *Colonies into Nation*, p. 144.

73. Quoted in Morris, *Peacemakers*, p. 459.

74. Dull, *A Diplomatic History*, p. 163.

75. Quoted in Merrill Jensen, *The New Nation: A History of the United States During the Confederation, 1781–1789* (New York: Alfred A. Knopf, 1950), p. 105.

76. Johnston, ed., *Correspondence of John Jay*, III, 154.

77. Quoted in Jensen, *The New Nation*, p. 154.

78. Quoted in Samuel Flagg Bemis, *Jay's Treaty: A Study in Commerce and Diplomacy* (New Haven: Yale University Press, 1962), p. 34.

79. William C. Stinchcombe, *The American Revolution and the French Alliance* (Syracuse: Syracuse University Press, 1969), p. 169.

80. Quoted in Kaplan, *Colonies into Nation*, pp. 160–161.

81. Quoted in Frederick W. Marks, III, *Independence on Trial: Foreign Affairs and the Making of the Constitution* (Baton Rouge: Louisiana State University Press, 1973), p. 135.

82. Julian P. Boyd, *Number Seven: Alexander Hamilton's Secret Attempts to Control American Foreign Policy* (Princeton: Princeton University Press, 1964), p. xi.

83. Quoted in Catherine Drinker Bowen, *Miracle at Philadelphia* (Boston: Little, Brown, 1966), p. 137.

84. Quoted in Jerald A. Combs, *The Jay Treaty: Political Battleground of the Founding Fathers* (Berkeley: University of California Press, 1970), p. 24.

85. Quoted in Charles R. Ritcheson, *Aftermath of Revolution: British Policy toward the United States, 1783–1795* (Dallas: Southern Methodist University Press, 1969), p. 44.

86. Quoted in Marks, *Independence on Trial*, p. 68.

87. John C. Fitzpatrick, ed., *The Writings of George Washington* (Washington: Government Printing Office, 1931–1944; 39 vols.), XXVII, 475.

88. Samuel Flagg Bemis, *Pinckney's Treaty: A Study of America's Advantage from Europe's Distress, 1783–1800* (Baltimore: The Johns Hopkins University Press, 1926), p. 84.

89. Quoted in Marks, *Independence on Trial*, p. 31.

90. Quoted in Lawrence S. Kaplan, *Jefferson and France: An Essay on Politics and Political Ideas* (New Haven: Yale University Press, 1963), p. 23.

91. Quoted in Kaplan, *Colonies into Nation*, p. 180.

92. *Diplomatic Correspondence of the United States of America, from the Signing of the Definitive Treaty of Peace, September 10, 1783, to the Adoption of the Constitution, March 4, 1789* (Washington: Blair and Ives, 1837; 3 vols.), I, 792.

93. Quoted in Marks, *Independence on Trial*, p. 48.

94. Article VI of the Constitution.

95. Lyman H. Butterfield, ed., *Letters of Benjamin Rush* (Princeton: Princeton University Press, 1951; 2 vols.), I, 475.

96. Quoted in Jacob Javits, *Who Makes War: The President Versus Congress* (New York: William Morrow, 1973), p. 13.

97. Quoted in Arthur M. Schlesinger, Jr., *The Imperial Presidency* (Boston: Houghton Mifflin, 1973), p. 4.

98. Jacob E. Cooke, ed., *The Federalist* (Middletown, Conn.: Wesleyan University Press, 1961), p. 64.

99. Quoted in Clinton Rossiter, *1787: The Grand Convention* (New York: Macmillan, 1966), p. 138.

100. Quoted in Varg, *Foreign Policies of the Founding Fathers,* p. 41.
101. Quoted in Van Alstyne, *Rising American Empire,* p. 69.
102. Merrill D. Peterson, "Thomas Jefferson and Commercial Policy, 1783–1793," *William and Mary Quarterly, XXII* (October, 1965), 592.
103. Quoted in Ernest R. May, *The Making of the Monroe Doctrine* (Cambridge, Mass.: Harvard University Press, 1975), p. 19.
104. Stinchcombe, *American Revolution and French Alliance,* p. 200.
105. Quoted *ibid.,* p. 205.
106. Quoted in Kate Mason Rowland, *The Life of George Mason* (New York: G. P. Putnam's Sons, 1892; 2 vols.), II, 47.
107. Julian Boyd, ed., *The Papers of Thomas Jefferson* (Princeton: Princeton University Press, 1950–1974; 19 vols.), VIII, 545.
108. Adams, *Works, VIII,* 235–236.

Chapter 2

Leopard **versus** *Chesapeake,* **1807.** This naval encounter highlighted once again the impressment issue in Anglo-American relations and nearly caused war. After the incident President Thomas Jefferson closed American ports to the Royal Navy, only to find that the British commanders haughtily anchored their ships in Chesapeake Bay. Jefferson probably could have obtained from Congress a declaration of war, but, preoccupied at the time by Aaron Burr's treason trial, he chose economic coercion over military retaliation. (Watercolor by Irwin J. Bevan, courtesy of the Mariners' Museum, Newport News, Virginia)

Independence and Expansion in a World at War, 1789–1815

DIPLOMATIC CROSSROAD: THE CHESAPEAKE AFFAIR, 1807

At 7:15 A.M. on the morning of June 22, 1807, the 40-gun American frigate *Chesapeake* weighed anchor from Hampton Roads, Virginia, and made sail under a pleasant southwesterly breeze. Commanded by Commodore James Barron, the *Chesapeake* was bound for the Mediterranean, where it would replace its sister vessel, the U.S.S. *Constitution*, as flagship of a small naval squadron that protected American merchantmen from the Barbary pirates. No one expected trouble. The ship's crew numbered 375, several of whom, it was rumored, were deserters from the British Navy who had enlisted on the *Chesapeake* under assumed names. A number of sick sailors, recovering from a drinking bout of the night before, were allowed by the ship's doctor to lie in the sunny air on the upper deck. The gun deck was cluttered with loose lumber. Cables were not stowed away. Four of the guns did not fit perfectly into their carriages. Only five of the powder horns used in priming the guns were actually filled. In fact, the crew had not been exercised at the guns during the ship's fitting out in Hampton Roads. Barron set sail anyway. His ship was already four months behind schedule and there would be ample opportunity for gunnery practice during the long sea voyage.

At 9:00 the *Chesapeake* passed Lynnhaven Bay, where two 74-gun British ships of the line, *Bellona* and *Melampus,* lay anchored. A rumor had circulated in Norfolk that the captain of the *Melampus* was threatening to seize from the *Chesapeake* three alleged deserters, but if Commodore Barron had heard the story, he took no special precautions. Neither British ship stirred. Soon after midday the *Chesapeake* sighted another ship off Cape Henry, the 50-gun frigate H.M.S. *Leopard.* At approximately 3:30 P.M., when both vessels were some ten miles southeast of Cape Henry, the *Leopard* came about and hailed that the British captain wanted to send dispatches to the Mediterranean through the courtesy of the American commodore. The *Chesapeake* hailed back: "We will heave to you and you can send your boat on board of us."[1] At this point Barron made a serious mistake.

James Barron (1769–1851). The commander of the *Chesapeake,* according to court-martial proceedings conducted in early 1808, had not prepared his ship properly for battle with the *Leopard.* Many of his fellow officers thought Barron had prematurely surrendered. The Navy suspended Barron for five years without pay. He returned to service but was given only shore duty. Years later he killed his chief nemesis, naval officer Stephen Decatur, in a duel, further bespoiling the reprimanded commander's career. (Library of Congress)

According to naval custom, a captain should never permit a foreign warship to approach alongside without first calling his crew to battle stations. The disorderly conditions on the *Chesapeake,* however, made it difficult to clear the guns quickly, and to Barron, the idea of a British naval attack in home waters seemed preposterous.

British Lieutenant John Meade came aboard at precisely 3:45. He handed Barron a copy of orders from Captain S. P. Humphreys, instructing him to search the *Chesapeake* for British deserters. Humphreys did not elaborate on his orders, except to "express a hope that every circumstance respecting them may be adjusted in a manner that the harmony subsisting between the two countries may remain undisturbed."[2] Barron replied correctly; he could never allow his crew to be mustered "by any other but their own officers. It is my disposition to preserve harmony, and I hope this answer . . . will prove satisfactory."[3] Meade returned to the *Leopard* by longboat. Barron now ordered the gun deck cleared for action.

The time was nearly 4:30. To prepare the frigate for battle required a full half hour. The sea was calm. The *Leopard,* less than a pistol shot away, moved closer. Captain Humphreys again used the hailing pipe: "Commodore Barron, you must be aware of the necessity I am under of complying with the orders of my commander-in-chief." Barron, now on deck where he could plainly see the *Leopard*'s guns, tried to gain time by shouting: "I do not hear what you say."[4] He ordered the men to their stations without the drumbeat. The *Leopard* fired a shot across the *Chesapeake*'s bow. Another shot followed a minute later. Then, from a distance of less than two hundred feet, the helpless *Chesapeake* was raked by an entire broad-side of solid shot and canister. The Americans could not fire back. The guns were loaded, but they could not discharge without lighted matches or heated logger-heads from the galley fires. Ammunition had to be brought by hand from the magazine. The *Leopard* poured in more broadsides at point-blank range. In ten minutes of barrage the *Chesapeake* was hulled twenty-two times. Its three masts were badly damaged. The American ship suffered three men killed, eight severely and ten slightly wounded, including Commodore Barron, who stood exposed on the quarterdeck throughout the cannonade. Finally, not wanting to sacrifice lives needlessly, Barron ordered the flag struck. The Americans salvaged a modicum of honor by firing a lone shot at the *Leopard.* A lieutenant had managed to discharge the gun by carrying a live coal in his fingers all the way from the galley. The eighteen-pound shot penetrated the *Leopard*'s hull, but fell harmlessly into the wardroom. The battle was over.

British boats again came alongside, and Captain Humphreys took only four sailors from the deserters and identifiable Englishmen aboard the *Chesapeake.* Of the four, three were undeniably Americans, deserters from the *Melampus* the pre-vious March. Two of these, it turned out, both blacks, had previously deserted from an American merchantman and had voluntarily enlisted in the Royal Navy in 1806. The fourth deserter was a surly Londoner, Jenkin Ratford (alias John Wilson), who had openly insulted his former British officers on the streets of Norfolk. The British found Ratford hiding in the *Chesapeake*'s coal hole and even-tually hanged him from a Halifax gallows, while the three Americans received lesser punishment. A few days after the *Chesapeake* had limped back to Hampton Roads, an American cutter carrying Vice-President George Clinton was fired upon by another British warship off the Virginia Capes.

Americans were angry when they heard about the *Chesapeake.* Heretofore the Royal Navy's practice of impressing alleged British sailors from American mer-chant ships had caused much diplomatic wrangling. Just a few months earlier, President Thomas Jefferson and Secretary of State James Madison had rejected a treaty with England largely because it failed to disavow "this authorized system of kidnapping upon the ocean."[5] British warships, skippered by arrogant officers, constantly stopped and searched merchantmen in American waters, and once the previous year H.M.S. *Leander* had killed an American when firing a shot across a merchantman's bow. But the *Chesapeake* affair was unprecedented. The British had deliberately attacked an American *naval* vessel, a virtual act of war.

Federalists and Republicans alike were shocked. In historian Henry Adams words, "the brand seethed and hissed like the glowing olive-stake of Ulysses in the Cyclops' eye, until the whole American people, like Cyclops, roared with pain and stood frantic on the shore, hurling abuse at their enemy, who taunted them from his safe ships."[6] The citizens of Hampton Roads expressed their resentment by destroying some two hundred water casks that were ready for delivery to the thirsty British squadron in Lynnhaven Bay. The British threatened retaliation. At a meeting of citizens in Baltimore, according to Senator Samuel Smith, "there appeared but one opinion—War—in case that satisfaction is not given."[7] Even in Boston, the stronghold of pro-British sentiment, a crowd of two thousand pledged resolutions in support of whatever action the federal government might take. President Jefferson's first step, on July 2, was to issue a proclamation closing American waters to British warships. Two weeks later he told the French minister:

"If the English do not give us the satisfaction we demand, we will take Canada."[8] Secretary of the Treasury Albert Gallatin believed that war would bring increased taxes, debts, and destruction, but that "all these evils" should not be "put in competition with the independence and honor of the nation." War with England, thought Gallatin, might "prevent our degenerating, like the Hollanders, into a nation of mere calculators."[9]

The *Chesapeake* affair did not lead to war—at least not immediately. Jefferson chose, in historian Bradford Perkins' phrase, "to play the part of a damper rather than a bellows."[10] Military preparations and diplomatic alternatives had to be tried first. Even before Congress convened late in the year, Jefferson moved energetically to strengthen American defenses. Without public fanfare, the President called all naval and merchant vessels home, ordered naval gunboats to be readied, armed seven coastal fortresses, sent field guns to various state militia, gave war warnings to all frontier posts, and informed state governors that he might call 100,000 militia members to federal service. In readying American ramparts, however, the Jefferson Administration discovered just how inadequate its defenses were. The Navy Department, it turned out, could not send a ship to the East Indies recalling American merchant ships because there were no funds for such a voyage. Even Washington seemed vulnerable to attack. Gallatin warned prophetically that the British could "land at Annapolis, march to the city, and re-embark before the militia could be collected to repel [them]."[11] When Congress met in December, 1807, however, Jefferson's republican ideology precluded any request for a large standing army, and the President asked for inexpensive coastal gunboats in preference to oceangoing frigates.

Jefferson's diplomacy also proved inadequate. The British government might have settled the matter amicably if the Americans had asked only for an apology and reparations for the *Chesapeake.* Foreign Minister George Canning told American minister James Monroe exactly that, in late July, 1807, but Jefferson insisted that England abandon impressment altogether. Canning was willing to disavow the incident but not the practice. As it turned out, a formal apology for the *Chesapeake* attack was not delivered and accepted until 1811, by which time America's wounded sense of honor and England's stubbornness made war almost impossible to avoid. The *Chesapeake* affair also had set in motion American thoughts about invading Canada, and the British, in turn, began to repair their alliances with the Indian tribes in the Ohio Valley. The British Indian agent Matthew Elliott openly encouraged the Shawnee chiefs Tecumseh and the Prophet to form a confederation of western tribes. In this way were maritime grievances linked to frontier friction. By 1812, most Americans could agree with Andrew Jackson's boast that "we are going to fight for the re-establishment of our national character . . . ; for the protection of our maritime citizens . . . ; [and for] some indemnity for past injuries . . . by the conquest of all the British dominions . . . of North America."[12]

EUROPE'S WARS, AMERICA'S CRISES

The *Chesapeake* affair came during the series of wars that engulfed Europe after 1789. These wars were initially advantageous to the United States. The economic prosperity of the young republic depended on the disposing of agricultural surpluses abroad on favorable terms, and war in Europe automatically created

Makers of American Foreign Policy from 1789 to 1815

Presidents	Secretaries of State
George Washington, 1789–1797	Thomas Jefferson, 1790–1794
	Edmund Randolph, 1794–1795
John Adams, 1797–1801	Timothy Pickering, 1795–1800
	John Marshall, 1800–1801
Thomas Jefferson, 1801–1809	James Madison, 1801–1809
James Madison, 1809–1817	Robert Smith, 1809–1811
	James Monroe, 1811–1817

trading opportunities for neutral carriers. American exports amounted to $20,750,000 in 1792, the last year of peace between France and England; by 1796 exports had jumped to $67,060,000. Europe's wars also gave the United States more diplomatic leverage with respect to territorial disputes in North America. Since England and Spain were embroiled with France, and both sets of belligerents desired American trade, the Administration of George Washington could proceed more forcefully in negotiating with Spain over the Mississippi and Florida, and with Great Britain over the still occupied northwest forts. Yet Europe's wars also posed the danger that the United States might get sucked in. France might demand American assistance under the terms of the 1778 alliance. England and Spain might fight rather than concede territorial claims in North America. Even if the United States maintained neutrality, belligerent nations might still disrupt America's neutral commerce. Americans differed over the proper response to Europe's wars, and the ensuing debate over foreign policy coincided with the rise of national political parties. The political and economic stakes were high indeed.

George Washington, whether as plantation manager, military commander, or president, always sought the best counsel before making decisions. Although Vice-President John Adams, Chief Justice John Jay, and Attorney General Edmund Randolph sometimes contributed recommendations, the making of foreign policy during Washington's first Administration often resembled an essay contest between Secretary of State Thomas Jefferson and Secretary of the Treasury Alexander Hamilton. Hamilton usually won, sometimes by using unscrupulous tactics, and around his successful policies coalesced the first national political party in the United States, the Federalist party. Although historians correctly use the term "Hamiltonian" foreign policy, Washington tried to remain above partisanship and accepted Hamilton's advice because he thought it in the national interest. However, the popular father of his country "was an *Aegis very essential to me,*" Hamilton later admitted.[13]

Hamilton dominated diplomacy because early in the Washington Administration he had, as treasury secretary, formulated and won congressional approval for a fiscal program with foreign policy implications. By funding the national debt at par, assuming the Revolutionary debts of several of the states, and paying the arrears on the national debt owed abroad, Hamilton hoped to attract financial support for the federal experiment from wealthier commercial interests. Such a program required revenue. Hamilton provided the necessary monies through a tariff on imports and a tax on shipping tonnage. The revenue laws, passed in July,

1789, levied a tax of fifty cents a ton on foreign vessels in American ports and attached a 10 percent higher tariff on imports in foreign bottoms. Such navigation laws served to stimulate American shipping by discriminating moderately against foreigners, but not enough to curtail trade. Hamilton particularly opposed discriminatory measures against England, such as the bill sponsored by James Madison in 1791 that would have prohibited imports from countries that forbade American imports in American bottoms (as England did with respect to Canada and the British West Indies). In Hamilton's eyes, any interference with Anglo-American commerce spelled disaster. Fully 90 percent of American imports came from England, more than half in British ships; nearly 50 percent of American exports went to British ports. Revenue would dry up if trade were curtailed. National credit, said Hamilton, would be "cut up . . . by the roots."[14] Accordingly, this brilliant bastard son of a West Indian planter spent the better part of his tenure at the Treasury Department defending the sanctity of Anglo-American trade, and hence, Anglo-American diplomatic cooperation.

Opposition to Hamilton's definition of the national interest quickly developed, particularly among Southern agrarian interests hoping to develop new markets for grain, cotton, and tobacco on the European continent. Echoing Jefferson, who resented Hamilton's encroachment on his prerogatives, Madison raised questions in Congress. Unlike the Federalists, Madison wanted to use commercial discrimination as a lever to obtain trade and territorial concessions from England. As spokesmen for Southern planters whose crops had long been shackled to British markets and British credit, Madison and Jefferson wanted to loosen Anglo-American patterns through favorable commercial treaties with other European states and by legislation favoring non-British shipping. Britain might retaliate, but, as Madison bragged: "The produce of this country is more necessary to the rest of the world than that of other countries is to America. . . . [England's] interests can be wounded almost mortally, while ours are invulnerable."[15] In particular, he calculated that the British West Indies, in the event of a European war, would starve without United States supplies. Even though Hamilton blocked Madison's navigation bill in the Senate, the mere threat of commercial reprisals induced the British to send their first formal minister, George Hammond, to the United States in October, 1791. Washington thereupon returned the compliment by sending former Governor of South Carolina Thomas Pinckney to the Court of St. James's.

The American split over commercial policy was exacerbated further by the French Revolution. The initial phase of the French upheaval, with familiar figures like Thomas Paine and the Marquis de Lafayette in positions of leadership, elicited almost universal approbation in America. Then came the spring of 1793 and news that King Louis XVI had been guillotined and France had declared war on England and Spain. While conservative Federalists recoiled at the republican terror in France, Jeffersonian Republicans cheered and began organizing popular societies in apparent imitation of the French Jacobin clubs. Caught up in the enthusiasm, Jefferson himself wrote: "My own affections have been deeply wounded by some of the martyrs to this cause [the executed victims in Paris], but rather than it should have failed I would have seen half the earth desolated; were there but an Adam and an Eve left in every country, and left free, it would be better than it now is."[16] Frightened Federalists began to suspect that the Jeffersonians sought to plunge the country into war on the side of France. The Jeffersonians, in turn, conjured up visions of plots by Federalists, and thought they wanted "to make a party in the confederacy against human liberty."[17] In actuality, the rising political passions in 1793 obscured the fact that neither party placed the interests of France or England above those of the United States. Although Hamilton sometimes talked indiscreetly to British diplomats, he did so in the belief that the twin American goals of commercial and territorial expansion could be best achieved in close relationship with Great Britain. As for Jefferson's celebrated Francophilism, French Minister Pierre Adet commented in 1796: "Jefferson I say is American and as such, he cannot be sincerely our friend. An American is the born enemy of all the European peoples."[18] Even though the country remained officially neutral, it seemed inevitable that Americans would favor one side or the other in the symbolic struggle between England and France, between monarchy and republicanism.

President Washington's proclamation of neutrality on April 22, 1793 received the unanimous backing of his Cabinet advisers. How to reconcile neutrality with the French alliance was another matter. In receiving France's new republican minister, Citizen Edmond Charles Genêt, Jefferson refuted Hamilton's arguments that the 1778 treaties had lapsed with the death of Louis XVI. Jefferson thereby set two important diplomatic precedents: American respect for the sanctity of treaties and quick diplomatic recognition of regimes that had de facto control over a country. The thirty-year-old Genêt eased his reception by not asking the United States to become a belligerent; he even offered new commercial concessions if American merchants would take over France's colonial trade with the West Indies. Exultant, Jefferson innocently noted: "He offers everything & asks nothing."[19]

Obstacles to Franco-American harmony quickly materialized. Genêt outfitted some fourteen privateers—privately owned American ships, equipped in American ports for war under French commission. Before long they had captured more than eighty British merchant ships, some of them taken within the American three-mile coastal limit. Such activities openly violated neutrality regulations announced in August. British minister Hammond protested and Jefferson warned Genêt, but pro-French juries often acquitted those Americans who were arrested. Genêt infuriated Jefferson by promising that a captured British prize, *Little Sarah*, would not be sent to sea as a privateer only a few hours before the vessel (renamed *Petite Democrate*) slipped down the Delaware River to embark on a career of destroying commerce. Not content with these embarrassments, Genêt also scurried about with plans for capturing Spanish-controlled Louisiana, an expedition comprised mostly of American volunteers and led by the drunken Revolutionary hero George Rogers Clark. Although the plan never reached fruition, the French envoy dramatically informed Paris: "I am arming the Canadians to throw off the yoke of England; I am arming the Kentuckians, and I am preparing an expedition by sea to support the descent on New Orleans."[20] Genêt also encouraged pro-French editorials in the press of the nation's capital, Philadelphia, hobnobbed with Republican leaders, and at one point addressed an appeal to the American people over the head of the President. Washington grew furious, and even Madison admitted that Genêt's "conduct has been that of a madman."[21]

The furor over Genêt abated somewhat by late summer of 1793, when an outbreak of yellow fever caused most government officials to leave Philadelphia. By this time Genêt had made himself so obnoxious that the Washington Administration, Jefferson included, agreed unanimously to ask the French government to recall its envoy. Meanwhile, Washington replaced Gouverneur Morris as American

Factionalism and Foreign Policy. In this Federalist cartoon of the 1790s, President George Washington attempts to advance toward the invading French ("Cannibals") at the left, but Thomas Jefferson, among others, restrains him. Differences over questions of foreign policy helped propel American leaders into the Federalist and Republican parties. (Courtesy of the New-York Historical Society, New York City)

minister in Paris. The wooden-legged Morris had proven himself a shrewd judge of the French Revolution, but had alienated his hosts by befriending French aristocrats, at one point even aiding in an abortive attempt to spirit the King and Queen out of France. The nomination of James Monroe, a firm Virginia Republican, to replace Morris temporarily patched up quarrels, as did the arrival of Genêt's successor, Joseph Fauchet, in February, 1794. As for Genêt, he never returned to France. By the time of his recall the French Revolution had moved inexorably to the left, the Girondins having been replaced by the Jacobins, and young Genêt was in danger of literally losing his head as well as his reputation. Washington relented and allowed Genêt to remain in America as a private citizen, whereupon the once stormy Frenchman moved to New York, married the daughter of Governor George Clinton, and lived quietly until his death in 1834.

COMMERCE, POLITICS, AND DIPLOMACY: JAY'S TREATY

No sooner had the crisis with France eased than the country found itself on the edge of war with England. Seizure of American commerce on the high seas and threats of Indian attacks from Canada touched off a war scare in the winter and early spring of 1794. Indignation raged in Congress when it learned in late February that British cruisers, under a secret order in council (Admiralty decree) declaring foodstuffs contraband, had seized more than 250 American merchantmen trading with the French West Indies. These maritime acts, coupled with an inflammatory speech to the western Indians by Lord Dorchester, governor general of Canada, posed a direct threat to the young republic. Congress responded, on March 26, 1794, by imposing a thirty-day embargo (later extended to sixty days) on all shipping in American ports bound for foreign destinations. Although ostensibly impartial, the legislation was aimed at England.

Cool heads sought to prevent a rupture. Fearful that the Republican majority in the House of Representatives would destroy trade and credit through permanent embargoes and thus cause war with England, Hamilton and other Federalists suggested a special mission to London. By a vote of 18 to 8, the Senate, on April 18, confirmed the appointment of John Jay. Historian Samuel Flagg Bemis has entitled Jay's subsequent agreement "Hamilton's Treaty."[22] Not only did the treasury secretary conceive the special mission, but he also drafted the bulk of Jay's instructions. Only after strenuous argument from Edmund Randolph, who had replaced Jefferson as secretary of state, was a reference inserted to "the possibility of sounding Russia, Sweden, or Denmark as to an alliance on the principles of the Armed Neutrality."[23] The Anglophilic Hamilton deliberately defused this menacing diplomatic weapon, which might have induced England to make concessions on neutral rights, when he leaked to British Minister Hammond the information that Washington's Cabinet, ever wary of entanglements, had actually decided not to join a neutral alliance. Aside from the stipulations forbidding any agreement that contradicted obligations under the 1778 alliance with France, and prohibiting any commercial treaty that failed to open the British West Indies to American shipping, the special minister's instructions afforded him considerable discretion. Moreover, Jay's concern for maintaining peace and commerce with Great Britain was almost as great as Hamilton's.

Amidst wine, dining, and British flattery, Jay negotiated the Treaty of Amity, Commerce, and Navigation, signed on November 19, 1794. England, locked in deadly combat with France, found it prudent to conciliate the United States on North American issues, but generally did not yield on questions involving its maritime supremacy. Jay's most important accomplishment was the British surrender of the northwest forts, which London had already promised to relinquish in the 1783 peace treaty. This time the redcoats actually left. Whitehall's abandonment of the west also aborted efforts to unite the Indians north and south of the Ohio against American encroachment. When General Anthony Wayne defeated the northern tribes in the Battle of Fallen Timbers in August, 1794, the British commander at nearby Fort Miami closed his gates to the retreating Indians. In the subsequent Treaty of Greenville, the Indians formally ceded much of what would become the states of Ohio and Indiana. The settlement kept the frontier relatively pacified for the next fifteen years.

Another British concession, the opening of the British East Indies to American commerce, held great promise for future trade with Asia. Jay also obtained trade with the British Isles on a most-favored-nation basis. As for the British West Indies, however, American shipping would be limited to vessels of less than seventy tons, and American export of certain staples, like cotton and sugar, was forbidden. Other controversial matters, including compensation for recent maritime seizures, pre-Revolutionary debts still owed by Americans, and the disputed northeast boundary of Maine, were to be decided by arbitration. In regard to neutral rights, Jay was forced to make concessions that violated the spirit, if not the letter, of America's treaty obligations to France. His treaty stipulated that under certain circumstances American foodstuffs bound for France might be seized and compensation offered and that French property on American ships constituted a fair prize. In this case, then, "free ships" no longer meant "free goods." The commercial clauses were to remain in effect for twelve years, thus making it impossible for Republicans to discriminate against the British. Finally, the treaty said nothing about impressment and abducted slaves. "A bolder party stroke was never struck," Jefferson grumbled. "For it certainly is an attempt of a party, which . . . lost their majority in one branch of the legislature, to make a law by the other branch of the executive, under color of a treaty, which shall bind up the hands of the adverse branch from ever restraining the commerce of their patron nation."[24]

Jefferson's discontent notwithstanding, Jay's Treaty was a milestone on the road to mature national sovereignty. Faced with the loss of American trade, England had compromised on territorial issues in North America. However, London would no more surrender maritime supremacy in 1794 than it would in 1807. Nonetheless, in view of the contempt England had shown American diplomacy since 1783, any concession by treaty constituted real proof that the United States could maintain its independence in a hostile world. By inaugurating a ten-year period of relatively amicable relations between England and the United States, Jay's Treaty gave the United States time in which to grow in territory, population, and national consciousness. When war came in 1812 the United States was able to fight more effectively than in 1794.

The treaty signed in November, 1794 arrived in Philadelphia on March 7, 1795. The Senate had just dispersed, so Washington did not actually submit the treaty for approval until early June. The senators debated in executive session, and only by eliminating Article XII (dealing with the West Indian trade restrictions) were the Federalists able to secure a bare two-thirds vote of 20 to 10 on June 24. Complications prevented the President's immediate signature. Washington was not sure whether he needed to resubmit the treaty to England (without Article XII) before formally ratifying it. While he considered this dilemma Jay's Treaty was leaked to the press. Critics quickly charged that Jay had surrendered American maritime rights for minor British concessions, and that the French alliance had been betrayed. Antitreaty manifestos and protest parades materialized in many towns and cities. In Philadelphia a mob hanged John Jay in effigy and stoned the residence of the British minister. A crowd also stoned Hamilton when he spoke in favor of the treaty in New York. In retreat he shouted: "If you use such striking arguments, I must retire."[25]

Federalist leaders quailed at the onslaught. Washington had to take action to put an end to the clamor and to protect his reputation. "If the President decides wrong, or does not decide *soon*," wrote Oliver Ellsworth of Connecticut, "his good fortune will forsake him."[26] While Washington pondered a decision at Mount Vernon during the summer of 1795, according to historian Joseph Charles, it seemed that the entire "inner circle of the Federalist Party fairly held its breath."[27] Yet the President withheld formal ratification—in part, because he was irked that the British had resumed seizures of American vessels carrying foodstuffs to France. Conferring almost exclusively with Randolph, he decided to wait for adequate British explanations.

Always a deliberate man, Washington might have avoided ratification indefinitely had not suspicions of treason intervened and thereby removed Edmund Randolph, an obstacle to peaceful relations with England. In March, 1795, a British man-of-war had captured a French corvette carrying dispatches from Minister Joseph Fauchet to Paris. Dispatch Number Ten recounted conversations in which Randolph had allegedly sought from Fauchet money for Republican leaders in Pennsylvania during the Whiskey Rebellion of 1794. The report of the conversation was confused and remains puzzling to scholars, but Foreign Minister William Grenville sensed his opportunity and sent Dispatch Number Ten to Minister Hammond with the instruction that "the communication of some of [the information] to well disposed persons in America may possibly be helpful to the King's service."[28] Hammond showed the dispatch to Secretary of War Timothy Pickering, a tall, pinch-faced New Englander and diehard Federalist who seemed convinced of Randolph's treason and who deliberately but subtly mistranslated certain French passages in Number Ten to make the evidence look more incriminating. Then he wrote carefully to Mount Vernon. "On the subject of the treaty," he informed Washington, "I confess that I feel extreme solicitude; and for a *special reason* which can be communicated to you only in person, I entreat that you return with all possible speed."[29]

Washington arrived in Philadelphia in August, read Pickering's translation of Number Ten, and apparently pronounced his secretary of state guilty without trial. He also decided to ratify Jay's Treaty. On August 18, 1795, the President put his official signature on the document. The next day he confronted Randolph. Pickering was in attendance, eyeing the victim like a hawk. Washington handed him Fauchet's dispatch, pronouncing coldly, "Mr. Randolph! here is a letter which I desire you to read, and make such explanations as you choose."[30] The young Virginian's defense was valiant, but foredoomed. Randolph then wrote a voluminous *Vindication,* which he hoped would redeem his name. Even though most modern scholars accept Randolph's innocence, he made the mistake of quarreling openly with the revered President Washington, and in the heated political atmosphere of 1795–1796 neither the Republicans nor the Federalists would take up his cause. Randolph resigned and returned to Virginia embittered.

The Republicans, while avoiding any identification with the fallen Randolph, made one last effort in the House of Representatives to negate Jay's Treaty by trying to block appropriations for its implementation. During the House debates in March, 1796, Republican leaders asked the President to release all official documents and correspondence relating to the treaty. In a precedent-setting decision, Washington categorically refused, citing the need for secrecy and the fact that the treatymaking power lay exclusively with the executive and Senate. The debate raged on. Federalist Fisher Ames of Massachusetts evoked the fear of Indian warfare in the Northwest if appropriations were rejected and British troops did not leave: "In the day time, your path through the woods will be ambushed; the darkness of midnight will glitter with the blaze of your dwellings. You are a father; the blood of your sons shall fatten your cornfield! You are a mother: the war-whoop shall wake the sleep of the cradle! . . . By rejecting the posts, we light the savage fires—we bind the victims."[31] Another Federalist wrote to his congressman: "If you do not give us your vote, your son shall not have my Polly."[32] A bare majority (51 to 48) of the House voted the necessary funds on April 30.

PINCKNEY'S TREATY, FRANCE, AND WASHINGTON'S FAREWELL

One reason why the House, despite a Republican majority, voted appropriations for Jay's Treaty was the fear that its negation might jeopardize the more popular Pinckney's Treaty with Spain. This treaty (sometimes called the Treaty of San Lorenzo) obtained everything that the United States had sought from Spain since the Revolution, and was especially pleasing to the South and West. Signed by Thomas Pinckney in Madrid on October 27, 1795, the treaty secured for American farmers free navigation of the Mississippi River and the right of depositing goods at New Orleans for transshipment. This privilege of deposit was stipulated to last for three years, renewable either at New Orleans or some other suitable place on the Mississippi. Spain also set the northern boundary of Florida at 31 degrees north latitude. The Senate approved the accord unanimously on March 3, 1796. With America's southeastern frontier now settled with Spain, a number of Republicans in the House did not want to risk losing a similarly favorable settlement in the Northwest by voting against the Jay Treaty. In the sense that they redeemed America's borderlands from foreign control, Jay's Treaty and Pinckney's Treaty were thought to stand together.

In actuality, the popular treaty with Spain seems to have been a by-product of Jay's handiwork in England. When Thomas Pinckney arrived in Spain in June, 1795, the Spanish knew of Jay's Treaty, but no one had yet seen the actual text. The Spanish Foreign Minister, Don Manuel de Godoy, feared that a military alliance had been signed between England and the United States. Spain's lightly garrisoned outposts in North America were already vulnerable to American settlers moving across the Alleghenies, and so an Anglo-American alliance would make Spanish territory indefensible. Better to make concessions to the grasping Americans and keep the peace. Godoy was in the process of extricating Spain from the war against France (effected in July, 1795), and he hoped to renew the old alliance with France. He feared England's wrath when Madrid switched sides: hence his willingness to appease the Americans. Historians have debated whether Godoy actually saw a copy of Jay's Treaty (and therefore knew that it was not a military alliance) before signing Pinckney's Treaty in October. Arthur P. Whitaker argues that Godoy did have an accurate text and thus Spain made a favorable treaty with the United States because it "had no stomach for dealing with the American frontiersman."[33] Samuel Flagg Bemis thinks Godoy did not know, thereby making European diplomatic pressure the major factor. Whatever the main reason, it is clear that Spain's power and attention were diverted from North America by the war in Europe; to use Bemis' famous phrase, it was a classic case of "America's advantage from Europe's distress."[34] European wars permitted American expansion.

If diplomatic advantages from Spain followed logically from the Jay Treaty, the pact generated only trouble with France. James Monroe, who had assured the French that Jay's instructions precluded any pact that violated American obligations to the 1778 alliance, had to bear the brunt of French outrage over the surrender of "free ships, free goods." Monroe had ingratiated himself with the French by hailing France's contributions to human liberty in a speech before the National Convention; he had been the only foreign diplomat to remain in Paris during the Reign of Terror. When news of Jay's Treaty reached Paris, however, poor Monroe made the mistake of predicting that the treaty would never be ratified. In July, 1796, the angry French government announced that American ships would no longer be protected under the neutral rights provisions of the 1778 treaty. To make matters worse, a disgruntled Washington ordered Monroe home on August 22. French agents in America, meanwhile, stepped up their efforts to wean American policy from its pro-British orientation. Minister Pierre Adet, imitating his predecessors Genêt and Fauchet, did his best to bring about "the right kind of revolution" by lobbying unsuccessfully in the House of Representatives against Jay's Treaty and openly backing Thomas Jefferson for the presidency.[35] Adet's electioneering efforts came to naught, however, and John Adams defeated Jefferson by an electoral vote of 71 to 68.

One of the reasons for Adams' victory over Jefferson was the publication of Washington's Farewell Address on September 19, 1796. It was timed for its political impact. To be sure, Washington, ever conscious of history's verdict, was setting down a political testament that he hoped would have lasting effect on posterity. At the same time, the first President and Hamilton, who revised Washington's draft of the speech, had French intrigues very much in mind in making the famous warning: "Against the insidious wiles of foreign influence . . . the jealousy of a free people ought to be *constantly* awake."

Read as a whole, Washington's valedictory stands as an eloquent statement of American diplomatic principles. It reiterated the "Great Rule" that "in extending our commercial relations" the United States should have "as little *political* connection as possible" with foreign nations. Like Thomas Paine, he posited the idea of American uniqueness. "Europe," said Washington, "has a set of primary interests which to us have none or a very remote relation. . . . Our detached and distant situation invites and enables us to pursue a different course." Then came perhaps his most memorable words: "'Tis our true policy to steer clear of permanent alliances with any portion of the foreign world. . . . Taking care always to keep ourselves . . . on a respectable defensive posture, we may safely trust to temporary

George Washington (1732–1799). The Virginia gentleman farmer and first President always maintained a regal, if not cold, countenance. His Farewell Address of 1796 proved once again that he was a supreme nationalist. (The Cleveland Museum of Art, Hinman B. Hurlbut Collection)

alliances for extraordinary emergencies." Significantly, Washington did not say "no entangling alliances ever," as later politicians sometimes mistakenly claimed.[36] Nor did he preclude westward expansion. Even though Washington seemed to fear a French connection more than a British involvement in 1796, the evenhandedness of his phraseology gave the Farewell Address an enduring quality. "Our country-men," Jefferson noted in agreement, "have divided themselves by such strong affections to the French and the English that nothing will secure us internally but a divorce from both nations."[37] The next four years would test the assumptions underlying Washington's advice.

THE XYZ AFFAIR AND THE QUASI-WAR WITH FRANCE

"My entrance into office," John Adams wrote, "is marked by a misunderstanding with France, which I shall endeavor to reconcile, provided that no violation of faith, no stain upon honor, is exacted. . . . America is not SCARED."[38] In July, 1796, some four months after Jay's Treaty had officially gone into effect, the French decreed that they would treat neutral vessels the way neutrals permitted England to treat them—that is, "free ships" would not guarantee "free goods." Shortly thereafter, French privateers and warships began seizing American merchantmen in the West Indies. There were 316 seizures by June, 1797. In addition, the five-man Directory, which now ruled France, had refused to receive Charles C. Pinckney, the South Carolina Federalist whom Washington had sent to replace James Monroe as American minister. Threatened with arrest, Pinckney had stalked off to the Netherlands, thus presenting Adams with a complete diplomatic rupture. Rejecting suggestions of war from bellicose Federalists, the new President dispatched a special commission to negotiate all outstanding differences with the French. To accomplish this delicate task, Adams named Pinckney, Federalist John Marshall of Virginia, and Massachusetts Republican Elbridge Gerry. Adams displayed his nonpartisanship by selecting Gerry, an old friend, only after Thomas Jefferson and James Madison had declined to serve.

The three American envoys arrived in Paris in October, 1797, whereupon they encountered perhaps the most fascinating, most unscrupulous diplomat of all time. The wily (the word was invented to describe him) Charles Maurice de Talley-rand-Périgord, formerly a bishop in the ancien régime, recently an exile for two years in the United States, had become French foreign minister that summer. Despite his firsthand acquaintance with Americans (indeed, he and Gouverneur Morris had once shared the same mistress in Paris), Talleyrand evinced little affection for France's sister republic. The United States, he once wrote, should not be treated "with greater respect than Geneva or Genoa."[39] Maritime pressure seemed a convenient way to persuade the Americans to acknowledge their com-mercial obligations to France under the treaty of 1778. The French still wanted the Americans to take over their carrying trade with the French West Indies, an impossible undertaking if the Americans refused to defend such commerce against the British. Talleyrand did not want open war, but as one of his diplomatic agents put it: "A little clandestine war, like England made on America for three years, would produce a constructive effect."[40] The war in Europe had begun to go well again for France under the young Corsican General Napoleon Bonaparte. Ameri-can questions were not deemed urgent. If Talleyrand could string out negotiations with the American commission, party divisions would reappear in the United

Talleyrand (1754–1838). The wily French statesman majored in survival during the stormy years of the French Revolution. His attempt to solicit bribes from American envoys in the XYZ Affair, it seems, was linked to secret land speculations Talleyrand made under an assumed name while he was living in exile in Pennsylvania in the early 1790s. (Prints Division, New York Public Library, Astor, Lenox and Tilden Foundations)

States, and France could easily make a favorable settlement. Or so Talleyrand thought.

Three French agents, later identified in the American dispatches as X, Y, and Z, soon approached the American commissioners as spokesmen for Talleyrand. The message, though indirect, was unmistakable. If the Americans expected serious and favorable negotiations, they should pay a bribe to the French foreign minister and arrange for a large loan to the French government. To the first request, Pinckney made his celebrated reply: "No; no; not a sixpence."[41] Contrary to legend, this initial attempt at bribery did not terminate negotiations. Conversations continued throughout the autumn and into the new year. Talleyrand was even suspected of employing a beautiful woman to work her charms on Gerry and Marshall. "Why will you not lend us money?" she asked at one point. "If you were to make us a loan, all matters will be adjusted. When you were contending your Revolution we lent you money."[42]

Talleyrand's methods were common enough in European chancelleries. The Americans refused to pay because they had no instructions, not solely because they were indignant. Gradually, however, they lost patience. Marshall correctly observed that "this haughty, ambitious government is not willing to come to an absolute rupture with America during the present state of the war with England but will not condescend to act with justice or to treat us as a free and independent nation."[43] In January, 1798, Marshall drew up a memorial, signed by Gerry and Pinckney, which recounted all American grievances against France, including the personal indignities gratuitously inflicted on the American commissioners. Talleyrand made no reply. The French issued new and harsher decrees that made a neutral cargo liable to capture if any part of it—a jug of rum, even an English-made compass or sextant—had British origins. Angry and frustrated, Marshall and Pinckney asked for their passports, although Gerry, a native of Marblehead, stayed another three months in a futile attempt to negotiate.

Rumors of French insolence began to filter back to the United States in early 1798. After receiving the first official dispatches from his three emissaries, Adams went before Congress on March 19. Pointing out that his peace overtures had been refused, the President asked for authority to arm merchant ships and for other defensive measures. Jeffersonian Republicans smelled a Federalist trap. The House of Representatives demanded that the President send it all relevant diplomatic correspondence. Adams, ignoring the precedent of Washington's refusal in the case of Jay's Treaty, sent all dispatches to the House, substituting the letters X, Y, and Z for the real names of Talleyrand's highwaymen. The country was soon aflame with the news. "Millions for defense but not one cent for tribute" (a phrase mistakenly attributed to Charles C. Pinckney) became a popular slogan, and John Marshall was hailed as a triumphant hero on his return to New York. Even the dour Adams aroused cheers when he promised Congress in June that he would never "send another minister to France without assurances that he will be received, respected, and honored as the representative of a great, free, powerful, and independent nation."[44] A frightened Jefferson observed: "All the passions are boiling over, and one who keeps himself cool and clear of the contagion, is so far below the point of ordinary conversation, that he finds himself insulted in every society."[45]

The young republic nearly went to war with France. In the summer of 1798 Congress passed a series of measures that amounted to "quasi-war." It declared all French treaties null and void, created a Navy Department, funded the construction of new warships, and authorized increases for the regular Army. George Washington came out of retirement to lead the new forces, although effective command, at Washington's request, rested in the hands of Inspector General Alexander Hamilton. Jeffersonians saw the Army, in conjunction with the new Alien and Sedition Laws directed against pro-French radicals, as suppression of political opposition; the Federalists meant "to arm one half of the people, for the purpose of keeping the other in awe."[46] As it was, Adams did not request, nor did Congress authorize, a declaration of war. The American Navy was ordered only to retaliate against attacking French warships and privateers. The quasi-war lasted more than two years, during which the Navy captured some eighty-five French armed vessels. The new frigates performed brilliantly, and such spectacular victories as that of the *Constellation* over the *Insurgente* helped to deter the French from widening hostilities. Adams was content with naval retaliation only. He correctly perceived that France, bogged down in campaigns in Europe and Egypt, would not respond with full-scale war or invasion. Adams saw no need to use the Army.

Federalist partisans, including a majority of Adams' Cabinet, were more warlike. Hamilton became particularly fascinated by a grand scheme promoted by Venezuelan revolutionary Francisco de Miranda, whereby the Americans would undertake a joint expedition with the British against both Spain and France in the Americas, thus securing the liberation of all Latin America, the acquisition of Florida and Louisiana for the United States, and military glory for Inspector General Hamilton. The idea of a British alliance intrigued Secretary Pickering, Treasury Secretary Oliver Wolcott, and other high Federalists, and Miranda hurried to London in the autumn of 1798 to elicit British cooperation.

The scheme failed. Adams, always suspicious of British wiles anyway, thought Miranda a "knight errant, as delirious as his immortal countryman, the ancient hero of La Manche."[47] The British, too, balked at aiding a new revolution, even

Alexander Hamilton (1755–1804). A controversial Founding Father, Hamilton served as General Washington's aide-de-camp during the Revolutionary War and as the nation's first secretary of the treasury. In the late 1790s, especially during the XYZ Affair, the pro-British Hamilton favored a muscular policy toward France. The fact that Hamilton, whom President John Adams called a "proud, spirited, conceited, aspiring Mortal," would assume effective command of a wartime army helped restrain Adams from a military solution to the XYZ Affair. Hamilton died after he was shot in a duel with Aaron Burr. (Library of Congress)

one aimed at reducing French and Spanish power in the New World. Enough Anglo-American cooperation did occur during the quasi-war (British naval convoys for American merchantmen, a temporary softening of British maritime practices, cordial personal relations between Minister Rufus King and Foreign Secretary Lord Grenville) for historian Bradford Perkins to dub this period the "first rapprochement."[48] The point is clear, however: the Adams Administration followed Washington's "Great Rule" by avoiding war with France or alliance with England.

Ironically enough, the individual most responsible for stopping full-scale war was the person who had initiated the crisis, Talleyrand. Throughout the summer and fall of 1798, first through the departing Elbridge Gerry, then through assurances to the American minister in the Netherlands, William Vans Murray, Talleyrand let it be known that France wanted peace. He promised Murray that any new envoy sent to make peace would "undoubtedly be received with the respect due to the representative of a free, independent, and powerful nation."[49] These were the same words Adams had used before Congress in June, 1798. To emphasize such assurances, the French repealed their decrees against American shipping and reined in their privateers.

Adams took the chance for peace. The President had received reports from his son John Quincy Adams, now American minister to Prussia, fully corroborating Murray's opinion that France was not bluffing and "a negotiation might be risked."[50] Always a solitary person, President Adams deliberated in private, shunned his Cabinet, and, on February 18, 1799, sent a message to the Senate nominating William Vans Murray as minister plenipotentiary to France. Abigail Adams wrote from Massachusetts: "It comes so sudden, was a measure so unexpected, that the whole community were [sic] like a flock of frightened pigeons." She correctly ranked it as "a master stroke of policy."[51]

Federalist partisans, their appetites whetted for war with France, reacted mindlessly, even threatening to delay Murray's confirmation until Adams nominated Oliver Ellsworth and William R. Davie, both Federalists, as additional plenipotentiaries. Secretary of State Pickering dragged his feet and managed to delay departure of the mission for several months. Adams eventually fired him. The President understood that his decision for peace meant political suicide, but he persisted anyway. Abigail wrote of her husband: "He has sustained the whole force of an unpopular measure which he knew would excite the passions of many, thwart the views of some, and showered down upon his head a torrent of invective produced by ignorance and malevolence and jealousy."[52] Years later Adams himself declared: "I desire no other inscription over my gravestone than: 'Here lies John Adams, who took upon himself the responsibility of the peace with France in the year 1800.'"[53]

The American commissioners arrived in Paris in March, 1800, and negotiations continued until the following autumn. Politics had again shifted in France. Napoleon Bonaparte had returned from Egypt, seized power in the coup d'état of 18 Brumaire, and was now first consul. Joseph Bonaparte, the future king of Spain, took charge of talks with the Americans. Although the war in Europe still raged fiercely, the new leadership had begun to think seriously of reconstituting France's empire in North America. Talleyrand, who had earlier approached the Spanish about Louisiana, encouraged Napoleon in this direction. The rebuilding of a French Empire required peace with Europe, and especially reconciliation with the United States. Napoleon's great victory at Marengo in June, 1800 made a European settlement possible by assuring French control of territory in Italy, which Spain might accept in lieu of Louisiana. One day after the Franco-American Treaty of Mortefontaine was signed, at Joseph Bonaparte's estate outside Paris, the French and Spanish, on October 1, 1800, concluded secret arrangements whereby Napoleon promised Spain the Italian Kingdom of Tuscany, or its equivalent, in exchange for Louisiana. Although American plenipotentiaries did not know about this so-called treaty of San Ildefonso, the French desire for Louisiana played an important, if silent, role nonetheless in the Franco-American accord.

The Treaty of Mortefontaine, or Convention of 1800, amounted to a horse trade. The American negotiators had presented two basic demands: the French were to nullify the 1778 treaties, and pay some $20,000,000 in compensation for illegal seizures of American cargoes. America, the French retorted, had itself invalidated the 1778 treaties by conceding maritime rights to the British in Jay's Treaty; thus French spoliations after 1795 were not illegal. The logjam broke when the Americans agreed to assume the claims of their own citizens, whereupon the French abrogated all previous treaties. Napoleon then suggested the insertion of a statement reaffirming American principles of neutral rights as enumerated in the Model Treaty and in the 1778 alliance. The Americans, seeing no entangling commitments, agreed. The formal signing of the treaty, on September 30, 1800, came amidst much splendor and pageantry. Nearly two hundred diplomats were treated to a deer hunt and huge banquet echoing with toasts to Franco-American harmony.

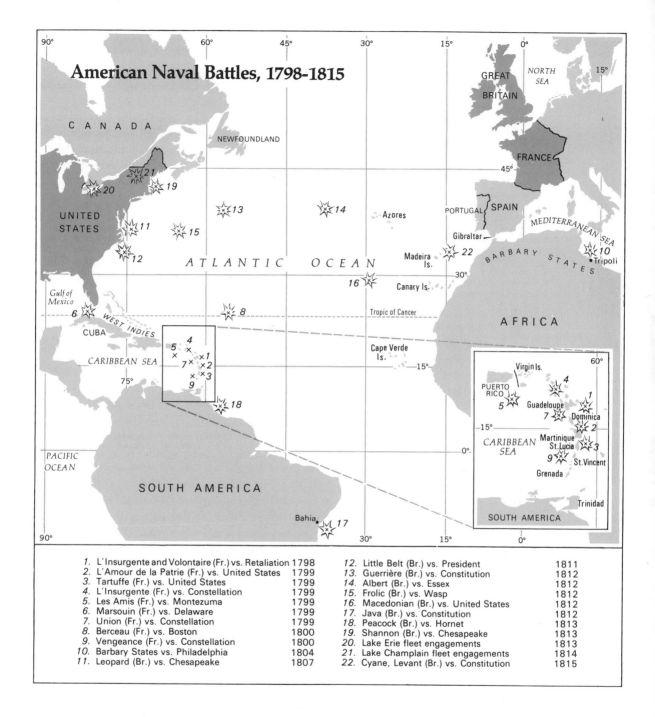

American Naval Battles, 1798-1815

1.	L'Insurgente and Volontaire (Fr.) vs. Retaliation	1798	12.	Little Belt (Br.) vs. President	1811
2.	L'Amour de la Patrie (Fr.) vs. United States	1799	13.	Guerrière (Br.) vs. Constitution	1812
3.	Tartuffe (Fr.) vs. United States	1799	14.	Albert (Br.) vs. Essex	1812
4.	L'Insurgente (Fr.) vs. Constellation	1799	15.	Frolic (Br.) vs. Wasp	1812
5.	Les Amis (Fr.) vs. Montezuma	1799	16.	Macedonian (Br.) vs. United States	1812
6.	Marsouin (Fr.) vs. Delaware	1799	17.	Java (Br.) vs. Constitution	1812
7.	Union (Fr.) vs. Constellation	1799	18.	Peacock (Br.) vs. Hornet	1813
8.	Berceau (Fr.) vs. Boston	1800	19.	Shannon (Br.) vs. Chesapeake	1813
9.	Vengeance (Fr.) vs. Constellation	1800	20.	Lake Erie fleet engagements	1813
10.	Barbary States vs. Philadelphia	1804	21.	Lake Champlain fleet engagements	1814
11.	Leopard (Br.) vs. Chesapeake	1807	22.	Cyane, Levant (Br.) vs. Constitution	1815

Napoleon, that "most skillful self possess [sic] Fencing master," as Murray called him, was trying to lull the Americans until his plans for Louisiana jelled.[54]

The peace of Mortefontaine, followed by Thomas Jefferson's victory in the presidential election of 1800, ended the Federalist era in American diplomacy. The administrations of George Washington and John Adams, despite internal debate and external pressures, pursued a consistent foreign policy. Seeking to maintain independence and honor and to expand trade and territorial boundaries, the young republic at times seemed to veer in a pro-French direction and on other occasions tilted toward the British. At every juncture, however, Washington and Adams escaped being pulled into the European maelstrom in alliance with either France or Britain. Like Jay's Treaty before it, the peace of Mortefontaine avoided a war that hotheaded partisans had advocated. Jefferson's Inaugural Address seemed to promise continuity. "We are all Federalists; we are all Republicans," he said. Slightly amending Washington's advice, the former Francophile pledged "peace, commerce, and honest friendship with all nations, entangling alliances with none."[55]

THE LOUISIANA PURCHASE AND EMPIRE FOR LIBERTY

For one who never traveled more than a hundred miles west of his beloved Monticello, the new President showed an intense interest in American expansion. A few months after his inauguration Jefferson told Monroe: "However our present interests may restrain us within our limits, it is impossible not to look forward to distant times when our rapid multiplication will expand it beyond those limits, & cover the whole northern if not the southern continent."[56] Jefferson primarily eyed the Mississippi Valley, but his vision also embraced the Pacific Coast, the Floridas, Cuba, and a Central American canal. So long as Spain occupied America's borderlands, standing, in Henry Adams' phrase, like a "huge, helpless, and profitable whale," Jefferson was in no hurry.[57] The rapid expansion of the American frontier population, hungry for new land and numbering some 900,000 inhabitants beyond the Alleghenies by 1800, would enable the United States to take over Spanish lands peacefully, "peice by peice [sic]."[58]

Then came rumors in the summer of 1801 about Spain's retrocession of Louisiana to France, along with news that England and France had made peace. Soon French ships were carrying an army to the New World, commanded by Napoleon's brother-in-law, Victor Emmanuel Leclerc, with orders to put down the black rebellion led by Toussaint L'Ouverture on Santo Domingo, and then, presumably, to occupy New Orleans, Louisiana, and perhaps the Floridas as well. American leaders grew alarmed. With Spain no longer controlling the Mississippi, Pinckney's Treaty would become obsolete. Even if the French did not encroach on American territory, their control of New Orleans and commerce on the Mississippi might provoke western farmers to either wage war or secede from the Union. As Madison put it: "The Mississippi is to them [the westerners] everything. It is the Hudson, the Delaware, the Potomac and all the navigable rivers of the Atlantic States formed into one stream."[59] Jefferson seemed willing to consider a veritable revolution in American foreign policy. In a letter of April, 1802 to Minister Robert Livingston in Paris, Jefferson warned that the day France took possession of New Orleans "we must marry ourselves to the British fleet and nation."[60] The President made sure that the warning became public knowledge in France.

Even the threat of an Anglo-American alliance made little impact on France during 1802. Livingston, who was himself hard of hearing, found Talleyrand deaf, dumb, and blind on the subject of Louisiana. The French foreign minister baldly denied the existence of a retrocession treaty for several months (the Spanish King did not actually sign the order of transfer until October, 1802), and then he refused to consider Livingston's offer to purchase New Orleans and West Florida. Napo-

**Thomas Jefferson
(1743–1826).** Before he became President in 1801 Jefferson had served as secretary of state. His presidency was plagued by the neutral rights question and distinguished by the Louisiana Purchase. This idealized view of the Virginian by Thaddeus Kosciuszko is titled "A Philosopher—A Patriot—and a Friend." (The Henry Francis du Pont Winterthur Museum)

leon, bent on reviving a grand French empire in America, redoubled his efforts to acquire the Floridas from Spain.

Tension in America nearly reached the snapping point when, on October 16, 1802, the Spanish intendant of Louisiana suddenly withdrew the American right of deposit at New Orleans, in direct violation of Pinckney's Treaty. Most Americans suspected Napoleon's hand in the plot. The riflemen of Tennessee and Kentucky talked of seizing New Orleans before the French could take formal possession. Some Federalists suddenly found themselves supporting the West and urging war to embarrass Jefferson. Alexander Hamilton exhorted the Administration "to seize at once on the Floridas and New Orleans, and then negotiate."[61] To calm the growing clamor and buy time for diplomacy, Jefferson, in January, 1803, nominated James Monroe as a special envoy to France and Spain, empowered to assist Livingston in purchasing New Orleans and Florida for $10 million. As the French minister reported to Talleyrand, the former governor of Virginia had *"carte blanche"* and would go to London if "badly received in Paris."[62] Congress provided more diplomatic muscle by authorizing the President to call some 80,000 militia members into federal service in case France proved unreasonable. Monroe finally embarked on March 8, arriving in Paris on April 12. The previous day Talleyrand had astonished Robert Livingston by offering to sell all Louisiana to the United States for $15 million.

The decision to relinquish Louisiana was solely Napoleon's. His motives were mixed. The French failure in Santo Domingo probably loomed largest, an especially distressing defeat for Napoleon as Leclerc's 30,000-man army melted away, victims of guerrilla attacks and yellow fever. When Bonaparte learned in January that his brother-in-law had also succumbed to fever, he burst out: "Damn sugar, damn coffee, damn colonies."[63] In the Napoleonic scheme of empire, Louisiana was to have been the source of supply for the sugar and coffee plantations of Santo Domingo, but without Santo Domingo, Louisiana became a liability. In the event of war with England Louisiana could be easily overrun, and Napoleon was already thinking of war. In historian Marshall Smelser's words, "he wished to get back to

New Orleans, 1803. The American eagle spreads its wings over the port of New Orleans at the mouth of the Mississippi River—a prize acquisition in the Louisiana Purchase. (Chicago Historical Society)

his glorious drums and trumpets, his drilling and killing of the fittest youth in Europe."[64] Hence, it made sense to sell Louisiana to the Americans rather than return it to Spain. The sale price would fill French coffers in preparation for the next campaigns, while at the same time eliminating American hostility.

The negotiations did not take long. Napoleon was eager to sell and the Americans eager to buy. Monroe and Livingston had no compunction about violating their instructions; instead of paying $10 million for New Orleans, they pledged $15 million for New Orleans and an undefined empire that lay entirely to the west of the Mississippi, including 50,000 new citizens of French-Spanish descent and about 150,000 Indians. The treaty, signed on April 30, 1803, stipulated that the United States was to receive Louisiana on the same terms that Spain had retroceded the territory to France. Livingston, wondering if any of West Florida came with the purchase, asked Talleyrand what the precise boundaries were. The Frenchman replied vaguely: "You have made a noble bargain for yourselves, and I suppose you will make the most of it."[65] This enigmatic remark provided the basis for future American claims to Spanish territory in Florida and Texas. As it was, acquiring some 828,000 square miles of territory at 3 cents an acre seemed an enormous achievement. Livingston observed, "from this day the United States take their place among the powers of the first rank."[66] Bonaparte remarked: "This accession of territory affirms forever the power of the United States, and I have just given England a maritime rival that sooner or later will lay low her pride."[67]

The treaty still had to be approved and ratified in Washington. Some Federalists, thinking that the addition of trans-Mississippi lands would tip the political balance

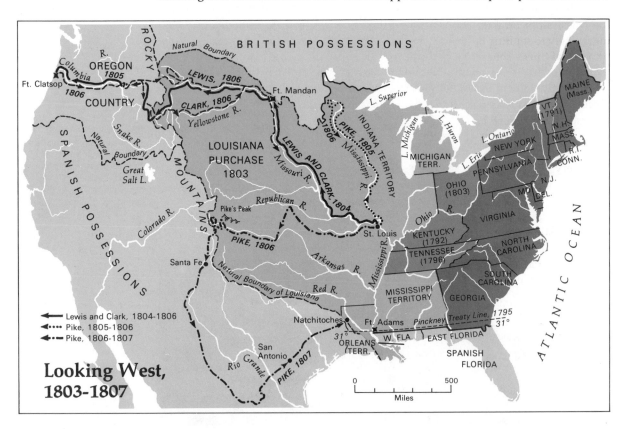

Looking West,
1803-1807

toward agrarians, attacked the treaty. "We are to give money of which we have too little for land of which we already have too much," bewailed one Bostonian.[68] Others accused Jefferson of being in cahoots with Napoleon. There was also the problem, particularly bothersome to Federalist Senator John Quincy Adams, of whether the Constitution, under the treaty power, permitted the incorporation of 50,000 Creoles into the Union without their consent. The President, however, shedding his reputation as a strict constitutionalist, told Madison "that the less we say about constitutional difficulties respecting Louisiana the better, and that what is necessary for surmounting them must be done sub silentio."[69] With the support of such prominent Federalists as Alexander Hamilton, Rufus King, and John Adams, the purchase passed the Senate 24 to 7 in October. The formal transfer of territory came at noon on December 20, 1803, in the Place d'Armée in New Orleans. As the French flag was hauled down and the Stars and Stripes climbed upward, the United States officially doubled its territorial domain.

The Spanish borderlands continued to attract American diplomatic interest for the next several years. Taking advantage of the ambiguous terms of the Louisiana Purchase, Jefferson hoped to harness French support to American agrarian migration and obtain West Florida and Texas from Spain. But Napoleon refused to help, and before long the maritime crisis with England forced Jefferson to defer expansion, although other Americans probed Spanish lands. In 1806–1807 an American military officer, Lieutenant Zebulon M. Pike, led a cartographic expedition up the Arkansas River into Spanish territory, failed to climb the mountain peak which bears his name, and was temporarily detained by Spanish troops for violating Spanish sovereignty. At this time, too, Aaron Burr and sixty followers went down the Mississippi on flatboats, ostensibly to capture Texas from the Spanish, but more likely to set Burr up as the emperor of a secessionist Louisiana. Whatever the purpose of Burr's conspiracy, Jefferson had his former vice-president arrested and took special care to keep the peace with Spain.

The most enduring example of Jefferson's interest in westward expansion during these years was his sponsorship of the Lewis and Clark Expedition. Conceived by Jefferson even before he considered the acquisition of Louisiana, the expedition was designed to find a useful route to the Pacific, to study geography, and to develop fur trade with the Indians. Leaving St. Louis in May, 1804, the "Corps of Discovery" went up the Missouri, crossed the Continental Divide, and followed the Snake and Columbia rivers to the Pacific (Seaside, Oregon today claims the "end of the trail"). Lewis and Clark returned along the same route, arriving at St. Louis in September, 1806. This epic exploration, which Jefferson took pains to publicize, stimulated interest in the rich furs and abundant fauna of the Rocky Mountains and suggested wrongly that the Missouri-Columbia route was a convenient waterway for trade with China. John Jacob Astor's American Fur Company was chartered in 1808, and, with Jefferson's encouragement, Astor projected a line of fortified posts from St. Louis to the Pacific. Only Astoria, at the mouth of the Columbia River, was completed by the outbreak of war in 1812.

Jefferson's efforts at territorial expansion were cut short by a growing crisis with England after 1805, but his optimism remained undimmed. He told Madison, shortly after leaving the White House in 1809, that the United States would become "such an empire for liberty as she has never surveyed since the creation; and I am persuaded that no constitution was ever so well calculated as ours for extensive empire and self-government."[70]

Canton, China, 1800. This Chinese painting of the wharf at the busy commercial port of Canton about 1800 shows the American flag, third from left, flying over *hongs,* or warehouses. Thirty-four American or "barbarian" vessels visited Canton in 1801 alone, attesting to the international character of American commercial relations. (Peabody Museum of Salem)

If Jefferson sought to expand American institutions on land, he also attempted to maintain free American commerce on the high seas. Until the Anglo-French war riveted all attention on the Atlantic, Jefferson eagerly employed the American Navy in the Mediterranean to protect trade against the depradations of the Barbary pirates. The war with Tripoli was especially satisfying to young America. A squadron consisting of the frigates *Constitution* and *Philadelphia* and six smaller vessels performed creditably under the command of Commodore Edward Preble in 1803 and 1804. The *Philadelphia,* however, ran aground while chasing pirates, and the ship and crew were captured. Lieutenant Stephen Decatur heroically slipped into Tripoli Harbor and burned the American vessel at night. In 1805 a contingent of Marines (seven in all) marched overland from Egypt and seized the port of Derna on the shores of Tripoli. The Sultan of Tripoli made peace shortly thereafter, but not until he was paid some $60,000 in tribute. The remainder of the Barbary pirates had to wait until the end of the War of 1812 for American retribution. Jefferson, even while he feared the effects of commercial prosperity on republican virtue, vigorously defended American rights on the high seas.

BLOCKADES AND IMPRESSMENT: THE PERILS OF NEUTRAL TRADE, 1803–1807

Some two weeks after unloading Louisiana on the Americans in the spring of 1803, Napoleon picked a quarrel with England over the insignificant island of Malta. War raged for twelve years, spreading over much of the world, and ending only with Bonaparte's lonely exile to St. Helena in 1815. The war transformed the

United States into the world's largest neutral carrier. Shipping boomed in America, expanding at a rate of seventy thousand tons annually. Particularly significant was the trade between French and Spanish ports in the West Indies and French and Spanish ports on the European continent. Because such direct trade violated Britain's arbitrary Rule of 1756 (which decreed that trade not open to a nation in time of peace could not be opened in time of war), American merchants usually "broke" the voyage by stopping at an American port and paying duties on the cargo, thus converting it to "free goods." The voyage would then continue until the "neutralized cargo" reached France or Spain. While direct American exports amounted to a steady $42 million annually in 1803–1805, the lucrative re-export trade soared from $13 million in 1803 to $36 million in 1804 to $53 million in 1805. A British diplomat angrily denounced the Americans, complaining that "there is not, thanks to our Tars, a single French or Spanish merchantman that now navigates these seas—& these Jews want to navigate for them."[71]

For more than two years neither the British nor the French interfered seriously with American commerce. Indeed, British admiralty courts in the case of the American ship *Polly* (1800) had not disputed the legality of the "broken voyage." But on October 21, 1805, Lord Horatio Nelson's black-hulled ships smashed the combined French and Spanish fleets off Trafalgar, thus establishing England's overwhelming control of the seas. Less than two months later Napoleon crushed the Russian and Austrian armies at Austerlitz, making him master of Europe. Neither the Tiger nor the Shark, each supreme in its own element, could fight the other directly. For the next several years commercial warfare dominated the struggle between England and France. In the ensuing web of blockades and counterblockades, America's neutral trade became inextricably ensnared.

The British decision in the *Essex* case, in May, 1805, signaled trouble. The American merchant brig *Essex* had been captured en route to Havana from Barcelona after having stopped (the "break" in the voyage) in Salem, Massachusetts. The British admiralty judge reversed the *Polly* decision, claiming that the *Essex* had not paid bona fide duties on its cargo. Thereafter American shippers had to prove that importation of enemy goods into the United States was in good faith, not merely a legal subterfuge to bypass the Rule of 1756. Under the new doctrine of the "continuous" voyage, trade carried by a neutral between a belligerent colonial port and home port violated British maritime regulations. Soon British cruisers lurked outside American harbors, practically blockading the coastline.

The British followed up the *Essex* decision with the Order in Council of May 16, 1806, calling for a complete blockade of Napoleonic Europe, from Brest to the Elbe River. Americans angrily complained that this was a "paper blockade" because British cruisers ranged far out to sea and did not actually deny access to enemy ports. Napoleon, "fleetless but well supplied with parchment and sealing wax," retaliated in November with his Berlin Decree, which created a paper blockade of the British Isles.[72] The decree declared that any ship that had previously touched at a British port was a lawful prize and its cargo forfeit. The London government struck back with two more orders in council (January and November, 1807), barring all trade with ports under French jurisdiction unless that shipping first passed through a system of British controls and taxes. England was in essence telling neutrals that they could trade with the continent of Europe only if they paid tribute first. Napoleon retaliated again, this time in the Milan Decree of December, 1807, which stated that any ship that paid taxes to the British, that submitted to

"John Bull Taking A Lunch." The Englishman enjoys a French warship for lunch. In a study of Republican rhetoric in 1811–12, Ronald L. Hatzenbuehler and Robert L. Ivie have shown that congressional "war hawks" projected a diabolic image of John Bull, depicting the covetous British "trampling on America's rights and wresting independence from its citizens in order to sate a bestial appetite for control of world commerce." (Library of Congress)

visit and search by British cruisers, or stopped at a British port, would be treated, ipso facto, as a British ship. The French Emperor was erecting what he called his "Continental System," a gigantic attempt to ruin England's export trade by closing off all European outlets. The Continental System never became fully effective, as Spain, Sweden, and Russia opened their ports to British goods at various intervals after 1807. John Quincy Adams likened the system to excluding "air from a bottle, by sealing up hermetically the mouth, while there was a great hole in the side."[73] Caught in the vise of French decrees and British orders in council, Yankee traders ran the risk of British seizure if they traded directly with French-controlled ports, whereas they incurred Napoleonic displeasure if they first submitted to British trade regulations.

"I consider Europe as a great mad-house," Jefferson lamented, "& in the present deranged state of their moral faculties to be pitied & avoided."[74] In the diplomatic protests that followed, American efforts were directed more at England than at France, because British maritime practices (particularly British warships operating in American waters) more directly jeopardized American commerce. The British, so absorbed in the life-or-death struggle against Napoleon, were hardly humble or apologetic toward Washington, which took offense easily. French seizures, numerous though they were, usually occurred in French ports and in the Caribbean, and were often shrouded in official verbiage that smacked of misunderstanding and promised rectification. With the Americans, Napoleon was tricky and evasive, but seldom arrogant.

Impressment, which rose to alarming proportions after 1803, and which exploded as an issue in the *Chesapeake* affair, helped focus resentment upon England rather than France. With American shipping expanding rapidly during this period, and with life on a British naval vessel resembling life in a British prison, English seamen in increasing numbers jumped ship, took advantage of liberal American naturalization laws, and then enlisted in the American merchant marine. To cite one example, the vessel carrying the new British minister Anthony Merry to America in the autumn of 1803 lost fourteen men to desertion when the ship touched port. By 1812, according to official British claims, some 20,000 English sailors were manning American vessels, approximately one-half of all able-bodied seamen then serving in the merchant marine. Since the British Navy required 10,000 new recruits annually to maintain full strength, the need to impress British deserters from American service became urgent. In carrying out impressment, however, British captains, in historian Paul Varg's phrase, "resorted to the scoop rather than the tweezers," and soon naturalized Americans by the hundreds were manning Royal Navy yardarms.[75] Altogether, according to James Monroe's figures in 1812, some 6,257 Americans were impressed after 1803, probably a more accurate estimate than the 1,600 conceded by the British.

Impressment was an explosive issue. The British could not accept any abridgment of a practice which they saw as vital to maritime supremacy. Americans admitted the British right to search for contraband or enemy personnel, but denied that this right justified the impressment of American citizens. "That an officer from a foreign ship," wrote Secretary of State James Madison in 1807, "should pronounce any person he pleased, on board an American ship on the high seas, not to be an American Citizen, but a British subject, & carry his interested decision on the most important of all subjects to a freeman, into execution on the spot . . . is anomalous in principle, . . . grievous in practice, and . . . abominable in abuse."[76]

Jefferson and Madison missed an opportunity to alleviate some of the controversy when they rejected the Monroe-Pinkney Treaty of December, 1806. Jefferson had sent William Pinkney, an able Maryland lawyer, to join James Monroe in London in an attempt, similar to the Jay mission of 1794, to settle all outstanding differences with England, including impressment and "broken" voyages. Jefferson and Madison attached a *sine qua non* to the instructions: the treaty must contain an explicit British disavowal of impressment. The British would make concessions on broken voyages and the re-export trade, but not on impressment. The most the British Cabinet could concede was a separate note, attached to the final treaty, promising "observance of the greatest caution in the impressing of British seamen; . . . the strictest care . . . to preserve the citizens of the United States from any molestation or injury; and . . . immediate and prompt redress . . . of injury sustained by them."[77] Here was a British promise to mitigate in practice what they would not surrender in principle. Mindful of growing anti-American sentiment in England, and fearful of repercussions from Napoleon's recent Berlin Decree, Pinkney and Monroe opted for half a loaf. Their treaty, signed on December 31, 1806, was probably the best bargain that the United States could have extracted from England during the Napoleonic Wars. Still, Jefferson refused to submit it to the Senate. He and Madison believed that the passage of time, plus the threat of American economic retaliation, would force the British to reconsider. Like John Adams in the Model Treaty of 1776, Jefferson and Madison thought that the attractions of American commerce, not to mention the rightness of American principles, would cause England to mend its ways. In Robert Rutland's apt phrase, they were "old-fashioned men still dreaming that Hobbes was wrong and Locke was right."[78]

"PEACEABLE COERCIONS" AND THE COMING OF THE WAR OF 1812

Anglo-American relations deteriorated steadily following the abortive Monroe-Pinkney Treaty. The *Chesapeake* episode of June, 1807 underscored the volatile nature of the impressment issue. "Never since the battle of Lexington," Jefferson wrote in July, "have I seen this country in such a state of exasperation as at present."[79] The President contemplated asking Congress for a declaration of war, but, owing partly to the country's lack of military and naval muscle, he sought another alternative. As he once put it, "those peaceable coercions which are in the power of every nation, if undertaken in concert & in time of peace, are more likely to produce the desired effect."[80] On December 22, 1807, he won congressional approval for the Embargo Act.

Evenhanded in principle, the embargo, in combination with a nonimportation measure against England, was aimed primarily at the British. The embargo's rules were simple: the export of goods anywhere, by sea or land, was virtually prohibited. Coastal American trade, however, continued with increasingly elaborate controls. Recorded American exports dropped 80 percent in 1808. American imports from Britain, not strictly enforced under the nonimportation act, decreased by 56 percent. One scholar has succinctly concluded that the embargo "stimulated manufactures, injured agriculture, and prostrated commerce."[81]

Domestic protest was loud and shrill. John Randolph, pointing to the loss of shipping and declining agricultural prices, charged his fellow Virginians with attempting to "cure the corns by cutting off the toes."[82] Numerous vituperative epistles reached the White House, including one of August, 1808:[83]

> Thomas Jefferson
> You are the damdest
> dog that God put life into
> God dam you.

Such dissent, when combined with widespread resistance to enforcement, caused Jeffersonians to despair. "I had rather encounter war itself than to display our impotence to enforce our laws," Secretary of the Treasury Albert Gallatin wrote dejectedly.[84] In New England, where Yankee merchants and sailors had long depended on commerce for their livelihood, the economy suffered badly. Ships rotted in harbor and grass grew on once busy wharves. Paranoid Federalists accused Jefferson of conspiring with Napoleon in initiating the embargo, and in the winter of 1808–1809 there were widespread rumors of secessionist conversations between New Englanders and British agents. "I did not expect a crop of so sudden and rank growth of fraud," wrote Jefferson, urging Congress to "legalize *all* means which may be necessary to obtain *its end*."[85] Despite the President's preference for war against England, his followers decided otherwise. On March 1, 1809, three days before Jefferson left the presidency, Congress replaced the embargo with the Non-Intercourse Act, thus freeing American exports to all ports except those controlled by England and France, and promising renewed trade with either belligerent if American neutral rights were respected.

Jefferson's embargo simply did not accomplish the desired diplomatic effect. The British government was initially delighted with the measure, inasmuch as it removed quarrels over neutral rights and gave British shippers a virtual monopoly over trade with Europe. Nonimportation limited trade with Britain, but alternative markets for British goods conveniently appeared in Spain (which revolted against Napoleonic rule in 1808) and Spain's Latin American colonies. As for the French, they continued to seize American ships, even those that evaded the British blockade, using the argument that such ships had to be British in disguise because American law prohibited their presence on the high seas. Rising food prices in England, plus the decline of manufacturing sales, might have tempted the British to

1809 Broadside. This Republican declaration praised Jefferson and Madison for lifting the Embargo, setting trade on a prosperous course again, and preserving American honor. Such praise was premature. (Courtesy of The New-York Historical Society, New York City)

Southwick & Pelsue, Printers

By the Virtue, Firmness and Patriotism of

JEFFERSON & MADISON,

Our Difficulties with England are settled—our Ships have been preserved, and our Seamen will, hereafter, be respected while sailing under our National Flag.

NEW-YORK, SATURDAY MORNING, APRIL 22, 1809.

IMPORTANT.

By the President of the United States.—A Proclamation.

WHEREAS it is provided by the 11th section of the act of Congreſs, entitled " An " act to interdict the commercial intercourſe between the United States and Great Bri- " tain and France, and their dependencies ; and for other purpoſes,"—and that " in " caſe either France or Great Britain ſhall ſo revoke or modify her edicts as that they " ſhall ceaſe to violate the neutral commerce of the United States," the Preſident is au- thoriſed to declare the ſame by proclamation, after which the trade ſuſpended by the ſaid act and by an act laying an Embargo, on all ſhips and veſſels in the ports and harbours of the United States and the ſeveral acts ſupplementary thereto may be renewed with the nation ſo doing. And whereas the Honourable David Montague Erſkine, his Britannic Majeſty's Envoy Extraordinary and Miniſter Plenipotentiary, has by the order and in the name of his ſovereign declared to this Government, that the Britiſh Orders in Council of January and November, 1807, will have been withdrawn, as reſpects the United States on the 10th day of June next. Now therefore I James Madiſon, Preſident of the United States, do hereby proclaim that the orders in council aforeſaid will have been withdrawn on the tenth day of June next; after which day the trade of the United States with Great Britain, as ſuſpended by the act of Congreſs above mentioned, and an act laying an embargo on all ſhips and veſſels in the ports and harbors of the United States, and the ſeveral acts ſupplementary thereto, may be renewed.

Given under my hand and the ſeal of the United States, at Waſhing- ton, the nineteenth day of April, in the year of our Lord, one (L. S) thouſand eight hundred and nine, and of the Independence of the United States, the thirty-third.

JAMES MADISON.

By the President,
RT. SMITH, *Secretary of State.*

---

appease their best trading partner if the embargo had lasted longer. Actually, the rising prices had attracted the most American violators in the last months of the embargo. Historian Burton Spivak has concluded that "it was the winter evasions and not the March repeal that spoiled [Jefferson's] dream."[86]

Non-intercourse was a face-saving substitute that actually favored the British more than the French. American ships could now clear port ostensibly for a neutral destination like Sweden but illegally take their cargo to Halifax in British Canada; vessels heading for French-controlled ports still had to face British block-ade ships. The new President, James Madison, nonetheless hoped to use non-intercourse to modify British policy. He found a willing collaborator in British Minister David M. Erskine. Married to an American wife, Erskine was the only British envoy in the early national period who developed cordial personal relations with his American hosts. When he came to Washington in 1806, he wanted very much to avoid war with America and, at Madison's urging, Erskine recommended repeal of the orders in council, provided that the United States keep non-intercourse against France. Foreign Minister Canning was agreeable if the United States promised to accept the Rule of 1756. Canning also stipulated that the Royal Navy should be allowed to seize any American vessel that violated the Non-Intercourse Act. Erskine proceeded to negotiate a treaty, although nothing explicit was said about the British Navy or the Rule of 1756. In late April, Madison issued a proclamation lifting non-intercourse against Britain on June 10, the date that England, according to the Erskine agreement, would repeal its orders in council. More than 600 American vessels laden with two years' accumulation of goods promptly set sail for British ports. Huzzas echoed from Maine to Georgia.

The joy soon whimpered away. When Canning learned that Erskine's agreement lacked the stipulations he had set, he repudiated the treaty and the "damned Scotch flunkey" who had negotiated it.[87] The foreign secretary, of course, allowed American ships still at sea to bring supplies to England. News of repudiation stunned Americans and angered Madison, who termed it a "mixture of fraud and folly."[88] The President quickly renewed non-intercourse, but the damage had been done. "We are not so well prepared for resistance as we were one year ago," Gallatin reported. "[Then] all or almost all our mercantile wealth was safe at home, our resources entire, and our finances sufficient. . . . Our property is now afloat; England relieved by our relaxations might stand two years of privations with ease; we have wasted our resources without any national unity."[89]

Canning aggravated matters further by replacing Erskine with Francis James ("Copenhagen") Jackson, a notorious diplomat whose mission to Denmark in 1807 had consisted of a brutal ultimatum followed by the destruction of the Danish capital by the guns of the British fleet.[90] Jackson's instructions, in Henry Adams' phrase, were "to propose nothing whatever."[91] The bumptious Briton managed to offend everyone in Washington, save for a handful of Federalists. Diplomacy got nowhere, as Jackson and Madison soon clashed over British charges that the Americans had consciously connived with Erskine to violate Canning's directions. "God damn Mr. Jackson," shouted one Kentuckian, "the President ought to . . . have him kicked from town to town until he is kicked out of the country. God damn him."[92] Madison finally declared Jackson *persona non grata;* London recalled him in April, 1810, and a replacement did not arrive for nearly two years.

The Non-Intercourse Act expired in the spring of 1810. A complicated piece of legislation known as Macon's Bill Number Two replaced it. The new law ostensibly removed all restrictions on American commerce, including trade with England and France; it also empowered the President to renew non-intercourse against one belligerent if the other gave up its punitive decrees. Madison noted that "public attention is beginning to fix itself on the proof . . . that the original sin agst. Neutrals lies with G.B. & that whilst she acknowledges it, she persists in it."[93] Here was an opportunity for Napoleon. Without actually stopping the seizure of American ships, he promised repeal of the Berlin and Milan decrees against American commerce, provided only that the United States "shall cause their rights to be respected by the English."[94] The French pledged to lift their decrees on

November 1, 1810. Whether or not Madison was trying to outfox Napoleon is a matter of scholarly debate, but the President assumed that the French promises were genuine. On November 2, 1810, without adequate proof that Napoleon had freed American shipping (he had not), the President proclaimed non-intercourse against Britain.

This time Madison's exercise in commercial coercion succeeded, but not quickly enough. The British, quite understandably, refused to be blackmailed into lifting their blockade while Napoleon pretended to revoke his decrees. Not only did the British not repeal their orders in council, they enforced them even more vigorously. (Altogether the French confiscated 558 American vessels in the period 1803–1812, as compared to 917 British seizures. In the years 1811–1812, however, French confiscations dwindled to a mere 34.) "The United States," wrote the new Secretary of State James Monroe, "cannot allow Great Britain to regulate their trade, nor can they be content with a trade to Great Britain only. . . . The United States are, therefore, reduced to the dilemma either of abandoning their commerce, or of resorting to other means more likely to obtain a respect for their rights."[95]

Indian troubles on the frontier also contributed to Anglo-American animosities. Beginning in 1806 two remarkable Shawnee Indians, Tecumseh and the Prophet, began to organize the western tribes against further white expansion. Americans had largely their own land grabbing and treaty breaking to account for Indian hostility, but frontier leaders were quick to attribute conspiratorial designs to the British in Canada, where Tecumseh's tribes received food and shelter (but not guns and ammunition, as Americans alleged). Finally, on November 7, 1811, an armed clash occurred at Tippecanoe Creek in what is now Indiana. American forces under General William Henry Harrison barely defeated a superior Indian concentration. Americans simply assumed that the British were stirring up the tribes, even though the opposite was true. Talk of taking Canada was heard in Congress and in the West. As Henry Clay put it: "Is it nothing to us to extinguish the torch that lights up savage warfare?"[96]

The United States thus moved inexorably, albeit haltingly, toward war in the winter and spring of 1812, not knowing that economic distress was finally causing Britannia to alter course. For, beginning in the autumn of 1810, a depression hit the British, accompanied by poor harvests, bread riots, unemployment, higher taxes, higher prices, and general unrest. British exports to the Continent dropped by one-third from 1809 to 1811, while exports to the United States were reduced by seven-eighths. Manufacturing interests began to put pressure on Parliament. A petition from Birmingham contained some 20,000 signatures on a sheet of paper fifty feet in length. On June 16, 1812, Foreign Minister Lord Castlereagh announced in Parliament that the orders in council would be immediately suspended. Two days later, however, without knowing of Castlereagh's action, the American Congress declared war against England.

WAR FOR SOVEREIGNTY BY LAND AND SEA

Because the vote for war was close (79 to 49 in the House, 19 to 13 in the Senate) and came after only two weeks of sharp debate, scholars have noted that had speedier transatlantic communications existed in 1812, war might have been prevented. True enough. But it does not necessarily follow that Americans went to war for imaginary, and therefore frivolous, reasons. The causes of the War of 1812 were numerous and compelling, and Madison gave a reasonably accurate listing in his war message of June 1. The President placed impressment first, spotlighting those hundreds of Americans "dragged on board ships of war of a foreign nation and exposed, under the severities of their discipline, to be exiled to the most distant and deadly climes, to risk their lives in the battles of their oppressors." Second, Madison mentioned British depradations against American commerce within sight of American harbors, as well as "pretended blockades" that disregarded all principles of international law. Third, he charged that Britain's orders in council waged war on American commerce in order to maintain "the monopoly which she covets for her own commerce and navigation." And last, Madison blamed the English for igniting "the warfare just renewed by the savages on one of our extensive frontiers."[97] Privately, without the need for presidential embellishment, Madison noted that Britain's conduct left the United States "no choice but between that [war] & the greater evil of a surrender of our sovereignty . . . , on which all nations whose agriculture & commerce are so closely allied, have an essential interest."[98]

Historians have speculated about the seeming contradiction between Madison's emphasis on maritime causes and the fact that a majority of war votes came from the agrarian South and West, not from the commercially minded Northeast. Some scholars, echoing John Randolph's contemporary charge that the "war hawks" were motivated by a "whip-poor-will cry" for Canada, have listed land hunger or a desire for territorial expansion as major causes of the war.[99] Part of the apparent paradox can be explained by delineating economic self-interest: the West and South were wracked by depression in 1812; eastern merchants, even with British and French depradations, were still making profits. Jeffersonian farmers and frontiersmen, many dependent on the export trade, blamed falling agricultural prices on the British blockade. As John C. Calhoun of South Carolina argued: "they see in the low price of the produce, the hand of foreign injustice; . . . they are not prepared for the colonial state to which again that Power is endeavoring to reduce us."[100] Westerners, moreover, perhaps imbued with a sense of frontier justice, were quick to protest such affronts to the national honor as impressment and the *Chesapeake* affair. The "war hawks" of the Twelfth Congress did talk of adding Florida and Canada to the American union, sometimes making spread-eagle statements that foreshadowed the Manifest Destiny arguments of the 1840s. Westerners focused on Canada in 1811–1812, in part because of their mistaken belief that England was stirring up the Indian tribes north of the Ohio River, but also because Canada was the only place to retaliate against British maritime practices. Matthew Clay of Virginia proclaimed, "We have the Canadas as much under our command as she [Great Britain] has the ocean; and the way to conquer her on the ocean is to drive her from our land."[101]

National honor served as another unifying force for war. The great bulk of the votes for war came from the same southern Republicans who had earlier supported the Embargo and Non-Intercourse laws. Commercial coercion had not worked. In historian Norman Risjord's words, "submission to the orders in council presaged a return to colonial status; war seemed the only alternative."[102] The real issue, wrote one Virginian in 1812, "has ceased to be a question merely relating to certain rights of commerce . . . —it is now clearly, positively, and directly *a question of independence;* that is to say, whether the U. States are an independent nation."[103]

Scholars have also stressed the importance of contingencies, emotions, and personalities. War might have occurred as early as 1807 over impressment and the *Chesapeake* affair, had not Jefferson and Madison chosen economic coercion rather than military retaliation. Even after the embargo failed, Madison persisted in economic pressure. Historian J. C. A. Stagg has shown that Madison quietly forged unity among "war hawks," "malcontents," and "Old Republicans" by gradually presenting war as the only logical alternative to commercial coercion. Many thought it necessary to invade Canada, which had developed as an alternative source of supplies for the West Indies and as a mecca for American smugglers after 1808. Indeed, Canada had "the potential to destroy the very basis of Madison's diplomacy of commercial restriction: his assumption that the British empire was dependent on the United States for 'necessaries.' "[104] Madison did ask Congress in November, 1811, to take preparatory measures, but he failed to get the votes. Federalists, unable to believe that the Administration would actually open hostilities after five years of half measures, initially supported preparedness to embarrass their opponents. But, as one Federalist lamented, "jests sometimes become serious & end in earnest."[105]

England also realized too late that the United States might actually fight. Preoccupied by the war against Napoleon and depression at home, the British were poorly served by their Minister, Augustus Foster, who fraternized too much with Federalists and did not take Madison's bellicose hints seriously. Usually inattentive to American relations anyway, British politicians became even more inward-looking at the close of 1810, when the aged George III finally went incurably insane upon the death of his favorite child. Several months were taken up with political debate over the accession of the Prince Regent, who was mistakenly thought to favor repeal of the orders in council. Later, in the spring of 1812, a lunatic assassinated Prime Minister Spencer Percival, thus delaying for another month the decision to lift the orders against American shipping. These distractions notwithstanding, perceptive reporting by American diplomats in England might have shown the signs that pointed to eventual repeal. Unfortunately, the capable William Pinkney had departed England in despair in February, 1811, and chargé d'affaires Jonathan Russell simply discounted the effect of protests and petitions on Parliament. Russell's last dispatches, which reached the United States on May 22, 1812, held out no promise that England would repeal her decrees. Madison and the "war hawks" made their decisions accordingly, in defense of American commerce, honor, and sovereignty.

Why did the United States not declare war against France as well? In a preliminary vote on June 12, a Federalist proposal to place France and England on the same belligerent footing failed of passage by a narrow 17 to 15 margin. The suspicious Federalists, citing Madison's false claim that France had repealed the Berlin and Milan decrees, subsequently charged that the declaration of war against England was made in collusion with Napoleon. Such was not the case. Madison and his Republican colleagues had no love for Napoleonic France; they knew that French cruisers were still seizing American merchantmen. Nevertheless, a triangular war seemed out of the question. "We resist the enterprises of England first," Jefferson observed, "because they first come vitally home to us, and our feelings repel the logic of bearing the lash of George III for fear of that of Bonaparte at some future day."[106] French outrages occurred in European waters. British press gangs roamed just off American shores, and British officers—not French—were thought to be stirring up the Indians in the Northwest. In Marshall Smelser's words: "Britain commanded the Americans as one commands lackeys. Napoleon appeared to treat the Americans as sovereign peers—while picking their pockets on the sly."[107] The United States could deal with Napoleon *after* it captured Canada. "As to France," Henry Clay explained, "we have no complaint . . . but of the past. Of England we have to complain in all the tenses."[108]

Madison was well aware of the potential advantages of co-belligerency with France. Napoleon's forces would keep the British bogged down in Spain. The French invasion of Russia, which began a week after the American declaration of war, might bring about the full application of the Continental System, thus putting added pressure on Britain. American cruisers and privateers, meanwhile, could use French ports to refit and sell their prizes. It was a policy dictated by American military weakness, reminiscent of American dependence on France during the Revolutionary War. But Madison shunned any formal alliance with France. Even in going to war with England, he tried to make the most of an independent foreign policy.

WARTIME DIPLOMACY AND THE PEACE OF GHENT

"At the moment of the declaration of war, the President regretted the necessity which produced it, looked to its termination, and provided for it."[109] Thus did Secretary of State Monroe write to the American chargé in London, Jonathan Russell, with instructions to seek an armistice, provided that England agreed to end impressment and revoke its orders in council. Several weeks after the Ameri-

Building the Frigate *Philadelphia*. Many Americans made their living from the seas. When their lucrative commerce was threatened by foreign warships, as it was during the 1790s and early 1800s, they prepared themselves for naval warfare. The citizens of Philadelphia raised the funds for the building of this American warship, launched in 1799. In an 1804 action against the Barbary pirates she was captured and burned. Other "gifts from seaport cities," as historian G. Terry Sharrer has put it, would go on to battle the British in the War of 1812. (Library of Congress)

can war declaration, news reached Washington of the British repeal of the orders in council. Hopes for a quick peace were dashed, however, when the British held stubbornly to their policy of impressment. "The Government could not consent to suspend the exercise of a right," Foreign Minister Castlereagh told Russell, "upon which the naval strength of the empire mainly depends."[110] The Americans also remained stubborn about impressment. Two years of war followed.

The next hint of peace came from remote St. Petersburg in the winter of 1812–1813. The Russian foreign minister offered mediation to American envoy John Quincy Adams, an offer which President Madison grasped eagerly. Without waiting for formal British agreement, Madison appointed Federalist James Bayard and Treasury Secretary Albert Gallatin to join Adams as peace commissioners in the Russian capital. The British politely put off their Russian ally, however, saying that the Anglo-American war had no bearing on the common struggle against Napoleon. It was not that British statesmen feared peace negotiations, but that they objected to Russian mediation. The flighty Tsar Alexander, in a moment of moral exultation, might find himself supporting the American position on maritime rights. "I fear the Emperor of Russia is half an American," Prime Minister Lord Liverpool complained.[111] The British told the Russians that they had no objection to treating directly with the Americans, but no one bothered to tell the three plenipotentiaries in St. Petersburg. Not until January, 1814 did Castlereagh formally propose direct negotiations to the United States, and even then he remained imprecise as to time and place.

In America during these months the war sputtered. Captain Oliver Hazard Perry's victory on Lake Erie, the recapture of Detroit, and the death of Tecumseh in 1813 effectively negated British and Indian efforts to roll back American expansion in the old Northwest and upper Louisiana. Elsewhere American forces found themselves constantly on the defensive. The conquest of Canada, contrary to Jefferson's boast, had not proven "a mere matter of marching."[112] American generals displayed incompetence, state militia units performed erratically, and the Canadians fought loyally under British command. The Madison Administration shuddered at the prospect of British reinforcements, soon to be shipped to North America after the defeat of Napoleon. At sea the Americans fared better, with swift Yankee frigates winning several ship-to-ship duels with British men-of-war, and numerous American privateers waging war against British maritime trade. All told, the Americans captured 1,408 British prizes. But even on the oceans British supremacy begin to assert itself by 1814 against the puny American Navy. The British blockade remained strong, and naval convoys kept commerce destruction to a tolerable minimum. The Royal Navy showed in 1814 that it could land troops almost anywhere on American shores, and in August, the island of Nantucket actually signed a separate peace with the British. Little wonder, then, that Madison welcomed Castlereagh's offer to negotiate. The President shrewdly added Jonathan Russell and Henry Clay to the three peace commissioners already in Europe. The appointment of Clay, the loudest "war hawk" of all, was calculated to provide insurance with Congress in case the peace treaty did not obtain the American war goals of 1812.

A diplomatic retreat seemed unavoidable. On June 27, 1814, just prior to the embarrassing British burning of Washington and a few weeks before peace negotiations began in Belgium, Secretary Monroe instructed the plenipotentiaries to "omit any stipulation on the subject of impressment," if such action would facilitate a peace settlement.[113] The American peacemakers paced for six weeks in the picturesque Flemish village of Ghent before the British delegation finally arrived on August 8. Castlereagh stalled in selecting and instructing his commissioners. Preoccupied with the more important European peace conference at Vienna (which Castlereagh attended in person), the British foreign secretary also thought that news of British military successes in North America would simplify diplomacy at Ghent. Meanwhile, like thoroughbred horses, the American delegates chafed and snapped at each other. The acerbic John Quincy Adams continually found fault with his colleagues' ideas and habits. Clay's predilection for poker, brandy, and cigars irritated the doughty New Englander, whose stoic regimen commenced each dawn with an hour of Bible study. Adams' icy disdain gradually melted, however, warmed by Clay's affability, Gallatin's tactful urbanity, and Bayard's good-humored patriotism. "We appear all to be animated by the same desire of *harmonizing* together," he wrote to his wife.[114]

The British peace proposals sorely tested American unity. By asking for the formation of a separate Indian buffer state in the Old Northwest, some adjustment in the Canadian-American boundary south of the Great Lakes, and a *quid pro quo* for renewing American fishing rights (which London claimed had lapsed during the war), the British nearly ended negotiations at the start. Of the Americans, only Clay, the self-proclaimed expert at the western game of brag, thought the British were bluffing. He was right. After a few weeks the Indian issue gradually disappeared. The British still insisted on boundary changes, direct access to the Mississippi, and compensation for fishing privileges. Adams experienced a sense of *déjà vu*. "The situation in which I am placed," he wrote to his father in Massachusetts, "often brings to mind that in which you were situated in the year 1782. . . . I am called upon to support the same interests, and in many respects, the same identical points and questions. . . . It is the boundary, the fisheries, and the Indian savages."[115] Next came a British demand for *uti possidetis*, or peace based upon the war map of the moment, meaning that the English would continue to hold eastern Maine and portions of American territory south of the Great Lakes. The Americans insisted on the 1783 boundary. News finally reached Ghent in late October that the British invasion of the Hudson Valley had been stopped dead at Plattsburgh, New York, and the amphibious attack on Baltimore had been repelled with the loss of one of England's best generals. Worse yet, President Madison had rallied support (even among New England Federalists) by violating diplomatic etiquette and publishing the initial British peace demands. "Mr. Madison has acted most scandalously," sniffed the Prime Minister, Lord Liverpool.[116]

Great Britain had a choice—either continue the war or accept a peace without territorial gain. Castlereagh was having a difficult time in Vienna, where the Prussians were hungrily eyeing Saxony and the Russians demanding all of Poland. The British Cabinet thereupon turned for advice to the Duke of Wellington, then in command of occupied and unruly Paris. The Iron Duke said that he would lead His Majesty's troops in America, if ordered, but it would be better, after the defeat at Plattsburgh, to negotiate peace on the terms *status quo ante bellum.* Lord Liverpool agreed, advising Castlereagh on November 18, 1814, to seek peace without any territorial additions.

European trouble once again proved an American blessing. Another month of speedy negotiations settled all remaining questions. Ironically enough, it was during this last phase that the one serious disagreement arose among the American delegates. The British, still hoping for a *quid pro quo* in return for American fishing rights, asked for access to the Mississippi River. When Adams, ever the protector of Yankee fishermen, seemed disposed to accept such a bargain, Jonathan Russell accused him of trying to "barter the patriotic blood of the West for blubber, and exchange ultra-Allegheny scalps for codfish."[117] Gallatin smoothed over the contretemps, however, by suggesting that any reference to the Mississippi and the fisheries be omitted from the final treaty. The British delegation agreed. And so, on the night before Christmas, 1814, in the residence of the British commissioners at Ghent, the treaty of peace was signed. "I hope," said Adams, "it will be the last treaty of peace between Great Britain and the United States."[118]

The pact was received with great rejoicing when it reached Washington in early February, 1815. The Senate voted approval 35–0, despite the fact that none of the ostensible causes of the war were mentioned in the treaty. Partly responsible for the euphoric atmosphere was the *previous* arrival of news concerning Andrew Jackson's smashing victory over the British at New Orleans on January 8, 1815. Many Americans believed erroneously that Jackson's achievement influenced the Ghent Treaty, and the Madison Administration was not averse to ending what had been an unpopular war in a blaze of military glory. News of Ghent and New Orleans also undermined any impact that delegates from the Hartford Convention might have had on American diplomacy. Composed of New England Federalists who opposed Madison's war against England, the Hartford Convention had sent delegates to Washington with proposals to amend the Constitution (among the suggestions was a sixty-day limit on embargoes and a two-thirds vote of Congress for war). Madison ignored the New Englanders, who slunk home in disgrace.

EUROPE'S WARS AND AMERICAN INDEPENDENCE, 1789–1815: THE LEGACY

The Peace of Ghent, coinciding with the end of the Napoleonic wars in Europe, marked the culmination of an important phase of American foreign policy. The United States, after 1793, had reacted to Europe's wars by trying to expand its commerce as a neutral carrier and enlarge its territory by playing upon European rivalries. American statesmen sought these goals without war or European entanglements until 1812, when the accumulation of grievances against America's neutral rights and a traditional interest in territorial gains catapulted an unprepared country into a second war of independence against Great Britain. The end of that Anglo-American conflict, combined with peace in Europe, made all questions of maritime rights academic. Thereafter, for the next thirty years or so, American relations with Europe focused almost exclusively on the matter of territorial expansion in the western hemisphere. A biographer of Madison has written, "the red sea of British dead created by the fire of Jackson's men [at New Orleans] dramatically and finally underscored American possession of the Western empire."[119]

By twentieth-century standards the War of 1812 seems inexpensive—only 2,260 battle deaths and $105 million in direct costs. Yet its consequences were large. Henry Clay thought that the country had gained "respectability and character abroad—security and confidence at home. . . . [O]ur character and Constitution are placed on a solid basis, never to be shaken."[120] Albert Gallatin's estimate was more balanced. "The War has been productive of evil & good," he wrote, "but I think the good preponderates. . . . Under our former system we were become too selfish. . . . The people . . . are more Americans: they feel & act more as a Nation, and I hope that the permanency of the Union is thereby better secured."[121] So impressed was the French minister in Washington that he characterized the naval victories of the Americans as "a prelude to the lofty destiny to which they are called," and concluded that "the war has given the Americans what they so essentially lacked, a national character founded on a glory common to all."[122]

This sense of national confidence and glory rested partly upon illusion. Jackson's heroics at New Orleans caused people to forget the burning of Washington, to forget that the war was a draw at best, hardly a spectacular success. The view arose, not easily dispelled, that "citizen soldiers" were a sufficient defense against European professionals, and that frontier captains were superior to West Point graduates. The lack of preparedness was forgotten. John Quincy Adams spoke only for himself in hoping that the United States would learn "caution against commencing War without a fair prospect of attaining its objects."[123] Forgotten, too, was the probability that, with more patience on the part of the Madison Administration, and less haughtiness and more attentiveness to American issues on the part of the British, the War of 1812 need never have been fought. The legitimate, if limited, naval successes of the war had a more enduring effect, as much of the wartime Navy was maintained after 1815. Less than a year after Ghent a squadron of ten vessels under Captain Stephen Decatur extracted favorable treaties from the Barbary sultans of Tripoli, Algiers, and Tunis, and in the ensuing decades naval officers continued to serve as advance agents of American empire. But even in naval matters the limits of American power were less remembered than the superpatriotism of Decatur's famous toast: "Our country! In her intercourse with foreign nations may she always be in the right; but our country, right or wrong."[124] The revulsion against the Federalists, furthermore, for their apparent lack of patriotic fervor, provided an ominous precedent for future opponents of American wars.

American gains were substantial nonetheless. Even if the British refused to revoke impressment in theory, the end of the war brought the release of hundreds of American citizens from British ships and British prisons. The defeat of Napoleon would have meant the end of impressment anyway, but at least the Americans had the satisfaction of vindicating their honor. Never again would the forceful abduction of American citizens on the high seas be a problem in Anglo-American relations. No longer could the northwest Indians rely on British support to oppose American expansion. Even if the peace settled no major issues by treaty, the United States, with its population doubling every 23 years, profited. In Henry Adams' words, "they gained their greatest triumph in referring all their disputes to be settled by time, the final negotiator, whose decision they could safely trust."[125] America's economic independence was thus established and its territorial integrity defended. However much the United States risked its diplomatic goals by going to war in 1812, the paradoxical effect of that war was to increase American self-confidence and to ensure European respect. The young republic still had not reached the rank of a great power by Europe's standards, but the war with England had shown that in North America the United States could not be treated like Geneva or Genoa.

The legacy of 1812 was most evident in Anglo-American relations. Britain, engaged in a life-or-death struggle with Napoleon, found the United States a tough adversary. As the Duke of Wellington recognized, Canada was useless as an offensive base and could be defended only with the greatest difficulty. There was also the matter of Anglo-American trade, as British exports to America rose substantially, thus presaging a commercial interdependence which, like Canada, served as a hostage to peaceful Anglo-American relations. Rivalry between the two

English-speaking nations did not end in 1815, of course, and Great Britain still stood as the chief barrier to American expansion. But after 1815 the former mother country chose to settle differences with the United States at the negotiating table, not on the battlefield. When the British West Indies were finally opened to American trade in 1830, an aging James Madison predicted that England could "no longer . . . continue mistress of the seas" and the "Trident must pass to this hemisphere."[126] He was right.[126]

FURTHER READING FOR THE PERIOD 1789–1815

General histories after 1789 include Henry Adams, *History of the United States During the Administrations of Jefferson and Madison* (1889–1891); Reginald Horsman, *The Diplomacy of the New Republic, 1776–1815* (1985); Lawrence S. Kaplan, *Colonies into Nation* (1972); Daniel G. Lang, *Foreign Policy in the Early Republic* (1985); Marshall Smelser, *The Democratic Republic, 1801–1815* (1968); and Paul A. Varg, *Foreign Policies of the Founding Fathers* (1970) and *New England and Foreign Relations, 1784–1850* (1983).

For the diplomacy of the Washington presidency see John R. Alden, *George Washington* (1984); Harry Ammon, *The Genet Mission* (1973); Samuel Flagg Bemis, *Jay's Treaty* (1962) and *Pinckney's Treaty* (1960); Julian P. Boyd, *Number 7* (1964); Joseph Charles, *The Origins of the American Party System* (1956); Jerald A. Combs, *The Jay Treaty* (1970); Alexander DeConde, *Entangling Alliance* (1958); Gilbert Lycan, *Alexander Hamilton and American Foreign Policy* (1970); Forrest McDonald, *The Presidency of George Washington* (1979); Charles R. Ritcheson, *Aftermath of Revolution* (1969); and Arthur P. Whitaker, *The Spanish-American Frontier, 1783–1795* (1927).

John Adams' diplomacy and the XYZ Affair are treated in Albert H. Bowman, *The Struggle for Neutrality* (1974); Ralph A. Brown, *The Presidency of John Adams* (1979); Alexander DeConde, *The Quasi-War* (1966); Lawrence S. Kaplan, *"Entangling Alliances with None"* (1987); Stephen Kurtz, *The Presidency of John Adams* (1957); and William Stinchcombe, *The XYZ Affair* (1981).

Jeffersonian foreign policy and expansionism are studied in Lance Banning, *The Jeffersonian Persuasion* (1978); Alexander DeConde, *This Affair of Louisiana* (1976); Robert M. Johnstone, Jr., *Jefferson and the Presidency* (1978); E. Wilson Lyon, *Louisiana in French Diplomacy, 1759–1804* (1934); Dumas Malone, *Jefferson the President* (1970); Drew R. McCoy, *The Elusive Republic* (1980); Forrest McDonald, *The Presidency of Thomas Jefferson* (1976); Merrill Peterson, *Thomas Jefferson and the New Nation* (1970); Malcolm J. Rohrbough, *The Trans-Appalachian Frontier* (1978); and Arthur P. Whitaker, *The Mississippi Question, 1795–1803* (1934).

Diplomatic issues leading to the War of 1812 are traced in Roger Brown, *The Republic in Peril: 1812* (1934); A. L. Burt, *The United States, Great Britain, and British North America* (1940); Clifford L. Egan, *Neither Peace Nor War: Franco-American Relations, 1803–1812* (1983); Ronald L. Hatzenbuehler and Robert L. Ivie, *Congress Declares War* (1983); Reginald Horsman, *The Causes of the War of 1812* (1962); Julius Pratt, *Expansionists of 1812* (1925); Bradford Perkins, *The First Rapprochement* (1955) and *Prologue to War* (1961); Robert A. Rutland, *Madison's Alternatives* (1975); Burton Spivak, *Jefferson's English Crisis* (1979); and J. C. A. Stagg, *Mr. Madison's War* (1983).

Wartime questions and the peacemaking at Ghent appear in James Banner, *To the Hartford Convention* (1970); Pierre Berton, *The Invasion of Canada, 1812–1813* (1980); Harrison Bird, *War for the West, 1790–1813* (1971); Fred L. Engleman, *The Peace of Christmas Eve* (1962); Bradford Perkins, *Castlereagh and Adams: England and the United States, 1812–1823* (1964); and Patrick C. T. White, *A Nation on Trial* (1965).

For aspects of expansionism, see John L. Allen, *Passage Through the Garden: Lewis and Clark and the Image of the American Northwest* (1975); Roy E. Appleman, *Lewis and Clark* (1975); James C. Bradford, ed., *Command Under Sail* (1985); Jonathan Goldstein, *Philadelphia and the China Trade, 1682–1846* (1978); Dorothy V. Jones, *License for Empire* (1982); David F. Long, *Nothing too Daring: A Biography of Commodore David Porter, 1780–1843* (1970); and Henry Savage, Jr., *Discovering America, 1700–1875* (1979).

Biographical studies of leading statesmen include Harry Ammon, *James Monroe* (1971); Samuel Flagg Bemis, *John Quincy Adams and the Foundations of American Foreign Policy* (1949); George A. Billias, *Elbridge Gerry* (1979); Irving Brant, *James Madison* (1941–1961); Gerald H. Clarfield, *Timothy Pickering and the American Republic* (1981); Jacob E. Cooke, *Alexander Hamilton* (1982); Robert Hendrickson, *The Rise and Fall of Alexander Hamilton* (1981); Peter P. Hill, *William Vans Murray* (1971); Ralph Ketcham, *James Madison* (1971); essays on Jefferson and Madison in Frank Merli and Theodore A. Wilson, eds., *Makers of American Diplomacy* (1974); Robert W. Remini, *Andrew Jackson and the Course of American Empire, 1767–1821* (1977); Raymond Walters, Jr., *Albert Gallatin* (1957); and Marvin R. Zahniser, *Charles Cotesworth Pinckney* (1967).

See also the General Bibliography and the following notes.

NOTES TO CHAPTER 2

1. Quoted in Henry Adams, *History of the United States During the Administrations of Jefferson and Madison* (New York: Charles Scribner's Sons, 1889–1891; 9 vols.), IV, 11.

2. *Ibid.*, p. 13.

3. *Ibid.*, p. 14.

4. *Ibid.*, pp. 15–16.

5. Quoted in Dumas Malone, *Jefferson and His Time* (Boston: Little, Brown, 1948–1974; 5 vols.), V, 401.

6. Adams, *History of Jefferson and Madison*, IV, 27.

7. Quoted in Malone, *Jefferson, V*, 425.

8. Quoted in R. Horsman, *The Causes of the War of 1812* (Philadelphia: University of Pennsylvania Press, 1962), p. 169.

9. Quoted in Adams, *History of Jefferson and Madison*, IV, 33.

10. Bradford Perkins, *Prologue to War: England and the United States, 1805–1812* (Berkeley: University of California Press, 1961), p. 144.

11. Quoted in Paul A. Varg, *Foreign Policies of the Founding Fathers* (Baltimore: Penguin Books, 1970), p. 192.

12. Quoted in Horsman, *Causes of the War of 1812*, p. 235.

13. Henry Cabot Lodge, ed., *The Works of Alexander Hamilton* (New York: G. P. Putnam's Sons, 1904; 12 vols.), X, 357.

14. Quoted in Samuel Flagg Bemis, *Jay's Treaty: A Study in Commerce and Diplomacy* (New Haven: Yale University Press, 1962; rev. ed.), p. 372.

15. Quoted in Jerald A. Combs, *The Jay Treaty: Political Battleground of the Founding Fathers* (Berkeley: University of California Press, 1970), p. 76.

16. A. A. Lipscomb, ed., *The Writings of Thomas Jefferson* (Washington: Thomas Jefferson Memorial Association, 1903–1904; 19 vols.), IX, 10.

17. Worthington C. Ford, ed., *Writings of Thomas Jefferson* (New York: G. P. Putnam's Sons, 1892–1899; 10 vols.), VI, 278.

18. Quoted in Lawrence S. Kaplan, *Colonies into Nation: American Diplomacy, 1763–1801* (New York: Macmillan, 1972), p. 219.

19. Lipscomb, *Writings of Jefferson*, IX, p. 97.

20. Quoted in Harry Ammon, *The Genet Mission* (New York: W. W. Norton, 1973), p. 86.

21. Quoted in Claude G. Bowers, *Jefferson and Hamilton: The Struggle for Democracy in America* (Boston: Houghton Mifflin, 1925), p. 229.

22. Bemis, *Jay's Treaty*, p. 373.

23. Quoted in John Garry Clifford, "A Muddy Middle of the Road: The Politics of Edmund Randolph, 1790–1795," *Virginia Magazine of History and Biography*, LXXX (July, 1972), 298.

24. Paul Leicester Ford, ed., *The Works of Thomas Jefferson* (New York: G. P. Putnam's Sons, 1904; 12 vols.), VIII, 193.

25. Quoted in Kaplan, *Colonies into Nation*, p. 243.

26. Quoted in Clifford, "Edmund Randolph," p. 306.

27. Joseph Charles, *The Origins of the American Party System* (Williamsburg: Institute of Early American History and Culture, 1956), p. 106.

28. Bernard Mayo, ed., "Instructions to the British Ministers to the United States, 1791–1812," *Annual Report of the American Historical Association for 1936* (Washington: Government Printing Office, 1941; 3 vols.), III, 83.

29. Quoted in John A. Carroll and Mary W. Ashworth, *George Washington: First in Peace* (New York: Charles Scribner's Sons, 1957), p. 278.

30. Quoted *ibid.*, p. 294.

31. Quoted in Combs, *The Jay Treaty*, p. 184.

32. *Ibid.*

33. Arthur P. Whitaker, *The Spanish-American Frontier, 1783–1795* (Boston: Houghton Mifflin, 1927), p. 220.

34. Samuel Flagg Bemis, *Pinckney's Treaty: A Study of America's Advantage from Europe's Distress* (New Haven: Yale University Press, 1962; rev. ed.).

35. Quoted in Henry Blumenthal, *France and the United States, Their Diplomatic Relations, 1789–1914* (Chapel Hill: The University of North Carolina Press, 1970), p. 14.

36. James D. Richardson, ed., *A Compilation of the Messages and Papers of the Presidents, 1789–1901* (Washington: Government Printing Office, 1896–1914; 10 vols.), I, 221–223.

37. Quoted in A. H. Bowman, *The Struggle for Neutrality* (Knoxville: University of Tennessee Press, 1974), pp. 268–269.

38. Quoted in Alexander DeConde, *The Quasi-War: The Politics and Diplomacy of the Undeclared War with France, 1797–1801* (New York: Charles Scribner's Sons, 1966), p. 3.

39. Quoted in William Stinchcombe, "Talleyrand and the American Negotiations of 1797–1798," *Journal of American History*, LXII (December, 1975), 578.

40. Quoted in Bowman, *The Struggle for Neutrality*, p. 277.

41. Walter Lowrie and Matthew St. Clair Clarke, eds., *American State Papers (Class I) Foreign Relations* (Washington: Government Printing Office, 1832–1859; 6 vols.), II, 161.

42. Quoted in DeConde, *Quasi-War*, p. 52.

43. Quoted in Kaplan, *Colonies into Nation*, p. 276.

44. Richardson, ed., *Messages of the Presidents*, I, 256.

45. Quoted in Varg, *Foreign Policies of the Founding Fathers*, p. 135.

46. Quoted in DeConde, *Quasi-War*, p. 99.

47. Quoted in Kaplan, *Colonies into Nation*, p. 282.

48. Bradford Perkins, *The First Rapprochement: England and the United States, 1795–1805* (Philadelphia: University of Pennsylvania Press, 1955).

49. Lowrie and Clarke, eds., *American State Papers, Foreign Relations*, II, 242.

50. Quoted in Page Smith, *John Adams* (Garden City: Doubleday, 1962; 2 vols.), II, 995.

51. Quoted *ibid.*, II, 1000.

52. Quoted *ibid.*, II, 1002.

53. Charles Francis Adams, ed., *The Works of John Adams* (Boston: Little, Brown, 1856; 10 vols.), X, 113.

54. Quoted in Peter P. Hill, *William Vans Murray, Federalist Diplomat: The Shaping of Peace with France, 1797–1801* (Syracuse: Syracuse University Press, 1971), p. 196.

55. Richardson, ed., *Messages of the Presidents*, I, 323.

56. Lipscomb, *Writings of Jefferson*, X, 296.

57. Adams, *History of Jefferson and Madison*, I, 340.

58. Quoted in Marshall Smelser, *The Democratic Republic, 1801–1815* (New York: Harper and Row, 1968), p. 87.

59. Gaillard Hunt, ed., *The Writings of James Madison* (New York: G. P. Putnam's Sons, 1900–1910; 9 vols.), VI, 462.

60. Quoted in Robert M. Johnstone, Jr., *Jefferson and the Presidency* (Ithaca: Cornell University Press, 1978), p. 69.

61. Quoted in Malone, *Jefferson and His Time*, IV, 277.

62. Quoted in Albert H. Bowman, "Pichon, the United States, and Louisiana," *Diplomatic History*, I (Summer, 1977), 266.

63. Quoted in E. W. Lyon, *Louisiana in French Diplomacy, 1759–1804* (Norman: University of Oklahoma Press, 1934), p. 194.

64. Smelser, *Democratic Republic*, p. 94.

65. Quoted in Alexander DeConde, *This Affair of Louisiana* (New York: Charles Scribner's Sons, 1976), p. 174.

66. Quoted in François de Barbé-Marbois, *History of Louisiana* (Philadelphia: J. B. Lippincott, 1830), pp. 310–311.

67. Quoted in Lyon, *Louisiana in French Diplomacy*, p. 206.

68. Quoted in Malone, *Jefferson and His Time*, IV, 297.

69. Quoted *ibid.*, p. 316.

70. Lipscomb, *Writings of Jefferson*, XII, 277.

71. Quoted in Clifford L. Egan, *Neither Peace Nor War: Franco-American Relations, 1803–1812* (Baton Rouge: Louisiana State University Press, 1983), p. 27.

72. Smelser, *Democratic Republic*, p. 148.

73. Charles F. Adams, ed., *Memoirs of John Quincy Adams* (Philadelphia: J. B. Lippincott, 1874–1877; 12 vols.), II, 92.

74. Quoted in Perkins, *Prologue to War*, p. 41.

75. Varg, *Foreign Policies of the Founding Fathers*, p. 173.

76. Quoted in Perkins, *Prologue to War*, p. 89.

77. Quoted in Varg, *Foreign Policies of the Founding Fathers*, p. 182.

78. Robert A. Rutland, *Madison's Alternatives: The Jeffersonian Republicans and the Coming of War, 1805–1812* (Philadelphia: J. B. Lippincott, 1975), p. 5.

79. Lipscomb, *Writings of Jefferson*, XI, 274.

80. Quoted in Horsman, *Causes of the War of 1812*, p. 59.

81. Walter W. Jennings, *The American Embargo, 1807–1809* (Iowa City: University of Iowa Studies in the Social Sciences, 1921), p. 231.

82. Quoted in Perkins, *Prologue to War*, p. 163.

83. Quoted in Robert H. Ferrell, ed., *Foundations of American Diplomacy, 1775–1872* (New York: Harper and Row, 1968), p. 6.

84. Quoted in Perkins, *Prologue to War*, p. 161.

85. Quoted in Richard Mannix, "Gallatin, Jefferson, and the Embargo of 1808." *Diplomatic History*, III (Spring, 1979), 168.

86. Burton Spivak, *Jefferson's English Crisis* (Charlottesville: University Press of Virginia, 1979), p. 203.

87. Quoted in Perkins, *Prologue to War*, p. 220.

88. Quoted in Smelser, *Democratic Republic*, p. 194.

89. Quoted in Ralph Ketcham, *James Madison: A Biography* (New York: Macmillan, 1971), p. 496.

90. Rutland, *Madison's Alternatives*, p. 25.

91. Adams, *History of Jefferson and Madison*, V, 103.

92. Quoted in Horsman, *Causes of the War of 1812*, p. 155.

93. Quoted in Rutland, *Madison's Alternatives*, p. 27.

94. Quoted in Roger H. Brown, *The Republic in Peril: 1812* (New York: Columbia University Press, 1964), p. 23.

95. Quoted in Varg, *Foreign Policies of the Founding Fathers*, p. 286.

96. Quoted in Perkins, *Prologue to War*, p. 283.

97. Richardson, ed., *Messages of the Presidents*, II, 484–490.

98. Quoted in Varg, *Foreign Policies of the Founding Fathers*, p. 292.

99. Quoted in Perkins, *Prologue to War*, p. 359.

100. *Annals of Congress*, 12 Cong., 1 Sess. (December 12, 1811), p. 482.

101. Quoted in Horsman, *Causes of the War of 1812*, p. 182.

102. Norman K. Risjord, "1812: Conservatives, War Hawks, and the Nation's Honor," *William and Mary Quarterly*, XVII (April, 1961), 200.

103. Quoted *ibid.*, p. 205.

104. J.C.A. Stagg, *Mr. Madison's War* (Princeton: Princeton University Press, 1983), p. 46.

105. Quoted in Perkins, *Prologue to War*, p. 434.

106. Quoted in Lawrence S. Kaplan, "France and Madison's Decision for War," *Mississippi Valley Historical Review*, L (March, 1964), 658.

107. Smelser, *Democratic Republic*, p. 223.

108. J. F. Hopkins, ed., *The Papers of Henry Clay* (Lexington, Ky,: University of Kentucky Press, 1959–1973; 5 vols.), I, 674.

109. Lowrie and Clarke, eds. *American State Papers, Foreign Relations*, III, 585–586.

110. *Ibid.*, III, 589–590.

111. Quoted in Bradford Perkins, *Castlereagh and Adams: England and the United States, 1812–1823* (Berkeley: University of California Press, 1965), p. 14.

112. Quoted in Adams, *History of Jefferson and Madison*, VI, 337.

113. Lowrie and Clarke, eds., *American State Papers, Foreign Relations*, III, 704.

114. Quoted in Perkins, *Castlereagh and Adams*, p. 49.

115. Quoted in Samuel Flagg Bemis, *John Quincy Adams and the Foundations of American Foreign Policy* (New York: Alfred A. Knopf, 1949), p. 196.

116. Quoted in Perkins, *Castlereagh and Adams*, p. 113.

117. Quoted *ibid.*, p. 124.

118. Quoted in Bemis, *John Quincy Adams*, p. 218.

119. Ketcham, *James Madison*, p. 596.

120. Quoted in Perkins, *Castlereagh and Adams*, p. 150.

121. Quoted in Raymond Walters, Jr., *Albert Gallatin: Jeffersonian Financier and Diplomat* (New York: Macmillan, 1957), p. 288.

122. Quoted in Ketcham, *James Madison*, pp. 597–598.

123. Quoted in Perkins, *Castlereagh and Adams*, p. 151.

124. Quoted in Charles J. Peterson, *The American Navy* (Philadelphia: James B. Smith, 1858), p. 287.

125. Adams, *History of Jefferson and Adams*, IX, 53.

126. Quoted in Stagg, *Mr. Madison's War*, p. 517.

Chapter 3

James K. Polk (1795–1849). Tennessean, graduate of the University of North Carolina, and a vigorous Democratic expansionist, Polk admired Andrew Jackson. As President, Polk cast his eyes on Mexican lands and helped spark war with Mexico to obtain them. (National Portrait Gallery, Smithsonian Institution)

Making Way for Continental Expansion, 1815-1848

DIPLOMATIC CROSSROAD: MEXICAN-AMERICAN WAR ON THE RIO GRANDE, 1846

The momentous order to march to the Rio Grande reached "Old Rough and Ready" General Zachary Taylor on February 3, 1846. Planning and reconnoitering took several weeks, so the first infantry brigades did not tramp out single file from Corpus Christi until March 9. The army averaged ten miles a day, through suffocating dust, across sunbaked soil, through ankle-deep sands, past occasional holes of brackish water, into areas that gradually became grasslands capable of supporting trees and other vegetation. Near a wide, marshy stream called the Arroyo Colorado, American troops nearly tangled with a Mexican cavalry force, but the numerically superior "gringoes" managed to cross unmolested. Late in the morning of March 28 Taylor's army reached its goal, an expansive area of plowed field on the north bank of the Rio Grande some 150 miles south of Corpus Christi. Across the 200 yards of mud-colored river was the Mexican town of Matamoros and its well-armed garrison of nearly 3,000 men. Taylor encamped, set up earthworks (later called Fort Texas), and waited.

The next three weeks were nervous, but peaceful. The initial parley between Taylor and the Mexicans had to be conducted in French because no American could speak Spanish and none of the Mexicans present had mastered English. Taylor assured the Mexicans that his advance to the Rio Grande was neither an invasion of Mexican soil nor a hostile act. The suspicious Mexicans reinforced their garrison with some 2,000 additional troops. Then, on April 24, Major General Mariano Arista arrived to assume command of the Division of the North and immediately notified Taylor that hostilities had begun. A force of Mexican cavalry, 1,600 strong, crossed the river at La Palangana, fourteen miles upstream from Matamoros. Taylor sent a detachment of dragoons to investigate, but they returned having seen nothing. That same evening, April 24, Taylor ordered out another cavalry force under Captain Seth B. Thornton. This time the Americans rode into an ambush. Thornton tried to fight his way free but lost 11 men killed.

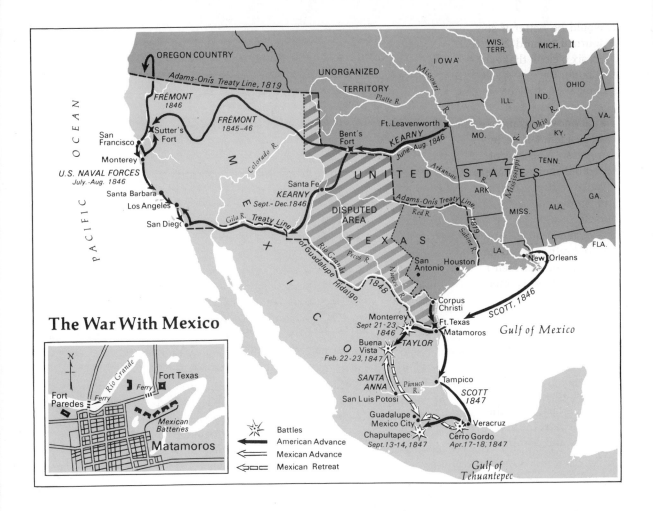

The War With Mexico

Battles ✦
American Advance ◄━━━
Mexican Advance ◄═══
Mexican Retreat ◁□□

The rest of his 63-man contingent was captured. News of the fight reached Taylor at reveille on April 26 when Thornton's guide returned to Fort Texas. "Hostilities may now be considered as commenced," an agitated Taylor immediately wrote to Washington.[1] His dispatch, which had to travel overland, took two weeks to reach the capital.

President James K. Polk was a stiff, angular man, with sharp grey eyes set in a sad, thin face. This hardworking, unhumorous chief executive had called a Cabinet meeting on Saturday, May 9. He was looking for an excuse to declare war on Mexico. Reviewing the diplomacy of the past year, which included the annexation of Texas, suspension of relations with Mexico, and abortive attempts to solve boundary disputes and to purchase California and New Mexico, Polk self-righteously told his Cabinet that "in my opinion we had ample cause of war, and that it was impossible that we could stand in *statu quo*, or that I could remain silent much longer; that I thought it was my duty to send a message to Congress very soon and recommend definitive measures."[2] He hoped that the Mexicans would commit an act of "aggression" against Taylor's army, but as yet nothing had happened. The Cabinet was polled. All agreed that a declaration of war should be sent to Congress by the following Tuesday, although Secretary of the Navy George Bancroft thought it would be better if some hostile act on the border had occurred. The Cabinet adjourned around 2:00 P.M., and Polk began to compose the war message.

At six o'clock that evening the news about the Rio Grande skirmish reached the White House. The Cabinet hastily reconvened. It reached a unanimous decision: submit a war message as quickly as possible. All day Sunday, except for two hours at church, Polk labored over his message, conferring with Cabinet colleagues, military advisers, and congressional leaders. "It was a day of great anxiety to me," the President wrote in his diary.[3] At noon on Monday he sent the message to Congress. "The cup of forbearance has been exhausted," Polk declared. "After reiterated menaces, Mexico has passed the boundary of the United States, has invaded our territory and shed American blood upon American soil." War exists, and "notwithstanding all our efforts to avoid it, exists by the act of Mexico herself." Accompanying the war message was a bill authorizing the President to accept militia and volunteers for military duty. The bill did not specifically declare war, but rather asked Congress to recognize that "by the act of . . . Mexico, a state of war exists between the government and the United States."[4]

A disciplined Democratic majority responded swiftly and efficiently to Polk's recommendations. Debate in the House was limited to two hours. Angry Whigs asked for time to examine documents that Polk sent with his message. Denied. The Speaker of the House repeatedly failed to recognize representatives who wanted to ask detailed questions about how the war started. Only by resorting to a parliamentary trick—by demanding permission to explain why they wanted to be excused from voting—did two dissenters gain the floor and proclaim Polk's war message an "utter falsehood." The House vote of 174 to 14 was a victory for stampede tactics. In the Senate the following day, notwithstanding a more prolonged debate, the vote was even more decisive in favor of the war bill, 40 to 2. The "haughty and dominating" majority again refused members time to study controversial questions.[5] Whigs and dissident Democrats, remembering the political fate of Federalists who had opposed the War of 1812, either voted aye or did not vote. Democratic Senator John C. Calhoun of South Carolina, who did not accept Polk's version of the Rio Grande as the Texas boundary, later insisted that fewer than 10 percent of his colleagues would have voted for the war bill if the issue had been fairly presented. Nonetheless, Calhoun sat silently in his seat when his name was called.

Thus began the Mexican War, a conflict that lasted nearly two years and added to the United States a vast domain, which included the present-day states of New Mexico, Arizona, California, Nevada, and Utah. Contemporaries called it "Mr. Polk's War," a most appropriate appellation. Despite backing from a unanimous Cabinet and an overwhelming congressional declaration, it was the plodding, secretive man from Tennessee who made the crucial decisions for war. It was Polk who unilaterally defined the geographic limits of Texas as including disputed land between the Nueces River and the Rio Grande. It was Polk who, as Commander-in-Chief, ordered General Taylor to the Rio Grande. It was Polk who decided that Mexico had fired the first shot. It was Polk who presented Congress with an accomplished fact. Despite congressional authorization, the rise of presidential war did not go unchallenged. Congressman John Quincy Adams, then in the last year of his distinguished life and himself once an advocate of expansion, was one of the few who voted against war. "It is now established as an irreversible precedent," Adams lamented, "that the President of the United States has but to declare that War exists, with any Nation upon Earth and the War is essentially declared. . . . It is not difficult to foresee what the ultimate issue will be to the people of Mexico, but what it will be to the People of the United States is beyond my foresight, and I turn my eyes away from it."[6] It was "Mr. Polk's War," but he could bring it off successfully because his aims reflected the grand hopes of expansionist America.

MANIFEST DESTINY OR MANIFEST DESIGN: THE ROOTS OF EXPANSIONISM

"Mr. Polk's War" on the Rio Grande came at a critical juncture and dramatized, in microcosm, some of the expansionist themes that dominated American foreign policy after the War of 1812. At the very time Taylor's troops were killing Mexicans in the Southwest, Polk was quietly settling a dispute with England over control of the Pacific Northwest. By dividing Oregon at 49 degrees north latitude in June, 1846, Polk temporarily abated the rivalry with England over the territory and commerce of North America. The anti-British fervor of the Revolutionary era remained strong in the 1830s and 1840s, and the fear of British encroachment in Texas and California contributed to the outbreak of war against Mexico. That the United States fought Mexico and not Britain in 1846 illustrated another theme: namely, American expansionists were more aggressive against weaker peoples like Spaniards, Mexicans, and Indians than against the stronger Britishers. According to the expansionist ideology, those peoples who neither improved the land they held nor developed effective political institutions had to make way for those who could. The lands Polk wanted from Mexico were lightly populated, and he assumed that American institutions could be easily assimilated. England, with greater power and similar traditions, could be a rival, but not a victim. Indeed, as Polk moved toward war in the winter of 1845–46 he invoked the precedent of the Monroe Doctrine in warning England against further expansion in North America, thus making explicit what had been implicit in 1823—that Europeans could not seize territory in the western hemisphere, but the United States could. Polk sincerely believed that Mexico fired the first shot on the Rio Grande, just as many Americans sincerely believed that God had destined the United States to control the entire continent. The sincerity of such beliefs did not stop expansionism from being both racist and imperialistic.

Continental expansion became the watchword in the three decades after 1815. Having defended their territorial integrity during the second war with Great Britain, American statesmen proceeded to acquire Florida, Texas, Oregon, and the Mexican cession, some 1,263,301 square miles. Population nearly trebled, from 8,419,000 in 1815 to 22,018,000 in 1848. American commerce expanded into new channels, notably Latin America and the Far East, with total exports climbing from $53 million in 1815 to $159 million in 1847. The gross output of farm production increased from $338 million in 1820 to $904 million thirty years later. The production of cotton, a vital ingredient in Anglo-American relations, rose from 209,000 bales in 1815 to 2,615,000 bales in 1847. The construction of canals and railroads created a transportation revolution that served to quicken American growth. It became the purpose of American diplomacy during these years to facilitate this expansion. *"On s'agrandit toujours un peu, dans ce monde"* ("Everyone always grows a little in this world"), said Tsar Alexander I of Russia after John

Within the illustration:

AIR LINE, through by daylight Passage $50.

My hair!! how the wind blows.

ROCKET LINE. through in advance of the Telegraph. Passengers not found, (if lost.)

Held on there I've paid my passage and I aint aboard.

Stand from under.

Bill. I'm afraid we cant get aboard.

Passage $125 and found (if lost)

I'm bound to go anyhow.

Quincy Adams told him of the American acquisition of Florida.[7] Americans were out to grow.

It is difficult to isolate the tangled roots of expansion—historical, economic, demographic, intellectual, strategic. Nor does it suffice to say that the United States, like Topsy, "just growed." To be sure, "extending the sphere" (in Madison's phrase) was nothing new, and much that occurred after 1815 derived from earlier precedents. Part of the rationale for acquiring Florida in 1819 followed the example of Louisiana: just as New Orleans under foreign control had blocked navigation of the Mississippi, so too did Spanish sovereignty over the mouths of the Pearl, Perdido, and Chattahoochee rivers make it difficult for American farmers upstream to get their produce to market. Moreover, Florida, just like New Orleans, might be ceded by Spain to a more dangerous power, hence the argument for possessing it before England or France could grab it. Memories of the Revolution of 1776, combined with opportunities for Latin American markets, helped bring about the Monroe Doctrine of 1823. By stipulating that Europe and the Americas had distinctly different political systems, Monroe's message recalled the isolationist principles of Paine's *Common Sense* and Washington's Farewell Address. There were echoes from the past in the Anglo-American trade rivalry in Latin America and in the attempts to gain equal access to the British West Indian trade in the 1820s. A more explicit reference to earlier concerns about neutral rights came in 1831 when President Andrew Jackson negotiated an agreement whereby France promised to pay an indemnity of 25 million francs for illegal seizures of American shipping in the years 1805–1812. When the French defaulted on an installment in 1834, Jackson is reported to have shouted: "I know them French. They won't pay unless they are made to."[8] The French paid. Undoubtedly, Jackson's pugnacity reflected good electioneering instincts, but it also served notice that the United States would

"The Way They Go to California." N. Currier's lithograph captures the frenzied American expansionist fever—in this case for California after the Mexican War. (Library of Congress)

insist on the right to expand its carrying trade in the event of another European conflagration.

Perhaps the most important element in expansion after 1815 was the growing vision of what was possible. As early as 1813 Jefferson himself envisioned *"American governments, no longer to be involved in the never-ceasing broils of Europe. . . . America has a hemisphere to itself. It must have a separate system of interest which must not be subordinated to those of Europe."*[9] But Jefferson thought in terms of separate and independent republics, not a grand republican empire ruled from Washington. Despite treaties in 1818 and 1819 that established a firm claim to the Pacific Coast, most Americans still thought of the Rocky Mountains as a "natural" boundary. Oregon was far away. It had taken Lewis and Clark eighteen months to travel to the Pacific from St. Louis. A sea voyage from Boston to the Pacific Coast lasted six to eight months, depending on the weather. Even Senator Thomas Hart Benton of Missouri, who would catch the Oregon "fever" with a vengeance in the 1840s, went on record in 1825 in favor of the Rocky Mountain limitation. "Along the back of this ridge," he intoned, "the Western limit of the republic should be drawn, and the statue of the fabled god, Terminus, should be raised upon its highest peak, never to be thrown down."[10]

"Manifest Destiny." John Gast's painting captures the ebullient spirit of the trek westward. Pioneers relentlessly move on, attracting railroads and driving out Native Americans, as "Columbia" majestically pulls telegraph wires across America. Recent scholars have emphasized the imperialist goals of American expansion. "Neither accidental nor innocent," writes Thomas Hietala, "the expansion to the Pacific represented not manifest destiny, but manifest design." (Collection of Harry T. Peters, Jr.)

Technology shrank geography and expanded horizons. Steamboats, canals, and railroads stimulated imaginations as well as commerce. Although there were still fewer than 5,000 miles of railroad track in the United States in 1845, plans for constructing transcontinental lines had already reached the drawing boards. The development of high-speed printing presses gave rise in the early 1840s to mass circulation newspapers, which in turn trumpeted expansionist rhetoric to a larger foreign policy public. Samuel Morse's invention of the telegraph, first put into operation in 1844, came at an opportune time. "The magnetic telegraph," boasted editor John L. O'Sullivan in 1845, "will enable the editors of the 'San Francisco Union,' the 'Astoria Evening Post,' or the 'Nootka Morning News,' to set up in type the first half of the President's Inaugural before the echoes of the latter half shall have died away beneath the lofty porch of the Capitol, as spoken from his lips."[11]

The same O'Sullivan, editor of the *Democratic Review,* gave the expansionist process a name in the summer of 1845. The United States, according to O'Sullivan, had the "manifest destiny to overspread the continent allotted by Providence to the free development of our yearly multiplying millions."[12] Although the geographical limits of the Temple of Freedom were not always clear—the Pacific? the continent? the hemisphere?—most believers in Manifest Destiny followed John Quincy Adams' notion, expressed in 1819, that the United States and North America were identical. Manifest Destiny meant republicanism, religious freedom, states' rights, free trade, cheap land. Manifest Destiny in its purest form did not envisage acquisition of territory by force. Peaceful occupation of uninhabited wilderness, followed by self-government on the American model and eventual annexation by mutual consent—this was the ideal. Neighboring peoples of Spanish and Indian heritage, given time and the American example, might qualify. The process was supposed to be almost automatic. "Go to the West," said an Indiana congressman in 1846,[13]

> and see a young man with his mate of eighteen; and [after] a lapse of thirty years, visit him again, and instead of two, you will find twenty-two. That is what I call the American multiplication table. We are now twenty millions strong; and how long, under this process of multiplication, will it take to cover the continent with our posterity, from the Isthmus of Darien to Behring's straits?

Unfortunately, reality did not match the ideal, as "Polk's War" on the Rio Grande sadly attested. Inevitably, racism betrayed Manifest Destiny. The racial thinking of the time posited Anglo-Saxon superiority as a proven scientific fact and thus denigrated groups that resisted the inexorable march of democratic institutions. Protestant missionaries who sought to assimilate Indians into white society, according to historian Robert Berkhofer, firmly believed that "any right-thinking savage should be able to recognize the superiority of Christian society," and thus any failures in the acculturation process were attributed to the victims.[14] Just as the negative stereotype of blacks in the nineteenth century justified slavery in the South and unequal treatment of freedmen in the North, and as the prevailing image of the Indians as savages justified their subjugation, so too did expansionists project their notions of racial superiority against Mexicans who were allegedly too cowardly to fight or too treacherous to win if they did fight. In historian Thomas Hietala's words, "manifest destiny, or rather manifest design, offered nothing to nonwhite peoples . . . but inevitable decline, expulsion, or final extinction."[15]

Yet in some ways American expansion seemed a natural, organic process. Americans always sought greater productivity through the cultivation of new lands. Problems generating from increased population, inadequate transportation, depressed agricultural prices, and general hard times also caused periodic migrations into new areas. Whether this movement was into American territory beyond the Alleghenies or into fertile lands under alien rule, the causes and results were similar. Once established, American settlers retained their distinctly Yankee customs and institutions; if under foreign rule, they rejected alien processes and virtually established American "colonies." Friends, relatives, and politicians at home directed American foreign policy toward the "protection" of their fellow countrymen, perhaps even incorporating them into the Temple of Freedom. Thus came the rhetoric of Manifest Destiny—the spread-eagle appeals to national prestige, the glittering description of natural resources and fertile lands. As the American "colonies" grew in size, so too did fears increase that some European power, probably perfidious England, would snatch the potential prize. If politicians sometimes exaggerated the extent to which England meddled in such places as California, Oregon, and Texas, the fact that British involvement did exist contributed to the expansionist momentum.

Population movements tended to come on the heels of economic downturns. The Panic of 1819, combined with Mexico's generous land policies, encouraged the first flood of immigration into Texas in the 1820s. Similarly, the severe economic depression in 1837–1842 stimulated more western farmers and southern planters to migrate westward. The population of Texas ballooned to 100,000 by 1845, and in far-off Oregon some 5,000 Americans had crossed the Rockies. Actually, settlement in California was still miniscule in 1845, but as one resident put it: "Once let the tide of emigration flow toward California, and the American population will soon be sufficiently numerous to play the Texas game."[16] It was this organic, seemingly inevitable process of agrarian migration that prompted John C. Calhoun in 1843 to advocate a "wise and masterly inactivity" on the part of the American government.[17] God and the passage of time seemed to smile benevolently upon American expansion. Force did not seem necessary—at least not in theory.

Makers of American Foreign Policy from 1815 to 1848

Presidents	Secretaries of State
James Madison, 1809–1817	James Monroe, 1811–1817
James Monroe, 1817–1825	John Quincy Adams, 1817–1825
John Quincy Adams, 1825–1829	Henry Clay, 1825–1829
Andrew Jackson, 1829–1837	Martin Van Buren, 1829–1831
	Edward Livingston, 1831–1833
	Louis McLane, 1833–1834
Martin Van Buren, 1837–1841	John Forsyth, 1834–1841
William H. Harrison, 1841	Daniel Webster, 1841–1843
John Tyler, 1841–1845	Abel P. Upshur, 1843–1844
	John C. Calhoun, 1844–1845
James K. Polk, 1845–1849	James Buchanan, 1845–1849

Heightened interest in the commercial potential of the Pacific also fueled expansion. Trade with Latin America reached a peak in the early 1830s, and merchants plying the west coast of South America made easy profits that could be used to purchase the products of East Asia. "The North American road to India" was Senator Benton's description of the Columbia River Valley during the 1840s.[18] Whaling, salmon fisheries, furs, the fabled China trade, commercial rivalry with Britain and Russia—all were stressed from the 1820s onward by publicists seeking to colonize Oregon as a means to commercial empire. The Columbia and Missouri rivers would link with the Mississippi. In historian Frederick Merk's words: "Furs from the Oregon Country would flow to China. In return teas, silks, and spices would move to St. Louis, the Venice of the New World. A modern Tyre would rise at the mouth of the Columbia."[19] American exports of Turkish opium through Cantonese middlemen also expanded trade with China in the 1820s and 1830s.

Just as the first wave of settlers reached Oregon in 1843, the British, victorious in the Opium War, were breaking down Chinese trade barriers. By the Treaty of Nanjing in 1842, Britain forced China to open five new coastal ports (Canton, Amoy, Ningbo, Fuzhou, and Shanghai) and grant broad rights of extraterritoriality (legal trials for foreigners in special courts of their own nationality). This was a signal for Americans to obtain their own treaty. President John Tyler entrusted Massachusetts Whig Caleb Cushing with the mission. Cushing, whose family was involved in the China trade, bought a special uniform of white pantaloons with gold stripes, white vest, blue coat with gilt buttons, and plumed headpiece, all presumably calculated to overawe the Chinese. His Treaty of Wangxia (1844) gained for the United States the same rights, on an unconditional most-favored-nation basis, that England had won in the Opium War. The ensuing influx of Yankee traders, missionaries, and diplomats created what historian Michael Hunt has called an "open door constituency" committed to "penetrating China and propagating at home a paternalistic vision . . . of defending and reforming China."[20]

The American Navy, although ranking only eighth in the world in 1836, also aided expansion. Its contribution came primarily in the cartographic and exploratory expeditions of such officers as Matthew Perry, Matthew Maury, and Charles Wilkes. Charting coastlines, publicizing points of commercial and strategic interest, recommending steps to Washington for increasing American commerce in the Pacific, these naval explorers became, in historian Geoffrey Smith's phrase, "'maritime frontiersmen,' mirror images of the thousands of mountain men, traders, pioneers, adventurers, and army surveyors who trekked westward to the Pacific."[21] Important in stimulating expansion was the publication of Lieutenant Wilkes's *Narrative of the United States Exploring Expedition during the Years 1838, 1839, 1840, 1841, 1842,* five weighty volumes containing accurate information about the Pacific Coast from Vancouver Island to Lower California. Wilkes's unqualified praise for San Francisco and the Strait of Juan de Fuca ("two of the finest ports in the world") sharply contrasted with his pessimistic dismissal of the Columbia River, with its shifting sandbars, as a viable commercial entrepôt. Once Wilkes's findings became known in 1842, American diplomats—particularly Daniel Webster—stepped up efforts to acquire either or both of these harbors. The main reason that American diplomacy pressed hard for the triangle of Oregon between

San Francisco in the 1840s. Ships at port attested to the trading activities that drew Americans to the Pacific before the frantic gold rush of 1849. (Courtesy, The Bancroft Library, University of California, Berkeley)

the Columbia and Fuca Strait was the need for a deep water port. Only seven Americans lived north of the Columbia River in 1845.

Commercial empire was even more exclusively the object in California. When a British naval officer entered San Francisco Bay in 1845, he exclaimed: "D–n it! is there nothing but Yankees here?"[22] The Americans were connected primarily with the Boston trading company of Bryant & Sturgis. Having pioneered the otter trade in the Pacific and opened an office in Portuguese Macao, Bryant & Sturgis began in the 1820s to shift from furs to hides, which it bought cheaply from Spanish missions and rancheros. The firm established an office in Santa Barbara in 1829, moving a few years later to Monterey. Thomas O. Larkin, later appointed the first American consul to California and a crucial figure in the diplomacy of 1845–1846, was associated with Bryant & Sturgis, as was Richard Henry Dana, the author of the epic narrative *Two Years Before the Mast*, depicting a voyage to California around Cape Horn. Altogether, there were some 25,000 persons in California in 1845, including 800 Americans. Its link with Mexico City, more than 1,500 miles away, was weak. Overland communications were extremely difficult, and courts, police, schools, and newspapers scarcely existed. American merchants, whalers, and sailors competed with their British counterparts. As the American minister to Mexico put it in 1842, California was "the richest, the most beautiful, the healthiest country in the world. . . . The harbor of St. [sic] Francisco is capacious enough to receive all the navies of the world, and the neighborhood furnishes live oak enough to build all the ships of those navies."[23] Daniel Webster, equally impressed, thought the port of San Francisco "twenty times as valuable to us as all Texas."[24]

Commercial opportunities also beckoned in Hawaii, which by the 1840s had become a piece of New England in the mid-Pacific. "Honolulu," Samuel Eliot Morison has written, "with merchant sailors rolling through its streets, shops fitted with Lowell shirtings, New England rum and Yankee notions, orthodox missionaries living in frame houses brought around the Horn, and a neo-classic meeting house built out of coral rocks, was becoming as Yankee as New Bedford."[25] While the Hawaiian archipelago did not become a formal part of the American empire until the 1890s, the absorption process was well underway several decades earlier.

Mercantile interest in the Pacific Coast was confined largely to New England and the Atlantic seaboard, but there were growing commercial interests in the Midwest which sought to link maritime trade to agrarian migrations. Farmers moving to Oregon had in mind an expanded market for their products in Asia, as did some Southerners, who saw the Chinese as potential buyers of cotton and tobacco. Politicians like Stephen Douglas, an agrarian spokesman, embraced projects linking the Mississippi Valley with the Pacific via a transcontinental railroad. Indeed, it was in January, 1845 that Asa Whitney, a New York merchant involved in the China trade, first proposed the idea of government land grants to any group undertaking to build a railroad from the Great Lakes to Oregon. Such schemes did not reach fruition until after the Civil War, but their existence in the era of Manifest Destiny testifies to the dual nature (maritime and agrarian) of continental expansion.

NIBBLING AND SWALLOWING FLORIDA

Following the Louisiana Purchase of 1803, American diplomats had tried to obtain part of the large tropical peninsula of Florida by arguing that it had always been a part of Louisiana. The Spanish rejected such notions. The first bite out of the territory did not come until September, 1810, when a group of American settlers revolted against Spanish rule, captured the fortress at Baton Rouge, and proclaimed the "Republic of West Florida." The Bourbon banner was replaced by a blue woolen flag with a single silver star. President James Madison immediately proclaimed West Florida part of the United States, although he actually sent troops to occupy an area only to the Pearl River. During the War of 1812 American soldiers occupied Mobile and all of West Florida to the Perdido River—the only tangible addition of territory resulting from that war.

It fell to the Monroe Administration (1817–1825) and Secretary of State John Quincy Adams to complete the absorption. Spanish Minister Don Luis de Onís proved himself a dogged, skillful advocate of a hopeless cause. Adams took the diplomatic offensive, arguing that Spain should cede East Florida to the United States because Spanish authorities had not prevented Indians from raiding into American territory (as stipulated in Pinckney's Treaty of 1795). Adams also blamed the Spanish for not returning thousands of escaped slaves and accused them of cooperating with British forces during the War of 1812. Onís was prepared to cede East Florida, but not without a *quid pro quo*. Faced with revolts in its South American empire, Spain wanted a promise from the United States neither to assist the revolutionaries nor to recognize their declared independence. Furthermore, Madrid instructed Onís to settle the disputed western boundary of Louisiana, and only to cede Florida in exchange for the best frontier that circumstances would admit. Adams, delighted to negotiate this second issue, urged that the boundary be set deep in the south at the Rio Grande, or at least the Colorado River of Texas. Onís, after first insisting on the Mississippi, moved grudgingly to the Mermentau and Calcasieu rivers in the middle of present-day Louisiana. The negotiators were far apart. "I have seen slippery diplomatists," Adams later observed, "but Onís is the first man I ever met who made it a point of honor to pass for more of a swindler than he was."[26]

The man who would break the impasse was in early 1818 bivouacked with three thousand troops at Big Creek, near the Georgia–Florida boundary. This was General Andrew Jackson, the hero of New Orleans, a volatile mixture of frontier passion and calculating ambition. Ostensibly under orders to pursue and punish Seminole Indians who had been using Spanish Florida as a base from which to raid American settlements, Jackson had suggested in a secret letter to Monroe that "the whole of East Florida [be] seized and held as indemnity for the outrages of Spain upon the property of our Citizens."[27] Whether or not Monroe or Secretary of War John C. Calhoun explicitly approved Jackson's proposal has never been determined. Jackson claimed they had; both denied it. What is known is that neither Monroe nor Calhoun ever told Jackson *not* to cross the border. To the pugnacious Tennessean, this silence from Washington constituted tacit agreement that the Spanish were every bit as much the enemy as were the Seminoles.

"Old Hickory" burst across the border in late March, 1818. On April 6 the Spanish garrison at St. Marks meekly surrendered. "My love," Jackson wrote to his wife, "I entered the Town of St. Marks on yesterday. . . . I found in St. Marks the noted Scotch villain Arbuthnot. . . . I hold him for trial."[28] Alexander Arbuthnot, in actuality, was a kindly, seventy-year-old British subject whose commercial dealings with the Indians were so scrupulously honest that his profit-minded superiors in England were annoyed with him. Convinced that Arbuthnot was in cahoots with the Seminoles, Jackson plunged into the jungle swamps looking for the main Indian camp. He found the camp, but not the Indians. He seized another Englishman lurking nearby, one Lieutenant Robert C. Ambrister, formerly of the British Royal Colonial Marines. Returning to St. Marks, Jackson convened a court martial, hanged Arbuthnot, and shot Ambrister, not at all perturbed that he was administering American "justice" on Spanish soil to two British citizens. "Old Hickory" next turned west toward Pensacola, where he felt certain that the "Red Sticks" were being fed and supplied by the Spanish governor. Pensacola capitulated quickly on May 28 and Jackson promptly took over the royal archives, replaced the governor with one of his own colonels, and declared in force the revenue laws of the United States. In two short months, although he killed or captured very few Indians, Jackson had occupied every important Spanish post in Florida except St. Augustine.

When news of Jackson's deeds reached Washington in early July, there was considerable embarrassment. Minister Onís roused John Quincy Adams from his early morning Bible study and demanded an indemnity, as well as punishment of Jackson. Calhoun and other Cabinet members suggested a court martial for the rambunctious general. Monroe, who disapproved less of what Jackson had done than the way he did it, quietly agreed to return the captured posts to Spain. But he did not censure Jackson and even offered to falsify some of the general's dispatches so that the invasion would appear in a more favorable light. Congress, led by Henry Clay, launched an investigation into the entire Florida undertaking. Only Adams stoutly defended Jackson.

When the British did not protest the murder of Arbuthnot and Ambrister, Monroe gave his secretary of state full backing. As usual, Adams thought that the best defense was a good offense, and thereupon drew up a memorable reply to Onís' demands for censure and indemnity. Self-defense was the motif. If Spain could not restrain her Indians, the United States would. A bit embarrassed by the lack of precedents in international law, Adams boldly claimed that the right of defensive invasion was "engraved in adamant on the common sense of mankind." Charging the Spanish with "impotence" rather than perfidy, the secretary demanded that "Spain must immediately make her election, either to place a force in Florida adequate at once to the protection of her territory and to the fulfillment of her engagements, or cede to the United States a province, of which she retains nothing but the nominal possession, but which is, in fact, a derelict, open to the occupancy of every enemy, civilized or savage, of the United States, and serving no other earthly purpose than as a post of annoyance to them."[29] This chauvinistic proclamation, which was presently published, impressed Thomas Jefferson as the greatest state paper in American history. Onís could make no effective rejoinder. Even worse, his superiors in Madrid reacted to Jackson's forays with instructions to cede Florida quickly and retreat to the best possible boundary between Louisiana and Mexico.

More negotiations followed, finally culminating in the Adams-Onís Treaty, signed in Washington on February 22, 1819. The United States acquired East Florida, tacit recognition that previously occupied West Florida was part of the Louisiana Purchase, and a new boundary line that began at the mouth of the Sabine River, moved stairstep fashion along various rivers in a northwesterly direction to the forty-second parallel, and then went straight west to the Pacific. Adams' initiative in running the boundary to the Pacific was entirely his own. While contemporaries considered the Rocky Mountains the natural boundary and dreamed of the Pacific Northwest as some future and separate American republic, Adams had his eyes fixed on the Columbia River Basin. It was a grand vision and a masterful diplomatic victory.

In return for these lucrative gains, Adams surrendered the vague claims for Texas arising from the Louisiana Purchase. As it turned out, Onís had instructions to retreat even on the Sabine boundary, but Monroe and the Cabinet thought that Florida was more important than Texas and did not press the matter. The United States also agreed to assume the claims of its own citizens against Spain, some five million dollars resulting from Franco-Spanish seizures of American shipping during the undeclared war of 1798–1800. The Transcontinental Treaty said nothing about American recognition of Spain's rebellious colonies. Partly because of this silence, and partly because of personal intrigues over royal land grants in Florida, Madrid dragged its feet over ratification. Adams staunchly resisted any hand-tying nonrecognition pledge. Two years passed before ratifications were exchanged in 1821.

Perhaps the importance of the Adams-Onís Treaty lay not in what was acquired in 1819, but in what it foreshadowed. Just as in his diplomacy with England in the Convention of 1818 (discussed on p. 100), Adams was projecting a continental vision. It did not matter if he and Onís were drawing lines across deserts that did not exist or around mountains that were not where maps said they should be. "It was . . . a battle between two kinds of imagination," historian George Dangerfield has written. "Onís was defending . . . a moribund, revolted, and helpless empire; Adams . . . was thinking and dreaming of an America of the future whose westward movement, in those days before the railroad, was hardly calculable."[30] Although the actual phrase was not coined until the 1840s, John Quincy Adams was the first to speak the language of Manifest Destiny. "The remainder of the continent shall ultimately be ours," he wrote at the time.[31]

A second, more disturbing precedent was the way in which Jackson's invasion of Florida had buttressed diplomacy. Spain's willingness to yield Florida, combined

John Quincy Adams (1767–1848). This daguerreotype photograph taken in 1843, near the end of Adams' distinguished career as diplomat, secretary of state, President, and congressman from Massachusetts, demonstrates well that his countenance was austere and gloomy indeed. (The Metropolitan Museum of Art, Gift of I. N. Phelps Stokes, Edward S. Hawes, Alice Mary Hawes, Marion Augusta Hawes, 1937)

with Britain's refusal to question the execution of Ambrister and Arbuthnot, minimized diplomatic repercussions. Nevertheless, as the congressional investigation into the affair revealed, Monroe and Jackson had virtually waged war without the sanction of Congress. According to Henry Clay, Monroe had assured the Congress that no Spanish forts would be seized if Jackson crossed the border in pursuit of Seminoles, but this was precisely what had occurred. It was, said Clay, "dangerous to permit this type of conduct to pass without comment by the House. Precedents, if bad, are fraught with the most dangerous consequences."[32] Clay may have been right in this instance, but he also wanted to become President. Contemporaries viewed the investigation as an attack on Clay's chief rival, Jackson. They also liked what the general had done. Thus, on February 8, 1819, after a twenty-seven-day debate, the four congressional resolutions condemning Jackson were defeated by comfortable margins. Jackson's popularity, of course, later carried him to the White House. Congress—not for the last time—voted to acquiesce in its own subordination.

THE MONROE DOCTRINE CLEARS THE WAY

The next notable milestone for expansion came with the Monroe Doctrine of 1823. At first glance, that remarkable statement of American diplomatic principles appears entirely anti-imperialist in intent—a stern warning to reactionary Europe not to interfere with revolutions in the New World, a gesture of solidarity and sympathy with the newly independent republics to the south. It was indeed a warning and a gesture, but motives more selfishly American were also involved. In saying "Thou Shalt Not" to Europe, James Monroe and John Quincy Adams were careful to exempt the United States. By facilitating commercial expansion into Latin America and landed expansion across the North American continent, the Monroe Doctrine became, in historian Richard Van Alstyne's words, "an official declaration fencing in the 'western hemisphere' as a United States sphere of influence."[33]

The Latin American revolutions (1808–1822) had a magnetic effect on the United States. The exploits of such Latin American leaders as Bolívar, San Martín, and O'Higgins rekindled memories of 1776. Henry Clay, in a famous oration in 1818, proclaimed that the Latin leaders "adopted our principles, copied our institutions and . . . employed the very language and sentiments of our revolutionary papers."[34] That the United States did not heed popular enthusiasms and immediately recognize the Latin American republics was due primarily to the calculating diplomacy of John Quincy Adams. Cynical and cautious, Adams "wished well" to the emerging Latin states, but doubted that they could "establish free or liberal institutions of government. . . . Arbitrary power, military and ecclesiastical, was stamped upon their education, upon their habits, and upon all their institutions. Civil dissension was infused into all their seminal principles."[35] So Adams carefully avoided recognition, thereby facilitating negotiations with Spain over the Transcontinental Treaty of 1819. Not until the spring of 1822, after the expulsion of Spanish armies from the New World, and following a sharp rise in United States trade with Latin America, did President Monroe extend formal recognition to the new governments of La Plata, Chile, Peru, Colombia, and Mexico. Adams instructed American diplomats to focus their energies on obtaining favorable trading rights. He did not want the new "republics" to exchange Spanish political domination for British commercial domination.

There were additional European threats. Following Napoleon's final defeat, European statesmen had endeavored to restore order and legitimacy to an international system thrown out of kilter by the French Revolution and the conquests of the Corsican usurper. Conservatism became the watchword, and by the Treaty of Paris of 1815 the members of the Quadruple Alliance (Austria, Prussia, Russia, and Britain) bound themselves to future diplomatic congresses for the maintenance of peace and the status quo. A penitent France formally joined the "Concert of Europe" in 1818, and the Quadruple Alliance turned into the Quintuple Alliance. The allies also signed in 1815 a vague agreement called the Holy Alliance. By 1819–1820 the Austrian Foreign Minister, Prince Klemens von Metternich, enthusiastically supported by Tsar Alexander I of Russia, had transformed both alliances into instruments for suppressing revolutions. At the Congress of Troppau in 1820 the Holy Allies agreed that if internal revolutions posed threats to neighboring states, "the powers bind themselves, by peaceful means, or if need be by arms, to bring back the guilty State into the bosom of the Great Alliance."[36] Thus, in due course, Austrian armies were sent to put down uprisings in Naples and Piedmont in 1821. The following year a French army marched across the Pyrenees in support of Spain's unstable Ferdinand VII, who was then being embarrassed by a liberal Constitutionalist government. Similarly, the Holy Allies gave diplomatic support to Ottoman Turkey in attempting to snuff out national revolutions in Greece and the Danubian principalities. Americans were particularly incensed at the betrayal of freedom in Greece. Would the Holy Alliance's zeal for putting down revolutions everywhere lead to the restoration of legitimate rule over the insurrectionist colonies of Spain in the New World?

British diplomacy during these years played an ambivalent and tortuous role. Foreign Secretary Castlereagh wanted very much to support the system devised at the Congress of Vienna and to preserve the grand coalition that had defeated Napoleon. The British had little sympathy for revolution per se. Nevertheless, confident of the stability of their own political institutions, and guarded by the English Channel and the Royal Navy, many Britons came to see the use of French and Austrian troops to suppress foreign revolts as upsetting the balance of power. When the Congress of Verona (1822) sanctioned the deployment of French military forces in Spain, something the British had fought the long and bitter Peninsular War (1809–1814) to prevent, England's withdrawal from the Holy Alliance became inevitable. The distraught Castlereagh committed suicide, and his successor, George Canning, promised a return to splendid isolation. Economic factors also influenced the British. Since 1808 British merchants had captured the lion's share of trade with Spanish ports in the New World. These lucrative commercial dealings had not sufficiently overcome London's antipathy to revolution so as to bring about formal recognition. The British, however, did fear that restoration of the Spanish colonies to Ferdinand VII might result in the elimination of British trade. As Canning later boasted, "I resolved that if France had Spain, it should not be Spain 'with the Indies.' I called the New World into existence to redress the balance of the old."[37]

Canning's determination to prevent any restoration in Spanish America led, in August, 1823, to a remarkable conversation with American Minister Richard Rush.

The two men were talking about the progress of French armies in Spain. Rush casually mentioned how confident he was that the British would never permit France to interfere with the independence of Latin America or to gain territory there by conquest or cession. Canning listened intently. What, he asked Rush, would the American government say to going hand in hand with England in such a policy? No concerted action would be necessary; if the French were simply told that the United States and Britain held the same opinions, would that not deter them? Both nations would also disavow any intention of obtaining territories for themselves. Four days later, Canning wrote Rush, "nothing would be more gratifying to me than to join you in such a work, and I am persuaded, there has seldom, in the history of the world, occurred an opportunity, when so small an effort of two friendly Governments, might produce so unequivocal a good and prevent such extensive calamities."[38] Rush was admirably cool. One of the most able diplomats of his generation, Rush told Canning that he lacked instructions to conclude such an agreement; nevertheless, if the foreign secretary agreed to recognize the independence of the new Latin republics, Rush would initial such a joint statement without specific authorization. A cautious Canning talked vaguely of future recognition, so Rush referred the matter to Washington.

Rush's dispatch arrived in early October and sparked one of the most momentous discussions in American history. Monroe sought the advice of Thomas Jefferson and James Madison. These two elder Virginians agreed with the President that the British proposal should be accepted. Jefferson's reply recalled memories of 1803, when the French seemed ready to take New Orleans. "Great Britain," he wrote, "is the nation which can do us the most harm of any one, or all on earth; and with her on our side we need not fear the whole world."[39] Madison also counseled that "with British cooperation we have nothing to fear from the rest of Europe."[40] Madison even suggested a joint statement with the British on behalf of Greek independence. Armed with these opinions, Monroe called a Cabinet meeting on November 7, fully prepared to embrace British cooperation.

John Quincy Adams, however, fought vigorously for a unilateral course. Adams did not trust the British. Hoping to compete successfully for Latin American markets, and not wanting to tie American hands in some future acquisition of, say, Texas or Cuba, the secretary of state argued that it would be more dignified and candid to make an independent declaration of principles to the Holy Alliance than "to come in as a cockboat in the wake of the British man-of-war."[41] In this and subsequent meetings Adams gradually won Monroe over. Complications arose when another dispatch from Rush reported that Canning had mysteriously lost interest in a joint declaration. (Rush did not know that Canning, on October 9, had made an agreement with the French, the so-called Polignac Memorandum, whereby the French "abjured any design" of acting against the former Spanish colonies in Latin America.[42]) News also arrived of the French capture of Cadiz, along with rumors that a French fleet might soon embark for the New World. Secretary of War Calhoun was "perfectly moonstruck" by the French threat and, according to Adams, "has so affected the President that he appeared entirely to despair of the cause of South America." Adams remained optimistic. He pointed out the competing national interests within the Holy Alliance, noted England's stake in Latin America, and sarcastically told Calhoun that "I no more believe that the Holy Allies will restore the Spanish dominion on the American continent than that the Chimborazo will sink beneath the ocean."[43] Adams won his point.

Monroe followed Adams' advice, notwithstanding a bleak report from his former minister to Spain predicting European intervention.

The next step was the declaration. Monroe's original draft followed Adams' previous arguments in the Cabinet, but it also included a ringing indictment of the French intervention in Spain and a statement favoring the independence of revolutionary Greece. Adams opposed both points. However much he deplored events in Spain and Greece, the secretary of state advocated isolation from European embroilments. He urged the President "to make an American cause and adhere inflexibly to that."[44] The offending passages were excised. The now famous Monroe Doctrine thus became part of the President's message to Congress of December 2, 1823. It contained three essential points: noncolonization, "hands off" the New World, and American noninvolvement in European quarrels.

The first point, noncolonization, was aimed specifically at Russia, and was a response to an announcement by the Tsar in 1821 that Russian dominion extended southward from Alaska along the Pacific to the fifty-first parallel. Adams had opposed this aggrandizement in a note to the Russian minister in the summer of 1823, so Monroe simply reiterated the axiom that "the American continents, by the free and independent condition which they have assumed and maintain, are henceforth not to be considered as subjects for future colonization by any Euro-

James Monroe (1758–1831). Before becoming President in 1817, the distinguished Virginian served as secretary of state (1811–1817). Sharing John Quincy Adams' nationalist perspective, Monroe helped shape the doctrine against European intrusions into Latin America. (The Metropolitan Museum of Art, Bequest of Seth Low, 1929. All rights reserved.)

pean powers." By implication, the noncolonization principle applied to England and the Holy Alliance, as well as to Russia.

Monroe's second principle, "hands off," was revealed in a lengthy discussion of possible intervention by the Holy Allies. Positing the notion of two different worlds, he observed that the monarchical system of the Old World "is essentially different from that of America." Monroe warned that "any attempt" by the Holy Alliance to "extend their system to any portion of this hemisphere" would be regarded as "dangerous to our peace and safety." In convoluted but striking language, the President declared:

> With the existing colonies or dependencies of any European power we have not interfered and shall not interfere. But with the Governments who have declared their independence . . . we could not view any interposition for the purpose of oppressing them, or controlling in any other manner their destiny, by any European power in any other light than as the manifestation of an unfriendly disposition toward the United States.

As for the final principle, abstention, Monroe echoed Washington's Farewell Address: "In the wars of the European powers in matters relating to themselves we have never taken any part, nor does it comport with our policy to do so."[45]

An implicit corollary to the Monroe Doctrine, though not mentioned in the address, was the principle of "no transfer." Earlier that same year, in response to reports that Britain might try to negotiate the cession of Cuba from Spain, Adams had informed both Spain and the Cubans that the United States opposed British annexation. "Cuba," Adams wrote in April, 1823, "forcibly disjoined from its own unnatural connection with Spain, and incapable of self-support, can only gravitate towards the North American Union, which by the same law of nature cannot cast her off from its bosom."[46] Thus, when read in the context of Adams' concern with Cuba, the noncolonization principle in the Monroe Doctrine also warned Spain against transferring its colony to England or to any other European power.

The immediate effect of the pronouncement was hardly earthshaking. Brave words, after all, would not prevent the dismemberment of Latin America. The Polignac Memorandum and the British Navy actually took care of such a contingency. The Holy Allies sniffed in contempt, calling Monroe's principles "haughty," "arrogant," "blustering," and "monstrous." Metternich ignored the "indecent declarations," as did the Tsar, who thought "the document in question . . . merits only the most profound contempt."[47] Canning was pleased at first, but soon realized that Monroe and Adams might steal his thunder and turn Latin gratitude into Yankee trade opportunities. Canning thereupon rushed copies of the Polignac Memorandum to Latin American capitals, where it was quickly learned that England, not the upstart Americans, had warned off the Holy Allies. Latin Americans at first received the Monroe Doctrine cordially. When Washington refused to negotiate military alliances with Colombia and Brazil, however, disillusionment quickly set in.

At home the response was enthusiastic. "The explicit and manly tone," reported the British chargé, "has evidently found in every bosom a chord which vibrates in strict unison with the sentiments so conveyed. It would, indeed, be difficult . . . to find a more perfect unanimity."[48] Such unanimous response derived from the anti-British, anti-European thrust of Monroe's warning. As Adams knew, it was fortunate that the United States did not have to back up words with deeds. The irony of Monroe's message, despite its anti-imperialist intent, was that later generations remembered the words in ways that justified American expansion in the name of hemispheric solidarity and republican principles. It was one thing to defend one's own territory, even to expand at the expense of Spaniards and Indians in North America, quite another to guarantee republican governments in other countries, including Latin America. The Boston *Advertiser* seemed a lone prophetic voice in 1823: "Is there anything in the Constitution which makes our Government the Guarantors of the Liberties of the World? Of the Wahabees? The Peruvians? The Chilese? The Mexicans or Colombians?"[49]

ANGLO-AMERICAN ACCOMMODATIONS AND TENSIONS

In the decades following the Monroe Doctrine, because of commercial rivalry in Latin America, squabbles over West Indian trade, political troubles in Canada, boundary disputes, and British attempts to suppress the international slave trade, most Americans continued to regard Britain as *the* principal threat to the national interest. As co-occupant of the North American continent, the strongest naval power in the world, and a commercial giant, only England could block American expansion.

Fortunately, just as in the 1790s, the intertwining of the two economies helped to countervail any impulse toward war. In 1825, for example, the United States exported $37 million in goods to England, out of total exports valued at $91 million; by 1836 the figures rose to $58 million and $124 million; in 1839 they stood at $57 million and $112 million. As for imports, the United States bought $37 million in goods from Britain in 1825, out of total imports of $90 million. In 1840 the figures were $33 million and $98 million. Imports from Britain during this period fluctuated between one-half and one-third of total American imports. While Britain was less dependent on the United States, its trade with America was still highly significant, especially as the burgeoning British textile industry came to depend on American cotton. In 1825, 18 percent of total British exports went to the United States; in 1840, 10 percent. In those same years England received 13 percent and 27 percent of her total imports from America. These figures, combined with the British decision in 1830 to open the West Indies to direct trade with the United States, reflected a growing British trend toward free trade, which in the 1840s resulted in the dismantling of imperial preference, repeal of the Corn Laws, and concentration on manufactured exports. American grain exports to England would grow considerably in the 1850s and 1860s. This economic interdependence, while hardly a guarantee against war, certainly acted as a brake against military hostilities. At the same time, expanding foreign trade created an intense commercial rivalry.

Ironically, the years immediately following the War of 1812 marked a high point in Anglo-American relations, thanks largely to the conciliatory diplomacy of John Quincy Adams and Lord Castlereagh. After signing the Treaty of Ghent, Adams, Albert Gallatin, and Henry Clay went directly to London and negotiated a commercial treaty with the British Board of Trade in 1815. It was a simple reciprocal trade agreement that repeated the terms of Jay's Treaty with respect to commercial intercourse between America and Great Britain. The British West Indies remained closed to American ships. The treaty also forbade discriminatory duties by either country against the ships or commerce of the other, thus tacitly conceding the failure of Jefferson's earlier attempts at "peaceable coercions." Nothing was said about impressment or neutral rights. This commercial convention was renewed in 1818 for ten more years.

War's end also found the British and Americans engaged in feverish warship construction on the Great Lakes, the beginnings of a naval race that neither London nor Washington could afford. Concerned about postwar finances and confident that the United States could build vessels quickly in a crisis, the Monroe Administration proposed a standstill agreement to the British. Much to the disappointment of the Canadians, Castlereagh agreed. By the Rush-Bagot agreement, negotiated in Washington in April, 1817, each country pledged to maintain not more than one armed ship on Lake Champlain, another on Lake Ontario, and two on all the other Great Lakes. The Rush-Bagot accord applied only to warships and left land fortifications intact. Not until the Treaty of Washington in 1871 did relations between Canada and the United States become amicable enough for the myth of the "unguarded frontier" to become reality.

The Convention of 1818, negotiated in London by Richard Rush and Albert Gallatin, dealt with the fisheries and the northwestern boundary. In an effort to settle the vaguely defined limits of the Louisiana Purchase, the Americans initially proposed to extend the Canadian-American boundary westward from the Lake of the Woods to the Pacific Ocean along the line of 49 degrees north latitude. Because Britain refused to abandon its claims to the Columbia River Basin, the convention stipulated that the boundary should run from Lake of the Woods to the "Stony Mountains" along the forty-ninth parallel. Beyond the Rockies, for a period of ten years, subject to renewal, the Oregon territory should remain "free and open" to both British and American citizens. As for the vexatious matter of the Atlantic fisheries, Gallatin and Rush won confirmation of the "liberty" to fish "for ever" along specific stretches of the Newfoundland and Labrador coasts, as well as to dry and cure fish along less extensive areas of the same coastline. Although the phrasing was vague enough to cause controversy in later decades, Secretary John Quincy Adams accepted the agreement as vindication of his family's honor. Not for nothing was the motto on the Adams family seal *Piscemur, venemur ut olim* ("We will fish and hunt as heretofore").

The fisheries question, one should hasten to add, was not definitively settled until 1910 in an arbitration before the Hague Court. Technically, the issue was probably the most complicated in nineteenth-century American diplomatic history. According to a story at Harvard University, the humorist Robert Benchley was once forced to answer an examination question on the North Atlantic fisheries in a course on American foreign policy. Benchley knew nothing about the fisheries. Undaunted, he wrote: "This question has long been discussed from the American and British points of view, but has anyone considered the viewpoint of the fish?"[50] Benchley proceeded to analyze the codfish question and was awarded, appropriately enough, the grade of "C".

Following the Monroe Doctrine, George Canning hoped to avoid unnecessary friction with Washington. "Let us hasten settlement, if we can," he wrote, "but let us postpone the day of difference, if it must come."[51] London's shift toward free trade finally opened the British West Indies to American merchants in 1830. But a series of crises disrupted relations. Most important was the Canadian rebellion of 1837, led by William Lyon Mackenzie. Many American volunteers joined the tumult. Coming a year after the Texas war for independence, the Canadian rebellion revived expansionist visions of 1812, particularly in areas along the Canadian-American border. Rensselaer Van Rensselaer, the drunken son of an American general, tried to become a Canadian version of Sam Houston, leading a motley group of Canadian patriots and American sympathizers on raids into Canada from New York. It was after one of these forays that Canadian soldiers, on December 29, 1837, struck Van Rensselaer's stronghold on Navy Island in the Niagara River, hoping to capture the rebel supply ship *Caroline*. The troops crossed to the American shore, found the 45-ton *Caroline*, set her afire, and cast her adrift to sink a short distance above the great falls. During the fracas an American, one Amos Durfee, was killed. Outrage gripped Americans along the border. Durfee's body was displayed before 3,000 mourners on the porch of the Buffalo city hall. The good citizens of Lewiston, New York made a bonfire of books by British authors. In May of 1838 some Americans boarded the Canadian steamboat *Sir Robert Peel*, plying the St. Lawrence River. They burned and looted the vessel, all the while shouting "Remember the Caroline!" Raids and counter-raids continued through 1838. Fortunately, the authorities in Washington maintained their equilibrium. President Martin Van Buren warned Americans against joining the rebellion and sent General Winfield Scott to the New York-Ontario border to restore quiet. Scott brooked no nonsense. "Except if it be over my body," he shouted to an unruly crowd, "you shall not pass this line—you shall not embark."[52] When Mackenzie and Van Rensselaer fled to the American border, they were quickly arrested, and the rebellion petered out.

A new crisis flared up in February, 1839 in northern Maine. The vast timberlands spanning the Maine–New Brunswick border had long been a subject of diplomatic dispute because of cartographic errors contained in the 1783 peace treaty. The matter had not seemed urgent until the mid-1830s, when the discovery of fertile soil in the Aroostook Valley brought an influx of settlers, rival claims, and occasional brawls. Soon axe-wielding lumberjacks were embroiled in the bizarre "Aroostook War." Maine mobilized its militia that winter, as did New Brunswick, and Congress appropriated some $10 million for defense. It seemed an opportunity to whip the "Warriors of Waterloo."[53] As the "Maine Battle Song" had it:[54]

> Britannia shall not rule the Maine,
> Nor shall she rule the water;
> They've sung that song full long enough,
> Much longer than they oughter.

The "war" did not last long. General Scott again rushed to the scene, and after a few tense weeks the British minister and Secretary of State John Forsyth negotiated a temporary armistice pending a final boundary settlement. The only American death came at the very end when a Maine militiaman, firing his musket in celebration of the peace, accidentally killed a farmer working his field.

Any possibility that the *Caroline* affair would be forgotten soon disappeared in November, 1840, when a Canadian named Alexander McLeod bragged in a Utica, New York saloon that he had personally killed Amos Durfee. McLeod was quickly arrested and charged with murder and arson. While this development brought huzzas from Americans remembering the *Caroline*, it aroused apoplectic roars from the British Foreign Secretary Lord Palmerston, who let it be known that McLeod's execution "would produce war, war immediate and frightful in its character, because it would be a war of retaliation and vengeance."[55] Daniel Webster was then secretary of state and anxious to avoid trouble, but the federal government did not have jurisdiction in the case. Fortunately for Anglo-American amity, McLeod told a different story sober than he had while drunk, the jury believed him, and he was acquitted.

Within a month of McLeod's acquittal, however, another crisis erupted. In November, 1841, a cargo of slaves being transported from Hampton Roads to New Orleans mutinied and took control of the American vessel *Creole*, killing one white man in the process. The slaves sought refuge at Nassau in the Bahamas, where British authorities liberated all but the actual murderers. Southerners were incensed. This was not the first time the British had refused to return escaped slaves. Moreover, the British efforts to suppress the international slave trade were constantly hampered by the unwillingness of the United States to allow its ships to be searched. This refusal to permit search stemmed in part from memories of impressment, but to the British, Uncle Sam was a crude and brutal defender of the inhumane traffic in human souls.

Thus, as the year 1842 approached, Anglo-American relations were beset with troubles. The northeastern boundary remained in contest. Britain had not apologized for the *Caroline* affair. There were rumblings over British interest in Oregon and Texas. Americans disliked British snobbery. British visitors, most notably Charles Dickens, wrote scathingly of American manners and morals. Britons were incensed over America's inadequate copyright laws. But the time seemed ripe for the settlement of many of these issues. A new Tory government took office in September, 1841, and Lord Aberdeen, a conciliatory man who had been a protégé of Castlereagh, replaced the cantankerous Palmerston at the Foreign Office. Aberdeen appointed as the new British minister to Washington the equally conciliatory Lord Ashburton. Only recently retired from the great financial house of Baring Brothers, Ashburton had married an American, and was so sympathetic to the United States that he had opposed British maritime restrictions against the U.S. before the War of 1812. Beetle-browed Daniel Webster reciprocated Ashburton's amicability. The secretary of state had known Ashburton for some years. Indeed, Webster had long been the American legal agent for the Baring firm, often earning several times his government salary through British commissions. Three years earlier the "godlike Daniel," an erudite and eloquent orator then at the peak of his political career, had toured England and was lionized as few American visitors had been. Opponents later charged that Webster sought appointment as minister to the Court of St. James's. Both men believed that reasonable compromise would serve the interests of their respective countries. The two diplomats therefore met leisurely for several weeks in the summer of 1842. There was little interchange of diplomatic notes, but much consumption of good food and drink. In this relaxed manner they produced the Webster-Ashburton Treaty, signed and approved in August.

The Anglo-American agreement drew a new Maine boundary. Far enough south not to block a military road the British wanted to build between New Brunswick and Quebec, the border was still considerably north of Britain's maximum demand. The United States received approximately 7,000 of the 12,000 square miles under dispute, although this was some 893 square miles less than had been

Daniel Webster (1782–1852). A famed constitutional lawyer from Massachusetts, Webster served as a member of Congress (1823–1827), a United States senator (1827–1841), and secretary of state (1841–1843). He helped settle the northeastern boundary dispute. As a senator again in 1845–1850, he opposed the acquisition of Texas and the Mexican War. From 1850 until his death, this imposing political figure sat once more as secretary of state. (National Portrait Gallery, Smithsonian Institution)

awarded by the King of the Netherlands in 1831 in his abortive attempt to arbitrate the controversy. Farther west Webster won most of the disputed territory near the headwaters of the Connecticut River, as well as a favorable boundary from Lake Superior to the Lake of the Woods. Included in the latter award, but largely unbeknownst at the time to the negotiators, was the valuable iron ore of the Mesabi Range in Minnesota. Although not part of the treaty per se, two inconclusive notes on the *Creole* and *Caroline* affairs were exchanged, burying the issues.

Characterized by compromise and cordial personal relations, Webster's discussions with Ashburton were simple compared to his diplomacy with Maine and Massachusetts. The Bay State had retained half ownership in Maine's public domain after the latter had become a separate state in 1820, and so Webster had to persuade both states to approve the new boundary with Canada. For this difficult task, the secretary of state resorted to some dubious cartographic persuasion. One of Webster's friends was Jared Sparks, a historian who later became president of Harvard. Sparks had been researching the diplomacy of the American Revolution in the British archives, and he told Webster he had seen the original map on which Benjamin Franklin had drawn a strong red line delineating the northeast boundary. From memory Sparks reproduced the line on a nineteenth-century map, and it corresponded closely to British claims. A second map turned up, older but still not genuine, also supporting the British position. Accepting both spurious maps as genuine, Webster sent Sparks to Augusta and Boston with this new "evidence" to persuade local officials to accept the treaty before the British decided to back out of the agreement. Webster also offered each state $150,000. Maine and Massachusetts then endorsed the Webster-Ashburton Treaty. The original maps used in the 1783 peace negotiations (four were later located) actually supported the American boundary claims. Palmerston had found one such map in 1839, but said nothing. With more effort Webster might have found a similar map which was discovered in the Jay family papers in 1843. Instead, it seems that 3,207,680 acres of woodland that belonged to the United States became a part of Canada.

CONTEST OVER OREGON

The Webster-Ashburton negotiations did not settle the question of Oregon. Webster proposed yielding Oregon north of the Columbia, if the British in return would persuade Mexico to sell California. Ashburton declined. That same year, 1842, saw the beginning of "Oregon fever," as farmers by the hundreds began to arrive in the lush valley of the Willamette River. Oregon suddenly became controversial. In 1843 the Senate passed a bill calling for the construction of forts along the Oregon route, but the House demurred. When rumors leaked of Webster's offer to surrender the territory north of the Columbia, numerous "Oregon conventions" met, especially in the Midwest, to reassert America's claim to 54° 40'. When Secretary of State John C. Calhoun again proposed to the British, in 1844, that Oregon be divided at the forty-ninth parallel, this too was considered betrayal by vociferous expansionists. The Democratic party platform of 1844 called for the "reoccupation" of Oregon and the party's candidate, James K. Polk, vowed to effect it.

Thomas Hart Benton (1782-1858). Rugged and rambunctious, a Missouri Senator from 1821 to 1851, this splashy orator pushed westward expansion with seldom-equaled intensity and fairmindedness. He championed the 49th-parallel compromise boundary for Oregon in 1846 and only reluctantly voted for war with Mexico because he considered the Nueces the true boundary. Ironically, some expansionists opposed a field command for Benton during the war because they believed, correctly, that he would oppose a large territorial indemnity from Mexico. (Library of Congress)

In actuality, war over Oregon was not as close as it appeared. The American population in Oregon, while increasing every year, still numbered only 5,000 persons in 1845, and all but a handful lived south of the Columbia River. In contrast, the 700-odd trappers and traders associated with the Hudson's Bay Company all lived north of the river. Four times, in 1818, 1824, 1826, and 1844, the British had proposed the Columbia as the boundary. Each time the United States had countered with 49 degrees. The dispute, by any dispassionate analysis, centered on the triangle northwest of the Columbia, including the deep water Strait of Juan de Fuca. Notwithstanding shouts of "Fifty-four forty or fight" from such ultras as Benton, only a minority of the Democratic party, mainly midwesterners, were ready to challenge England. Southern Democrats cared more for Texas than Oregon. A few Whigs, like Webster, wanted Pacific ports, but not at the risk of war. Even though Polk had been elected on an expansionist platform, the new President had ample opportunity to settle the Oregon boundary through diplomacy.

Polk began badly. Bound by the Democratic platform to assert full American claims, he announced in his inaugural address (March 4, 1845) that the American title to the whole of Oregon was "clear and unquestionable."[56] This claim, coming in an official state paper, raised British hackles. Polk, it seems, was talking more for domestic consumption, for in July he had Secretary of State James Buchanan propose the forty-ninth parallel (including the southern tip of Vancouver Island) as a fair compromise. Buchanan explained that the President "found himself embarrassed, if not committed, by the acts of his predecessors."[57] Buchanan's offer, however, did not include free navigation of the Columbia River, and this omission, coupled with Polk's earlier blustering about 54° 40', unfortunately caused the British Minister, Richard Pakenham, to reject the proposal without referring it to London. Polk waited several weeks. Then, on August 30, after rejecting the advice of Buchanan—who wanted to temporize because of tensions with Mexico over Texas—the President withdrew his offer and reasserted American claims to 54° 40'.

Polk increased the pressure further in his annual message to Congress of December, 1845. Laying claim again to all of Oregon, Polk recommended giving Britain the necessary year's notice for ending joint occupation. This was a virtual ultimatum, and he hinted at military measures to protect Americans in Oregon. Polk also made specific reference to the Monroe Doctrine. "The United States," he said, "cannot in silence permit any European interference on the North American continent, and should any such interference be attempted [the United States] will be ready to resist it at any and all hazards."[58] Polk had Texas and California in mind, in addition to Oregon, but the "European" power being warned was clearly Britain.

For the next five months, while Congress debated the ending of joint occupation, Polk remained publicly adamant for 54° 40'. Twice the British offered to arbitrate; each time the United States refused. Privately, however, perhaps influenced by the growing likelihood of war with Mexico, Polk began to drop hints that the United States would resume negotiations if the British made a reasonable counterproposal. Lord Aberdeen sincerely wanted a settlement, but he could not afford to retreat in the face of Yankee braggadocio. Moving carefully, the foreign secretary already had begun a propaganda campaign in the London *Times* and other journals designed to prepare public opinion for the loss of the Columbia River triangle. He was greatly aided in this effort when the Hudson's Bay Company, faced with the flood of American settlers into the Willamette Valley, decided in 1845 to abandon the "trapped-out" southern part of Oregon and move its main depot from Port Vancouver on the Columbia River north to Vancouver Island. Still, the British statesman told the United States government that he would no longer oppose offensive military preparations in Canada, including the immediate dispatch of "thirty sail of the line. . . ." When this news reached Washington in late February, 1846, Polk replied that if the British proposed "extending the boundary to the Pacific by the forty-ninth parallel and the Strait of Fuca," he would send the proposition to the Senate, "though with reluctance."[59]

The British proposal came on June 6, 1846, but because it guaranteed free navigation of the Columbia to the Hudson's Bay Company, Polk found it distasteful. Nevertheless, on the advice of his Cabinet and Senator Benton, he decided on an unusual procedure. Before signing or rejecting the treaty, he submitted it to the Senate for *previous* advice. This procedure placed responsibility for the settlement squarely on the Senate and absolved Polk from his ignominious retreat from 54° 40'. On June 12, the Senate advised Polk, by a vote of 38 to 12, to accept the British offer. On June 15 the President formally signed the treaty, which the Senate then approved, 41-14, three days later. Of course, one major reason Polk and the Senate were so willing to compromise was the fact that war with Mexico had begun some six weeks earlier.

TAKING TEXAS

It was the acquisition of Texas that brought about the Mexican War. The United States had confirmed Spanish claims to this northernmost province of Mexico in the Adams-Onís Treaty of 1819, but the self-denial was only temporary. After Mexico won independence from Spain in 1821, two American ministers attempted to purchase the area. The first, South Carolinian Joel Poinsett, involved himself in local politics in the late 1820s and tried to work through friendly liberals in the Mexican Congress. His successor, Anthony ("What a scamp!") Butler, an unscrupulous crony of Andrew Jackson, tried bribery. Both efforts came to naught. As in the case of Oregon and Florida, transborder migration became the chief engine of American expansion.

Large-scale American settlement did not begin until the 1820s. Spanish authorities, in 1821, hoping to build up Texas as a buffer against American expansion, had encouraged immigration through generous grants of land. Moses Austin, a Connecticut Yankee from Missouri, and his son Stephen undertook to become the first *empresarios* by pledging to bring in 300 families, who, in turn, were required to swear allegiance to Spain and the Catholic faith. After Mexico gained independence in 1821, the new government confirmed these grants and issued others. Within a decade more than 20,000 Americans had crossed into Texas seeking homesteads—more people than had settled in the previous three centuries. Most were slaveholders seeking the fertile delta soil along the Gulf Coast to grow cotton. Under such circumstances, according to historian Gene M. Brack, "it did not take long for Mexicans to discern the similarity of American attitudes towards blacks, Indians, and Mexicans."[60]

Friction was inevitable. The newcomers, required by law to become Roman Catholics and Mexican citizens, were predominantly Protestants who never ceased to think of themselves as Americans. There was sporadic trouble over immigration, tariffs, slavery, and Mexican army garrisons. Finally, General Antonio Lopez de Santa Anna seized dictatorial power in 1834 and attempted to establish a strong centralized government in Mexico City. Regarding this as a violation of their rights under the Mexican Constitution of 1824, Texans submitted a "Declaration of Causes" that resembled the "Declaration of Rights and Grievances" of 1775. By the autumn of 1835, Texans had skirmished with local Mexican soldiers, set up a provisional government, and begun raising an army under the leadership of Sam Houston.

Santa Anna responded by leading a huge force north across the Rio Grande. At the old Alamo mission in San Antonio, some 200 Texans stood off 5,000 Mexicans for nearly two weeks. Then, on March 6, 1836, with the Mexican bugles sounding "no quarter," Santa Anna's forces broke through the Alamo's defenses and killed every one of the resisters, including the legendary Davy Crockett and James Bowie. Three weeks later another Texan force, numbering some 400 recent volunteers from the United States, surrendered at Goliad. More than 300 were promptly shot. These atrocities enraged the North Americans and hundreds of volunteers flocked to Sam Houston's army, which continued to retreat eastward. The showdown came on April 21, 1836, when Houston's army, now numbering 800 men, turned and attacked the Mexican main force near the ferry of the San Jacinto River, not far from the present-day site of Houston, Texas. With a makeshift band playing the ballad "Will You Come to the Bower I Have Shaded for You," the Texans charged across an open field, yelling "Remember the Alamo," and routed the Mexicans, killing about 630. Taken by surprise when the Texans attacked during afternoon siesta, Santa Anna was found hiding in a clump of long grass, dressed in a blue shirt, white pants, and red carpet slippers. Instead of hanging Santa Anna from the nearest tree, Houston extracted a treaty from the Mexican leader that recognized Texas' independence and set a southern and western boundary at the Rio Grande. Mexico repudiated this agreement after Santa Anna's release, but for all practical purposes the battle of San Jacinto ensured Texas' independence.

Texas sought immediate annexation to the United States. Houston's good friend President Andrew Jackson certainly wanted Texas and had tried to purchase the territory from Mexico, but by 1836 Texas had become a hot potato politically. The problem was slavery. Even a fervent continentalist like John Quincy Adams was beginning to see that expansion westward meant the expansion of slavery as well as free institutions. The balance in 1836 stood at thirteen slave states and thirteen free states. No one ever accused Andrew Jackson of being a poor politician, and so "Old Hickory" tiptoed quietly. Not until the last days of his Administration, some eleven months after San Jacinto, did Jackson even recognize Texas' independence. Jackson's chosen successor, Martin Van Buren, also refused to consider annexation for fear of rousing abolitionist zealots. The annexation issue slumbered until 1843, when unpopular President John Tyler, having everything to gain and nothing to lose, seized upon Texas as a vehicle for lifting his political fortunes. Tyler successfully negotiated an annexation treaty with the Texans and submitted it to the Senate in April, 1844, just prior to the presidential nominating conventions.

Tyler, and later Polk, hoped to gain support for the absorption of Texas by playing on fears of British intrusion. Having recognized Texan independence in 1840, Britain had developed a clear interest in maintaining that independence. Motives in London were mixed. Paramount was the hope that an independent Texas would block American expansion, perhaps in time to serve as a balance in the classic European model. Further, Texas could offer an alternative supply of cotton for England's textile factories. A low-tariff Lone Star Republic might grow into a large British market and, by example, stimulate Southern states to push harder in Washington for tariff reduction. Certain Britishers also hoped that Texas might be persuaded to abolish slavery, an illusion that Texan leaders manipulated to gain British support against Mexico. Such help was forthcoming, as England in 1842 arranged a truce between Texas and Mexico. Later, in the spring of 1844, Lord Aberdeen toyed with the idea of an international agreement whereby Mexico would recognize Texas; and England, France, and, he hoped, the United States would guarantee the independence and existing borders of both Texas and Mexico. The scheme collapsed when Mexico stubbornly refused any dealings with Texas. Not until May, 1845, after a resolution for annexation had already passed the United States Congress, did Mexico agree to recognize Texas, but by then it was too late.

Those foreign maneuvers, however legal and aboveboard, alarmed American expansionists. By nurturing such anxieties, the Tyler Administration might have achieved annexation in 1844 had not Calhoun injudiciously boasted that annexation was "the most effectual, if not the only means of guarding against the threatened danger" of abolition under British tutelage.[61] Calhoun went on to defend slavery with pseudo-scientific arguments that offended the British far less than they antagonized abolitionists and free soilers in the North. Accordingly, when the Senate took its final vote on June 8, 1844, the tally was 35 to 16, a two-thirds majority *against* annexation. The hapless Tyler won neither the Whig nor Democratic nomination that summer.

Texas and annexation did, however, become a central feature of the 1844 presidential campaign. Nominating James K. Polk of Tennessee, a disciple of Jackson, the Democrats fervently embraced expansion. The party platform promised the "reoccupation of Oregon and the re-annexation of Texas," giving rise to the myth that somehow the United States once owned Texas and perhaps John Quincy Adams had given it back to Spain in 1819. The Whigs chose Henry Clay, who opposed taking Texas if it meant war. It was a fierce campaign, full of expansive oratory, and Texas loomed as the central issue. Polk won by a close margin: 1,337,000 to 1,299,000 in the popular vote and 170 to 105 in the electoral college. Although people at the time considered the Democratic victory a mandate for expansion, other factors, including an abolitionist third-party candidate who took key votes from Clay in the decisive state of New York, explain Polk's victory. Whatever the reasons for their choice, the voters, in one of the rare presidential elections in which foreign policy issues predominated, had elected the candidate who would bring war. If Clay had won in 1844, he almost certainly would have kept peace with Mexico.

Even before Polk took office, the annexationists acted. Unable to win a two-thirds Senate majority for a treaty, lame-duck Tyler suggested annexation by joint resolution (simple majorities of both houses). Opponents howled. Albert Gallatin called it "an undisguised usurpation of power," and John Quincy Adams grumbled about the "apoplexy of the Constitution."[62] But the annexationists had the votes—120–98 in the House, 27–25 in the Senate—and on March 1, 1845, three days before leaving office, Tyler signed the fateful measure. Five days later the Mexican minister in Washington asked for his passports and went home.

Polk did not inherit an inevitable conflict with Mexico. Rather, the President made decisions and carried them out in ways that exacerbated already existing tension and made war difficult to avoid. Mexico had stated unequivocally that it would sever diplomatic relations if Texas were annexed to the United States, but Polk compounded the problem by supporting Texas' flimsy claim to the Rio Grande as its southern and western boundary. Except for the treaty extracted from Santa Anna in 1836, the Nueces River had always stood as the accepted boundary, and during the nine years of Texas' independence no move had been made to occupy the disputed territory south of Corpus Christi. Nevertheless, during the negotiations to complete annexation in the summer of 1845, Polk's emissaries apparently urged Texas President Anson Jones to seize all territory to the Rio Grande. Polk's orders to American military and naval forces, though couched in defensive terms, were aimed at preventing any Mexican retaliation. At this time, too, the President sent secret orders to Commodore John D. Sloat, commander of the Pacific Squadron, to capture the main ports of California in the event that Mexico attacked Texas. Whether Polk actively sought to provoke war, or was merely using force to buttress diplomacy, he was making unilateral decisions that disregarded Mexican sensibilities and ignored congressional prerogatives.

When Mexico failed to retaliate, Polk again turned to diplomacy. He had received word from the American consul in Mexico City that the government, while furious at annexation, was unprepared for war and would receive a special emissary to discuss Texas. Polk sent John Slidell, a Louisiana Democrat, as a full Minister Plenipotentiary empowered to re-establish formal relations and to negotiate on issues other than Texas. California now loomed large in Polk's mind, even larger than Texas. No sooner had the President instructed Slidell to purchase New Mexico and California for $25 million (Slidell could go as high as $40 million) than a report arrived from Consul Thomas Larkin in Monterey describing in lurid terms British machinations to turn California into a protectorate. Since Polk had no way of knowing that Larkin was reporting false rumors and exaggerating local British activities, this information only increased his resolve to obtain California. He ordered Larkin to propagandize among the Californians for annexation to the United States and for resistance against the British. Similar orders went to Lieutenant John C. Frémont, head of a United States Army exploring party in eastern California. Frémont, the son-in-law of expansionist Senator Thomas Hart Benton, interpreted his instructions as a command to foment insurrection among American settlers, and this he proceeded to do in the summer of 1846.

Slidell's mission, meanwhile, was a complete failure. When he reached Mexico City in early December, 1845, officials refused to receive him because, they said, his title of Minister Plenipotentiary suggested prior acceptance of Texas' annexation. Actually, even if Slidell had made the monetary offer for California, no Mexican government would sell territory to the United States in the highly charged atmosphere of 1845–1846. Too many Mexicans remembered the bizarre incident in 1842, when Commodore Thomas ap Catesby Jones, mistakenly believing that war had broken out, sailed into Monterey harbor and forced the astonished authorities to surrender. Jones discovered his error, apologized, and sailed away, leaving the Mexicans understandably angry. Any offer to purchase California, coming so closely on the heels of Texas' annexation, was out of the question. War seemed preferable. Some Mexican leaders thought that their large professional army stood an excellent chance of beating the corrupt, land-grabbing Yankees. "Depend upon it," Slidell arrogantly reported, "we can never get along well with them, until we have given them a good drubbing."[63]

Polk responded on January 13, 1846, as we have seen, by ordering General Taylor to move south from Corpus Christi and occupy the left bank of the Rio Grande. Even though Polk initially regarded this action as added pressure on Mexico to negotiate, Mexicans interpreted it as heralding a war of aggression. Taylor blockaded Matamoros, itself an act of war under international law. The Mexicans retaliated. The first clash occurred on April 24, and Polk was able to present Congress with a fait accompli.

WARTIME DIPLOMACY AND THE PEACE

Polk never wanted a long war. California and the Rio Grande boundary were his principal objectives, and he was willing to explore diplomatic alternatives. Shortly after hostilities broke out, the President was approached by an emissary of Santa Anna, then living in exile in Havana. The former dictator promised Polk that if the United States helped him to return to Mexico he would undertake to give Polk the territory he desired. Terms were worked out, and in August, 1846 Santa Anna was permitted to slip through the American naval blockade and land at Veracruz. A revolution propitiously occurred in Mexico City and Santa Anna was named President. Instead of making peace, however, the self-proclaimed Napoleon of the West organized an army and marched north to fight General Taylor. More than a year passed before Polk understood that he had been doublecrossed. As late as General Scott's campaign to capture Mexico City in the autumn of 1847, Polk was still hoping to bribe Santa Anna into a settlement. The Mexican took the money, but kept fighting.

An even more bizarre diplomatic opportunity presented itself in November, 1846 in the persons of Moses Y. Beach and Jane McManus Storms. Beach, the Democratic editor of the *New York Sun* and a chief drum-beater for Manifest Destiny, had contacts in the Mexican army and the Catholic hierarchy in Mexico City. He suggested to Polk that he be sent as a confidential agent to Mexico, empowered to negotiate a suitable peace which would include, in addition to Texas and California, the right to build a canal across the Isthmus of Tehuantepec. Polk agreed, thinking that it would be a "good joke" if Beach were to succeed.[64] Beach then journeyed to Veracruz and Mexico City, accompanied by Mrs. Storms, a beautiful and adventuresome journalist whose greatest notoriety had come some twelve years before when she was named co-respondent in the divorce trial of seventy-seven-year-old Aaron Burr. Once in the Mexican capital, the two Americans rashly joined a clerical uprising against Santa Anna, only to have the dictator suddenly arrive on the scene, claiming to have beaten back Taylor's army at Buena Vista. The revolution collapsed, along with hopes for a quick peace. Beach and Storms fled.

The President finally decided in the spring of 1847 to send an accredited State Department representative along with Scott's army. At first he thought of Secretary Buchanan, but negotiations might take months and such an important Cabinet member could not be spared. He settled on Nicholas P. Trist, the chief clerk of the State Department, a man of impeccable Democratic credentials (he had once been Andrew Jackson's private secretary and had married a granddaughter of Thomas Jefferson). Trist, Polk thought, could be easily managed and would keep a watchful eye on the politically ambitious Scott, a Whig. The President immediately regretted his choice. In May Trist reached the American Army, then marching toward the plain of Central Mexico. He soon quarrelled furiously with General Scott, who resented Trist's power to decide when hostilities should cease. The two men did not speak to one another for six weeks, communicating only through vituperative letters, some up to thirty pages in length. Then Trist fell ill, and Scott chivalrously sent a special jar of guava marmalade to speed his recovery. Overnight the two prickly prima donnas resolved to work together.

By this time, September, 1847, Scott's troops had battered their way to Mexico City, and the diplomat and warrior were trying to conclude peace with any Mexican faction that would treat. Polk, suspicious at the political implications of the Scott-Trist entente and angry that Trist had forwarded to Washington a Mexican peace proposal that still insisted on the Nueces as the Texas boundary, summarily recalled his unruly representative. The President now seemed in no hurry to conclude peace. Military successes had made it possible to obtain more

Americans Enter Mexico City, 1847. General Winfield Scott triumphantly parades in the plaza as an American flag flies over the palace at the right. One Mexican, at the left with stone in hand, did not appreciate the ceremonies. (Library of Congress)

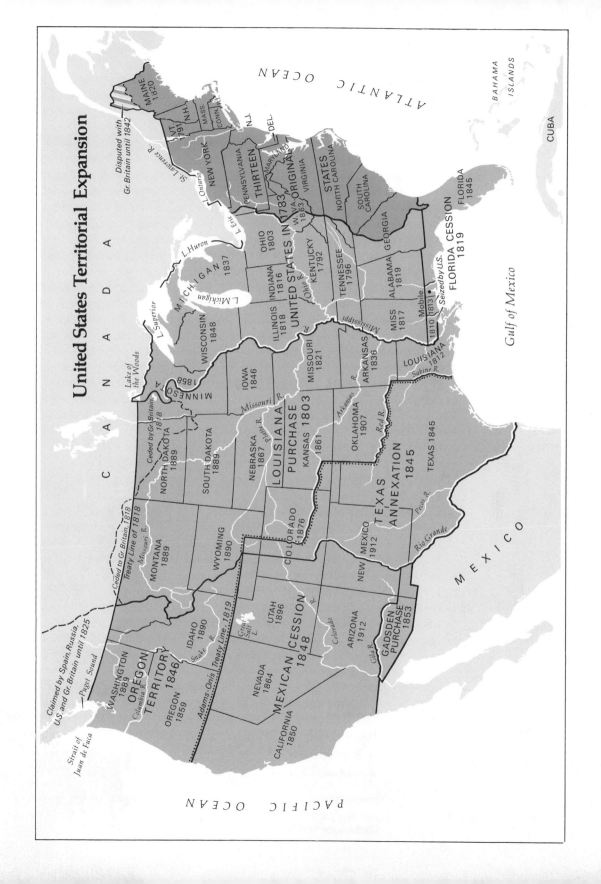

United States Territorial Expansion

ATLANTIC OCEAN

BAHAMA ISLANDS

CUBA

CANADA

Disputed with Gr. Britain until 1842

MAINE 1820

N.H.

VT. 1791

MASS.

CONN. R.I.

N.J.

DEL.

St. Lawrence R.

L. Ontario

L. Erie

NEW YORK

PENNSYLVANIA

MARYLAND

THIRTEEN

ORIGINAL

W. VA. 1863

VIRGINIA

UNITED STATES IN 1783

STATES

NORTH CAROLINA

SOUTH CAROLINA

GEORGIA

FLORIDA 1845

FLORIDA CESSION 1819

Seized by U.S.

Gulf of Mexico

L. Huron

L. Michigan

L. Superior

MICHIGAN 1837

OHIO 1803

INDIANA 1816

ILLINOIS 1818

Ohio R.

KENTUCKY 1792

TENNESSEE 1796

ALABAMA 1819

MISS 1817

Mobile 1810 1813

WISCONSIN 1848

Lake of the Woods

Ceded by Gr. Britain 1818

MINNESOTA 1858

IOWA 1846

Missouri

MISSOURI 1821

ARKANSAS 1836

LOUISIANA 1812

Sabine R.

LOUISIANA

Mississippi

Ceded to Gr. Britain 1818

Treaty Line of 1818

NORTH DAKOTA 1889

SOUTH DAKOTA 1889

Missouri R.

NEBRASKA 1867

Platte R.

LOUISIANA PURCHASE 1803

KANSAS 1861

Arkansas R.

OKLAHOMA 1907

Red R.

TEXAS 1845

Pecos R.

TEXAS ANNEXATION 1845

Claimed by Spain, Russia, U.S. and Gr. Britain until 1825

Puget Sound

Strait of Juan de Fuca

MONTANA 1889

WYOMING 1890

COLORADO 1876

NEW MEXICO 1912

Rio Grande

MEXICO

WASHINGTON 1889

OREGON TERRITORY 1846

Columbia R.

Adams-Onis

OREGON 1859

IDAHO 1890

Snak R.

Treaty Line...1819

Great Salt L.

UTAH 1896

MEXICAN CESSION 1848

ARIZONA 1912

Colorado R.

Gila R.

GADSDEN PURCHASE 1853

NEVADA 1864

CALIFORNIA 1850

PACIFIC OCEAN

territory than he had originally sought—perhaps Lower as well as Upper California, the Isthmus of Tehuantepec, and the provinces north of the Sierra Madre. Polk even contemplated the absorption of all Mexico. Lewis Cass, a Michigan Democrat, grandly declared: "To attempt to prevent the American people from taking possession of Mexico, if they demand it, would be as futile . . . as to undertake to stop the rushing of the cataract of Niagara."[65]

Nicholas Trist thereupon did an extraordinary thing. He refused to be recalled. Trist, as historian Frederick Merk has pointed out, was a true believer in the vision of Manifest Destiny, "confident that Mexico, left to herself, would someday enter the temple of freedom."[66] But such a process could not be forced. Reconciliation had to come first. Any peace that demanded too much would violate this canon. Even before he received his recall notice, Trist had begun negotiations with a moderate faction that had come to power. These Mexicans urged him to remain. Scott concurred. His mind made up, Trist informed Polk, in a bristling sixty-five-page letter, that he was continuing peace talks under his original instructions. Polk grew splenetic. "I have never in my life felt so indignant," he told his diary.[67]

In due course Trist negotiated his peace treaty, signed on February 2, 1848, at Guadalupe Hidalgo, near Mexico City. According to its terms Mexico ceded California and New Mexico to the United States and confirmed the annexation of Texas with the Rio Grande as the boundary. In return, the United States was to pay $15 million and assume the claims of American citizens totaling another $3.25 million. When the treaty arrived in Washington, the President reluctantly decided to submit it to the Senate, notwithstanding that "Mr. Trist has acted very badly." The territorial gains were all that Slidell had been empowered to obtain in his 1845–1846 mission. "If I were now to reject a treaty," Polk explained to the Cabinet, "made upon my own terms, as authorized in April last, with the unanimous approbation of the Cabinet, the probability is that Congress would not grant either men or money to prosecute the war."[68] The Whig-dominated Senate had just passed a resolution praising General Taylor's victories in "a war unnecessarily and unconstitutionally begun by the President of the United States." Congress had repeatedly voted men and supplies for the army, but Polk did not want to risk his gains. The treaty passed the Senate, 38 to 14, on March 10, 1848. A Whig critic cynically commented that the peace "negotiated by an unauthorized agent, with an unacknowledged government, submitted by an accidental President, to a dissatisfied Senate, has, notwithstanding these objections in form, been confirmed."[69]

The antiwar movement had made little impact. In Congress this opposition consisted largely of Whigs and Calhoun Democrats. The target of criticism at the outset was the questionable way in which Polk had begun the war, but it soon shifted to attempts to bar slavery from any territorial gains, and, finally, after Scott's victorious march to the Halls of Montezuma, opposition to any Administration effort to take "All Mexico." The Wilmot Proviso was the most ominous war protest. Attached as a rider to the war appropriation bill of August, 1846 by Democrat David Wilmot of Pennsylvania, the proviso held that none of the territory acquired from Mexico should be open to slavery. Its supporters were almost exclusively Northerners, and a coalition of Southern Whigs and Administration Democrats was sufficient to defeat it. Nonetheless, the Wilmot Proviso was introduced again and again, never passing, but sparking ever increasing debate, causing Southerners like Calhoun to despair of the Union. Polk struck back at his critics by suggesting that they were aiding the enemy, a stinging charge using the

Abraham Lincoln (1809–1865). As a one-term Whig member of Congress from Illinois, Lincoln strongly opposed the extension of slavery into new territories and believed that President Polk had provoked Mexico into war. Lincoln dismissed Polk's attempt to blame the start of the war on Mexico as the "'half insane mumbling of a fever-dream" by a man whose mind had been "tasked beyond its power." This 1846 Daguerreotype photo by N. H. Shepherd is the earliest-known of Lincoln. (Library of Congress)

Constitution's definition of treason. Few critics chose to risk voting against military supplies. Americans believed that a war, right or wrong, which Congress had voted, must be upheld.

THE LESSONS AND COSTS OF CONTINENTAL EXPANSION, 1815–1848

The United States acquired more than 500,000 square miles of territory in the war against Mexico, which young Congressman Abraham Lincoln labeled "a war of conquest."[70] This accession, combined with the Oregon settlement with England, completed the continental expansion of the 1840s. Polk did not obtain "All Mexico," nor did he fight for "Fifty-four forty," but he had taken what he wanted: Texas and California. The casualties: 1,721 Americans killed in battle and 11,550 deaths from other causes, mainly disease. About 50,000 Mexicans died.

The war brought other ugly consequences that could not be easily quantified. The arrogant rationalizations for expansion appalled an old Jeffersonian like Albert Gallatin, who noted in 1848: "All these allegations of superiority of race and destiny neither require nor deserve any answer; they are pretences [sic] . . . to disguise ambitions, cupidity, or silly vanity."[71] Ralph Waldo Emerson had pre-

"The Trail of Tears." Robert Lindneux's poignant painting of Indian removal illustrates a tragic consequence of United States expansion. Of the 100,000 Indians transported beyond the Mississippi in 1824–1845, perhaps one-fourth to one-third died during or shortly after the forced marches. "Why do not the Americans take the Indian names?" asked one foreign visitor to the United States during this period. "They have robbed the Indians of everything else." (From the original oil painting at Woolaroc Museum, Bartlesville, Oklahoma)

dicted in 1847 that the United States would gobble Mexican territory "as the man swallows arsenic, which brings him down in turn."[72] Indeed, debates over the Wilmot Proviso raised the all-important question whether the new territories would be free or slave. It took two more decades and a bloody civil war to answer the question. In fact, the issue of race in the 1850s blocked any possibility that the United States might acquire additional territories in the Caribbean or Pacific. Such potential prizes as Cuba or Hawaii had racially mixed populations, and thus seemed less adaptable to American settlers and institutions than did the lightly populated prairies of North America. Opponents of slavery became opponents of expansion.

The American Indian became another victim of westward expansion. "Land enough—Land enough! Make way, I say, for the young American Buffalo!" shouted one fervent orator for Manifest Destiny in 1844.[73] It was the Indian who had to give way. While Americans in the 1820s and 1830s sought fertile lands in Texas and Oregon, other farmers were encroaching on Indian lands east of the Mississippi. Despite solemn treaty commitments, those years saw the removal of most of the tribes in the Old Northwest and Southwest to new reservations in

Missouri and Oklahoma. It was a brutal process—a "trail of tears." Indians were uprooted, forced to march thousands of miles, robbed by federal and state officials, ravaged by disease. Some tribes resisted, as evidenced by the Black Hawk War of 1832 and the guerrilla warfare waged by the Seminoles in the Everglades for nearly a decade. In the case of the Creeks, the population in 1860 was only 40 percent of what it had been 30 years earlier. Other tribes suffered similar losses. Native Americans beyond the Mississippi and Missouri rivers would feel the pinch of empire after 1848.

The costs of American expansion for Mexico were also easily overlooked at the time. The loser in a disastrous war, Mexico suffered 50,000 dead, relinquished more than half its national territory, and saw large amounts of real estate, foodstuffs, art treasures, and livestock destroyed by the invading armies. The American invaders treated Mexicans as they did the Indians—as racial inferiors. General John Quitman, temporarily the governor of Mexico City, called Mexico's 8,000,000 inhabitants "beasts of burden, with as little intellect as the asses whose burdens they share."[74] Then, too, Mexican politics, stormy since independence, grew even more tumultuous, and the country had to endure another 25 years of rebellion, civil war, and foreign intervention before a degree of national unity could be attained under the authoritarian regime of Porfirio Díaz. The war increased the disparity in size, power, and population between the United States and Mexico, thus creating a set of national attitudes that would bring mixed results in the twentieth century.

The success of continental expansion left one obvious imprint on the United States—that of increased power. To be sure, the Mexican War did not propel the United States into great power status; it would take another half-century, industrialization, and a war with Spain to achieve such ranking. Nonetheless, the nation had grown from a third-rate to a second-rate power, capable of challenging any of the European giants within its own hemisphere. The evolution of the Monroe Doctrine mirrored this growth. President Monroe had hurled his defiant message in 1823 without the power to enforce it. When Britain seized the Falkland Islands in 1833 and the French bombarded Mexican ports in 1838, American statesmen did nothing. In 1842, however, President Tyler specifically warned England and France against annexing Hawaii. Three years later Polk arrogantly invoked the Monroe Doctrine in proclaiming American rights to Texas, California, and Oregon. As American power continued to increase after 1848, as economic interests began to focus on the Caribbean and the possibility of an isthmian canal, American statesmen would also invoke the Monroe Doctrine. The same mixture of motive that operated in the 1820s would continue—namely, a genuine desire to forestall European intervention, combined with a wish to extend American influence, political and economic, throughout the hemisphere.

Few persons would deny that continental expansion served American interests. One opponent of the Mexican War suggested: "If just men should ever again come into power, I believe they ought not to hesitate to retrocede to Mexico the country of which we have most unjustly despoiled her."[75] Just or not, no American President has ever offered to return Mexican lands. The attitude of the Whig party was indicative. Approximately 90 percent of the Whigs in Congress in 1845 opposed territorial expansion. Once war with Mexico was declared, however, with Whig generals Scott and Taylor gaining popular laurels, Whigs voted for war supplies and eventually accepted the Treaty of Guadalupe Hidalgo. The commercial attractions of the Pacific Coast salved many Whig consciences. The real debate was not over the fact of continental expansion, but the way it was accomplished. The rhetoric of Manifest Destiny envisioned a peaceful extension of American institutions across the continent—yet war had occurred. Many still asked if it was necessary to resort to force.

Polk told one congressman in 1846 that "the only way to treat John Bull was to look him straight in the eye."[76] This was the diplomacy of eyeball-to-eyeball confrontation. Polk's resolute style seemed successful with both Britain and Mexico. The Tennessean's "lessons" for later American diplomats take on added importance when one considers his high reputation in the twentieth century. Theodore Roosevelt saw in Polk a model for reasserting strong executive leadership in foreign policy. In 1919 Justin H. Smith published his Pulitzer prize-winning history of the Mexican War, defending Polk at every turn. A poll of historians in the early 1960s ranked him eighth in importance among American Presidents, just ahead of Harry Truman.

In point of fact, Polk was probably lucky. Unlike John Quincy Adams, whose forceful diplomacy against Spain and the Holy Allies was based on a shrewd understanding of international power realities, Polk moved against Mexico and Britain without careful thought of consequences. Regarding Oregon, his initial call for 54° 40' unnecessarily heightened jingo fevers on both sides of the Atlantic and postponed any settlement until the spring of 1846. In view of the concurrent crisis with Mexico, such a delay invited the disastrous possibility of a war on two fronts. Nor was England's decision to settle at the forty-ninth parallel the beneficent result of "looking John Bull straight in the eye." British conciliation was due more to troubles at home—the potato famine in Ireland, tensions with France, political turmoil over repeal of the Corn Laws. Aberdeen's sobering presence also helped. Had Palmerston become foreign secretary (as he very nearly did, in January, 1846), Polk's "eyeball" tactics might have meant war. Given the flood of American immigration into the Pacific Northwest in 1844–1846, Calhoun's policy of "masterly inactivity" would almost certainly have produced a favorable settlement without risking war. Polk apparently had not heard what Castlereagh said a generation earlier: "You need not trouble yourselves about Oregon, you will conquer Oregon in your bedchambers."[77]

"Masterly inactivity" might have worked with Mexico as well. Polk did not want war so much as he desired the fruits of war. He wanted California, New Mexico, and the Rio Grande boundary, and, suspicious of British intrigues, he was in a hurry. Slidell's offer to purchase the territory was genuine and, in Polk's narrow mind, generous, but it completely disregarded Mexican nationalist sensibilities. Keeping Taylor's army at Corpus Christi would have protected Texas with little provocation to Mexico. Negotiations could resume when tempers cooled. Whether Mexico would have ever released the territories is, of course, an open question. As for California, Polk should have understood, after a careful reading of all diplomatic correspondence, that England had no serious intention of seizing that lucrative prize. The obvious alternative was to wait, and see if the influx of American settlers would make California another Texas or Oregon. Annexation might have come peacefully—perhaps, as historian David Pletcher has suggested, during some subsequent European crisis like the Crimean War. As it turned out, Polk's decision for war in the spring of 1846 was reckless, coming as it did while tensions with England were still acute. War risked all the expansionist goals. A major Mexican victory (and Santa Anna nearly won the battle of Buena Vista) might have brought a European loan to Mexico, military stalemate, and possible British mediation. California might have been lost. Polk was also lucky that his repudiated agent, Trist, made a treaty of peace when he did. The capture of Mexico City and the successful negotiations that quickly followed obscured the fact that insistence on "All Mexico" might have led to the kind of protracted guerrilla war against United States occupation forces that Mexicans waged against French armies twenty years later. Overall, if Polk truly believed in Manifest Destiny, it seems strange that he tried to hurry what Americans thought was inevitable. But, because Polk ultimately succeeded in pushing American borders to the Pacific, the blemishes in his diplomatic record will probably continue to be covered with the cosmetic cream of national celebration.

FURTHER READING FOR THE PERIOD 1815–1848

For general studies, American expansion, Manifest Destiny, and leaders before mid-century, see Irving Bartlett, *Daniel Webster* (1978); Maurice G. Baxter, *One and Inseparable: Daniel Webster and the Union* (1984); John M. Belohlavek, *"Let the Eagle Soar!" The Foreign Policy of Andrew Jackson* (1985); Ray A. Billington, *Westward Expansion* (1974); Kinley J. Brauer, *Cotton versus Conscience: Massachusetts Whig Politics and Southwestern Expansion, 1843–1848* (1967); Richard Drinnon, *Facing West* (1980); William H. Goetzmann, *When the Eagle Screamed: The Romantic Horizon in American Diplomacy, 1800–1860* (1966); Norman A. Graebner, ed., *Manifest Destiny* (1968); Thomas R. Hietala, *Manifest Design* (1985); Reginald Horsman, *Race and Manifest Destiny* (1981); Walter LaFeber, ed., *John Quincy Adams and American Continental Empire* (1965); Frederick Merk, *Manifest Destiny and Mission in American History* (1963) and *The Monroe Doctrine and American Expansionism, 1843–1849* (1966); Vincent Ponko, *Ships, Seas, and Scientists: U. S. Naval Exploration and Discovery in the Nineteenth Century* (1974); essays on Adams, Wilkes, and Polk in Frank Merli and Theodore A. Wilson, eds., *Makers of American Diplomacy* (1974); Paul Pappas, *The United States and the Greek War for Independence, 1821–1828* (1985); Robert V. Remini, *Andrew Jackson and the Course of American Freedom, 1822–1832* (1981); Leonard L. Richards, *The Life and Times of Congressman John Quincy Adams* (1986); Michael P. Rogin, *Fathers and Sons: Andrew Jackson and the Subjugation of the American Indian* (1975); Malcolm J. Rohrbough, *The Trans-Appalachian Frontier* (1978); Henry Savage, Jr., *Discovering America, 1700–1875* (1978); John H. Schroeder, *Shaping a Maritime Empire* (1985); William Stanton, *The Great United States Exploring Expedition of 1838–1842* (1975); Richard W. Van Alstyne, *The Rising American Empire* (1960); Paul A. Varg, *United States Foreign Relations, 1820–1860* (1979); Herman J. Viola and Carolyn Margolis, eds., *Magnificent Voyagers* (1985); and Albert Weinberg, *Manifest Destiny* (1935).

The acquisition of Florida, Latin American issues, and the formulation of the Monroe Doctrine are studied in Harry Ammon, "The Monroe Doctrine: Domestic Politics or National Decision?" *Diplomatic History* (1981); Samuel Flagg Bemis, *John Quincy Adams and the Foundations of American Foreign Policy* (1949); Philip C. Brooks, *Diplomacy and the Borderlands: The Adams-Onís Treaty of 1819* (1939); George Dangerfield, *The Awakening of American Nationalism, 1815–1828* (1965) and *The Era of Good Feelings* (1952); Ernest May, *The Making of the Monroe Doctrine* (1975); Bradford Perkins, *Castlereagh and Adams* (1964); Dexter Perkins, *The Monroe Doctrine, 1823–1826* (1927) and *A History of the Monroe Doctrine* (1955); and Arthur P. Whitaker, *The United States and the Independence of Latin America* (1941).

Anglo-American crises, including the Oregon question, appear in Ray A. Billington, *The Far Western Frontier* (1956); Charles C. Campbell, *From Revolution to Rapprochement: The United States and Great Britain, 1783–1900* (1974); Norman A. Graebner, *Empire on the Pacific*

(1955); Howard Jones, *To the Webster-Ashburton Treaty* (1977); Wilbur D. Jones, *Lord Aberdeen and the Americas* (1958) and *The American Problem in British Diplomacy, 1841–1861* (1974); and Frederick Merk, *Albert Gallatin and the Oregon Problem* (1950) and *The Oregon Question* (1967). Also see Howard Kushner, *Conflict on the Northwest Coast: American-Russian Rivalry in the Pacific Northwest, 1790–1867* (1975).

For early American interest in China and its trade, see Warren I. Cohen, *America's Response to China* (1980); Jonathan Goldstein, *Philadelphia and the China Trade, 1682–1846* (1978); Michael Hunt, *The Making of a Special Relationship* (1983); Edward Ingram, *The Beginning of the Great Game in Asia, 1828–1834* (1978); and Kenneth W. Rea, *Early Sino-American Relations, 1841–1912* (1977).

Texas and the Mexican War receive scrutiny in Ephraim D. Adams, *British Interests and Activities in Texas, 1838–1846* (1910); William C. Binkley, *The Texas Revolution* (1952); Gene Brack, *Mexico Views Manifest Destiny, 1821–1846* (1975); J. D. P. Fuller, *The Movement for the Acquisition of All Mexico, 1846–1848* (1936); Norman Graebner, "Lessons of the Mexican War," *Pacific Historical Review* (1978) and "The Mexican War," *Pacific Historical Review* (1980); Neal Harlow, *California Conquered* (1982); Robert W. Johannsen, *To the Halls of Montezuma: The Mexican War in the American Imagination* (1985); Ernest M. Lander, Jr., *Reluctant Imperialists: Calhoun, the South Carolinians, and the Mexican War* (1980); David M. Pletcher, *The Diplomacy of Annexation: Texas, Oregon, and the Mexican War* (1973); Glenn W. Price, *Origins of the War with Mexico: The Polk-Stockton Intrigue* (1967); John H. Schroeder, *Mr. Polk's War: American Opposition and Dissent, 1846-1848* (1973); Charles G. Sellers, *James K. Polk: Continentalist, 1843-1846* (1966); and David J. Weber, *The Mexican Frontier, 1821-1846* (1982).

See also the General Bibliography and the following notes.

NOTES TO CHAPTER 3

1. Quoted in David M. Pletcher, *The Diplomacy of Annexation: Texas, Oregon, and the Mexican War* (Columbia: University of Missouri Press, 1973), p. 377.

2. Milo M. Quaife, ed., *The Diary of James K. Polk, 1845–1849* (Chicago: A. C. McClurg, 1919; 4 vols.), I, 384.

3. *Ibid.*, I, 389–390.

4. James D. Richardson, ed., *A Compilation of the Messages and Papers of the Presidents, 1789–1897* (Washington: Government Printing Office, 1897–1900; 9 vols.), IV, 442.

5. Quoted in Frederick Merk, *Manifest Destiny and Mission in American History* (New York: Vintage Books, 1963), p. 90.

6. Quoted in Arthur M. Schlesinger, Jr., *The Imperial Presidency* (Boston: Houghton Mifflin, 1973), pp. 41–42.

7. Quoted in Charles F. Adams, ed., *Memoirs of John Quincy Adams* (Philadelphia: J. B. Lippincott & Company, 1874–1877; 12 vols.), II, 261.

8. Quoted in John M. Belohlavek, *"Let the Eagle Soar!"* (Lincoln: University of Nebraska Press, 1985), p. 115.

9. Quoted in Arthur P. Whitaker, *The Western Hemisphere Idea: Its Rise and Decline* (Ithaca: Cornell University Press, 1954), p. 29.

10. Quoted in Frederick Merk, *Albert Gallatin and the Oregon Problem* (Cambridge: Harvard University Press, 1950), p. 13.

11. *Democratic Review*, XVII (July–August, 1845), 9.

12. *Ibid.*, p. 5.

13. *Congressional Globe*, 29 Cong., 1 Sess. (January 10, 1846), p. 180.

14. Robert F. Berkhofer, Jr., *Salvation and the Savage: An Analysis of Protestant Missions and the American Indian Response, 1787–1862* (New York: Knopf, 1976), p. 14.

15. Thomas R. Hietala, *Manifest Design: Anxious Aggrandisement in Late Jacksonian America* (Ithaca: Cornell University Press, 1985), p. 172.

16. Quoted in Norman Graebner, ed., *Manifest Destiny* (Indianapolis: Bobbs-Merrill, 1968), p. xxxvii.

17. *Congressional Globe*, 27 Cong., 3 Sess. (January 4, 1843), p. 139.

18. Quoted in William H. Goetzmann, *When the Eagle Screamed: The Romantic Horizon in American Diplomacy, 1800–1860* (New York: John Wiley & Sons, 1966), pp. xvii, 43.

19. Merk, *Gallatin and the Oregon Problem*, pp. 15–16.

20. Michael H. Hunt, *The Making of a Special Relationship: The United States and China to 1914* (New York: Columbia University Press, 1983), p. xi.

21. Geoffrey S. Smith, "Charles Wilkes and the Growth of American Naval Diplomacy," in Frank J. Merli and Theodore A. Wilson, eds., *Makers of American Diplomacy* (New York: Charles Scribner's Sons, 1974), p. 143.

22. Quoted in Norman A. Graebner, *Empire on the Pacific: A Study in American Continental Expansion* (New York: Ronald Press, 1955), p. 79.

23. Quoted in Sidney Lens, *The Forging of the American Empire* (New York: Thomas Y. Crowell, 1971), p. 121.

24. Fletcher Webster, ed., *The Private Correspondence of Daniel Webster* (Boston: Little, Brown, 1857; 2 vols.), II, 204.

25. Samuel Eliot Morison, *Maritime History of Massachusetts, 1783–1860* (Boston: Houghton Mifflin, 1923), p. 264.

26. Worthington C. Ford, ed., *The Writings of John Quincy Adams* (New York: Macmillan, 1913–1917; 7 vols.), VII, 167.

27. John S. Bassett, ed., *Correspondence of Andrew Jackson* (Washington: Carnegie Institution of Washington, 1926–35; 6 vols.), II, 346.

28. Quoted in Marquis James, *The Life of Andrew Jackson* (Indianapolis: Bobbs-Merrill, 1938; 2 vols. in one), p. 288.

29. Quoted in Samuel Flagg Bemis, *John Quincy Adams and the Foundations of American Foreign Policy* (New York: A. A. Knopf, 1949), p. 327.

30. George Dangerfield, *The Awakening of American Nationalism, 1815–1828* (New York: Harper and Row, 1965), p. 66.

31. Quoted in Graebner, *Manifest Destiny*, p. xxiv.

32. Quoted in Jacob K. Javits, *Who Makes War: The President Versus Congress* (New York: William Morrow, 1973), p. 74.

33. Richard Van Alstyne, *The Rising American Empire* (Chicago: Quadrangle Books, 1965), p. 99.

34. *Annals of Congress*, 15 Cong., 1 Sess. (March, 1818), II, 1482.

35. Adams, *Memoirs of John Quincy Adams*, V, 325.

36. Quoted in Charles K. Webster, *The Foreign Policy of Castlereagh: 1815–1822* (London: G. Bell and Sons, 1963), p. 295.

37. Quoted in Harold W. V. Temperley, *The Foreign Policy of Canning, 1822–1827* (London: G. Bell and Sons, 1925), pp. 380–381.

38. Quoted in Dangerfield, *Awakening of American Nationalism*, p. 177.

39. Paul L. Ford, ed., *The Works of Thomas Jefferson* (New York: G. P. Putnam's Sons, 1904–1905; 12 vols.), XII, 319.

40. *Letters and Other Writings of James Madison* (Philadelphia: J. B. Lippincott, 1865; 4 vols.), III, 339.

41. Quoted in Ernest A. May, *The Making of the Monroe Doctrine* (Cambridge, Mass.: Harvard University Press, 1975), p. 199.

42. Quoted in Dexter Perkins, *The Monroe Doctrine, 1823–1826* (Cambridge: Harvard University Press, 1927), p. 118.

43. Adams, *Memoirs of John Quincy Adams*, VI, 186.

44. *Ibid.*, VI, 198.

45. Richardson, ed., *Messages of the Presidents*, II, 209, 217–219.

46. Ford, *Writings of John Quincy Adams*, VI, 371–372.

47. Quoted in Perkins, *The Monroe Doctrine*, pp. 166–168.

48. Quoted in Charles K. Webster, ed., *Great Britain and the Independence of Latin America, 1812–1830* (London: Oxford University Press, 1938), II, 508.

49. Quoted in Perkins, *The Monroe Doctrine*, p. 146.

50. Quoted in Richard M. Dorson, *American Folklore* (Chicago: University of Chicago Press, 1959), pp. 256–257.

51. Quoted in Bradford Perkins, *Castlereagh and Adams: England and the United States, 1812–1823* (Berkeley: University of California Press, 1964), p. 346.

52. Quoted in Howard Jones, *To the Webster-Ashburton Treaty* (Chapel Hill: University of North Carolina Press, 1977), p. 30.

53. Quoted in Howard Jones, "Anglophobia and the Aroostook War," *New England Quarterly*, XLVII (December, 1975), 527.

54. Quoted in John F. Sprague, *The Northeastern Boundary Controversy and the Aroostook War* (Dover, Maine: The Observer Press, 1910), pp. 110–111.

55. Quoted in Charles S. Campbell, *From Revolution to Rapprochement* (New York: Wiley, 1974), pp. 56–57.

56. Richardson, ed., *Messages of the Presidents*, IV, 381.

57. Quoted in Campbell, *Revolution to Rapprochement*, p. 66.

58. Richardson, ed., *Messages of the Presidents*, IV, 398.

59. Quoted in Campbell, *From Revolution to Rapprochement*, p. 70.

60. Gene M. Brack, *Mexico Views Manifest Destiny, 1821–1846* (Albuquerque: University of New Mexico Press, 1975), p. 170.

61. Quoted in Charles M. Wiltse, *John C. Calhoun: Sectionalist, 1840–1850* (Indianapolis: Bobbs-Merrill, 1951), pp. 169–70.

62. Quoted in Schlesinger, *Imperial Presidency*, pp. 40–41.

63. Quoted in Norman Graebner, "The Mexican War: A Study in Causation," *Pacific Historical Review*, XLIX (August, 1980), 416.

64. Quaife, *Diary of James K. Polk*, II, 477.

65. *Congressional Globe*, 30 Cong., 1 Sess. (December 30, 1847), p. 79.

66. Merk, *Manifest Destiny and Mission*, p. 181.

67. Quaife, *Diary of James K. Polk*, III, 201.

68. *Ibid.*, III, 346–351.

69. Bayard Tuckerman, ed., *The Diary of Philip Hone, 1828–1851* (New York: Dodd, Mead, 1889; 2 vols.), II, 347.

70. Quoted in Ramon E. Ruiz, "A Commentary on Morality: Lincoln, Justin H. Smith, and the Mexican War," *Journal of the Illinois State Historical Society*, LXIX (February, 1976), 29.

71. Quoted in Reginald Horsman, "Scientific Racism and the American Indian in the Mid-Nineteenth Century," *American Quarterly*, XXVII (May, 1975), 168.

72. Quoted in John H. Schroeder, *Mr. Polk's War: American Opposition and Dissent, 1846–1848* (Madison: University of Wisconsin Press, 1973), p. 117.

73. Quoted in Albert K. Weinberg, *Manifest Destiny* (Baltimore: The Johns Hopkins University Press, 1935), p. 119.

74. Quoted in Blanche Wiesen Cook, "American Justification for Military Massacres from the Pequot War to Mylai," *Peace and Change, III* (Summer–Fall, 1975), 9.

75. Quoted in Schroeder, *Mr. Polk's War*, p. 159.

76. Quaife, *Diary of James K. Polk*, I, 155.

77. Quoted in Pletcher, *Diplomacy of Annexation*, p. 103.

Chapter 4

"Black Ship." In 1853 and 1854 Commodore Matthew C. Perry entered Tokyo Bay with a fleet that included two coal-powered, steam-driven side-wheelers, the *Susquehanna* and the *Mississippi*. Both ships later served in the Civil War blockade against the Confederacy. Here one of the ships is sketched as a dragonlike vessel billowing the black smoke that so alarmed this Japanese artist and his countrymen. (Courtesy, The Mariners' Museum, Newport News, Virginia)

Sputtering Expansionism, Sectionalism, and Civil War Diplomacy, 1848–1865

DIPLOMATIC CROSSROAD: COMMODORE PERRY'S "OPENING" OF JAPAN, 1853–1854

On July 14, 1853, as the early morning sun burned the summer haze off the Bay of Yedo (Tokyo), Commodore Matthew C. Perry paid careful attention to combing his dark, curly hair. An unsmiling person with scowling, bushy eyebrows, Perry grew anxious as he pulled on his uncomfortable full dress uniform. On the beach, five to seven thousand Japanese troops awaited him. Perry armed every man in his landing party, including the forty musicians, with swords, pistols, or muskets. The flag bearer was sternly warned not to let the Japanese capture the American ensign. Perry had already positioned his ships across the bay with loaded guns aimed at surrounding forts. With all precautions taken and spirits running high, Perry, accompanied by fifteen launches and cutters, began the short journey in his official barge over smooth water to the shore. Dour as always, the commodore was nonetheless resplendent in gold braid, bright buttons, and ceremonial sword. All the trappings were "but for effect," he noted.[1]

For Perry, appearances counted. He came from a long line of successful naval officers. His older brother, Oliver Hazard Perry, had gained a national reputation during the War of 1812. Matthew was noted for spending hours grooming himself and surrounding himself with bodyguards, secretaries, and aides. An unrelenting disciplinarian, he thought lashings a proper punishment. On one occasion he slugged a sailor to make his point stick. "Old Bruin," like most seasoned officers, had wanted to command the prestigious and salubrious Mediterranean Squadron. In early 1852, however, he was ordered to command the distant East India Squadron. Disappointed but loyal, Perry took the command seriously. He was an expansionist, and expansion into Asia came logically on the heels of the victory over Mexico, the absorption of California, and the Oregon settlement. The Orient was nearer to America than ever before, and it seemed inevitable that Americans would penetrate it. "Our people must naturally be drawn into the contest for empire," Perry wrote in the spring of 1852.[2]

The fifty-seven-year-old officer's special assignment was the "opening" of Japan to Westerners. Washington sought trading and coaling ports and the protection of American sailors, often shipwrecked from whaling vessels. Congressional backing for the venture was stimulated by the New England whaling industry and by some American manufacturers. Perry read everything he could about Japan. Like most Americans, he thought the Japanese "a weak and semi-barbarous people" who might have to be "severely chastised" if they did not accede to American requests.[3] Except for a single port, Nagasaki, where the Dutch traded, few Westerners were welcome in a Japan governed by feudal lords bent on maintaining their isolation from "barbarian" whites. Herman Melville in *Moby Dick* called Japan the "double-bolted land."[4] American Commodore James Biddle had visited Japan in 1846 and had been rudely shoved by a Japanese official and his ship unceremoniously towed out to sea. Perry would tolerate no such indignities. Unlike Biddle, Perry would not permit Japanese "sightseers" aboard or Japanese guard boats around his ships.

Perry had a distinct psychological advantage. Two of his four warships were steam-powered, belching clouds of black smoke. The Japanese had never seen such vessels before, and when the two steamers appeared on the horizon, in July, 1853, the Japanese thought them afire, "a conflagration on the sea."[5] One feared that Japan was being invaded by "barbarians . . . in floating volcanoes."[6] For a week, in early July, the terrifying "black fleet" rested in the Bay of Yedo. The commodore, as if to illustrate his exalted importance, remained secluded on his flagship, the U.S.S. *Susquehanna,* allowing no Japanese on board. He sent word that he would meet only with the highest officials and threatened to sail directly to Tokyo. Also admirers of pomp and ceremony, the Japanese decided upon a polite and cool reception for the imposing American. On July 14, accompanied by a thirteen-gun salute, about four hundred armed personnel, two heavily armed black bodyguards, and a band playing "Hail, Columbia!" Perry landed from his barge and handed the Japanese officials a letter from President Millard Fillmore. "Our steamships can go from California to Japan in eighteen days," Fillmore boasted. "I am desirous that our two countries should trade with each other, for the benefit both of Japan and the United States." He told the Japanese to revise their laws to permit American trade and to treat shipwrecked American seamen "with kindness," adding, "we are very much in earnest in this." Finally, he asked for coaling stations for American ships. The Japanese sternly replied that the impertinent letter was received "in opposition to Japanese law" and that Perry could now "depart." Jilted and apparently deflated, Perry remarked that his fleet would leave in a few days. But, he warned, he would return next year for an answer to the President's letter. When asked if he would bring all four vessels, he replied, "all of them and probably more."[7] Although he accomplished little by his bluff, Perry was satisfied that he had not suffered any indignities.

Perry's second ceremonial landing of March 8, 1854 was more impressive. This time three steamers in a total of nine warships anchored at bay. One crew member described the "long line of boats crowded with men glittering with bayonets, the brass . . . guns blazing in the sun ready to vomit forth death and destruction."[8] Perry disembarked to a seventeen-gun salute and the playing of "The Star Spangled Banner" by three fully armed bands. Five hundred seamen marched with him. Although the Japanese had resisted negotiations (Perry sat in the harbor for two weeks before the March 8 event), they received the commodore

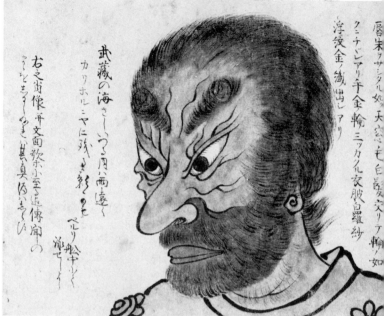

Matthew C. Perry (1794–1858). A career naval officer born in Newport, Rhode Island, Matthew was the younger brother of Oliver Hazard Perry, the hero of the battle of Lake Erie in the War of 1812. The exaggerated Japanese sketch of Matthew does not convey the majesty Perry himself surely admired in the American painting by John Beaufain Irving. Matthew Perry advocated what historian Geoffrey Smith has called "maritime Manifest Destiny." (Honolulu Academy of Arts, Gift of Mrs. Walter F. Dillingham in memory of Alice Perry Grew, 1960; and U.S. Naval Academy Museum)

courteously. Banquets, *sumo* wrestling, and an American minstrel entertained guests and hosts. Gifts were exchanged. The Japanese offered precious art objects; the Americans, reflecting their burgeoning industrial economy at home, provided the curious Japanese with a quarter-scale railroad train and a telegraph system. Both were conspicuously set up on shore. The berobed Japanese enjoyed themselves immensely. The commodore also handed over a copy of a history of the war with Mexico, which included dramatic sketches of the American fleet bombarding Veracruz. Perry complained privately that the American gifts were worth more than the Japanese offerings.

Although instructed to negotiate an expansion of commercial relations between the two countries, Perry settled for less. The Japanese protested that they did not need foreign products. "You are right," said Perry. "Commerce brings profits to a country, but it does not concern human life. I shall not insist upon it."[9] The Treaty of Kanagawa, signed on March 31, 1854, guaranteed protection for shipwrecked American crews, opened up two ports for obtaining coal and other supplies, and established consular privileges at these ports. But the treaty had shortcomings. The two ports, Shimoda and Hakodate, were relatively inaccessible and unimportant. And, although Japan granted the United States most-favored-nation treatment, there was no binding provision for beginning trade. Perry had fallen short of his instructions; he had "opened up" Japan only slightly.

One member of the expedition wrote that the Perry mission was "the beginning of American interference in Asia,"[10] and another began his diary with these pompous words: "The American Eagle allows little birds to sing."[11] Similar chauvinism was expressed in the hero's welcome accorded Perry in the United States, in April, 1855. The New York Chamber of Commerce presented him with a 381-piece silver dinner service, Boston merchants pinned a medal on him, and Congress voted him a bonus of $20,000. There was even talk about a presidential candidacy. The Senate ratified the treaty unanimously. Apparently everybody thought Perry had opened Japan to trade. Secretary of the Navy James C. Dobbin had earlier congratulated the commodore for having "secured for your country, for commerce, and for civilization, a triumph the blessings of which may be enjoyed by generations yet unborn."[12] Surely, his admirers thought, "Old Bruin" had accomplished more than appeared on paper. Perry himself later admitted that his treaty was not a "commercial compact." Commerce would result, he said, if the United States followed up with "corresponding acts . . . of national probity." Nonetheless, he envisioned "that the people of America will, in some form or other, extend their dominion and their power, until they shall have brought within their mighty embrace the Islands of the great Pacific, and place the Saxon race upon the eastern shores of Asia."[13]

SECTIONALISM AND SPUTTERING EXPANSIONISM

Perry's excursion to Japan grew out of the 1840s spirit of expansionism that had generated the Oregon settlement, the Mexican War, and visions of a Pacific empire. After that successful war, with California firmly a part of the Union and with a long, unbroken Pacific coastline, expansionists dreamed of strengthening links with Asia. With new and faster steamships, with the valuable ports of San Diego and San Francisco, with already existing commercial and missionary ties, with the possibility of a canal across Central America and a transcontinental railroad to reduce the travel time between New York City and San Francisco, with the population of San Francisco ballooning (in part because of the gold rush of 1849)—with all of these changes and aspirations, American interest in Asia flamed anew after 1848. Lieutenant John Rodgers, who headed the United States Surveying Expedition to the North Pacific Ocean in 1853–1856, predicted great trade with the Chinese: "We shall carry to Europe their teas and silks. . . . The results are so vast as to dazzle sober calculation."[14]

This interest in Asia was nothing new. The first American ship to China sailed in the 1780s and American businessmen were trading in Canton at the turn of the century. Caleb Cushing, the first American commissioner to China, secured trading privileges in five ports from China by the Treaty of 1844. The "aim of the Western trading powers in China," according to historian John K. Fairbank, "was to trade but not to govern."[15] By the early 1850s Americans carried about one-third of China's trade with the West. The United States was not a major player in Asian politics, however. As junior partners, Americans usually trailed behind the British, who were not averse to using military force to build up imperial privileges: for

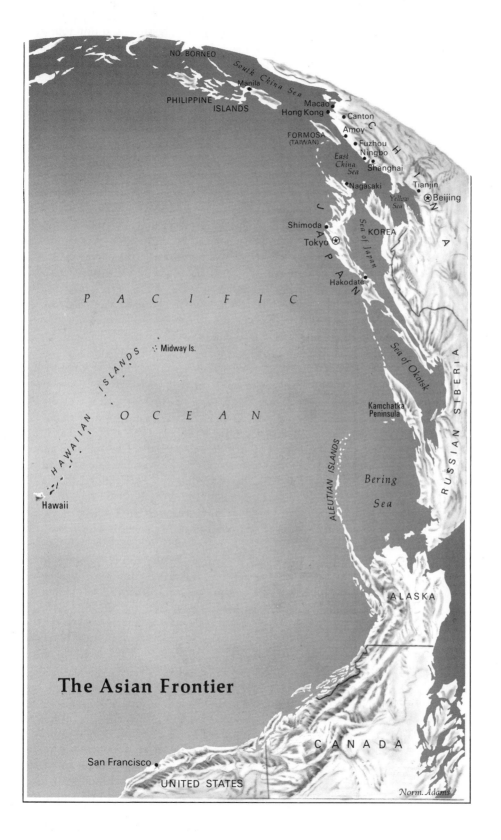

NO. BORNEO

South China Sea

Manila

PHILIPPINE
ISLANDS

Macao
Hong Kong

Canton

Amoy

C

FORMOSA
(TAIWAN)

Fuzhou
Ningbo

*East
China
Sea*

Shanghai

H

Nagasaki

Tianjin

*Yellow
Sea*

Beijing

N

Shimoda

Tokyo

J
A
P
A
N

KOREA

Sea of Japan

Hakodate

A

P A C I F I C

Midway Is.

Sea of Okotsk

O C E A N

Kamchatka
Peninsula

RUSSIAN SIBERIA

HAWAIIAN ISLANDS

*Bering
Sea*

ALEUTIAN ISLANDS

Hawaii

ALASKA

The Asian Frontier

C A N A D A

San Francisco

UNITED STATES

Norm. Adams

example, the Opium War enabled Cushing to negotiate the Treaty of Wangxia The Americans, complained a Chinese official in Shanghai, "do no more than follow in England's wake and utilize her strength."[16] Although the United States proved much less warlike than the other Western powers in Asia, and did not gobble up territory as had Britain (India), the Netherlands (East Indies), and Portugal (Macao), Asians could only view America as another nation of grasping white foreigners wishing to deny them their sovereignty and dignity.

In 1858, during a civil war called the Taiping Rebellion, France and Britain further gouged China by opening ten new treaty ports. Once again practicing what some historians call "hitchhiking imperialism," the United States gained access to eleven more ports and low tariffs in the dictated Treaty of Tianjin (Tientsin). In Japan, where the United States in 1856 sent Townsend Harris as consul to capitalize on Perry's expedition, the gains were less impressive, but nonetheless important. Isolated at the post of Shimoda, Harris patiently waited for an opportunity to negotiate a commercial treaty. Lacking the naval power exerted by the westerners in China and displayed by Perry in 1854, Harris could not threaten Japanese leaders, who resented his very presence; but he pressed his case in a prime early example of what would later become known as "personal diplomacy." In 1858 his tenacity paid off in a treaty wherein Japan opened other ports, provided for freedom of trade, and created a tariff schedule. The next year Harris became minister to Japan and established an American legation in Tokyo.

Despite these evidences of American expansion in the Orient in the 1850s, for statesmen and Americans generally, writes historian Charles E. Neu, "Asia remained an abstract idea, a distant area that was only one part of a worldwide commercial empire."[17] The euphoria following Perry's drama soon evaporated. The State Department gave little guidance to its representatives in the Far East, who therefore often acted on their own: in 1856, for example, Commodore James Armstrong's ships destroyed five Chinese forts near Canton after a cannon fired on an American vessel. President Franklin Pierce thereupon reprimanded the naval officer. As another example of America's secondary interest in Asia, Rodgers of the North Pacific Surveying Expedition found upon returning to San Francisco in 1856 that he could not complete his survey of trade routes because his funds had run out and he could obtain no more. Even Perry, who had requested twelve warships for his presidentially authorized expedition to Japan in 1854, was given only four.

America's relative inattention to Asian affairs reflected the general waning of American expansionism and Manifest Destiny after the Mexican War. Talk of annexing Canada subsided. Even in Latin America, an area of prime focus, expansionist ventures sputtered and imperial ambitions dissipated. Attempts to grab Cuba collapsed and cries for grabbing more territory from Mexico were muffled. Notions of planting an American colony in slaveholding Brazil enjoyed some currency, after an exploration directed by Lieutenant Matthew F. Maury, but nothing came of the hopes. Washington did persuade Mexico to negotiate the Gadsden Purchase of 1853, which added 29,640 square miles to the United States at a cost of $10 million for a potential railroad route to the Pacific Coast—the only land acquired by the United States in the period from the Mexican War to the end of the Civil War. Yet trade continued to expand abroad, sustaining faltering hopes for an ever growing empire. "There is not in the history of the Roman Empire," asserted Senator William H. Seward of New York in 1850, "an ambition for aggrandizement so marked as that which has characterized the American people."[18]

Yet such hungering was starved in the 1850s and early 1860s. The reason lay at home, in the heated sectional debates over chattel slavery that drew the nation into the Civil War.

The divisive issue of slavery curbed Northern appetites for ventures into Latin America, where the "peculiar institution" might flourish and slave states might arise to vote with the South. Many residents of the latter, having beaten back restrictions like the Wilmot Proviso, continued the cry for empire, hoping to enhance their declining political status and mollify the threat to slavery, "the cornerstone of their way of life."[19] Northern leaders regretted that Manifest Destiny had fallen victim to the crude aspirations of slavemasters. Slavery, said Abraham Lincoln in 1854, "deprives our republican example of its just influence in the world—enables the enemies of free institutions to taunt us as hypocrites."[20] Badly divided at home by insistent Northern abolitionists and Southern "fire-eaters," the United States could not successfully undertake further bold schemes in international affairs, because it could not reach a foreign policy consensus. Intensely preoccupied as Americans were by the Compromise of 1850, the Fugitive Slave Act, "bleeding Kansas," the Dred Scott decision, the commercial and financial panic of 1857, the Lincoln-Douglas debates, John Brown's raid, the formation of the new Republican party, and the 1860 election of Abraham Lincoln, they gave less and less attention to foreign policy questions.

Some Americans, however, at the very time their own nation was being torn apart by sectional differences after the Mexican War, joined the nationalistic "Young America" movement. They identified the revolutions of 1848 in Europe as evidence of New World, republican influences on the Old, and applauded Camillo Bensi di Cavour, Giuseppe Mazzini, and Giuseppe Garibaldi of Italy and Lajos Kossuth of Hungary, whose short-lived rebellions against entrenched conservatism and monarchy kindled American sympathies. In late 1850 Whig Secretary of State Daniel Webster, for example, lectured the Hapsburg government, claiming that, compared to the mighty United States, Austria was "but a patch on the earth's surface."[21] Concerned about bitter division at home over the expansion of slavery, he hoped his public rebuke to the government that had crushed the Hungarian revolution would "touch the national pride, and make a man feel *sheepish* and look *silly* who should speak of disunion."[22] In other words, Webster sought to use a nationalist movement abroad to generate nationalism at home. When Kossuth excited the United States in 1851–1852 during a rousing visit, Webster once again applied his exceptional oratorical abilities on behalf of liberty and American nationalism. In the 1852 Democratic party platform, the rallying cry was "Young America." The following year, "Young America" advocate and Democratic Secretary of State William Marcy ordered a new dress code for American diplomats; they were to wear the "simple dress of an American citizen" to reflect America's "republican institutions."[23] But the "Young America" movement was no formula for perpetuating the ebullient nationalism and Manifest Destiny of the 1840s. "Young America" fell into the hands of Democratic party expansionists, many of whom favored the extension of slavery. An incongruity impressed some observers: "Young America" advocates championed liberty abroad, while at home they denied it to black human beings under the repressive system of slavery.

Scholars generally agree that political leadership in the United States between the Mexican War and Civil War was undistinguished, quite mediocre and un-imaginative. Contemporary historian George Bancroft thought it "feeble and

"Young America" and John C. Frémont (1813–1890). The explorer Frémont led a military force into northern California and helped ignite the Bear Flag Revolt in June, 1846. After fighting as an officer in the Mexican War, more explorations, farming, and a short tenure as a California senator, he became the new Republican Party's first candidate for President in 1856. Here he is idolized on the cover of sheet music as a rugged representative of "Young America." (National Portrait Gallery, Smithsonian Institution)

Makers of American Foreign Policy from 1848 to 1865

Presidents	*Secretaries of State*
James K. Polk, 1845–1849	James Buchanan, 1845–1849
Zachary Taylor, 1849–1850	John M. Clayton, 1849–1850
Millard Fillmore, 1850–1853	Daniel Webster, 1850–1852
	Edward Everett, 1852–1853
Franklin Pierce, 1853–1857	William L. Marcy, 1853–1857
James Buchanan, 1857–1861	Lewis Cass, 1857–1860
	Jeremiah S. Black, 1860–1861
Abraham Lincoln, 1861–1865	William H. Seward, 1861–1869

incompetent."[24] Allan Nevins later identified a "special weakness" of Democratic President Franklin Pierce: "a tendency to rash pyrotechnics."[25] The presidents and secretaries of state conducted a blustering foreign policy, often playing to domestic political currents through bombastic rhetoric. Few had diplomatic experience. One writer in 1853 was satisfied that whether American foreign affairs were "directed by a sot or a simpleton, they will continue to grow and expand by a law of nature and a decree of Providence."[26] But inept leaders muddled relations with Spain, crudely grasped at an elusive Cuba, permitted filibusters to alienate Latin America, squabbled clumsily with Britain in Central America, meddled with emotion but without power in European revolutions, followed the British in humiliating the Chinese, and gave halfhearted attention to Japan after "opening" it. President Abraham Lincoln and his inveterately expansionistic secretary of state, William H. Seward, certainly raised the level of competence in Washington, despite Seward's suggestion in 1861 that the United States provoke a foreign dispute to galvanize nationalism at home and forestall Southern secession. The two managed to win the Civil War and contain it as a "localized" conflict, avoiding the world war it might have become. In doing so they preserved American power, thereby permitting the United States to resume its expansionist course after the fratricidal conflict.

THE SOUTH'S DREAM OF EMPIRE: FILIBUSTERING AND SLAVE EXPANSION

Many Southern leaders tried to exploit Manifest Destiny for territorial conquest in the Caribbean. They failed largely because they aroused domestic opposition by insisting that slavery be permitted to expand into new lands; they failed because they dressed expansionism in sectional garb. In the 1850s Northern expansionists parted company with Southern sectionalists and steadfastly opposed ventures into Latin America that might add slave territories to the Union. At the same time, some Northern expansionists, like Seward—then senator from New York—hoped that the abolition of slavery would eliminate Northern opposition to expansion into the Caribbean and Mexico. The paradox was striking: Southern expansionists sought a larger empire for the United States while at the same time they denigrated the supremacy of the federal government itself, during the heated debates of the 1850s that led to the Civil War. "You are looking toward Mexico, Nicaragua, and Brazil," Congressman Thomas Corwin of Ohio lectured his Southern colleagues, "while you are not sure you will have a government to which these could be ceded."[27]

For Southerners, expansion seemed essential. Since the Missouri Compromise of 1820, they had witnessed a profound shift in both the political and economic balance to the North, the free states. Under the Compromise of 1850, the territories seized from Mexico were given instructions: California would enter the Union as a free state, and the rest of the Mexican cession could determine whether it wished to be slave or free (the concept of "popular sovereignty"). A strong majority of Southern congressmen voted against the compromise bill and looked upon its

The Southern Perspective on Expansion

passage as further evidence of their diminishing political power. Potential slave states had to be found to right the balance. Tropical states where black slaves could toil under white mastery had long been part of the Southern imagination, but now, in the 1850s, the matter became urgent. The message was sent out by belligerent voices like those of James D. E. B. DeBow, in his widely read *DeBow's Review,* and the Knights of the Golden Circle, a secret society of several thousand members, many of them prominent politicians pledged to tropical expansion. The Gulf of Mexico, DeBow opined, was the "great *Southern sea.*"[28] The vision of expanded slavery took in Cuba, Mexico, and Central America. "With swelling hearts and suppressed impatience they await our coming," proclaimed a Southern congressman, "and with joyous shouts of 'Welcome! Welcome!' will they receive us."[29]

Yet Southern expansionists could not realize their dreams through diplomacy. Stymied by the Northern rejection of their proslave imperialist aspirations, many Southerners supported the filibusters, those dramatic warriors who attempted to grab territories through unauthorized and illegal attacks upon sovereign nations recognized by the United States. Most of the filibustering bands originated in New Orleans, were "Southern" in goals and personnel, and employed the rhetoric of Manifest Destiny for sectional purposes. Narciso López, John A. Quitman, and William Walker led the ill-fated ventures.

Venezuelan by birth, General Narciso López had been a Spanish military officer and Cuban businessman before his attempted invasion of Cuba in 1849. Married into a proslave aristocratic Cuban family, he came to believe he was the island's savior from the perfidies of mother Spain. He wished to free Cuba and annex it to the United States. Using New York City and New Orleans as bases, López sought supporters. He hired some desperate-looking veterans from the Mexican War, promising them "plunder, women, drink, and tobacco"; each soldier would receive a $1000 bonus and 160 acres of Cuban land if the expedition succeeded.[30] López gathered his several hundred mercenaries at Round Island, off the Louisiana coast, but in September, 1849 the United States Navy blockaded the isle and foiled his plans.

López reached for support elsewhere in the South. He won over Southern expansionists like John A. Quitman, a wealthy sugar and cotton planter, former general in the Mexican War, and governor of Mississippi (1850–1851); the editor of the *New Orleans Delta,* Laurence J. Sigur; a former senator and cotton planter from Mississippi, John Henderson; and editor John L. O'Sullivan of Manifest Destiny fame. In May, 1850, disguised as emigrants to California, the filibusters of the López expedition departed New Orleans. On May 19 they landed at Cárdenas, but beat a hasty retreat when superior Spanish forces confronted them. López hurriedly charted a course to the United States, where American officials prosecuted him for violating the Neutrality Act of 1818, which forbade military expeditions from American soil against nations at peace with the United States. In New Orleans, López, Quitman, Henderson, Sigur, and O'Sullivan, among others, were put on trial. After three mistrials for Henderson, the federal government dropped charges against the others. Ever adventuresome, López in August, 1851 launched another attack against Cuba with 500 followers, called by black abolitionist leader Frederick Douglass "freebooters, pirates, and plunderers."[31] Federal officials in New Orleans obligingly looked the other way. The flamboyant filibuster carried a proclamation: "The star of Cuba . . . will rise beautiful and shining perchance to be admitted gloriously into the splendid North American constellation according to its inevitable destiny."[32] López himself was denied glory. Having garnered little Cuban backing, he and his half-starved and undermanned contingent were captured. Among them was Colonel William Crittenden of Kentucky, nephew of the attorney general of the United States. López, Crittenden, and fifty of the mercenaries were executed.

Undeterred by the debacle of the López expedition, DeBow proclaimed that the American "lust for dominion" over Cuba remained an American sentiment.[33] And riots against Spanish property broke out in New Orleans. Secretary of State Daniel Webster apologized in early 1852 and paid $25,000 to Spain for damage to its consulate in New Orleans. Quitman, who had resigned his governorship in 1851 because of the filibustering flap, grew angry. He detested the Compromise of 1850 and feared that Spain might free slaves in Cuba, constituting a "fatal stab" at Southern institutions.[34] Indeed, he thought a "strong negro or mongrel empire" might arise in Cuba to thwart Southern expansion.[35] Quitman plotted a new journey. In 1854 he agreed to command an expedition of 3,000 men, but financial shortages, lack of support in Cuba, and hostility from Washington persuaded him to scotch his mission in early 1855. Quitman thereupon retired from filibustering, futilely complaining about the "humbug administration" in Washington.[36]

Then came William Walker, the "grey-eyed man of destiny."[37] Restless and reckless, Tennessean Walker earned a physician's degree from the University of Pennsylvania, studied medicine in Paris, practiced law in Louisiana, and edited a Southern journal before he embarked on schemes in Mexico and Nicaragua. Attracted to California in 1850 by the euphoric gold rush, Walker hatched plans for an invasion of Lower California, which was indisputably Mexican territory. At age twenty-nine, in 1853, this man of small figure and simple dress marched into Mexican lands and captured the territorial capital of La Paz. In early 1853, however, the expedition collapsed from discontent among his followers and faulty organization. Tried for violating the Neutrality Act, Walker was acquitted by an admiring San Francisco jury.

William Walker (1824–1860). The most infamous of American filibusters terrorized Latin American nations, ruled Nicaragua for a short time, and flouted United States law—all by the age of 36. He fell before a firing squad and remains buried in an unmarked grave in Honduras. (Smithsonian Institution)

"Once more aiding the stars," the man of destiny next eyed Nicaragua, then a country of some mention as a route for an isthmian canal.[38] Hardly the agent of benevolent, democratic Manifest Destiny that his admirers attempted to portray, the persevering Walker became a petty tyrant who "ruled with a rod of iron."[39] He sought to subjugate Nicaragua in 1855, 1857, 1858, and 1860. He plundered and killed. In the first expedition, leading men whom he described as "tired of the humdrum of common life," he proclaimed himself president of the country.[40] Apparently under the influence of Pierre Soulé, he then instituted slavery. The American minister in Nicaragua, North Carolinian plantation owner and slaveholder John Hill Wheeler, abetted Walker in this adventure, since he was convinced that the "rich soil so well adapted to the culture of cotton, sugar, rice, corn, cocoa, indigo, etc. can never be developed without slave labor."[41] Walker dreamed beyond Nicaragua; he wanted to build a Central American federation and then attack Cuba. Thinking that the decision would be politically popular, and finding no other Nicaraguan government in existence, the Pierce Administration recognized Walker's regime in 1856. But the filibuster soon wobbled. Walker alienated the native population through pillaging and dictatorial orders, and his soldiers fell victim to frequent drunkenness and disease. He then alienated transportation magnate Cornelius Vanderbilt, who had interests in Nicaragua; the influential "Commodore" backed Honduras, Guatemala, San Salvador, and Costa

Rica when they took up arms against the intruding adventurer. In May of 1857 Walker fled to the United States.

The famed filibuster tried to return to Nicaragua in November, 1857, but United States naval officers arrested him near Greytown. He escaped prosecution. Walker's third futile effort, in 1858, ended ingloriously on a coral reef near British Honduras, where his ship went aground. Still claiming to be the legitimate president of Nicaragua, the irrepressible Walker headed for his adopted country once again in the spring of 1860. This time he attacked Honduras first. Honduran troops inflicted heavy casualties, and Walker soon surrendered to an unsympathetic British official, who turned him over to Honduran officers. "Will the South stand by and permit him to be shot down like a dog?" exhorted one Southern woman. "If so, let her renounce forever her reputation for chivalry, valor, policy, or pride!"[42] Such appeals went unheeded, and Walker was executed by a firing squad on September 12, 1860.

William Walker, like the other filibusters, aroused considerable enthusiasm in the South among prominent politicians, planters, and editors. He symbolized for many the survival of slavery and hence the Southern way of life. Although Southerners came to adopt Walker as a tool of expansion, it does not appear that he was committed to either Southern expansion or slavery. His was a story of personal ambition, from which sectionalists hoped to benefit. Hindered by Northern opponents from territorial gains through diplomacy or war, the ardent defenders of the "peculiar institution" turned to the illegal machinations and drama of the filibusters. They would also turn to civil war in 1861. "As dream and reality met," historian Robert E. May has written, "the South's grandiose vision of empire dissolved in the blood of war."[43]

CUBA BY HOOK OR BY CROOK

Cuba, the Pearl of the Antilles, lay too close to the United States to escape the latter's expansionist urges. Spain once called it the "Ever Faithful Isle" because, unlike other Spanish possessions in the New World, Cuba did not revolt against Madrid in the stormy decades of the early nineteenth century. Like a "coy temptress," to use historian William H. Goetzmann's words, Cuba attracted American attention.[44] A rich producer of sugar, Cuba drew American businessmen and traders as the United States became the island's largest commercial partner. Slave revolts in the 1830s and 1840s, as well as anticolonial rebellions in the following decade, aroused Americans, especially those who wished to abolish slavery. Slaveholders in Cuba had a notorious reputation as cruel masters. A corrupt and inept Spanish administration heightened Cuba's plight and gained American sympathies. One prominent twentieth-century historian, Allan Nevins, has described Spanish rule in Cuba as "an outrage upon the name of Christian civilization."[45] Caught up in the ideology of Manifest Destiny, Americans believed that inevitably, by "natural growth," Cuba would be taken under their eagle's outstretched wings.[46] Or, to use a metaphor of the times: "The fruit will fall into our hands when it is ripe, without an officious shaking of the tree. Cuba will be ours, and Canada and Mexico, too—if we want them—in due season, and without the wicked imperative of a war."[47]

Some Americans tried to hurry the ripening process. In 1848 President James K. Polk, looking for other fruits to match Oregon and the Mexican cession, contemplated purchasing Cuba from Spain for $100 million. But Spanish resistance and the ardent opposition of France and Britain blocked him. In the late 1840s and early 1850s the question of the annexation of Cuba to the United States became ensnarled in the debate over slavery and its expansion. Southern defenders of the "peculiar institution" increasingly included Cuba in their dreams of a Caribbean empire wherein slavery might flourish. Filibustering expeditions like those of Narciso López fired Southern hopes for the absorption of Cuba.

In 1852 Britain and France asked the United States to join them in a three-power statement to disavow "all intention of obtaining possession" of Cuba.[48] Unwilling to be bound by such a self-denying agreement, Washington rejected the overture. President Millard Fillmore told the French and British ministers that "this question would fall like a bomb in the midst of the electoral agitation for the presidency" and divide North from South.[49] Secretary of State Edward Everett, who seemed to be "hunting larks with an elephant rifle," informed London and Paris that the United States did not "covet" Cuba, but the status of the island was "mainly an American question."[50] He went on to extoll the island's strategic and commercial value, deprecating at the same time the Cuban slave trade. By quoting Washington's Farewell Address and Jefferson's aversion to "entangling alliances," Everett shunned any hint of a pact with European nations. One thing was evident: the United States would not permit the transfer of Cuba to any other power. European capitals thought Everett's statements pompous and alarming, with their allusions to United States pre-eminence in the Caribbean. Lord Palmerston, ever mindful that British colonies in the West Indies lay in the path of American growth, angrily berated officials in his government who argued that Britain should concede Cuba to the United States. No, that "would be like propitiating an animal of Prey by giving him one of one's Travelling Companions. It would increase his desire for similar food and spur him on to obtain it."[51]

Fillmore's successor coveted Cuba. In his inaugural address, Franklin Pierce asserted that he would not be "controlled by any timid forebodings of evil from Cuba."[52] Backed by expansionists Secretary of State William L. Marcy (secretary of war under Polk), Minister to Britain James Buchanan (secretary of state under Polk), Minister to Spain Pierre Soulé (ardent defender of slavery from Louisiana), and Minister to France John Y. Mason (attorney general under Polk), Pierce played to the desire for Cuba of the Southern wing of the Democratic party. Soulé was impetuous, stubborn, and vain, "of swarthy complexion, black flashing eyes, and Frenchified dress and speech."[53] Born in France, schooled as a lawyer, and elected United States senator from Louisiana, the hotheaded minister became a central figure in the American quest for Cuba. Within weeks of his arrival in Madrid, Soulé wounded the French ambassador in a duel. Convinced that the United States could satisfy its "lusty appetite" for expansion by taking Cuba, this misplaced "diplomat" seemed to take every opportunity to make himself irritable to the Spanish, thereby thwarting the American goal of obtaining Cuba.[54]

Secretary Marcy believed that decrepit Spain would perceive the wisdom of selling its rebellious colony. He instructed Soulé to inquire discreetly about sale. "Discreetly," however, was not a word in Soulé's vocabulary. In February of 1854, an American merchant ship, the *Black Warrior*, was seized at Havana for violating port regulations. Apparently seeing an opportunity to force Cuba from Spain through a threat of war, President Pierce demanded a $100,000 indemnity (raised to $300,000 soon after) for the vessel's owners and heated up American fevers for

"**Master Jonathan Tries To Smoke a Cuba, But It Doesn't Agree With Him!**" America's trouble with Spanish-controlled, slavery-plagued Cuba was depicted in this mocking British cartoon. The Ostend Manifesto debacle of 1854 was particularly discomforting to the United States. (*Punch*, 1850)

revenge by sending a belligerent anti-Spanish message to Congress. Pierce thus fed Soulé's intemperance. The haughty minister thereupon demanded an apology from the Spanish government for an affront to the American flag. The Spanish agreed to restore the ship to its owner and pay a smaller indemnity, but Marcy found the Spanish reply full of "evasions" and called it a "disingenuous perversion of language."[55]

The much inflated *Black Warrior* affair was soon overshadowed by a new, rash attempt to annex Cuba. Marcy instructed Soulé in April of 1854 to try to buy Cuba for $130 million or less. Failing that, "you will then direct your efforts to the next desirable object which is to detach that island from the Spanish dominion and from all dependence on any European power."[56] Then, in August, the secretary told Soulé to meet with ministers Buchanan and Mason to discuss the question of annexation. The three expansionists relished the chance; they met in October at Ostend, Belgium, and then at Aix-la-Chapelle in Rhenish Prussia, where they created the remarkable confidential document known as the Ostend Manifesto. The three emissaries agreed that Cuba should be purchased for no more than $120 million. But if Madrid refused to sell, "by every law, human and divine, we shall be justified in wresting it from Spain if we possess the power."[57] The manifesto found its way into the press and the Pierce Administration was soon accused of propagating a Southern slave conspiracy. The Free Soil party thought the document "the highwayman's plea, that might makes right."[58] Reeling from the loud criticism hurled by antislavery forces, the Pierce Administration tried to place blame on Soulé. Fearing that Soulé would "break" more "ground" on behalf of the "robber doctrine," a relieved President Pierce accepted his resignation.[59] The "gasconading" Soulé returned home ignobly in early 1855.[60]

One author of the Ostend Manifesto, James Buchanan, became President in 1857. After his nomination as the Democratic candidate, he remarked that "if I can be instrumental in settling the slavery question . . . , and then add Cuba to the Union, I shall be willing to give up the ghost."[61] He appointed a Wall Street banker, the American representative of the Rothschilds, August Belmont, as minister to Spain. Belmont was a noted advocate of bribing Spanish officials to acquire Cuba and the Senate rejected him. Thereupon, in his annual message to

Congress in December, 1858, the President praised the commercial and strategic virtues of Cuba, urged its purchase, and asked Congress to appropriate a large sum to be put at his own disposal for this purpose. The Senate Foreign Relations Committee then issued a favorable report that declared the "law of our national existence is growth. We cannot if we would, disobey it."[62] The fruit was ripe for plucking. If the United States did not act, a European power might. The report also recommended an appropriation of $30 million—some of it no doubt for bribes of Spanish public officials. But Republican abolitionists who opposed annexation would have none of it and delayed action until Congress adjourned.

A slow learner, Buchanan appealed to Congress to pass the "Thirty Million Dollar Bill" again in his annual messages of 1859 and 1860. In the presidential election of 1860, however, Abraham Lincoln, a firm opponent of slave expansion, was elected, thus killing possibilities of annexing Cuba. By then the acquisition of Cuba had become solely the pet project of the South. One Southerner waxed erotic: "Who can object if he throws his arms around the Queen of the Antilles, as she sits, like Cleopatra's burning throne, upon the silver waves, breathing her spicy, tropic breath, and pouting her rosy, sugared lips. Who can object? None. She is of age—take her Uncle Sam."[63] But the objections were vociferous, Uncle Sam spurned an embrace, and the South learned by 1860 that its expansionist passions were frustrated.

NUDGING THE BRITISH OUT OF CENTRAL AMERICA

Great Britain kept a worried and watchful eye on United States attempts, official and unofficial, to expand in the Caribbean and Central America. At the close of the Mexican War, Anglo-American relations seemed on the eve of improvement. In 1842 Webster and Ashburton had drawn the Maine boundary and a line from Lake Superior to Lake of the Woods, and in 1846 President Polk had compromised on Oregon. As the danger of war over the Canadian-American border declined, the "Atlantic economy" revived.[64] In the mid-1840s the growth of trade between the United States and Britain had resumed, after a decade of sluggishness; by the 1850s the United States supplied Britain with 50 percent of its imports and 80 percent of its raw cotton, the basis of England's largest export industry. Forty percent of all American imports originated in Great Britain, and America's expanding economy attracted surplus British capital, especially during the railroad building boom of the 1840s. "Increased Commercial Intercourse may add to the Links of mutual Interest," Britain's Viscount Henry John Palmerston observed. But he also warned acidly that "commercial Interest is a Link that snaps under the Pressure of National Passions."[65]

In the 1840s and 1850s, as we have seen, American passions were aroused by dreams of expansion into Central America and the Caribbean. A treaty negotiated with New Granada (later Colombia) in 1846 and ratified in 1848 granted the United States extensive transit rights across the Isthmus of Panama, one of the more promising railroad and canal routes in Central America. Alarmed by this intrusion upon their maritime supremacy in the Caribbean, the British struck back. In January, 1848, they seized a Nicaraguan town at the mouth of the San Juan River. Renamed Greytown, this port controlled the most feasible transisthmian canal route, given the technology of the time. When added to the British protectorate over the Mosquito Indians inhabiting Nicaragua's eastern coast, possession of Belize (later British Honduras) and the Bay Islands, and the Royal Naval base at nearby Jamaica, Greytown accorded Great Britain a substantial position in Central America.

In the same month that the British took Greytown, John Marshall discovered gold at Sutter's mill in California. The great gold rush soon swelled California's population by 100,000 and led to admission of the Golden State to the Union in 1850. Most of the "Forty-niners" reached San Francisco by steamship. The trek included arduous overland travel through Nicaragua or Panama. For many Americans, construction of an efficient isthmian canal or railway suddenly became a matter of domestic urgency. But the conspicuous British presence in Central America precluded unilateral United States action. Whig Secretary of State John M. Clayton therefore proposed "a great highway" across the isthmus, "to be dedicated especially by Great Britain and the United States, to the equal benefit and advantage of all the nations of the world."[66]

Acerbic Foreign Secretary Palmerston, or Lord "Pumicestone," who thought "these Yankees are most disagreeable Fellows to have to do with about any American Question," respected the ability of the "ingenious Rogues" to deny to his Canadian provinces their much desired commercial reciprocity.[67] Thus he graciously told Clayton that Britain had "no selfish or exclusive views" about the isthmus. Like Clayton, he hoped "that any undertaking of this sort . . . should be generally open to and available to all the nations of the world."[68] To confirm this understanding, he sent Sir Henry Bulwer to Washington in December, 1849. Both Bulwer and Clayton hoped to neutralize isthmian transit. But Zachary Taylor's Administration also wanted British abandonment of Greytown and the Mosquito Coast. What followed was, as the *Times* of London put it, a struggle "for generalship in the use of terms"—what historian Charles S. Campbell has called "a treaty in obscure language."[69] The Clayton-Bulwer Pact of April 19, 1850 stipulated that neither Great Britain nor the United States alone would ever monopolize or fortify a canal in Central America, and that neither would "colonize, or assume, or exercise any dominion over . . . any part of Central America."[70]

This superficial, self-denying clause invited conflicting interpretations, as became apparent during the exchange of ratifications. On July 4, 1850, Bulwer informed Clayton that Britain did not believe the treaty included "whatever is Her Majesty's settlement at Honduras, nor whatever are the Dependencies of that settlement."[71] Having deftly exempted Belize and the Bay Islands from the terms of the Clayton-Bulwer Treaty, Britain thereafter excluded the Mosquito protectorate and Greytown, arguing that the treaty referred only to the acquisition of *new* territory. Despite London's verbal agility, the treaty in effect meant that "Britain could hardly turn around in Central America without being charged by Americans with violating its provisions."[72] Nonetheless, as Bulwer accurately perceived, the agreement defused Anglo-American tension and seemed "to bind the United States against further annexation."[73] As British historian Kenneth Bourne concludes, "considering that the American administration was . . . tackling the British in an area where they were already well entrenched, the Americans appeared to have scored a considerable success in facilitating the construction of a canal free from the threat of British control."[74]

That canal would await the twentieth century, but American enterprise soon began to saturate Central America. Cornelius Vanderbilt organized an interoceanic steamship and railroad connection through Nicaragua, and other entrepreneurs

Lord Palmerston (1784–1865). Henry John Temple, 3rd Viscount Palmerston, dominated English politics as foreign secretary (1830–1834, 1835–1841, 1846–1851) and prime minister (1855–1858, 1859–1865). "His dominance," biographer Donald Southgate has written, "coincided with Britannia ruling the waves and London ruling the exchanges . . . ." Able, self-confident, forthright, and frequently irritating, "Old Pam" struggled especially to keep peace in Europe. He bristled against Americans who eyed British interests in the western hemisphere. (Mansell Collection, Ltd.)

completed a railroad across Panama in 1855. However, the flag did not follow investors into Central America. The deepening domestic crisis over the expansion of slavery prevented President Franklin Pierce and his successor, James Buchanan, from doing much more than nipping verbally at the heels of the gradually retreating British. For his part, Lord Palmerston continued to berate the "vulgar minded Bullies" of North America, from whom "nothing is gained by submission to Insult & wrong."[75] But in 1854, when the U.S.S. *Cyane* bombarded Greytown in an excessive reprisal for an insult to an American diplomat and President Pierce refused to disavow the attack, London quietly let the matter drop.

The costly Crimean War (1854–1856), which pitted England and France against Russia, drained London's political and military energy and made a showdown with the United States over Central America unthinkable. As British soldiers fell like flies before Sebastopol in the Crimea, the desperate English government sent agents to the United States to recruit replacements, leading Secretary of State William Marcy to dismiss the British minister. Even Palmerston recognized his country's precarious position and recommended "some little Flourish" addressed to the "free, enlightened and Generous Race . . . of the great North American Union" as a means of dampening Marcy's "Bunkum vapouring" against Great Britain.[76]

Marcy had helped induce Palmerston's restraint by negotiating a long-desired reciprocity treaty in 1854. In 1852 the British had begun to interpret the Convention of 1818 very strictly and along the maritime provinces of British North America had seized some American fishing vessels. While hotheads in Massachusetts called for war and Matthew C. Perry steamed north in the *Mississippi*, President Millard Fillmore announced his willingness to settle the outstanding issues of fishing rights, free navigation of the St. Lawrence, and reciprocity with Canada. In May, 1854, London sent the Governor-General of Canada, Lord Elgin, to negotiate with Marcy. His lordship was shrewd and the environment highly congenial. "Lord Elgin pretends to drink immensely," his secretary recorded, "but I watched him [at a party], and I don't believe he drank a glass between two and twelve. He is the most thorough *diplomat* possible,—never loses sight for a moment of his object, and while he is chaffing the Yankees and slapping them on the back, he is systematically pursuing that object."[77] The "objects" of the two diplomats meshed and they signed the Marcy-Elgin Treaty on June 5, 1854. Americans could now navigate the St. Lawrence without restriction and fish within three miles of British North America, while Canadians could send duty-free a wide variety of agricultural products into the United States. The Marcy-Elgin Treaty, like the Webster-Ashburton Treaty and the Oregon settlement, contributed to tranquillity along the great northern border of the United States.

That Anglo-American relations in the 1850s ended with a whimper and not a bang was in large measure due to the deepening American crisis over the expansion of slavery. But a British reappraisal following the Crimean War also facilitated Anglo-American détente. Always the bellwether of official British opinion, Lord Palmerston wrote in December, 1857, in regard to Central America, that the Americans "are on the Spot, strong, deeply interested in the matter, totally unscrupulous and dishonest and determined somehow or other to carry their Point. We are far away, weak from Distance, controlled by the Indifference of the Nation . . . and by its Strong commercial Interest in maintaining Peace with the United States."[78] When he became Prime Minister in June, 1859, he quickly relinquished the Bay Islands to Honduras and the Mosquito Coast to Nicaragua. According to historian Kenneth Bourne, this retreat held great symbolic importance: "Had not the Civil War intervened, the [rapprochement] era of 1895–1902 might in many respects have been anticipated by some thirty years. Even as it was, Great Britain was never again seriously to challenge American expansion."[79] Without war the United States had gradually nudged Britain out of Central America. The Civil War, however, was to raise new issues in Anglo-American relations.

1861: YEAR OF CRISES

William H. Seward (1801–1872). Graduate of Union College, New York state politician, lawyer, United States senator (1849–1861), and secretary of state (1861–1869), Seward had wanted to be President but lost the Republican nomination to Abraham Lincoln in 1860. He spent the Civil War years trying to preserve the Union by keeping the European powers neutral.

On April 12, 1861, at Charleston, South Carolina, Brigadier General Pierre G. T. Beauregard's Provisional Forces of the Confederate States opened fire on the federal garrison barricaded in Fort Sumter. With this defiant act the rebellious South forced Abraham Lincoln to choose between secession and civil war. Sworn to defend the Constitution, and conscious that his task was "greater than that which rested upon Washington," the new Republican President called for 75,000 militiamen to suppress the insurrection.[80]

For support, Lincoln leaned upon a factious Cabinet of politically ambitious men, headed by a secretary of state who thought himself far abler and more sophisticated than his chief. Convinced that his superior wisdom entitled him to act as prime minister to a hesitant President, William Henry Seward concocted plans to "wrap the world in flames" in order to melt domestic disunity in the furnace of foreign war.[81] On April 1, he sent Lincoln a memorandum titled "Some Thoughts for the President's Consideration." He criticized Lincoln for being "without a policy either domestic or foreign" and proposed hostility or war against Britain, France, Russia, and Spain. The next day Seward responded to Spain's reannexation of Santo Domingo with a threat of war. Spain ignored the bombastic secretary of state and Lincoln cautioned him that he himself would formulate policy with "the advice of all the Cabinet."[82]

Scarcely deterred, Seward challenged Great Britain's interpretation of international maritime law. He successfully urged Lincoln to proclaim a blockade of the Southern ports as a matter of domestic policy. Britain quite properly interpreted the Union blockade as the act of a nation at war, insisted that the blockade must effectively close Southern harbors to be legally binding upon neutral shippers, and recognized the belligerent status of the Confederacy. With equal logic, Confederate President Jefferson Davis met Lincoln's blockade by calling for privateers, an historic mode of American naval warfare.

In the 1856 Declaration of Paris following the Crimean War, Great Britain and France had codified the rules of maritime warfare and outlawed privateering. The United States had refused to sign away its favorite naval strategy, but the Confederacy's resort to privateering impelled Seward to inform the British Minister, Lord Richard Lyons, that he wished belatedly to initial the covenant. Lyons welcomed United States adherence, but noted Washington's lack of authority to obligate the South. When Seward remonstrated that the Confederate States were not independent, Lyons coolly exposed the fatal political inconsistency of Lincoln's maritime strategy: "Very well. If they are not independent then the President's proclamation of blockade is not binding. A blockade, according to the convention, applies only to two nations at war." Seward went into a lather: "Europe must

"King Cotton Bound; or, the Modern Prometheus." In Greek mythology, Prometheus was the creator and savior of mankind whom Zeus chained to a mountain peak. In this rendition by the British humor magazine, *Punch,* the Northern eagle picks at the Confederate "King Cotton," manacled by the naval blockade. Although the mythical character was later freed, in this cartoon the monarch appears doomed. (*Punch,* 1861)

interpret the law our way or we'll declare war, [and] commission enough privateers to prey on English commerce on every sea."[83]

Seward spoke from weakness and the British knew it. The Union had twice the population of the South and produced 92 percent of all goods manufactured in the United States. But the North faced the difficult military challenge of subduing 9,000,000 hostile people and sealing off innumerable harbors strung along 3,500 miles of coastline. To blockade this coast, Secretary of the Navy Gideon Welles could muster only 42 operational warships, and of these only 8 were in home waters. British statesmen thought it implausible that Lincoln could reconstruct the Union against such odds.

The economic balance sheet also seemed to work against the North. Prior to the Civil War, British subjects invested widely in American securities, sent at least 25 percent of their annual exports to the United States, and depended on America for 55 percent of all foodstuffs imported each year. But these economic ties favoring the industrial North and farming West paled beside the South's share of over 70 percent of the British market for raw cotton, the staple undergirding an industrial and commercial empire employing between 4 and 5 million people. Were the cotton trade interrupted, worried Britishers predicted, England would become economically prostrate. As a Southern planter and politician bragged, cotton was "the king who can shake the jewels in the crown of Queen Victoria."[84]

Jefferson Davis moved quickly to convert economic advantage into political impregnability. In March he despatched three ministers to Europe to seek full

Charleston, South Carolina. Its wharves piled with cotton for export, this Southern city governed by wealthy planters and gentlemen relied heavily on the cotton trade for prosperity. In 1860 Charleston ranked third behind New Orleans and Mobile as a cotton-exporting port. (Library of Congress)

diplomatic recognition, or even intervention, in exchange for an uninterrupted supply of cotton, free trade with the Confederacy, and expansion of European power throughout the western hemisphere. From Washington, Lyons counseled the British foreign secretary to receive the Southern commissioners informally, and a worried Lord John Russell replied, "I shall see the Southerners when they come, but not officially, and keep them at a proper distance."[85]

To parry this diplomatic thrust, Seward sped Charles Francis Adams to the Court of St. James's. Described by a contemporary Northern diplomat as "the Archbishop of antislavery," Adams was the son of the author of the Monroe Doctrine and grandson of the diplomat who had helped make peace with England in 1783.[86] Aloof, cool, steeped in the traditions of diplomacy, and serenely confident that his appointment would lead him to the presidency, Adams ultimately insulated London from Seward's highly charged flashes without deviating from the secretary's goals. Historian Jay Monaghan has compared Adams to his adversary, British Foreign Secretary Russell: "The two men were equally cold, formal, diplomatic, and almost equally British. A diamond come to cut a diamond."[87]

Adams arrived in London on May 14, 1861, dismayed to learn that England had proclaimed itself neutral and had recognized Confederate belligerency. Fortunately, the British government had also forbidden its subjects to supply ammunition or privateers to either side. Adams sought an early audience with Lord Russell to determine the extent of British recognition of the Southern commissioners. The foreign secretary vaguely admitted that he had received them "some time ago" and "once more sometime since," but he concluded, "I have no intention of seeing them any more." For the time being, Adams had to content himself with this "provokingly diplomatic" reassurance.[88] His secretary and son, Henry Adams, thought there were sufficient grounds for severing diplomatic relations, but he and his father rejected such action as the "extreme of shallowness and folly," because a war with England, added to the Civil War, "would grind us all into rags in America."[89]

A process of amelioration then began on both sides of the Atlantic. On May 21, Seward drafted a hostile dispatch for Adams, threatening to declare war if Britain recognized Confederate independence, only to have Lincoln pencil out the most warlike phrases and insist that the message be sent for Adams' guidance rather than as an ultimatum to Lord Russell. Even when toned down, Dispatch No. 10 struck Adams' son Henry as "so arrogant in tone and so extraordinary and unparalleled in its demands that it leaves no doubt in my mind that our Government wishes to face a war with all Europe."[90] As Adams quietly pocketed the diplomatic bombshell, reverses at the front rendered the secretary's threats of war with Europe ridiculous. On July 21, 1861, at Manassas Junction, Virginia, Confederate troops stampeded a Union army into full retreat north.

The summer and fall of 1861 brought further encouragement to Confederate statesmen. In England James D. Bulloch, head of the Confederacy's overseas secret service, contracted for the construction of two sloops. Disguised as merchant ships until their departure from British waters, in order to circumvent the neutrality proclamation, the *Florida* and *Alabama* promised to play havoc with Northern commerce. In August the *Bermuda,* a blockade runner laden with war material for Savannah, dashed from the Thames. Russell snidely deflected Adams' protest with an invitation to sign the Declaration of Paris. To exploit this favorable drift of events, President Davis sent two fresh and aggressive ministers to Europe, the aristocratic James M. Mason of Virginia and John Slidell, the political boss of Louisiana and Polk's emissary to Mexico in 1845. On October 11, they boarded the Confederate steamer *Nashville* at Charleston to begin the first leg of their journey.

Hoping to avoid capture by crossing the Atlantic under a neutral flag, Mason and Slidell transferred to the British mail steamer *Trent* in Havana. Captain Charles Wilkes, one of the United States Navy's most audacious officers, learned of their plans and intercepted the *Trent* as it left Cuban waters on November 8, 1861. Since the British vessel carried Confederate mail, Wilkes could have seized it as a prize. But instead, he hauled Mason and Slidell aboard the U.S.S. *San Jacinto* and allowed the *Trent* to continue its voyage, an act reminiscent of the British practice of impressment before the War of 1812. When Washington learned of this bold stroke, crowds cheered the hero of the *Trent* and Congress passed a resolution of thanks for Wilkes, but diplomats and senators worried that the capture of Mason and Slidell might spark war with Great Britain. European ministers in the capital city unanimously decried the illegality of the seizure, and the Chairman of the Senate Foreign Relations Committee, Charles Sumner, urged immediate release of the two Confederates. Lincoln himself feared Mason and Slidell might become "white elephants," but believed he could not free the prisoners without inviting overwhelming popular disapproval.[91]

News of Wilkes's audacity reached London on November 27, igniting a panic on the stock exchange and fanning fears of war. The *Morning Post* echoed Prime Minister Palmerston's typically British confidence in the Royal Navy. "In one month we could sweep all the *San Jacintos* from the seas, blockade the Northern ports, and turn to a direct and speedy issue the tide of the [civil] war now raging."[92] Palmerston began emergency Cabinet meetings on November 29, reportedly opening one of them with the angry expostulation, "I don't know whether you are going to stand this, but I'll be damned if I do!"[93] At a meeting on November 30, the Cabinet called for "ample reparation for this act of violence committed by an officer of the United States Navy against a neutral and friendly nation." Lord Lyons was instructed to demand the release of Mason and Slidell and a formal apology "for the insult offered to the British flag." These instructions were rushed to Windsor Castle for review and approval by Queen Victoria's consort, Prince Albert, a staunch advocate of Anglo-American peace. He devised a loophole allowing the United States government, if it wished, to deny that Wilkes had acted under instructions, "or, if he did, that he misapprehended them." In revised instructions reflecting Albert's determination to maintain pacific relations with the United States, Lord Russell directed Lyons "to abstain from anything like menace" when insisting on freedom for Mason and Slidell and "to be rather easy about the apology."[94]

As the watered-down ultimatum crossed the Atlantic, British merchants profiting from trade with the Union joined Manchester liberals in an effort to quiet popular indignation. Some tough realists in the War Office and Admiralty tempered their enthusiasm for war with concern over the vulnerability of Canada and invulnerability of Boston and New York. They also feared marauding Yankee cruisers that might elude a British "blockade and prowl about the ocean in quest of prey." Albert's death from typhoid on December 14 further sobered the national mood. Two days later, Russell advised the Prime Minister to be restrained: "I incline more and more to the opinion that if the [American] answer is a reasoning, and not a blunt offensive answer, we should send once more across the Atlantic to ask compliance. . . . I do not think the country would approve an immediate declaration of war."[95]

Lyons informally delivered the ultimatum to Seward on December 19. While the President and secretary of state debated their response, pressure mounted for capitulation. From London, Charles Francis Adams warned of implacable British determination to see Mason and Slidell free. The French minister in Washington advised that the Franco-American tradition of neutrality prescribed safe passage for enemy civilians aboard neutral vessels. Charles Sumner chastised irresponsible war hawks who seemed willing to invite the shelling of American cities by British guns. So unanimous and ominous were the warnings of British resolve that Lincoln and Seward decided to defuse the crisis. Characterized by historian Gordon H. Warren as "a monument to illogic," Seward's reply to Lord Lyons defended Wilkes's right to stop, search, and seize the *Trent,* but admitted that the American naval officer had erred in not taking the vessel into port for hearings before a legal tribunal. The secretary thus disavowed Wilkes, congratulated the British for accepting American views on impressment, and "cheerfully liberated" the two Confederates.[96]

The successful conclusion of the *Trent* affair by no means eliminated all tension with Europe. During the crisis, Britain, France, and Spain had landed troops at Veracruz, Mexico, ostensibly to compel payment of interest on a $65 million foreign debt. Lord Russell had cautiously invited American participation in this intervention, although stipulating that his invitation did not constitute acceptance of "the extravagant pretensions" of the Monroe Doctrine. On December 4, 1861, Seward declined to participate but acknowledged the right of the powers to collect debts forcibly, provided they did not harbor political or territorial ambitions in Mexico. American fears of European plots to implant a monarchical government in Latin America were realistic. In early 1862, Prime Minister Palmerston thought "the monarchy scheme if it could be carried out . . . would be a great blessing for Mexico. . . . It would also stop the North Americans . . . in their absorption of Mexico."[97] However, the foreign office soon perceived the even more enticing opportunity to prevent Napoleon III from tampering with the continental European balance of power by allowing him to become mired down in Mexican affairs.

In April, 1862, Britain and Spain made separate arrangements for Mexican payment of their debts and withdrew from the joint venture. They left French troops to inch their way westward toward Mexico City, where Napoleon hoped to install a puppet government under Archduke Ferdinand Maximilian, an unemployed brother of the Austrian Emperor. Fierce Mexican resistance obliged Napoleon to commit increasingly large numbers of men, delaying occupation of the capital city until June of 1863. This entrapment forced Napoleon to follow Britain's lead in Civil War diplomacy, despite his own romantic predilection toward mediation in favor of the South. As historian David Crook observes, "balance of power considerations dramatized the dangers of playing solitaire in overseas adventures to the neglect of French security in Europe."[98]

"LOOKERS ON" ACROSS THE ATLANTIC

For the first nine months of 1862 British policymakers warily viewed the bloody contest. Along the Southern coast the Union's tightening blockade locked up Confederate privateers and drove neutral shipping to uneconomical, shallow draft steamers. In Tennessee an unknown general, Ulysses S. Grant, chased the rebels from Forts Donelson and Henry. Admiral David G. Farragut captured New Orleans in April, opening the Mississippi River to a campaign that would finally sever Texas and the West from the Confederacy. However, neither North nor South could score a decisive victory in the critical Eastern theater. General George B. McClellan faltered and retreated outside Richmond in July, 1862, just as Virginia's Robert E. Lee pulled back after the bloodletting at Antietam two months later. Always mindful of the vulnerability of Canada, and confident that the stalemate ultimately would exhaust Northern stamina and lead to a permanent separation of the sections, the British looked to their own interests.

From the beginning Great Britain prudently acquiesced in the Union blockade, accumulating precedents useful for future conflicts when once again England would be a belligerent and the United States neutral. The Crown's law office advised Russell that it was "highly desirable at present to avoid discussions upon abstract principles of International Law," even though the Union appeared "to have acted liberally in regard to this blockade."[99] A spokesman for the government raised the crucial question in Parliament: "how would it have been if . . . we had been the first . . . to say that the United States as a belligerent Power should not exercise all belligerent rights in the ordinary manner, because we wanted cotton?"[100]

During the first year of the blockade, in fact, England did not "want" raw cotton. The bumper American crop of 1860 provided 1.6 million bales for the saturated

Lancashire mills in 1861, and production of cotton textiles far exceeded demand. Reflecting the prevalent anticipation of an early end to the Civil War, British cotton manufacturers complacently counted on their stockpiled raw cotton to carry them through a short-term crisis, which they alleviated by laying off workers and curtailing inflated production. As the military deadlock deepened in 1862, the textile producers began to fear future shortages and energetically stimulated development of alternative sources of fiber, notably in Egypt and India. These new fields began to yield amply by 1863. In France, mill owners proved less resourceful, but Napoleon's insistence on following British policy toward the Civil War prevented the Confederacy from capitalizing upon discontent in the French cotton industry. As a close student of Civil War diplomacy has concluded, "King Cotton theory was a washout in the first year of the war, a phony threat to those in the know."[101]

The Confederacy fared better in maritime Liverpool. Contemptuous of the blockade and the Queen's neutrality proclamation, Liverpool shipping interests sought to recoup from the costly disruption of trade with the South by building blockade runners, commerce raiders, and rams for English adventurers and the South's James D. Bulloch. The blockade runners returned high profits to builders, skippers, and crews. Of 2742 runs attempted during the war, steam-driven runners completed 2525, or 92 percent. However, these vessels were of light tonnage, and a substantial percentage of the successful runs occurred during the largely ineffective first year of the blockade. Moreover, greed for profits induced many Southern shippers to import luxury items rather than military materiel, thus wasting precious cargo space and draining off scarce Southern capital.

Commerce raiders presented a greater threat to the Union. James D. Bulloch contracted for these vessels and disguised them as cargo ships during construction in order to circumvent the British neutrality proclamation, which forbade outfitting warships for either belligerent. In March of 1862 the *Oreto,* to be renamed *Florida* once at sea, slipped from Liverpool. Charles Francis Adams protested vainly and pleaded with Lord Russell to detain a larger second vessel, "Number 290," then nearing completion. On July 31, Russell grudgingly concluded the new ship was intended to be a Confederate commerce raider, but his order to seize it arrived a day after the "290," an alias for *Alabama,* had sailed. Under the command of the South's most gifted naval officer, Raphael Semmes, the C.S.S. *Alabama* sank nineteen Union merchantmen in its first three months at sea. Together with the *Florida* and lesser destroyers, it preyed on worldwide Union commerce, driving Northern merchants to flags of foreign registry and sharply accelerating a scarcely noticed prewar decline in the American merchant marine. Adams ultimately obtained redress for the United States, but only after the guns of war had stilled.

Two months after the *Alabama's* escape, Adams and the Union faced "the very crisis of our fate."[102] Awed by the Second Battle of Bull Run and the endless rivers of blood irrigating North America, Lord Russell proposed to Palmerston an Anglo-French mediation "with a view to the recognition of the independence of the Confederates."[103] Cotton shortages—the worst of the war—and fear of riots by unemployed Lancashire operatives added impetus to Russell's proposal, and at first the Prime Minister, whom Henry Adams considered "as callous as a rhinoceros," seemed receptive.[104] Unfortunately for the foreign secretary, however, France at that moment was caught in a cabinet crisis stemming from Napoleon's Mexican schemes and the Emperor's vacillation toward Italy, where a near civil war erupted in August. The Quai d'Orsay therefore hesitated, and from St. Petersburg came a resounding endorsement of the North and reunion, which the Tsar favored as a check on British supremacy in the Atlantic. News of Lee's reversal at Antietam and retreat south across the Potomac finally inclined the Prime Minister "to change the opinion on which I wrote you when the Confederates seemed to carry all before them." He had now "very much come back to our original view of the matter, that we must continue to be lookers on till the war shall have taken a more decided turn."[105] This repudiation on October 22, 1862, of both mediation and recognition of Confederate independence duly determined the policy Great Britain followed for the remainder of the war.

Lincoln did all he could to insure continued European neutrality. Aware of Britain's ingrained hatred of slavery and Palmerston's abhorrence of the "diabolical Slave Trade," he issued the Emancipation Proclamation on September 22.[106] This historic gesture set January 1, 1863, as the date for freedom of slaves in areas not controlled by the Union—in short, only in districts still in rebellion. The Great Emancipator thought "it is a momentous thing to be the instrument under Providence for the liberation of a race."[107] But Palmerston sniffed that the proclamation was "trash," and Lord Russell, by then on the defensive, cynically observed of the limited manumission, "the right of slavery is made the reward of loyalty."[108] Even the workers of Lancashire evinced apathy or opposition to the emancipation. Yet some British publicists could thereafter denounce British mediation or forcible intervention on behalf of the Confederacy as "immoral."[109] As one historian judiciously writes, "much evidence still stands to the effect that the northern image improved, in the long run, after Lincoln adopted a war aim more intelligible to European opinion."[110]

As 1863 opened, Britain's cautious policy of watchful waiting was reinforced by a Polish uprising against Russian rule, which threatened general war and destruction of the critical European balance of power. Charles Francis Adams welcomed the "favorable interlude" of European disorder and waited impatiently for Union victories to give him real diplomatic clout.[111] In March, Henry Adams wrote his brother in the Union army that the diplomats needed encouragement from "military heroes," so that "we should be the cocks of the walk in England. . . . Couldn't some of you give us just one leetle sugar-plum? We are shocking dry."[112] Then in July came the good news; the Northern armies had held at Gettysburg and Grant had won control of the Mississippi River at Vicksburg. As Confederate bonds plummeted thirty-two points on the London market, Minister Adams pressed Lord Russell to seize two ironclad, steam-driven vessels nearing completion at the Laird yards in Liverpool. These shallow draft warships mounted seven-foot iron rams, theoretically an ideal weapon for piercing the wooden hulls of the Union's blockaders. Bulloch had ordered construction of the Laird rams, but he had so cleverly covered his tracks that the Pasha of Egypt appeared to be their legal owner. Since the rams lacked guns and the Crown lacked proof of Confederate ownership, Russell's law officers could not find them in violation of British neutrality. Russell, however, dared not disregard Adams' increasingly shrill warnings, nor the Union's midsummer military victories. On September 3, 1863, he prudently detained the rams. Should the purchasers successfully claim damages in British courts, he wrote Palmerston, "we have satisfied the opinion which prevails here as well as in America that that kind of neutral hostility should not be allowed to go on without some attempt to stop it."[113]

Charles Francis Adams (1807–1886). Son of John Quincy Adams, graduate of Harvard, and Republican congressman from Massachusetts before Lincoln appointed him minister to Great Britain (1861–1868), the suave and self-possessed diplomat labored diligently to keep London neutral during the Civil War. (Portrait by William Morris Hunt, Courtesy of Harvard University Portrait Collection)

Unaware of the foreign secretary's concession, Adams on September 5 penned a scathing note warning that if the rams were not halted, "it would be superfluous in me to point out to your lordship that this is war!"[114] Palmerston bridled at Adams' "insolent threats of war" and thought Russell should "say to him in civil terms, 'You be damned.'"[115] But the Prime Minister's private irritation did not detract from Adams' successful elimination of the Confederacy's last threat to the blockade, a triumph his son Henry immodestly recorded as a second Vicksburg victory. Indeed, the "American Minister had trumped their [the British] best card and won the game."[116]

Northern morale also received a boost from the visit of the Russian Baltic and Pacific squadrons to New York and San Francisco in September and October of 1863. Fearful of war with England over Poland, Russia sent its ships in the hope that they could operate against the Royal Navy from the ice-free American ports. Northerners, however, wishfully interpreted the visit as a sign of St. Petersburg's support for their cause. Secretary of the Navy Gideon Welles thought "our Russian friends are rendering us a great service."[117]

In 1863, too, the troops of Napoleon III finally fought their way into Mexico City. In July, the victorious French Emperor proclaimed a Mexican monarchy under Austrian Archduke Maximilian. Secretary Seward immediately recalled his minister, and denied recognition to Maximilian when the hapless claimant to the shaky new throne arrived in Mexico in July, 1864. By then Sherman was marching through Georgia and Grant was creeping bloodily toward Richmond. The apparently inevitable Union triumph would place a huge army and one of the world's largest navies along the border of Napoleon's puppet state. In April the United States Congress passed a resolution condemning the French invasion of Mexico. But Lincoln's Administration, hoping to avoid confrontation with France, disavowed the measure, confident in Seward's words that "those who are most impatient for the defeat of European and monarchical designs in Mexico might well be content to abide the effects which must result from the ever-increasing expansion of the American people westward and southward."[118] Napoleon began to scale down his commitment, intending to remove all but 20,000 French troops from Mexico by 1867. He also curried favor with Washington by directing Maximilian not to receive any Confederate ministers, and to appease Seward further he seized two Confederate rams under construction at Nantes in May, 1864. A month later the U.S.S. *Kearsarge* sank the C.S.S. *Alabama* within sight of Cherbourg. The diplomatic and naval isolation of the Confederacy was complete. "King Cotton" had failed. Confederate diplomacy, lacking decisive support from the battlefield, did not win European capitals to its cause. The "War Between the States" had remained just that.

"A POWER OF THE FIRST CLASS": THE EXPANSIONIST REVIVAL

When the guns of the Civil War quieted at Appomattox in April, 1865, Americans took account of their recent past and their apparently dim future. Over six hundred thousand countrymen lay dead and hundreds of thousands nursed disfiguring wounds. The war cost at least twenty billion dollars in destroyed property and expenditures. The American merchant marine was in a shambles, and commerce was badly disrupted. The eleven Confederate states suffered heavy economic losses, as a dislocated population and labor force, including four million former slaves, looked upon trampled and denuded agricultural fields and burned-out cities. Although the Union was whole once again, regional bitterness persisted. The wrenching Civil War experience and the necessity of postwar reconstruction suggested indeed that sectionalism would continue to impede traditional United States expansion abroad.

Countervailing evidence, however, indicated that the expansionism that had flourished in the 1840s and was muted in the 1850s would enjoy a rebirth. Ideas of Manifest Destiny about the natural growth of the United States into new territories survived. Although trade had been thrown askew, Northern commerce in wheat with England expanded greatly during the war, and prospects for a renewal of the cotton trade were good. Measurable economic changes held foreign policy implications. During the war Northern politicians established high tariffs to protect Northern manufacturers, stabilized the banking system, passed the Homestead Act to settle western lands and the Morrill Act to build land-grant colleges, and provided for the construction of a transcontinental railroad. Although historians differ over the economic impact of the Civil War on the North, it was evident that large federal expenditures of about $2 million a day generated capital accumulation and stimulated some industries. In so doing, the Civil War helped spur the "industrial revolution" of the late nineteenth century in America, which increasingly shifted the character of American foreign trade from agricultural to industrial goods and prompted the sale of surplus production overseas. Conspicuous industrial might was also a component of American power in the eyes of other nations. Because Northern diplomacy and European caution had prevented the Civil War from becoming an international conflict, these economic gains could be registered, insuring opportunities for expansion.

Once freed from the constraints of war, Secretary of State William H. Seward envisioned a larger American empire. Noted as an expansionist before the Civil War, Seward during the war had bristled over the intrusion of domestic affairs in his grand vision for continued expansion of the United States. In 1853 Seward had proclaimed that the boundary of the United States "shall be extended so that it shall greet the sun when he touches the tropics and when he sends his gleaming rays towards the polar circle, and shall include even distant islands in either ocean."[119] In 1865 Seward turned his attention southward, intent upon driving the French and Maximilian from Mexico, annexing territories, and building naval bases in the Caribbean. Santo Domingo, which Spain had cast off again in July, 1865, became one of Seward's first targets. The British, when they began their retreat from Central America in the late 1850s, had predicted that the United States would eventually "overrun" neighbors just as it had done with Louisiana, Texas, and California.[120] *The Spectator* summed up the postwar reality: "Nobody doubts any more that the Union is a power of the first class, a nation which it is very dangerous to offend and almost impossible to attack."[121]

The British had good reason to be sensitive about the United States. Northern anger toward London was bitter, especially over the depradations of the *Alabama* and the seeming British tolerance of Southern secession. Also, Anglo-American competition in Central America and the Caribbean joined competition in the Pacific and Asia to propel London and Washington along a collision course. Reciprocity with Canada was breaking down, and the Agreement of 1854 was abrogated in 1866. A new generation of American Anglophobes vowed to twist the British lion's tail. Some Americans insisted that Britannia relinquish Canada to the

United States as proper repentance for British sins in the Civil War. If the British reaped intense American hostility, they also carried away from the scrape some welcomed precedents in international law. The seafaring British acquiesced in the tortuous American rendering of maritime rights during the Civil War. The Lincoln Administration reversed the traditional American view of neutral rights and adopted what had been the British position. Seward insisted that the war was a *domestic* conflict, yet the United States declared a paper-thin blockade under *international* law. Not only did this behavior constitute a glaring contradiction; it also proved to be a violation of international law, for blockades must be effective. Seward also condemned Confederate privateering and commerce raiding. He even reversed the hallowed American doctrine that neutral shipping was immune to capture when traveling between neutral ports, regardless of the ultimate destination of the cargo: in 1863 he implicitly approved the capture of the *Peterhoff,* a British steamer loaded with Confederate goods en route to Matamoros, Mexico. The United States, it seemed to Britons, had repudiated principles thought worthy to fight over in 1812. During the period of American neutrality in the First World War (1914–1917), the British dusted off their history tomes and reminded Washington of Seward's Civil War policies. The legacy of the Civil War had a long reach indeed.

FURTHER READING FOR THE PERIOD 1848–1865

For general works and the expansionist issues of the 1850s, especially in the western hemisphere, see James C. Bradford, ed., *Captains of the Old Steam Navy: Makers of the American Naval Tradition, 1840–1880* (1986); Charles H. Brown, *Agents of Manifest Destiny: The Lives and Times of the Filibusters* (1980); Craig L. Dozier, *Nicaragua's Mosquito Shore* (1985); Amos A. Ettinger, *The Mission to Spain of Pierre Soulé, 1853–1855* (1932); Philip Foner, *A History of Cuba and Its Relations with the United States* (1962–1963); Norman A. Graebner, ed., *Manifest Destiny* (1968); Lester D. Langley, *The Cuban Policy of the United States* (1968) and *Struggle for the American Mediterranean: United States-European Rivalry in the Gulf-Caribbean, 1776–1894* (1976); Robert E. May, *The Southern Dream of a Caribbean Empire, 1854–1861* (1973) and *John A. Quitman* (1985); Donothon C. Olliff, *Reforma Mexico and the United States* (1981); Dexter Perkins, *The Monroe Doctrine, 1826–1867* (1933); Lester B. Shippee, *Canadian-American Relations, 1849–1874* (1939); Richard W. Van Alstyne, "Empire in Midpassage, 1845–1867," in William A. Williams, ed., *From Colony to Empire* (1972) and *The Rising American Empire* (1960); Paul A. Varg, *United States Foreign Relations, 1820–1860* (1979); and Donald Warner, *The Idea of Continental Union: Agitation for the Annexation of Canada to the United States, 1849–1893* (1960).

Principal makers of American diplomacy are examined in K. Jack Bauer, *Zachary Taylor* (1985); Samuel Flagg Bemis, ed., *The American Secretaries of State and Their Diplomacy* (1927–1960); David Donald, *Charles Sumner and the Rights of Man* (1970); Holman Hamilton, *Zachary Taylor* (1941–1951); Philip S. Klein, *President James Buchanan* (1962); Jay Monaghan, *Diplomat in Carpet Slippers* (1945) (Lincoln); Roy F. Nichols, *Franklin Pierce* (1958); John Niven, *Gideon Welles, Lincoln's Secretary of the Navy* (1973); Ernest N. Paolino, *The Foundations of the American Empire* (1973) (Seward); Kenneth E. Shewmaker, "Daniel Webster and the Politics of Foreign Policy, 1850–1852," *Journal of American History* (1976); and Glyndon G. Van Deusen, *William Henry Seward* (1967).

For Asia, see Warren I. Cohen, *America's Response to China* (1980); Foster R. Dulles, *China and America* (1946) and *Yankee and Samurai* (1965); Michael Hunt, *The Making of a Special Relationship* (1983) (China); John K. Fairbank, *Trade and Diplomacy on the China Coast* (1953); Gerald S. Graham, *The China Station* (1978); Curtis T. Henson, Jr., *Commissioners and Commodores: The East India Squadron and American Diplomacy in China* (1982); Samuel E. Morison,

"Old Bruin" (1967); Charles Neu, *The Troubled Encounter: The United States and Japan* (1975); William L. Neumann, *America Encounters Japan* (1963); Richard W. Van Alstyne, *The United States and East Asia* (1973); and Arthur Walworth, *Black Ships Off Japan* (1946).

The Anglo-American relationship is the subject of H. C. Allen, *Great Britain and the United States* (1955); Kenneth Bourne, *Britain and the Balance of Power in North America* (1967); Charles S. Campbell, *From Revolution to Rapproachement* (1974); Wilbur D. Jones, *The American Problem in British Diplomacy* (1974); and H. G. Nicholas, *The United States and Britain* (1975).

For European issues, see Henry M. Adams, *Prussian-American Relations, 1775–1871* (1960); Henry Blumenthal, *A Reappraisal of Franco-American Relations, 1830–1871* (1959) and *France and the United States* (1970); Alan Dowty, *The Limits of American Isolation* (1971) (Crimean War); James A. Field, Jr., *America and the Mediterranean World, 1776–1882* (1969); and Donald M. Spencer, *Louis Kossuth and Young America* (1977).

For the Union and Confederate foreign policies during the Civil War, especially naval questions and maritime rights, see works cited above and Ephraim D. Adams, *Great Britain and the American Civil War* (1925); Stuart Anderson, "1861: Blockade vs. Closing the Confederate Ports," *Military Affairs* (1977); Stuart L. Bernath, *Squall Across the Atlantic: American Civil War Prize Cases and Diplomacy* (1970); Henry Blumenthal, "Confederate Diplomacy," *Journal of Southern History* (1966); Kinley J. Brauer, "The Slavery Problem in the Diplomacy of the American Civil War," *Pacific Historical Review* (1977); Lynn M. Case and Warren F. Spencer, *The United States and France* (1970); Adrian Cook, *The Alabama Claims* (1975); David P. Crook, *Diplomacy During the American Civil War* (1975) and *The North, the South, and the Powers, 1861–1865* (1974); Charles P. Cullop, *Confederate Propaganda in Europe* (1969); Norman B. Ferris, *The "Trent" Affair* (1977) and *Desperate Diplomacy: William H. Seward's Foreign Policy, 1861* (1975); Norman A. Graebner, "Northern Diplomacy and European Neutrality," in David Donald, ed., *Why the North Won the Civil War* (1960); Alfred J. Hanna and Kathryn A. Hanna, *Napoleon III and Mexico* (1971); Brian Jenkins, *Britain and the War for the Union* (1974–1980); Frank J. Merli, *Great Britain and the Confederate Navy* (1970); Frank L. and Harriet Owsley, *King Cotton Diplomacy* (1959); Carlton Savage, *Policy of the United States toward Maritime Commerce in War* (1934); Thomas D. Schoonover, *Dollars over Dominion* (1978) (Mexico); Warren F. Spencer, *The Confederate Navy in Europe* (1983); Emory M. Thomas, *The Confederate Nation, 1861–1865* (1979); Gordon H. Warren, *Fountain of Discontent: The Trent Affair and Freedom of the Seas* (1981); Robin Winks, *Canada and the United States* (1960); and Albert A. Woldman, *Lincoln and the Russians* (1952).

See also the General Bibliography and the following notes.

NOTES TO CHAPTER 4

1. Quoted in Arthur Walworth, *Black Ships Off Japan* (New York: Alfred A. Knopf, 1946), p. 96.
2. Quoted in William L. Neumann, *America Encounters Japan: From Perry to MacArthur* (Baltimore: The Johns Hopkins University Press, 1963), p. 30.
3. Quoted in Henry F. Graff, *Bluejackets with Perry in Japan* (New York: New York Public Library, 1952), p. 68.
4. Quoted in Shunsuke Kamei, "The Sacred Land of Liberty: Images of America in Nineteenth Century Japan," in Akira Iriye, ed., *Mutual Images: Essays in American-Japanese Relations* (Cambridge, Mass.: Harvard University Press, 1975), p. 55.
5. Quoted in Oliver Statler, *The Black Ship Scroll* (Tokyo: John Weatherhill, 1963), p. 8.
6. Quoted in Walworth, *Black Ships Off Japan*, p. 71.
7. Francis L. Hawks, ed., *Narrative of the Expedition of an American Squadron to the China Seas and Japan* (Washington: Beverley Tucker, Senate Printer, 1856; 3 vols.), I, 256–257, 261, 263.
8. Quoted in Graff, *Bluejackets with Perry*, p. 127.
9. Quoted in Samuel Eliot Morison, *"Old Bruin": Commodore Matthew C. Perry, 1794–1858* (Boston: Little Brown, 1967), p. 371.
10. Quoted in Neumann, *America Encounters Japan*, p. 40.
11. Quoted in Graff, *Bluejackets with Perry*, p. 68.
12. Quoted in Morison, *"Old Bruin,"* p. 411.
13. Quoted *ibid.*, pp. 417, 425, 429.
14. Quoted in Richard W. Van Alstyne, *The Rising American Empire* (New York: W. W. Norton, 1974 [1960]), p. 175.

15. John K. Fairbank, *Trade and Diplomacy on the China Coast* (Cambridge, Mass.: Harvard University Press, 1953; 2 vols.), I, 208.

16. Quoted in Warren I. Cohen, *America's Response to China*, (New York: John Wiley & Sons, 1980; 2nd. ed.), p. 22.

17. Charles E. Neu, *The Troubled Encounter: The United States and Japan* (New York: John Wiley & Sons, 1975), p. 9.

18. Quoted in Richard W. Van Alstyne, "Empire in Midpassage, 1845–1867," in William A. Williams, ed., *From Colony to Empire* (New York: John Wiley & Sons, 1972), p. 119.

19. Eugene D. Genovese, *The Political Economy of Slavery* (New York: Vintage Books, 1967), p. 270.

20. Quoted in Eric Foner, *Free Labor, Free Soil, Free Men* (New York: Oxford University Press, 1970), p. 72.

21. Quoted in Kenneth E. Shewmaker, "Daniel Webster and the Politics of Foreign Policy, 1850–1852," *Journal of American History*, LXIII (September, 1976), 308.

22. Quoted in George T. Curtis, *Life of Daniel Webster* (New York: D. Appleton, 1870; 2 vols.), II, 537.

23. Quoted in Robert R. Davis, Jr., "Diplomatic Plumage: American Court Dress in the National Period," *American Quarterly*, XX (Summer, 1968), 173.

24. Quoted in Russell B. Nye, *George Bancroft: Brahmin Rebel* (New York: Alfred A. Knopf, 1944), p. 205.

25. Quoted in Allan Nevins, *Ordeal of the Union* (New York: Charles Scribner's Sons, 1947; 2 vols.), II, 347.

26. Quoted in Albert K. Weinberg, *Manifest Destiny* (Chicago: Quadrangle Books, 1963 [1935]), pp. 201–202.

27. Quoted in David Potter, *The Impending Crisis, 1848–1861* (New York: Harper & Row, 1976), p. 198.

28. Quoted in Robert F. Durden, "J. D. B. DeBow: Convolutions of a Slavery Expansionist," *Journal of Southern History*, XVII (November, 1951), 450.

29. Quoted in Robert E. May, *The Southern Dream of a Caribbean Empire, 1854–1861* (Baton Rouge: Louisiana State University Press, 1973), p. 5.

30. Quoted in Philip S. Foner, *A History of Cuba and Its Relations with the United States* (New York: International Publishers, 1962–1963; 2 vols.), II, 43.

31. Quoted *ibid.*, p. 64.

32. Quoted *ibid.*, p. 59.

33. Quoted in Durden, "J. D. B. DeBow," p. 451.

34. Quoted in C. Stanley Urban, "The Abortive Quitman Filibustering Expedition, 1853–1855," *Journal of Mississippi History*, XVIII (July, 1956), 177.

35. Quoted in C. Stanley Urban, "The Africanization of Cuba Scare, 1853–1855," *Hispanic American Historical Review*, XXXVII (February, 1957), 37.

36. Quoted in May, *Southern Dream*, p. 75.

37. Quoted in William H. Goetzmann, *When the Eagle Screamed: The Romantic Horizon in American Diplomacy, 1800–1860* (New York: John Wiley & Sons, 1966), p. 87.

38. Quoted in Roy F. Nichols, *Franklin Pierce: Young Hickory of the Granite Hills* (Philadelphia: University of Pennsylvania Press, 1931), p. 459.

39. William O. Scroggs, *Filibusters and Financiers: The Story of William Walker and His Associates* (New York: Macmillan, 1916), p. 241.

40. Quoted in May, *Southern Dream*, p. 91.

41. Quoted in Randall O. Hudson, "The Filibuster Minister: The Career of John Hill Wheeler as United States Minister to Nicaragua, 1854–1856," *North Carolina Historical Review*, XLIX (July, 1972), 295.

42. Quoted in May, *Southern Dream*, pp. 131–132.

43. *Ibid.*, p. 244.

44. Goetzmann, *When the Eagle Screamed*, p. 78.

45. Nevins, *Ordeal of the Union*, II, 63.

46. Quoted in Weinberg, *Manifest Destiny*, p. 190.

47. Parke Goodwin, quoted in Norman A. Graebner, ed., *Manifest Destiny* (Indianapolis: Bobbs-Merrill, 1968), p. lxiv.

48. Quoted in John A. Logan, Jr., *No Transfer: An American Security Principle* (New Haven: Yale University Press, 1961), p. 227.

49. Quoted in Basil Rauch, *American Interest in Cuba, 1848–1855* (New York: Columbia University Press, 1948), p. 176.

50. Foster Stearns, "Edward Everett," in Samuel Flagg Bemis, ed., *American Secretaries of State and Their Diplomacy* (New York: Cooper Square Publishers, 1963; 18 vols.), VI, 135, and John Bassett Moore, *A Digest of International Law* (Washington, D.C.: Government Printing Office, 1906; 8 vols.), VI, 462.

51. Quoted in Gavin B. Henderson, "Southern Designs on Cuba, 1854–1857 and Some European Opinions," *Journal of Southern History*, V (August, 1939), 385.

52. Quoted in Lester D. Langley, *The Cuban Policy of the United States* (New York: John Wiley & Sons, 1968), p. 37.

53. Quoted in J. Preston Moore, "Pierre Soulé: Southern Expansionist and Promoter," *Journal of Southern History*, XXI (1955), 205–206.

54. Quoted *ibid.*, p. 207.

55. Quoted in Amos A. Ettinger, *The Mission to Spain of Pierre Soulé, 1853–1855* (New Haven: Yale University Press, 1932), p. 378.

56. Quoted in Henry B. Learned, "William Learned Marcy," in Bemis, ed., *American Secretaries of State*, VI, 193.

57. Quoted in Ruhl J. Bartlett, ed., *The Record of American Diplomacy* (New York: Alfred A. Knopf, 1960; 3rd ed.), p. 241.

58. Quoted in Henderson, "Southern Designs," p. 374.

59. Quoted in Ivor D. Spencer, *The Victor and the Spoils: A Life of William L. Marcy* (Providence: Brown University Press, 1959), pp. 338–339.

60. Nichols, *Franklin Pierce*, p. 371.

61. Quoted in Philip S. Klein, *President James Buchanan: A Biography* (University Park: Pennsylvania State University Press, 1962), p. 324.

62. Quoted in Graebner, *Manifest Destiny*, p. 298.

63. Quoted in May, *Southern Dream*, p. 7.

64. Quoted in H. G. Nicholas, *The United States and Britain* (Chicago: University of Chicago Press, 1975), p. 22.

65. Quoted in Philip Guedalla, ed., *Gladstone and Palmerston* (New York: Kraus Reprint, 1971 [1928]), p. 208.

66. United States Senate, Executive Document 27 [Serial 660], 32 Cong., 2 Sess., p. 30.

67. Quoted in Kenneth Bourne, *The Foreign Policy of Victorian England, 1830–1902* (Oxford: Clarendon Press, 1970), p. 334.

68. Quoted in Wilbur D. Jones, *The American Problem in British*

Diplomacy, 1841–1861 (Athens: University of Georgia Press, 1974), p. 75.

69. Quoted in Mary W. Williams, *Anglo-American Isthmian Diplomacy, 1815–1915* (Washington: American Historical Association, 1916), p. 92, and Charles S. Campbell, *From Revolution to Rapprochement: The United States and Great Britain, 1783–1900* (New York: John Wiley & Sons, 1974), p. 81.

70. Hunter Miller, ed., *Treaties and Other International Acts of the United States of America* (Washington: Government Printing Office, 1931–1948; 8 vols.), V, 672.

71. *Ibid.*, p. 685.

72. Jones, *American Problem*, p. 88.

73. Quoted in Richard A. Van Alstyne, "The Clayton-Bulwer Treaty, 1850–60," *Journal of Modern History*, XI (June, 1939), 156.

74. Kenneth Bourne, *Britain and the Balance of Power in North America, 1815–1908* (London: Longmans, Green, 1967), p. 177.

75. Quoted *ibid.*, p. 182.

76. Quoted *ibid.*, p. 189.

77. Quoted in Margaret O. W. Oliphant, *Memoir of the Life of Laurence Oliphant and of Alice Oliphant, His Wife* (Edinburgh: William Blackwood and Sons, 1891; 2 vols.), I, 120.

78. Quoted in H. C. Allen, *Great Britain and the United States* (New York: St. Martin's Press, 1955), p. 423.

79. Kenneth Bourne, "The Clayton-Bulwer Treaty and the Decline of British Opposition to the Territorial Expansion of the United States, 1857–60," *Journal of Modern History*, XXXIII (September, 1961), 289.

80. Quoted in Allan Nevins, *The Coming Fury* (Garden City, N.Y.: Doubleday, 1961), p. 217.

81. Jay Monaghan, *Diplomat in Carpet Slippers: Abraham Lincoln Deals with Foreign Affairs* (Indianapolis: Charter Books, 1945), p. 58.

82. Quoted in John G. Nicolay and John Hay, *Abraham Lincoln: A History* (New York: The Century, 1890; 10 vols.), III, 445–449.

83. Quoted in Monaghan, *Diplomat in Carpet Slippers*, p. 82.

84. S. R. Cockerill, quoted in Frank L. Owsley and Harriet C. Owsley, *King Cotton Diplomacy: Foreign Relations of the Confederate States of America* (Chicago: University of Chicago Press, 1959; rev. ed.), p. 19.

85. Quoted in Norman A. Graebner, "Northern Diplomacy and European Neutrality," in David Donald, ed., *Why the North Won the Civil War* (Baton Rouge: Louisiana State University Press, 1960), p. 56.

86. Quoted in Monaghan, *Diplomat in Carpet Slippers*, p. 26.

87. *Ibid.*, p. 100

88. Quoted *ibid.*, p. 102.

89. Worthington C. Ford, ed., *Letters of Henry Adams* (Boston: Houghton Mifflin, 1930–1938; 2 vols.), I, 92.

90. Quoted *ibid.*, p. 93.

91. Quoted in Allan Nevins, *The War for the Union* (New York: Charles Scribner's Sons, 1959–1971; 4 vols.), I, 392.

92. Quoted in David P. Crook, *The North, the South, and the Powers* (New York: John Wiley & Sons, 1974), p. 130.

93. Quoted in Bourne, *Britain and Balance of Power*, p. 219.

94. Quoted in Crook, *The North, the South, and the Powers*, pp. 132, 133–134.

95. Quoted *ibid.*, pp. 147, 140.

96. Gordon H. Warren, *Fountain of Discontent: The Trent Affair and Freedom of the Seas* (Boston: Northeastern University Press, 1981), p. 184.

97. Quoted in Crook, *The North, the South, and the Powers*, pp. 93, 184.

98. *Ibid.*, p. 182.

99. *Ibid.*, p. 176.

100. *Ibid.*, p. 179.

101. David P. Crook, *Diplomacy During the American Civil War* (New York: John Wiley & Sons, 1975), p. 74.

102. Quoted in Crook, *Diplomacy*, p. 93.

103. Quoted in Emory M. Thomas, *The Confederate Nation, 1861–1865* (New York: Harper & Row, 1979), p. 179.

104. Ford, *Letters of Henry Adams*, I, 122.

105. Quoted in Norman A. Graebner, "European Interventionism and the Crisis of 1862," *Journal of the Illinois State Historical Society*, LXIX (February, 1976), 43.

106. Quoted in Campbell, *From Revolution to Rapprochement*, p. 79.

107. Quoted in Monaghan, *Diplomat in Carpet Slippers*, p. 273.

108. Quoted in Robert H. Jones, *Disrupted Decades: The Civil War and Reconstruction Years* (New York: Charles Scribner's Sons, 1973), p. 376 and Crook, *Diplomacy*, p. 96.

109. Quoted in Crook, *Diplomacy*, p. 97.

110. Crook, *The North, the South, and the Powers*, p. 237.

111. Quoted in Crook, *Diplomacy*, p. 123.

112. Ford, *Letters of Henry Adams*, I, 96.

113. Quoted in Monaghan, *Diplomat in Carpet Slippers*, p. 328.

114. Quoted in Frank J. Merli, *Great Britain and the Confederate Navy, 1861–1865* (Bloomington: Indiana University Press, 1970), p. 201.

115. Quoted in Owsley and Owsley, *King Cotton Diplomacy*, p. 402.

116. Henry Adams, *The Education of Henry Adams: An Autobiography* (Boston: Houghton Mifflin, 1961 [1918]), p. 174.

117. Quoted in Howard K. Beale, ed., *Diary of Gideon Welles* (New York: W. W. Norton, 1960; 3 vols.), I, 484.

118. Quoted in Crook, *Diplomacy*, p. 164.

119. Quoted in Ernest N. Paolino, *The Foundations of the American Empire: William Henry Seward and U.S. Foreign Policy* (Ithaca: Cornell University Press, 1973), p. 7.

120. Lord Clarendon quoted in Bourne, *The Balance of Power in North America*, p. 202.

121. Quoted in H. C. Allen, "Civil War, Reconstruction, and Great Britain," in Harold Hyman, ed., *Heard Round the World: The Impact Abroad of the Civil War* (New York: Alfred A. Knopf, 1969), p. 35.

Chapter 5

Annexation Demonstration, Dominican Republic. James Taylor's watercolor of a Dominican rally in favor of the nation's annexation to the United States captured the moment but did not move the question. (Library of Congress)

Global Rivalry and
Regional Power, 1865–1895

DIPLOMATIC CROSSROAD:
THE FOILED GRAB OF SANTO DOMINGO, 1869–1870

President Ulysses S. Grant was infatuated with his pet project as he walked from the White House across Lafayette Park to the elegant brick home of the Chairman of the Senate Foreign Relations Committee, Charles Sumner. The flattery of senatorial egos sometimes brought fruitful results, and in this case Grant was reaching for a two-thirds vote. Politics was politics, after all. On the evening of January 2, 1870, in Washington, Sumner was offering good food and conversation to two politicos when Grant appeared, uninvited and unexpected. Several awkward moments passed before the President revealed his mission to the powerful senator from Massachusetts. Would Sumner support an annexation treaty for the Dominican Republic? Grant seemed impatient and only briefly sketched his case for this imperialistic scheme. Sumner said simply that he would study the matter. Yet Grant, indulging in a bit of wishful thinking, left persuaded that the senator would back the project. An American land grab seemed imminent—at least Grant thought so.

The Dominican Republic, which shared the island of Hispaniola with Haiti, was constantly strife-torn and invariably ruled by the unscrupulous, and had long been within the United States' expansionistic vision. The navy coveted the harbor at Samaná Bay, a choice strategic site in the Caribbean. The country's raw materials, especially timber and minerals, and its undeveloped status invited the attention of foreign businessmen; others thought of Santo Domingo as a potential sanitarium for isthmian canal workers struck by yellow fever. The Caribbean, in any case, was destined to become an American lake. Dominican President Buenaventura Baez, "an active intriguer of sinister talents," seemed eager to sell off his country.[1]

In July of 1869, Grant's personal secretary, General Orville Babcock, had gone to Santo Domingo to reconnoiter this "Gibraltar of the New World." Later exposed as a member of the Whiskey Ring, which defrauded the United States Treasury of millions of dollars, Babcock was also looking for personal profit in the Dominican Republic. He befriended William Cazneau and Joseph Fabens, two American speculators and sometime diplomatic agents who owned key Dominican port facilities, mines, and banks. They also represented a steamship company that sought traffic between New York and the island. With Cazneau and Fabens in the wings, and American warships in Dominican waters, Babcock and Baez struck a deal in two treaties signed on November 29, 1869. In the first, the United States agreed to annex the Dominican Republic and assume its national debt of $1.5 million. The second treaty promised that if the United States Senate refused to take all of the country, Samaná Bay could be had for $2 million. After the signing, Babcock and Fabens prematurely hoisted the American flag at Samaná.

Babcock had done his work well, and Grant began to lobby for annexation. His visit to Sumner's house was a calculated step to build support. Yet the independent-minded Sumner remained noncommittal for months. The more Sumner and his colleagues heard, the more they recoiled from the untidy affair. Baez was a corrupt money-grabber about to be driven from office by rebels, who were being harassed in turn by the United States Navy. Baez may have remained in power only because the United States backed him. Babcock was still a military officer, not a diplomatic official. Fabens and Cazneau were notorious schemers who had obviously enthralled Grant and his advisers with their Dominican scenario. Finally, Haiti and Santo Domingo were nearly at war. Sumner grumbled about these unsavory facts. Other skeptics sniffed another scandal like that which had tarnished the Alaska purchase.

Grant grew annoyed with Sumner's inertia and worked vigorously for the treaty by personally lobbying senators. He warned reluctant Cabinet members, who had not been consulted on annexation, to back the treaty or resign. The indignant but cautious Secretary of State, Hamilton Fish, whose department had been bypassed in the rush to get Santo Domingo, threatened to quit, but a sense of loyalty and Grant's personal appeal kept him at his post. Fish opposed annexation but favored American hegemony over the country in the form of a "protectorate." He could not persuade the stubborn President, who seemed bent on total victory or total defeat. On March 15, 1870, the Foreign Relations Committee, by a 5-2 vote, with Sumner in the lead, disapproved the treaty. Days later, Sumner launched the debate on the Senate floor, disparaging annexation but favoring a "free confederacy" in the West Indies where the "black race should predominate" and be protected by the United States.[2]

Annexationists countered that absorption of the island would ensure a steady flow of raw materials to the United States. They displayed pieces of Dominican hemp to prove their point and two senators performed an impromptu tug-of-war to demonstrate the fiber's strength. Another predicted that the spindles of New England textile mills would whirl once the Dominicans began to buy American cotton goods. Anti-imperialists retorted that the island was infested with Spanish-speaking Catholics and nonwhites, two groups out of favor in white Anglo-Saxon Protestant America; that annexation would spur the building of a larger navy, which would in turn entangle the United States in foreign troubles; that Americans were acting too much like colonizing Europeans; and that Congress had a constitutional duty to check such presidential schemes.

**Ulysses S. Grant
(1822–1885).** Graduate of the United States Military Academy, soldier in the Mexican War, and Civil War general before becoming President, Grant worked hard but unsuccessfully for the annexation of the Dominican Republic. (Library of Congress)

To regain the offensive, Grant on May 31 sent a special message to Congress extolling the virtues of the tiny island nation. It read like an expansionist's shopping list: raw materials from mines and forests, excellent harbors, a naval base, national security, a market for American products, and a site from which to help settle the revolution raging in Cuba. America had to keep its word as recorded by the two treaties. Without evidence, the President warned that if the United States did not take Santo Domingo, some other country would and the Monroe Doctrine would be violated. He even had the audacity to report the result of a farcical rigged plebiscite in which the Dominicans registered their support for selling themselves to the United States by the highly suspicious vote of 15,169 to 11.

Sumner would not budge. Personal feuding complicated this issue. Grant had always considered Sumner an arrogant Yankee and a political challenger. Sumner had been cool to Grant's nomination in 1868, had opposed some of the President's appointees, and was linked to the radical wing of the Republican party—a faction to which Grant never warmed. Grant also felt betrayed, remembering that night in January when he believed Sumner had given his word of support. Sumner, for his part, had little respect for the error-prone and intellectually inferior Grant and probably felt pique at not having been named to the post of secretary of state. Sumner's explosive temper, florid rhetoric, and attitude of intellectual certainty "excited obstinacy, anger and contempt" in Grant, noted Charles Francis Adams. Editor E. L. Godkin of *The Nation* remarked that Sumner "works his adjectives so hard that if they ever catch him alone, they will murder him."[3] The senator, commented one of his friends, treated "difference of opinion almost as moral delinquency."[4] The Dominican annexation treaty brought such personal antagonisms and different styles to the forefront.

In late June, the Senate voted 28-28 on the treaty of annexation, well short of the two-thirds vote required for ratification. "I will not allow Mr. Sumner to ride over me," Grant fumed.[5] The President and loyal Republicans vowed to strip Sumner of his chairmanship of the Foreign Relations Committee. Sumner began to lose support among his colleagues when he refused to approve a commission to study Dominican annexation. The senator saw it as a trick, a "dance of blood," and said so dramatically in his famous "Naboth's Vineyard" speech (referring to the Biblical story of King Ahab, who coveted his neighbor's vineyard). Delivered to the Senate on December 21, 1870, this intense oration reminded listeners of those pre–Civil War days when Sumner had blasted the defenders of slavery. Now Sumner scorned Cazneau and Fabens as "political jockeys" who had "seduced" Babcock. Santo Domingo, he insisted, belonged to the "colored" Dominicans and "our duty is as plain as the Ten Commandments. Kindness, beneficence, assistance, aid, help, protection, all that is implied in good neighborhood, these we must give freely, bountifully, but their independence is as sacred to them as ours is to us."[6] The Senate, nonetheless, voted 32-9 to establish the commission (it issued a favorable report in early 1871). Many senators voted "aye" not because they supported annexation, but because the commission was a face-saving device for Grant and a rebuke to the carping Sumner. In March, 1871, the Republican caucus voted 26-21 to remove Sumner altogether from the Foreign Relations Committee. Sumner, ill and irascible, had been duly punished for his opposition. Yet he still savored his victory over the Dominican land grab scheme. Grant could only walk through Lafayette Park, shake his fist at Sumner's house, and snap: "That man who lives up there has abused me in a way which I never suffered from any other man living."[7]

Charles Sumner (1811–1874). Harvard graduate, lawyer, abolitionist, critic of the Mexican War, Senator from Massachusetts, and Chairman of the Foreign Relations Committee (1861-1871), the strong-willed Sumner blocked attempts to annex the Dominican Republic and harassed England over the *Alabama* claims. (National Portrait Gallery, Smithsonian Institution)

The foiled grab of Santo Domingo, coming so soon after the Civil War, suggests that the sectional conflict was but a brief interlude in the continuity of expansion. To be sure, most Americans in the late 1860s were not thinking about the Caribbean or other foreign-policy issues, preoccupied as they were with healing the wounds of war, reconstructing a fractured nation, and settling the trans-Mississippi west. And, although the soaring oratory of "Manifest Destiny" sounded again through the late nineteenth century, the United States lacked well-defined, sustained foreign "policies" and only haltingly promoted overseas expansion and empire. As the Dominican episode illustrates, domestic politics, personal whims and antagonisms, and tensions between the executive and legislative branches could intrude. Uncertainties and hesitancies abounded, too, because strong anti-imperialist sentiment warned that an overseas empire would undermine institutions at home, invite perpetual war, and violate honored principles like self-determination. Also, the United States simply lacked the power to work its will in some parts of the world. American diplomats, consuls, and naval officers were active on a global scale, but American power was confined largely to the Western Hemisphere and parts of the Pacific.

Still, the direction of American foreign policy after the Civil War quickly became unmistakable: Americans intended to exert their influence beyond the continental United States. The more concerted, less restrained, and less erratic foreign policy that emerged in the 1890s consummated an imperial trend evident intermittently but persistently since the 1860s. Before the Civil War, American expansion was both commercial and territorial. The commercial expansion was global and largely maritime; the territorial expansion was regional and limited to areas contiguous to the United States (see Chapters 3 and 4). After the Civil War, expansion became primarily economic. As Secretary of State James G. Blaine said, the United States was more interested in the "annexation of trade" than in the annexation of territory.[8] The United States did seek and take a few territories in the 1865–1895 period, of course. Unlike the pre–Civil War additions, these annexed territories were noncontiguous to the United States and they remained in a long-term colonial status.

Although most Americans applauded economic expansion, many were uneasy with overseas imperialism—the imposition of control over other peoples, denying them the freedom to make their own choices, undermining their sovereignty. The critical factor in empire-building was power—the power to make others move the way the imperial state dictated. Imperialism took several forms, both formal (annexation, colonialism, or military occupation) and informal (the threat of intervention or economic or political manipulation). For example, the American economic domination of a country through trade and investment constituted informal imperialism, even though the United States did not officially annex the territory and make it a colony. Santo Domingo, to cite a case, was never formally taken by the United States, but by the early twentieth century, after years of private American economic expansion into the island, it had become subservient to the United States and hence part of the informal American empire. There was a significant difference between imperialism and expansionism. The latter referred only to the outward movement of goods, dollars, ships, people, and ideas. In the period after the Civil War, the United States was demonstrably expansionist. In some instances, this expansion became imperialism.

The expansionist impulse was fueled by a reinvigorated nationalism. After the Civil War, national leaders sought to narrow sectional divisions. The 1876 centennial celebration emphasized national unity. Confederate and Union soldiers met on former battlefields to exchange flags. New patriotic associations emerged to champion nationalism: Colonial Dames of America (1890), Daughters of the American Revolution (1890), and Society of Colonial Wars (1893). In the international rivalry for influence, Americans bragged about their exceptionalism. They were a special people, even God-favored, who had attained impressive material success and as an industrial power would soon surpass Great Britain and Germany. Americans also spoke about their mission to direct others. Nurturing a vague sense of Anglo-Saxonism—a racial view that Anglo-Saxons, meaning the main stock of Americans, were a breed specially equipped to judge, reform, and lead inferiors—they talked about regenerating the world. The prevalence of Social Darwinist thought—that by the natural order of things some people were meant to survive and others to fail—encouraged notions of national superiority. Nationalism also harbored a religious component. "Don't stay in this country theorizing, when a hundred thousand heathen a day are dying without hope because we are not there teaching the Gospel to them," boomed the traveling secretary of the Student Volunteer Movement, founded by college students in the late 1880s.[9] Said the Reverend Josiah Strong, author of the influential book *Our Country* (1885), "As America goes, so goes the world."[10]

The nationalistic argument for expansion and empire seemed all the more urgent when Americans anticipated the closing of the frontier at home. In 1893 Professor Frederick Jackson Turner postulated his thesis that an ever-expanding continental frontier had shaped the American character. Now that "frontier has gone, and with its going has closed the first period of American history." Turner

"The Stride of a Century." This Currier & Ives print captured the centennial spirit of 1876, which generated American nationalism and a celebration of the "progress" of the United States. (Library of Congress)

did not explicitly say that a new frontier had to be found overseas, but he doubted that "the expansive character of American life has now entirely ceased. Movement has been its dominant fact, and, unless this training has no effect upon a people, the American energy will continually demand a wider field for its exercise."[11]

The imperialism of the European powers and Japan also stimulated American nationalism and aroused the American competitive instinct. The imperialists began to carve up Asia and Africa into colonies and exclusive spheres of influence, and Americans feared being shut out. When Europeans threatened to capture parts of the Pacific and Latin America where Americans had already driven in some stakes, the United States reacted with flexed muscles and warned away the intruders.

ECONOMIC EXPANSION AND FOREIGN POLICY

When nationalistic Americans boasted about their country, they especially celebrated its economic success. After the Civil War the United States enjoyed unprecedented economic growth. Railroads knit the nation together, creating a coast-to-coast marketplace. Bold entrepreneurs like John D. Rockefeller and Andrew Carnegie built huge corporations whose assets and incomes dwarfed those of many of the world's nations. In the process of industrialization, inventors like Thomas Edison and George Westinghouse pioneered whole new enterprises—in their case, electricity. The advent and spread of the telegraph and telephone linked Americans together in a national communications network. Sprawling, busy cities became the centers of rapidly expanding manufacturing production. The federal government, through subsidies, land grants, loans, tariffs, and tax relief, stimulated the growth of American business. Not all went well, of course. Economic instability (major depressions in 1873–1878 and 1893–1897), the finan-

United States Trade Expansion, 1865–1914

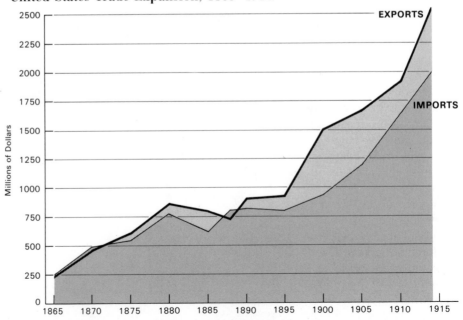

cial insolvency of railroads, farm indebtedness, inhumane working conditions, child labor, political corruption, business abuses necessitating antitrust and regulatory measures, discriminatory wages favoring men over women in the same jobs, and the failure of consumption to keep pace with production in the age of the "robber barons" tarnished the American record. Still, the United States by 1900 had become an economic giant rivaling Great Britain and Germany. Steel production increased from 77,000 tons in 1870 to 11,227,000 tons in 1900; wheat and corn output more than doubled in the same period. From the early 1870s to 1900 the gross national product more than doubled. Proud Americans preferred to emphasize this impressive data and to hide the embarrassing blemishes.

Foreign trade constituted an important part of the nation's economic growth. American exports expanded from $234 million in 1865 to $1.5 billion in 1900. Most American goods went to Europe, Britain, and Canada, but a slight shift toward Latin America and Asia took place through the late nineteenth century. Although exports of manufactured items increased, becoming predominant for the first time in 1913, agricultural goods (cereals, cotton, meat, and dairy products) accounted for about three-quarters of the total in 1870 and about two-thirds in 1900. From 1874 until 1934, with the one exception of 1888, the United States enjoyed a favorable balance of trade (exports exceeded imports).

Growing American productive efficiency, a decline in prices that made American goods less expensive in the world market, the high quality of American products, and improvements in transportation (steamships and the Suez Canal) help explain this impressive upturn in foreign trade. Improvements in communications also facilitated economic expansion. In 1866, through the persevering efforts of Cyrus Field, an underwater transatlantic cable linked European and American telegraph networks. James A. Scrymser, backed by J. P. Morgan's capital, connected the United States telegraph system with Latin America. He first wired Florida to Havana, Cuba, and then, in 1881, Galveston, Texas, to Mexico City. By 1883 Americans could communicate directly with Brazil; in 1890 Scrymser's lines reached Chile. By hooking into British cables, Americans could "talk" with Asian cities as well. Whereas the transfer of information had once taken days and weeks, it could now flow around the world more cheaply and securely in hours. Businessmen, diplomats, naval officers, and journalists worked the new communications system to seize opportunities. Technology was shrinking the globe.

Although exports represented a very small percentage (between 6 and 7 percent) of the gross national product, and although the great majority of American businessmen concentrated on the domestic market, American prosperity and key segments of the economy came to rely on foreign sales. It became popular to think that surplus production or the "glut" had to be exported to avert economic calamity at home. "We have advanced in manufactures, as in agriculture," Secretary of State William M. Evarts remarked in 1880, "until we are being forced outward by the irresistible pressure of our internal development."[12] America had to open new foreign markets, the economist David A. Wells warned, or "we are certain to be smothered in our own grease."[13]

Farmers were especially alert to the glut thesis, for the American marketplace could not absorb their bounty. Producers of cotton, tobacco, and wheat counted on foreign markets. Over half of the cotton crop was exported each year, and wheat growers in the period 1873–1882 received about a third of their gross annual income from exports. Wisconsin cheesemakers shipped to Britain; the Swift and Armour meat companies sold refrigerated beef in Europe; and "Quaker" oats became an international food. To sell American grain in Asia, James J. Hill of the Great Northern Railroad distributed cookbooks translated into several languages.

American business leaders like Hill looked to foreign markets for profits. Rockefeller's Standard Oil sold abroad, notably in Germany, England, Cuba, and Mexico. By the 1890s about half of all American petroleum was exported. By the mid-1880s one-third of the New York Life Insurance Company's business lay outside the United States and Canada. Cyrus McCormick of International Harvester sent his "reaper kings" into Russian fields, and by the turn of the century his company's foreign sales accounted for about 20 percent of its business. Metal-products firms like National Cash Register and Remington were active globally. Alexander Graham Bell and Thomas Edison collaborated in 1880 to install England's first telephone system. By the turn of the century, 50 percent of America's copper and 15 percent of its iron and steel were sold abroad, making many workers in those industries dependent upon exports. Singer's sewing machines seemed to be everywhere, from Scandinavia to Russia to Latin America. In 1879 Singer sold more machines overseas than at home. In the 1890s Singer ran more than forty large retail stores in Russia alone, and it dominated world markets. Some Europeans warned against an American "commercial invasion."[14]

Official Washington subsidized American exhibitions in foreign trade fairs and assisted business in other ways to expand abroad. Consular-service officers prepared reports on commercial prospects, and naval officers scouted markets and protected merchants. The government provided help in expanding the telegraph, negotiated reciprocity treaties to open trade doors, and kept up the drumbeat of patriotic rhetoric about the wonders of the export market. But the government's record was mixed. Until the 1890s economic expansion derived primarily from the activities of private companies and individuals, not from governmental policies. Washington neglected the merchant marine, letting it decline to a point where, by the turn of the century, only about 10 percent of American trade was carried by American ships. And Congress was slow to improve the American Navy (see pp. 161–163). The diplomatic corps and consular service were bespotted by the spoils system; too many political hacks rather than professionals filled their ranks. Washington also maintained a high-tariff policy, with rates reaching a peak in the 1890 McKinley Tariff (average duties of 49 percent). This exclusionist policy may

Singer Sewing Machine Advertisement. Selling "all over the world," the Singer Company, like many other large American businesses, enjoyed major foreign sales. In 1890 Singer accounted for three-quarters of all sewing machines sold in the world. (Courtesy of the New-York Historical Society, New York City)

have slowed the pace of economic expansion by stimulating foreign retaliatory tariffs against American products.

How significant were foreign commerce and investments (American capital invested abroad equalled $700 million in 1897) to the American economy? The statistics presented above tell only part of the story. The rest lies in perception—what prominent Americans *believed*. They believed that the economic health of the nation depended upon selling their surplus production in foreign markets. During depressions especially, goods stacked up at home could be peddled abroad, thus stimulating the American economy and perhaps even heading off the social and political unrest that feeds on economic crisis. How, then, did foreign trade and this belief in its necessity and significance affect American foreign policy? Hypothetically, even if only 1 percent of American goods was marketed abroad and exports represented only 1 percent of the gross national product, foreign trade would be inescapably intertwined with foreign policy and thus a factor of importance. Anticipating conflicts and wars, the Navy's Policy Board in 1890 concluded: "In the adjustment of our trade with a neighbor we are certain to reach out and obstruct the interest of foreign nations."[15] And even if all the efforts to expand trade delivered minimal results, the quest itself would necessitate naval and diplomatic activity.

Put another way: Why did American leaders believe foreign trade was important? First, exports meant profits. That was the pocketbook issue. Second, exports might relieve social unrest at home caused by overproduction and unemployment. Third, economic ties could lead to political influence (as in Hawaii and Mexico) without the formal necessity of military occupation and management. Fourth, foreign trade, hand-in-hand with religious missionary work, could promote "civilization" and human uplift. Fifth, economic expansion helped spread the American way of life, creating a world more hospitable to Americans. Sixth and last—to return to the theme of nationalism—foreign trade, if it conquered new markets abroad and helped bring prosperity to the United States, enhanced national pride at a time of international rivalry. Foreign trade, then, held an importance beyond statistics. It became an intricate part of American "greatness"; leaders believed it important to the national interest.

TOWARD COMMAND OF THE SEAS: NAVAL EXPANSION

In the late nineteenth century a popular doctrine gradually fixed itself in American thinking: to protect the nation's expanding overseas commerce, deemed vital to America's well-being, a larger navy had to be built. The Navy, explained Commodore Robert W. Shufeldt in popular language, was "the pioneer of commerce."[16] To fuel and repair ships in distant waters, naval stations and colonies had to be acquired. To ensure that foreigners did not endanger American merchants, property, investments, and trade, American warships had to be on patrol, ready to use force to protect United States interests and prestige in an era of intense international rivalry. "In the pursuit of new channels the trader," Shufeldt told a congressman, "needs the constant protection of the flag and the gun. He deals with barbarous tribes—men who appreciate only the argument of physical force. . . . The man-of-war precedes the merchantman and impresses rude people."[17] The commodore's graphic definition of "showing the flag" carried historical resonance. Since the end of the War of 1812, the United States had been stationing warships in Latin America, Africa, and Asia to protect the American merchant marine and merchants. New to the 1880s and 1890s was the shrinking theater of free operations, as European imperialists hastened to seize colonies and close out other foreigners. For the United States Navy, then, the next enemy might be an imperial European navy rather than a truculent "mob" in an Asian port. The need for new strategies and technologies became obvious.

The United States moved decisively, if slowly, to improve its navy as an instrument and protector of expansion abroad. The American Navy hesitantly evolved from sail-driven and wooden-hulled ships to steam-powered and steel-clad vessels in the thirty years following the Civil War. Its mission ultimately shifted from coastal defense to the command of the seas. By European standards, the entire American military before the 1890s was small. The Army demobilized after the Civil War, then killed or tamed Indians on the frontier under a strategy of "annihilation," and shrunk to below 30,000 troops.[18] The Navy concentrated on defending the long American coastline and protecting American life and property abroad. For these tasks, the American military seemed adequate at the time. The nation was, after all, basically secure. The European powers, feuding in the Old World, did not threaten America. Even the most bellicose European militarist would have been deterred by the difficulties of transporting an expeditionary force across the Atlantic and then supplying it in the United States, whose tremendous size and fiercely independent population could swallow alien armies. General Philip H. Sheridan, noting that it would take a foreign army of 1.5 million men to conquer the United States, assured Americans that they should not "be much alarmed about the probability of wars with foreign powers" on American soil.[19] The Navy, however diminutive in European eyes, could punish the unarmed peoples of what is now called the Third World, and it was substantial enough to chase pirates, protect missionaries and traders, and chart unexplored regions. Until the United States could acquire faraway fueling stations for taking on coal, having a fleet of long-range, steam-driven vessels did not make much sense.

In the 1880s and 1890s, as American expansionism and imperialism accelerated, and overseas commitments increased, a bigger, modern navy became imperative. Young naval officers—"armed progressives"—joined politicians, shipbuilders, armaments manufacturers, and commercial expansionists to lobby for an expanded fleet.[20] Naval leaders made it known that the navy was not keeping pace with European technological advances in hulls, engines, and guns and that the government-operated shipyards, dominated by the political spoils system, were corrupt and inefficient. They buttonholed members of Congress about the need for higher appropriations to launch significant naval improvements. As the Europeans built fast, heavily armed, well-armored battleships, America's slower, wooden cruisers and gunboats became laughably obsolete—mere floating museums, snickered European officers. Proud nationalists who shouted claims of American supremacy for almost everything else could not tolerate their nation's comparatively low naval ranking. They demanded better.

Rear Admiral Stephen B. Luce, father of the modern American Navy, became an effective naval politician. He founded the Naval War College in 1884, instilled greater professionalism, and encouraged officers like Captain Alfred T. Mahan to disseminate their ideas. Essentially summarizing the thinking of others, Mahan earned an international reputation for popularizing the relationship between a

Alfred Thayer Mahan (1840–1914). Graduate of the United States Naval Academy, this bookish officer, historian, and respected naval politician articulated the necessity for overseas expansion and a large Navy. He became world famous for his writings. Oxford and Cambridge Universities gave him honorary degrees, and German and Japanese leaders read his many statements. *(American Review of Reviews,* 1894)

navy and expansion. An instructor at the Naval War College, Mahan published his lectures in 1890 as *The Influence of Sea Power upon History*. British, German, and Japanese leaders read the book, but, most important, it became a treasured volume in the libraries of American imperialists like Henry Cabot Lodge and Theodore Roosevelt. Mahan's thesis was direct: a nation's greatness depended upon its sea power. Victory in war and a vigorous foreign trade, two measurements of greatness, depended upon an efficient and strong navy. Ships of war, in turn, required fueling stations or "resting places" and colonies, which would further enhance foreign commerce and national power.[21] The loop was closed: great navies required colonies; colonies begat great navies. The United States could not stand aside from the international race for greatness.

The American naval revival began in earnest during the 1880s. In 1883 Congress funded the *Atlanta, Boston,* and *Chicago*—steel-hulled, steam-powered cruisers. Between 1884 and 1889, money was appropriated for thirty more vessels, including the battleship *Maine.* Secretary of the Navy Benjamin F. Tracy (1889–1893) wanted seagoing battleships for this "New Navy"—soon the *Oregon, Indiana, Massachusetts,* and *Iowa* joined the fleet bearing the names of states to rally public support for naval expansion. In the process the government, military, and industry forged a partnership that would grow through the twentieth century. By 1893 the Navy ranked seventh in the world. Anti-imperialists presciently warned that this larger navy would propel Americans into a larger empire. "New Navy" ships in fact figured in the imperialist ventures of the 1890s: the *Boston* and its crew helped attach Hawaii to the United States; the *Maine*'s destruction in the harbor of Havana helped move the United States toward war with Spain; the 14,000-mile race of the battleship *Oregon* from the Pacific Coast to Cuba in 1898 fired desire for a canal across Central America; and the cruiser *Olympia* carried Commodore George Dewey into Manila Bay to help seize the Philippines from Spain. Secretary Tracy predicted, "The sea will be the future seat of empire. And we shall rule it as certainly as the sun doth rise."[22]

SECRETARY WILLIAM H. SEWARD EYES THE FUTURE

Secretary of State William Henry Seward (1861–1869) provided a connection between prewar and postwar expansionist thinking and behavior. During the Civil War he had to worry about keeping the European powers out of the internecine crisis (see Chapter 4). But after the war, this vain, confident, and intelligent Republican leader enthusiastically redirected United States foreign policy toward his vision of an American empire. As historian Walter LaFeber has noted, "In the unfolding drama of the new empire William Henry Seward appears as the prince of the players."[23] The secretary foresaw a coordinated empire tied together by superior American institutions and commerce. Latin America, the Pacific islands, Asia, and Canada, Seward prophesied, would eventually gravitate toward the United States because of the contagion of American greatness and because of some immeasurable will of God. Wars of conquest were unnecessary; commerce would bind the distant areas together. Seward once speculated that Mexico would be an appropriate location for the new imperial capital. He indicated the means for acquiring this empire: improved foreign trade, immigration to provide cheap labor for productive American factories, high tariff for the protection of American industry, liberal federal land policies to open the American West to

Makers of American Foreign Policy from 1865 to 1895

Presidents	Secretaries of State
Andrew Johnson, 1865-1869	William H. Seward, 1861-1869
Ulysses S. Grant, 1869-1877	Elihu B. Washburne, 1869
	Hamilton Fish, 1869-1877
Rutherford B. Hayes, 1877-1881	William M. Evarts, 1877-1881
James A. Garfield, 1881	James G. Blaine, 1881
Chester A. Arthur, 1881-1885	Frederick T. Freylinghuysen, 1881-1885
Grover Cleveland, 1885-1889	Thomas F. Bayard, 1885-1889
Benjamin Harrison, 1889-1893	James G. Blaine, 1889-1892
	John W. Foster, 1892-1893
Grover Cleveland, 1893-1897	Walter Q. Gresham, 1893-1895
	Richard Olney, 1895-1897

economic development, globe-circling telegraph systems, transcontinental rail-roads, a Central American canal, and, of course, the annexation of noncontiguous territories.

In 1865 the ambitious secretary began negotiations with Denmark to purchase the Danish West Indies (Virgin Islands), whose excellent harbors were potential naval stations for the protection of American trade. Two years later the islanders voted for American annexation. Seward raised his offer to $7.5 million for two of the islands, St. Thomas and St. John, but a combination of bad weather and heated politics undercut the treaty Seward signed with Copenhagen in October, 1867. When a hurricane and tidal wave wracked St. Thomas, critics poked fun at Seward's request for "footholds." The treaty also suffered the misfortune of being introduced at the time that President Andrew Johnson faced impeachment, and Seward himself lost credit with the Senate by supporting Johnson's unpopular Reconstruction policies. Incoming President Grant shelved the treaty, and the Virgin Islanders had to wait until 1917 for American overlordship.

Seward also wanted a piece of Santo Domingo. In 1866 he offered two million dollars for Samaná Bay, but the proposed deal remained open when he left office. Seward's vision encompassed Haiti (which he thought of annexing outright), some small Spanish, French, and Swedish islands in the Caribbean, revolution-torn Cuba, Iceland and Greenland (both of which he hoped to buy), Honduras' Tigre Island, and Hawaii, fast becoming Americanized as more sugar was planted and more churches were built. Seward's imperialist ambitions went unfulfilled in his day, but the secretary did achieve two real estate transactions. One acquisition was minor. The Midway Islands, some one thousand miles from Hawaii, were seized in August, 1867, by an American naval officer. Most Americans never heard again about these tiny imperial outposts until the great American-Japanese naval battle there in 1942.

More significant, attractive, and controversial was Seward's purchase of Alaska. Russia had put Alaska up for sale because it was proving unprofitable as colonial property, and because the Tsar feared that Britain would seize the unde-fended territory if the British and Russians tangled in a future war. Then, too, Russia seemed resigned to the inevitable. "The ultimate rule of the United States over the whole of America is so natural," the governor of Eastern Siberia told the

Tsar, "that we must ourselves sooner or later recede."[24] Edouard de Stoeckl, the Russian Minister to the United States who negotiated the transfer, later agreed: "In American eyes this continent is their patrimony. Their destiny (manifest destiny as they call it) is to always expand."[25] American fur traders, whalers, and fishermen had been exploiting the area's natural resources for decades. Why not cultivate a "friend," concede the inevitable, and sell the 591,000 square miles (twice the size of Texas) to the United States? Seward alertly followed up well-placed Russian hints and quietly began negotiations in Washington. The Cabinet and President remained largely ignorant of the talks, until they and the Congress were presented with a hastily drawn treaty and a bill for $7.2 million—not an inconsequential sum in March, 1867. One Treasury official estimated that the United States actually paid $43.4 million: $7.2 million in principal, $12.5 million in Army and Navy expenses, and $23.7 million in lost interest on the principal had the money remained in the Treasury for twenty-five years. It was, nevertheless, a substantial bargain.

Contemporary critics howled, anyway, especially because Seward had ignored Congress. Although some quipped about "Johnson's Polar Bear Garden," Seward astutely won over Charles Sumner, who began to applaud Alaska's commercial potential and natural resources. Sumner's influence, a vigorous propaganda program, in which Seward compared Alaska to the Louisiana Purchase, the Russian minister's hiring of lobbyists and bribing of some congressmen, and the exhilaration over expanding American boundaries—all combined to carry the treaty through the Senate only ten days after it was signed. The House stalled, delaying fifteen months before voting the funds, but by then Seward had already ordered the Stars and Stripes raised over his imperial catch.

Seward acquired fewer territories than he desired, largely because of domestic obstacles. He was a Republican supporter of Democratic President Johnson and evinced little sympathy for the plight of freedmen in the South. Displaying their disapproval, angry Radical Republicans called for Seward's ouster from the Cabinet and helped block his imperialistic schemes. Some people soured on expansion because of the corruption attending the annexation of Alaska. Reconstruction, railroad growth, an inflated economy, landless freedmen, a recalcitrant South—such issues compelled many Americans to look inward and to skimp on foreign adventures that cost money. A nation that had just freed its slaves after a bloody civil war was not about to acquire Cuba, in which slavery flourished. Seward could only lament "how sadly domestic disturbances of ours demoralize the National ambition."[26]

The secretary's ambition was blocked, too, because articulate anti-imperialists like Senator Justin Morrill (Vermont), the author Mark Twain, and the editor E. L. Godkin spoke out. They called for the development of America's existing lands and for an American showcase of domestic social, political, and economic improvements as the best way to persuade other people to adopt American institutions. Whereas some imperialists were racists who wanted to subjugate "inferior" people, some anti-imperialists made racist arguments against adding more non-whites to the American population. Godkin opposed the annexation of Santo Domingo, because that country harbored tens of thousands of Catholic, Spanish-speaking blacks who might seek United States citizenship. Other anti-imperialists insisted that colonialism violated the principle of self-government and increased the threat of foreign wars. Such men and ideas, joined to the partisan struggle

William H. Seward (1801-1872). Once freed from the restraints of the Civil War, Secretary of State Seward vigorously pursued an enlargement of the American empire. One scholar, Stephen Oates, has described Seward: he "resembled a jocular bird chewing on a Havana cigar. . . . A chain talker, he entertained guests at his house on Lafayette Square with a regular Niagara flood of chatter, gossip, and uninhibited profanity." (National Archives)

over Reconstruction, helped thwart Seward's efforts to create a larger empire. He was moving too fast for most Americans. When asked about the most important moment of his political career, Seward did not hesitate to say the purchase of Alaska—"but it will take the people a generation to find it out."[27]

NORTH AMERICAN RIVALS: GREAT BRITAIN, CANADA, AND THE UNITED STATES

Anglo-American and Canadian-American tensions, so evident before and during the Civil War, persisted in the 1865–1895 period. Union leaders remained irate over Britain's favoritism toward the South during the Civil War, especially the outfitting of Confederate vessels in British ports. At the end of the war, Seward filed damage claims against the British, even proposing at one point that Britain cede to the United States British Columbia or the Bahama Islands in lieu of a cash settlement. The secretary was also annoyed that British officials would not permit American soldiers to pursue the destitute Sioux Indians into Canadian territory. Canadians and Americans squabbled over the Fenian raids, tariffs, boundaries, fishing rights in the North Atlantic, and seal hunting. The neighbors to the north bristled upon hearing renewed and arrogant predictions that the United States would one day absorb Canada.

Although annexationist rhetoric echoed throughout the United States, only the hottest of heads urged American force to attach Canada to the Union. Pure Manifest Destiny doctrine, after all, prescribed patience until the inevitable "Americanization" of Canadians. And while Americans were busy settling their own West, there seemed no hurry. A military attack would no doubt have precipitated war with Great Britain, and even though "twisting the Lion's tail" became popular politics in the United States, few politicians wanted to invite British naval assaults upon the Gulf and East Coasts. Another reason for not "taking" Canada was the resistance of infant Canadian nationalism. Disputing William Seward, Canadians did not consider themselves a mere gap in the United States empire. Canadian nationalists like John A. Macdonald actually thought of themselves as British North Americans. They were put off by the political scandals, racial and ethnic prejudices, and flashy materialism of Gilded Age America. Macdonald became his nation's first Prime Minister when the Dominion of Canada came into being on July 1, 1867 as a confederation of provinces. The movement toward nationhood had received major stimulus from the annexationist rumblings in the United States, for the Dominion was Canada's way of resisting the American challenge.

In the late nineteenth century Anglo-Canadian-American relations moved from crisis to crisis. In 1866, armed forces of the Fenian Brotherhood, an Irish-American society of some 10,000 members organized to promote Irish independence from Britain, attacked Canada from Vermont. Seward wanted Canada, but not through such methods. He sent troops to the border to squelch further skirmishes, but both London and Ottawa believed he had acted too slowly.

Canada soon became entangled in another Anglo-American dispute: the question of the English-built Confederate ships (especially the *Alabama*) that had disrupted Union shipping during the Civil War. The irrepressible Charles Sumner added the naval damages to indirect damages that he derived by calculating that the Civil War was protracted for two years by British material help to and sympathy for the South; he totaled up a bill of $2.125 billion. One irate British diplomat shamelessly explained that Sumner "was fool enough some year or so ago to marry a young and pretty widow. She found that he was not gifted with 'full powers' and has left him. . . . He therefore makes up by vigour of tongue for his want of capacity in other organs.''[28] Some Americans thought the transfer of Canada to the United States would erase the debt. A Joint High Commission convened in Washington from February to May, 1871; it produced the Washington Treaty dated May 8. The British expressed regret for the actions of British-built Confederate raiders, and the signatories agreed to establish a tribunal to determine damages and claims. That commission finally issued its decision in December, 1872: Britain must pay the United States $15.5 million. "As the price of conciliating the United States, and protecting British naval interests," historian David P. Crook has written, "it was a bargain."[29]

The Washington Treaty attempted to settle two other Anglo-American disputes. Nestled between Vancouver Island (British Columbia) and territorial Washington in the Straits of Fuca were the San Juan Islands, claimed by both the United States and Britain on the basis of confusing geographical language in the Treaty of 1846. It was not much of an issue, except perhaps to the local inhabitants. The Treaty of Washington provided for arbitration by the German Emperor, who decreed in 1872 that the islands belonged to the United States.

Another long-standing dispute was more rancorous and more serious—the rights of American fishermen in North Atlantic waters. The Washington Treaty gave permission to Yankee fishermen to cast their nets in British North American waters and allowed Canadians to fish the coastal regions of the United States above 39 degrees north latitude. Macdonald grumbled that the British were conceding too much to the Americans. But the Prime Minister recognized Canadian weakness—the federation, he admitted, had not yet "hardened from gristle into bone."[30] When Macdonald reluctantly signed the Washington Treaty, he eyed Secretary of State Fish and snapped: "Here go the fisheries." Fish replied that "you get a good equivalent for them." "No," retorted the Canadian, "we give them away."[31] In 1877 a fisheries commission ruled that the United States should pay $5.5 million for the privilege of fishing in Canadian waters. The bill was paid, but in 1885, in protest against the award, the United States reactivated the fish war by unilaterally abrogating that part of the Washington Treaty dealing with fishing rights. The Canadians thereupon began seizing American vessels. New negotiations became testy. The Americans, fumed a prominent British diplomat, were "a bunch of dishonest tricksters."[32] An Anglo-American fisheries treaty of 1888 never passed the Senate and President Grover Cleveland threatened an economic embargo of Canada, but an interim agreement cooled tempers.

About the same time, British Minister Sir Lionel Sackville-West committed a sin of the first order for a diplomat—he became involved in American politics. When in 1888 a Republican pretending to be a former Englishman asked Sackville-West whether he should vote for the Republican candidate Benjamin Harrison or the Democrat Grover Cleveland, the careless diplomat recommended Cleveland as the politician more friendly to Britain. Gleeful Republicans printed and distributed copies of Sackville-West's indiscreet letter. Cleveland sent Sackville-West home just before the President lost his reelection bid. The Prime Minister, Lord Salisbury, revealed British pique by not dispatching a new minister until March of the next year.

Hardly quieted down after the Sackville-West incident and the fisheries dispute, Anglo-American rivalry turned toward the issue of seals in the Bering Sea near Alaska. "Amphibious is the fur seal, ubiquitous and carnivorous, uniparous, gregarious and withal polygamous," eminent historian Samuel Flagg Bemis has written.[33] Most of the seal herds lived in the Pribilof Islands near the Aleutians. American law forbade the killing of female or young seals and limited the slaughter of males. Yet foreign hunters slaughtered at will when the animals wandered on the high seas in search of food. In 1889 President Harrison warned Canadians against "pelagic" sealing (killing animals in ocean waters). When several Canadian sealing boats were seized in international waters, London and Ottawa protested. In mid-1890 the British sent four warships to the disputed region as Canadian sealers shot seals to death. American cutters made no arrests this time. In 1891 a temporary agreement halting pelagic sealing for a year was struck, and after another dispute the next year, London and Washington agreed to create an arbitral tribunal. In 1893 the arbiters handed Americans a defeat, for it permitted pelagic sealing within prescribed limits. The herd further declined in number. Not until 1911 did Russia, Japan, Britain, and the United States set strict regulations to protect the furry creatures.

CONTENDING WITH ASIA: CHINA, JAPAN, AND KOREA

With its vast territory, huge population, and tributary states, China attracted foreigners eager to sell, buy, invest, convert, and dominate. Although some Chinese leaders considered Americans less bullying than British gunboat diplomatists, the Chinese viewed all Westerners as barbarians. One diplomat regretted having to meet with his Western counterparts, for it was like "associating with dog and swine—a misfortune in a man's life."[34] And the more favorable image of Americans steadily diminished, because the United States demanded the same privileges China granted to other nations: open ports, low tariffs, and extraterritoriality (the exemption of foreigners from the legal jurisdiction of the country in which they resided). Before the 1890s the United States largely followed the British lead. Americans protested gunboat diplomacy—evident, for example, in 1860 when British and French forces occupied Beijing (Peking), but, practicing "hitchhiking" or "jackal" diplomacy, they seized opportunities created by the guns of other Westerners to expand trade and missionary work. Americans were not passive. The Asiatic squadron, for example, cruised the China seas to protect American lives and commerce.

In 1870, 50 American companies were operating in China, but that number dropped to 31 a decade later as some of the great merchant houses closed down. American exports to China slumped to $1 million in 1880; and although they rose to $3 million in 1890 and $15 million in 1900, trade with China claimed a miniscule part of American overseas commerce. Cotton goods and kerosene constituted the largest exports. "It is my dream," cried the governor of Georgia in 1878, to see "in every valley . . . a cotton factory to convert the raw material of the neighborhood into fabrics which shall warm the limbs of Japanese and Chinese."[35] Cheap, coarse cloth from United States mills soon undercut finer British textiles and came to dominate the Chinese market and to account for about half of the American industry's foreign sales. Kerosene also became big business in China; Standard Oil of New York advertised widely, and to improve sales, introduced small, inexpensive lamps. American investments in China remained modest, growing to less than $20 million by 1900.

Protestant missionaries, another American presence in China, steadily expanded their work, moving from treaty ports to the interior. They first visited China in the 1830s; by 1889 five hundred of them, mostly women, carried Christian teachings to "the heathen Chinee." By 1900 their number had grown to more than a thousand. They not only gained converts; they also helped promote American products simply by using them in front of curious Chinese. In some cases, religious missionaries and economic expansionists joined hands, as when Singer executives and missionaries championed the "civilizing medium" of the sewing machine.[36] "Fancy what would happen to the cotton trade if every Chinese wore a shirt!" remarked Charles Denby, who represented the State Department in China for 1885–1898. "Well, the missionaries are teaching them to wear shirts."[37] Before the mid-1890s, however, American commercial and missionary activities in China never matched such inflated rhetoric.

Between 1850 and 1900 about half a million Chinese, mostly males, emigrated to the United States. Many returned home after several years and most sent money home after first paying travel debts. They mined, built railroads, farmed, and laundered. By the mid-1870s about 150,000 Chinese resided in the United States, with the largest percentage in the San Francisco area. Wherever they settled, the Chinese formed close-knit communities, or "Chinatowns." Many joined secret societies and sought to preserve their cultural identity. Sinophobia on the West Coast wreaked hatreds and violence on the expatriate Chinese and spawned laws to exclude Asian immigrants. Americans in California called the Chinese "coolies" and spawned myths about filthy, rat-eating, opium-drunk "Mongolians" who threatened American culture by refusing to assimilate. Especially in times of economic bust in a frontier setting, Sinophobia flourished. White laborers complained that Chinese workers ate little and depressed wages. Anti-coolie clubs formed, and in the 1870s the Irish immigrant Dennis Kearney's Workingmen's Party became an instrument for Sinophobia. Anti-Chinese violence flared through the 1860s and 1870s; riots rocked Los Angeles in 1870 and San Francisco seven years later. Everyone came to know what "a Chinaman's chance" meant. In October of 1880, three thousand white men attacked the Chinese district of Denver, killing one resident, beating others, destroying property. Five years later

"Pacific Chivalry." How Californians handled the Chinese. (*Harper's Weekly*, 1869)

at Rock Springs, in the Wyoming Territory, white miners invaded Chinatown because Chinese laborers would not join them in a strike. The Chinese miners fled, but many were shot; others burned to death in fires set to raze the Chinese community. When it was over, 28 mutilated Chinese bodies lay in the debris. The Chinese minister to the United States protested the massacre, calling the local judicial proceedings, in which none of the rioters was punished, a "burlesque."[38] Congress eventually paid an indemnity of $148,000 to Chinese who had lost property.

As riots continued in other Western cities and towns, Washington strongly lectured the Western states against violence but informed Chinese diplomats that the federal government had no legal jurisdiction. At the same time, American officials petitioned Beijing to protect Americans in China against multiplying anti-foreign acts. As symbols of outside assaults upon China's integrity, missionaries received the brunt of nativist hostility and violence. By undermining the authority of local elites and by seeking Christian converts who necessarily fractured the local society, missionaries became subversive "foreign devils" around whom circled myths about exotic sexual and medical practices. An increasing number of antimissionary riots erupted in the 1880s and 1890s, prompting religious elders to appeal for official American protection.

Washington and Beijing became preoccupied with threats to one another's nationals and Chinese immigration to the United States. Anson Burlingame, American minister to China (1861–1867), went to work for the Chinese government after his retirement with an assignment to reduce Western intrusions. With Secretary Seward he negotiated the 1868 Burlingame Treaty, providing for free immigration between the two nations and the stationing of Chinese consuls in the United States (to look after Chinese subjects). Seward welcomed the pact as a step toward improved trade. But Sinophobia undercut the treaty. Politicians from the West lobbied hard for laws to restrict Chinese immigration. In 1879, Congress legislated that only fifteen Chinese could arrive on any one ship in the United States. President Rutherford B. Hayes vetoed the measure as a violation of the Burlingame Treaty. A new immigration treaty negotiated with China in 1880 permitted the United States to suspend, but not prohibit, Chinese immigration. Two years later Congress suspended Chinese immigration for ten years and denied Chinese immigrants American citizenship. These provisions would be renewed again and again. The Chinese population in the United States decreased after the early 1880s, but it always remained a target of Sinophobia. China found it impossible to protect its people in the United States or to challenge American immigration policy.

The Sino-Japanese War of 1894–1895 revealed the fragility of Chinese-American relations. Japan coveted Korea, an isolated nation nominally under China's control. Although Washington advised Japan to avoid war and offered good offices to mediate the dispute, American diplomats did little else. They settled into a policy of neutrality as Japanese forces crushed Chinese resistance. Americans, including the missionaries, seemed to favor a Japanese triumph to force China into the modern age. Victorious Japan soon dominated Korea, and China lay humiliated, all the more vulnerable to Western and Japanese imperialists. In the late 1890s, to protect their interests in China, Americans turned to the Open Door policy (see Chapter 6).

By that time Japan was quite a different nation from the one Commodore Matthew C. Perry had "opened" in the 1850s (see Chapter 4). In 1863–1864, despite the Civil War, the United States Navy deployed one dilapidated warship along-side British, French, and Dutch vessels to punish the Japanese for their antifor-eign riots and harassment of merchant ships. At Shimonoseki this firepower de-stroyed forts and boats, opening the strait to trade once again. Internally divided and militarily weak, the Japanese could not resist the $3,000,000 indemnity forced on them by the Western powers. (The United States received $780,000 of the amount but returned it to Japan in 1883.) Then, in the Convention of 1866, Japan reluctantly bestowed commercial favors on the Western nations in the form of low tariffs. By the late 1890s, America's trade with Japan surpassed its trade with China but still constituted only about 2 percent of total United States foreign commerce. Soon the Japanese consciously adopted a policy of "westernization," persuading some Americans that the Japanese, unlike the Chinese, were "civil-ized." Japan demonstrated its "progress" by thoroughly defeating the Chinese in the Sino-Japanese War of 1894–1895, thereby emerging as a major Asian power and a threat to American interests.

Korea became one of Japan's victims. This kingdom, called the "hermit nation" because of its self-imposed isolation, was technically a dependency of China—a tributary state that relied on Beijing to handle its external relations. But China's weakness denied Korea any protection from the predatory Japanese and Western-ers, including the French, who used gunboats in the 1860s to protest Korea's mistreatment of missionaries. Secretary Seward hoped to trade with the king-dom, but the fate of the merchant ship *General Sherman* revealed obstacles. In 1866, without Korean permission, the trading schooner pushed upriver. Its cap-tain became embroiled in a dispute with villagers, who burned the ship and killed all aboard. The following year, Commodore Robert Shufeldt investigated; he rec-ommended a punitive force to teach Korea the lesson "taught to other Eastern

Korea, 1871. Although the United States held negligi-ble interests in Korea, it sought to open the isolated kingdom to American com-merce. The Koreans at first resisted Western intrusions. When American warships entered their waters in 1871, the Koreans fired upon them. The American retaliation annihilated the defenders' forts and killed scores. (National Archives)

nations, that it can no longer maintain that contemptuous exclusiveness. . . .''[39] Not until 1871 did the United States retaliate. That year a mission, headed by the American minister to China and buttressed by five warships, sought not only to deal with the *General Sherman* incident but also to establish commercial relations and to guarantee the protection of shipwrecked Americans. When the fleet sailed up the Han River, its advance party was fired upon. After the Koreans refused to apologize, American guns bombarded their forts, killing at least 300 defenders. Still the Koreans refused to negotiate a treaty with the intruding Americans.

Japan battered Korea's gates open. In 1876 the Japanese coerced Korea into a treaty that recognized its independence from China. Four years later, near the end of a government-sponsored two-year expedition to Asia and Africa to scout trading opportunities, Commodore Shufeldt arrived in Korea aboard the U.S.S. *Ticonderoga*. An ardent commercial expansionist, the navy officer hoped to open Korea as Perry had opened Japan years before, but the Koreans rejected his over-tures. About this time, China began to encourage Western contacts with Korea in order to thwart the Japanese—"to play off the foreign enemies one against the other," reasoned China's chief diplomat.[40] In 1882 the dogged Shufeldt returned to Korea and negotiated a Korean-American treaty providing for American diplo-matic representation (a legation in Seoul) and trade relations. The Treaty of Che-mulpo passed the Senate the following year. Throughout the 1880s American businessmen built trade links; even Thomas Edison signed a contract for the in-stallation of electric lights in the royal residence. For the United States, however, Korea constituted a peripheral interest, and Washington could not prevent it from moving into Japan's orbit.

PACIFIC PRIZES: HAWAII AND SAMOA

Hawaii, that commercial and naval jewel in the Pacific, was linked in the Ameri-can mind to Asia. The Hawaiian (or Sandwich) Islands sat as convenient stations on the way to Asian markets. The undeveloped port of Pearl Harbor was an admiral's dream, and sugar had become big business. American missionaries ac-quired converts and property. The United States had repeatedly emphasized that, although it was not itself ready to annex the islands, no other power would be permitted to do so. In 1875, the United States virtually bound Hawaii to the American economy through a reciprocity treaty. Under this arrangement, Hawai-ian sugar could enter the United States duty free, provided Hawaii did not grant territory to another country. Secretary of State James G. Blaine was explicit in 1881 when he warned the British to stay out of Hawaii, which was "essentially a part of the American system of states, and a key to the North Pacific trade."[41] In 1887, Hawaii granted the United States naval rights to Pearl Harbor, prompting Britain to call futilely for Hawaiian neutrality and equal commercial accessibility for all nations. Nor did Japan, whose nationals made up about 40 percent of the islands' population, look kindly on American advances.

Reflecting the long-standing American interest in Hawaii, Secretary Blaine noted that "Hawaii may come up for decision at any unexpected hour, and I hope we shall be prepared to decide it in the affirmative."[42] Like the expansionists of the 1840s, Americans hurried the hour. At the start of the decade Congress changed tariff laws, removing the special privilege for Hawaiian sugar. Sugar shipments to the United States soon declined. Hawaiian producers screamed in economic pain and plotted revolution against the anti-American, despotic native government of Queen Liliuokalani. The revolutionaries were influential wealthy white planters, who comprised a distinct minority of the population, but they owned a major part of the islands' land. Most of the 3,000 Americans in Hawaii's population of approximately 100,000 sought annexation to the United States to remove tariffs on sugar exports to mainland markets.

On January 16, 1893, the businessmen-revolutionaries bloodlessly toppled the Queen from her throne and proclaimed a provisional government. The revolution could not have succeeded without the assistance of American Minister John L. Stevens and the men of the U.S.S. *Boston*. An active partisan for annexation, Stevens sent 164 armed bluejackets from the American cruiser into Honolulu. They did not bivouac near American property to protect it, the announced pretext for landing, but quickly deployed to within a few hundred yards of the monarch's palace. Sipping lemonade while at the same time ostentatiously brandishing Gatling guns and cannon, the troops by their very presence forced the Queen to give up. Minister Stevens recognized the provisional government, declared an American protectorate, and warned the State Department that the British might exploit this opportunity if the United States did not. The "Hawaiian pear is now fully ripe, and this is the golden hour for the United States to pluck it."[43] Native Hawaiians were never asked if they wished to be absorbed by the United States.

Although President Harrison had not authorized Stevens to intervene so directly, he accepted the result and in February signed a treaty of annexation with a "Hawaiian" commission (four Americans and one Englishman). Before the Senate could act, Grover Cleveland had replaced Harrison in the White House. A few days after taking office, Cleveland withdrew the treaty for reflection and ordered an investigator, former Congressman James H. Blount, to the islands. Blount's report confirmed that the revolution was carried out with Stevens' collusion and that the majority of Hawaiians had never been consulted about annexation. Although an expansionist, Cleveland opposed taking colonies. He also worried about some prickly questions. What would Southern Democrats think of incorporating a multiracial population in the Union? Could Hawaii, an overseas territory, ever become a state? What would happen if native Hawaiians revolted against their white rulers? Why stir up another heated issue when the United States was already beset at home by Chinese immigration, agricultural depression, and labor protests? Secretary of State Walter Q. Gresham, himself an expansionist willing to annex territories if legal processes were observed, said that he was "unalterably opposed to stealing territory, or of annexing a people against their consent, and the people of Hawaii do not favor annexation."[44] Cleveland killed the treaty. The white leaders in Hawaii thus had to wait for a more friendly President in Washington and for more propitious world events to persuade the United States to annex the islands (see Chapter 6).

Other imperialistic nations had cast longing eyes upon Hawaii, and international rivalry throughout the Pacific was keen. Germany, Britain, and the United States collided in Samoa, a group of fourteen volcanic islands lying 4,000 miles from San Francisco along the trade route between the United States and Australia. American whalers had long been stopping there, and in 1839 Charles Wilkes of the United States Navy had surveyed the islands as part of his exploring expedition in the Pacific. After the Civil War, nationals of the three great powers scrambled for privileges, urged their governments to annex Samoa, and exploited

**"Two Good Old
Friends."** In this German
cartoon, John Bull and
Uncle Sam try to balance
their Pacific interests in
Samoa and Hawaii while
the native inhabitants feel
the weight of imperialism.
(*Kladderadatsch* in *Review
of Reviews,* 1893)

the chaotic and often violent tribal politics that had earned Samoans some notoriety as the "Irishmen of the Pacific." At stake were coconut plantations, national
pride stimulated by the three-cornered rivalry, and the excellent ports of Apia and
Pago Pago. In 1872 a tribal chief granted the United States the right to build a
naval station at Pago Pago. This pact died because the Senate took no action on it
and Grant, timid after the defeat of his Dominican scheme, did not push it. In
1878 a new treaty was signed and ratified; it gave Americans privileges at Pago
Pago, and it provided for American good offices in disputes between Samoa and
outside nations, which were also collecting treaties of privilege.

In 1885–1886, after years of German intrigue, Secretary of State Thomas F. Bay-
ard launched a more active American diplomacy toward Samoa. He protested to
Berlin that "the United States had assumed the position of a benevolent protector,
and the German intervention would mean the virtual displacement of the United
States from that preferred status."[45] In 1887 Bayard convened a three-power
Washington Conference, but it could not reach agreement. When Germany
landed marines on Samoa, Washington dispatched a warship. The English and
Americans in Samoa refused to pay taxes to the German-dominated government.
German Chancellor Otto von Bismarck remarked that "we must show sharp
teeth."[46] Eager for a "bit of a spar with Germany," Theodore Roosevelt admitted
that the Germans might burn New York City.[47] But, he reasoned, the calamity

would persuade Americans to bolster coastal defenses. In early 1889 an aroused Congress authorized half a million dollars to protect Americans and their Samoan property and another $100,000 to build a naval station at Pago Pago. Whether boldness or bluff, this American action prodded Bismarck to seek a peaceful solution. Peace was also encouraged by a typhoon that devastated Samoa and wrecked most of the American, British, and German warships. After that disaster, nobody had the weapons in Samoa with which to fight a war. At the Berlin Conference of 1889, the three powers carved Samoa into a tripartite protectorate (the United States got Pago Pago) and forced an unpopular king on the Samoans. The writer Robert Louis Stevenson, a prominent resident of the islands, protested this violation of native sovereignty, this "Triple-Headed Ass."[48] Ten years later, in the aftermath of the Spanish-American-Cuban-Filipino War, the United States and Germany formally partitioned Samoa into colonies, with Britain compensated by other Pacific acquisitions.

PROBING THE "DARK CONTINENT": AMERICANS IN AFRICA

Before the Civil War, American ships and merchant traders, especially from Salem, Massachusetts, were conspicuous in Africa. But conflict disrupted old trading patterns, lower transportation costs made European goods less expensive, and discriminatory trade practices stymied Yankee competition. As a result, the American presence on the "Dark Continent" shrank in the late nineteenth century. American adventurers, explorers, mining engineers, and traders, and a few naval officers dispatched to identify prospects for foreign commerce kept some American interest in Africa alive. The Navy's West African squadron was also positioned to protect American lives and property. But official Washington took few steps to advance American interests in the vast land that the European imperial powers were rushing to conquer.

American tobacco, kerosene, and rum nevertheless continued to claim a good share of African markets. In Zanzibar, American cotton goods were preferred; in exchange, East African gum copal and ivory were shipped to New England factories. When, in the early 1880s, tribal warfare in Tanganyika interrupted the ivory trade, Connecticut plants had to shut down. In West Africa, where Americans had once been active in the slave trade and where many consular agents had long handled American commercial interests, British tariffs hurt American trade—for example, tobacco and rum on the Gold Coast and in Sierra Leone. Higher tariffs in French West Africa also diminished American commerce. By the end of the century, American trade with the continent had become inconsequential.

Such a decline might not have occurred had Washington heeded Commodore Shufeldt's recommendations. In 1879 the State and Navy Departments ordered him to sail the U.S.S. *Ticonderoga* to Africa and Asia for "the encouragement and extension of American commerce."[49] Shufeldt wrote detailed reports on economic opportunities, port facilities, and laws. He introduced American products to Africans and negotiated trade treaties. For American surplus goods, he advised, "Africa with its teeming population presents a tempting field. . . ."[50] He warned that the British and other imperialists were working to drive Americans from the continent. Washington officials read and listened, but seldom acted.

Americans nonetheless became fascinated with black Africa because individuals bent on adventure, fame, and wealth popularized it. Foremost among them was Henry V. Stanley, an immigrant from Wales who claimed he was a naturalized American. While working for the *New York Herald*, after stints in both the Confederate and Union armies, Stanley was directed by the newspaper's owner to depart for Africa and find Dr. David Livingston, the missionary-explorer who in 1866 had disappeared into central Africa while searching for the Nile's source. Stanley arrived in Zanzibar in 1871 and began to write dramatic stories about Africa. With an American flag at the head of his large expedition, he cut across Tanganyika and found Livingston, who appreciated Stanley's supplies and medicine but insisted on continuing his quest for the great river's headwaters. Three years later Stanley led another venture into the African interior; in his 999-day trek through the wilderness he battled hostile Africans and mapped the territory, making the Congo basin and himself internationally famous. Congress even voted him a resolution of thanks.

King Leopold II of Belgium saw in Stanley an instrument to bring his small nation a large empire. Unable to compete with the more powerful European imperialists, Leopold struck on the idea of forming an organization whose announced philanthropic purpose was ending the slave trade and protecting legitimate commerce, but whose real objective was obtaining an imperial foothold for Belgium in the Congo. The King hired Stanley, who negotiated with African leaders in the region to gain their allegiance to the international organization. Leopold also secured the services of Henry S. Sanford, a former American minister to Belgium who sought personal commercial gain from enlarged United States trade in the region. Working to thwart the encroaching Europeans, Sanford lobbied in Washington for American support of the principle of free trade in the Congo. In 1884 Sanford succeeded when the United States recognized the *Association Internationale du Congo* as sovereign over the area.

The United States then found itself in the midst of an international dispute, for other European nations claimed parts of the Congo. To head off a clash, the European rivals convened in Berlin in the fall of 1884. Washington sent two delegates, one of whom was Sanford; Stanley advised the American diplomats. The conferees signed an agreement that recognized the international association's (and hence Leopold's) authority over the Congo and ensured an open trade door. But the new President, Grover Cleveland, adhering to the tradition of avoiding entanglements with Europeans, withdrew the accord from the Senate. Still, the United States abided by its terms and in 1890 sent representatives to another Congo conference that elaborated upon the Berlin agreement. Thus American commercial interests, however small, were protected by American diplomacy for an open door in the Congo.

American Christian missionaries also entered Africa. By the end of the century the American Board of Commissioners for Foreign Missions had built schools, hospitals, and a seminary for training an African clergy. Its missionaries established stations in South Africa, Mozambique, and Angola, and translated the Bible into Zulu. Baptists sought converts in Nigeria and Lutherans opened missions in Madagascar. The African Methodist Episcopal Church, a major black church in the United States, was active in Liberia, Sierra Leone, and South Africa. In the 1890s, one of its bishops, the black nationalist Henry Turner, urged segregated and disenfranchised American blacks to emigrate to Africa. Hundreds did.

American prospectors and mining engineers flocked to the gold and diamond regions of South Africa. One of the fortune seekers, Jerome L. Babe, arrived in

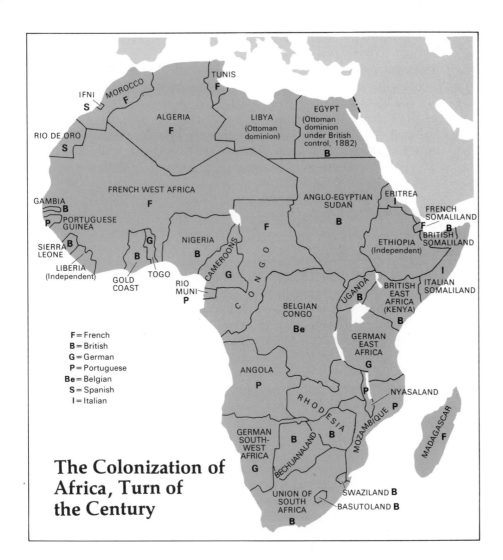

IFNI
MOROCCO
S
F
TUNIS
F
ALGERIA
F
LIBYA
(Ottoman
dominion)
EGYPT
(Ottoman
dominion
under British
control, 1882)
B
RIO DE ORO
S
FRENCH WEST AFRICA
F
ANGLO-EGYPTIAN
SUDAN
B
ERITREA
FRENCH
SOMALILAND
F B
GAMBIA
B
P PORTUGUESE
GUINEA
SIERRA B
LEONE
G
NIGERIA
B
CAMEROONS
G
C
O
N
G
O
ETHIOPIA
(Independent)
BRITISH
SOMALILAND
B
LIBERIA
(Independent)
GOLD
COAST
TOGO
RIO
MUNI
P
UGANDA
B
BRITISH
EAST
AFRICA
(KENYA)
B
ITALIAN
SOMALILAND
I
BELGIAN
CONGO
Be
GERMAN
EAST
AFRICA
G
F = French
B = British
G = German
P = Portuguese
Be = Belgian
S = Spanish
I = Italian
ANGOLA
P
RHODESIA
P
NYASALAND
MOZAMBIQUE P
MADAGASCAR
F

The Colonization of Africa, Turn of the Century

GERMAN
SOUTH-
WEST
AFRICA
G
BECHUANALAND
B
SWAZILAND B
UNION OF
SOUTH
AFRICA
B
BASUTOLAND B

1870 as a salesman for the Winchester Repeating Arms Company and reporter for the *New York World*. He stayed on to invent a screening apparatus for diamond mining and to buy and sell the precious stones. Hamilton Smith was a self-taught engineer from Kentucky; his reports on gold helped encourage large Rothschild investments. An unusual group of Americans, over twenty in number, became soldiers of fortune for Egypt before Britain occupied the country in 1882.

For Americans Liberia was the best-known African area. Settled in 1821 and governed by American blacks under the auspices of the American Colonization Society, Liberia was frequently bedeviled by internal strife and French and British nibblings at its territory. The United States, in 1875 and again in 1879, displayed its warships to help the Americo-Liberians quell rebellions by indigenous Africans. In the 1880s and 1890s British and French forces coerced Liberia into ceding land. Washington appealed for imperial restraint but refused to employ its meager power in the area to halt imperial ambitions. Perhaps America's patronage, however minimal, forestalled full-scale European domination of that African nation.

With the United States as an interested observer, whites carved up Africa—the British took Egypt, Sierra Leone, and the Gold Coast; the Germans feasted on East Africa and Southwest Africa; the French grabbed Tunis and West Africa; the Portuguese absorbed Angola and Mozambique; and the Belgians gained their Congo (see map). By 1895 most of Africa was partitioned. Washington worried, as always, that the colonial enclaves would be closed to American trade, and, as at the Berlin conference over a decade earlier, constantly reminded the European imperialists to keep the door open.

REGIONAL POWER: THE UNITED STATES IN LATIN AMERICA

During this period the United States was more active in Latin America than in any other part of the world. Americans challenged the French and British, established and expanded trade and investment links, intervened in inter-American disputes and revolutions, floated its warships in troubled waters to "show the flag," tried to annex territories, sought canal routes across Central America, lectured everybody about the supremacy of the Monroe Doctrine, and organized the Pan American movement. In 1881 *The Times* of London observed: "The United States are indisputably the chief power in the New World." Knowing something about imperialism, the newspaper predicted that the "time must arrive when the weaker States in their neighborhood will be absorbed by them."[51]

European competitors persisted in meddling in Latin American affairs, but when the French in 1861 intervened militarily in Mexico and placed the young Archduke Ferdinand Maximilian of Austria on a Mexican throne, the Civil War-wracked United States could do little more than protest. Seward was angry, of course. The intervention seemed to threaten American security and expansion and to hurl a blatant challenge at the Monroe Doctrine. Seward first sent arms to the forces of former Mexican President Benito Juárez. Once the Civil War subsided, President Andrew Johnson ordered 52,000 American soldiers to Texas. Under the command of General Philip Sheridan, the troops staged military maneuvers along the Mexican border to buttress Washington's diplomatic demands for a French exit. In early 1866 Seward firmly asked Napoleon III when the French military would be withdrawn. Facing opposition at home and Prussian competition in Europe, harassed by guerrillas in Mexico, and faced by a noisy, well-armed, and victorious United States, the Emperor decided to recall his troops. The hapless and abandoned "archdupe" Maximilian fell in 1867 before a Mexican firing squad. Americans believed, much too simply, that they had forced France out and that the Monroe Doctrine, although not mentioned by name in this crisis, had been reinvigorated.

Another, but different, challenge sprang from Cuba, long a part of America's expansionist vision. From 1868 to 1878 the Spanish-owned island, with its dreaded slavery, was bloodied by revolution. President Grant thought of recognizing the belligerency of the Cuban rebels, but Secretary Fish, wanting trade rather than war or territory in Latin America, dissuaded him. American hearts went out to the underdog Cubans as they and the Spanish mauled one another. The *Virginius* affair of 1873 ignited American protests. That Cuban-owned, gun-

Hamilton Fish (1808–1893). Graduate of Columbia University and lawyer, Fish served as a United States senator from New York (1851–1857) and opposed the expansion of slavery in the 1850s. More patient and tactful than President Grant, he recorded some achievements during his tenure as secretary of state (1869–1877): the Washington Treaty, nonintervention in the Cuban rebellion, and a reciprocity treaty with Hawaii. (*Harper's Weekly*, 1869)

running vessel was captured by the Spanish, who shot as "pirates" fifty-three of the passengers and crewmen, some of whom were United States citizens. As Americans shouted for revenge, the levelheaded Fish demanded and got an apology and indemnity from Madrid of $80,000. Cuba continued to bleed until 1878, when the rebellion ended and slavery was abolished. From then until 1895, when a new revolution erupted, Cubans suffered; and they schemed to push the Spanish out just as the Americans were coming in as investors and traders.

American economic interests were an important source of United States influence in Cuba and elsewhere in Latin America. American investments in and trade with Latin American countries were conspicuous: in Cuba (sugar and mines), Guatemala (the United States handled 64 percent of the country's trade by 1885), and Mexico (railroads and mines). In Mexico, according to the historian Karl M. Schmitt, the United States "reduced its neighbor virtually to an economic satellite. . . . By the mid-1880s its economic stake in Mexico surpassed both the French and the British, which had been dominant in the country."[52] By the early 1890s, the United States was buying 75 percent of Mexico's exports and supplying about 50 percent of its imports. The long and stable regime of the dictator Porfirio Diaz (1876–1910) invited this foreign economic penetration. By 1890, American citizens had invested some $250 million in Latin America. Still, the region took just 5 percent of total American exports that year. Most United States trade remained with Europe. Although these economic ties with Latin America comprised a small part of United States total world economic relationships, for countries like Cuba and Mexico such ties were vital; they therefore drew the United States into the internal affairs of these countries. American economic interests also drew the United States into a Brazilian civil war in 1893–1894, where Washington sent a naval fleet to break a blockade.

Central America attracted considerable American interest because of prospects for an isthmian canal linking the Pacific Ocean and the Gulf of Mexico, thereby greatly reducing commercial and naval travel time between the eastern seaboard and Asian markets. The gala opening of the Suez Canal in 1869 spurred American canal enthusiasts. Panama and Nicaragua were identified as possible sites. The problem was the Clayton-Bulwer Treaty (1850), which held that a Central American canal had to be jointly controlled by Britain and the United States. Washington resented this limitation on American expansion, and when President Rutherford Hayes learned in 1880 that Ferdinand de Lesseps, builder of the Suez Canal, would attempt to construct a canal through Panama, he sent two warships to demonstrate United States concern. "A canal under American control, or no canal," exclaimed Hayes.[53] In 1881 Secretary Blaine forcefully but futilely asked the British to abrogate the Clayton-Bulwer treaty, claiming that the United States "with respect to European states, will not consent to perpetuate any treaty that impeaches our right and long-established claim to priority on the American continent."[54] Three years later, in overt violation of the treaty, the United States signed a canal treaty with Nicaragua, although President Cleveland withdrew the offending pact when he took office. The movement led by naval officers, businessmen, and diplomats for an exclusive United States canal was nevertheless well under way. It was evident that someday it would be built; until that time other nations would be warned away. Meanwhile, Central American conditions would have to be stabilized, as in Panama in 1873 and 1885, when American troops went ashore to protect American property threatened by civil war. In the latter year an

American warship under the command of Alfred Thayer Mahan was ordered to display United States power to Guatemala, whose invasion of El Salvador threatened American-owned property, including James A. Scrymser's Central and South American Telegraph Company.

The convocation of the first Pan American Conference in Washington in 1889 bore further witness to the growing United States influence in Latin America. "Jingo Jim" Blaine, hoping to expand American trade and boost his presidential aspirations, had first recommended such a conference in 1881, but his departure in that year from the secretaryship of state left the question open until his return (1889–1892). The conference attracted representatives from seventeen countries. Six of the ten United States delegates were businessmen. After a grand tour of America's impressive industrial establishments in forty-one cities, the conferees assembled in Washington to hear Blaine's appeal for "enlightened and enlarged intercourse."[55] Unlike similar conferences in the twentieth century, the United States was not able to dictate the results of the conclave. Argentina stood as a tenacious opponent of hemispheric union; the Argentines suspected that Pan Americanism was a United States ruse to gain commercial domination. Blaine's ideas for a low-tariff zone and for compulsory arbitration of disputes were rejected, although the International Bureau of American Republics (later called the Pan American Union) was organized and reciprocity treaties to expand trade were encouraged. The conference also promoted inter-American steamship lines and railroads and established machinery to discuss commercial questions.

The Pan American Union amounted to little in its early days. Its most significant impact was on the Washington landscape, where, with major financial help from the steel baron Andrew Carnegie, the Pan American Union put up one of the most impressive buildings in the nation's capital. Pan Americanism did not mean hemispheric unity; rather it represented growing United States influence among neighbors to the south. For that reason European powers were disturbed by it.

Crises with Chile in 1891 and with Venezuela in 1895 (see Chapter 6) demonstrated United States determination to dominate the western hemisphere. Chilean-American relations steadily deteriorated, in part because the United States had clumsily attempted to end the War of the Pacific (1879–1883), in which Chile battled Bolivia and Peru to win nitrate-rich territory. Then, at the Pan American Conference, Chile had stood as a fearless critic of the United States. When civil war ripped through Chile in early 1891, the United States backed the sitting government, which had tried to assume dictatorial powers. The United States Navy seized arms purchased in the United States and destined for the rebels. When the victorious revolutionary Congressionalists took office, President Benjamin Harrison at first would not grant them recognition, muttering haughtily that "sometime it may be necessary to instruct them" on "how to use victory with dignity and moderation."[56] The United States had sided with the losers; anti-Yankeeism naturally festered in the winners. To make matters worse, Washington suspected that the British, ever the competitor in Latin America, were cementing close ties with the new Chilean regime.

An incident in October, 1891, after the end of the civil war, nearly exploded into a Chilean-American war. At Valparaiso, a major port for North American traders, one of the ships of the United States Pacific Squadron, the heavily armed *Baltimore*, anchored in the harbor. "She can whip any that can catch her and run away

James G. Blaine (1830–1893). Republican congressman and senator from Maine and secretary of state (1881, 1889–1892), Blaine's diplomatic record included the expansion and defense of United States interests in Latin America. (Library of Congress)

from any that can whip her," bragged Secretary of the Navy Tracy.[57] Commanded by Captain Winfield S. Schley, whose classmates at the Naval Academy included Mahan and George Dewey, the ship had been dispatched to protect American interests during the civil war. On October 16 its crew went ashore on liberty. The exuberant sailors gave local taverns and brothels considerable business. Outside the True Blue Saloon, rum-drunk Americans and anti-Yankee Chileans quarreled, fists flew, and knives slashed. Two Americans died, others were wounded, and some were arrested.

President Harrison, a former military man himself, reacted bitterly against this affront to the American uniform, especially when the Chilean government did not hurry to apologize. Captain Robley D. ("Fighting Bob") Evans of the *Yorktown*, also in Chilean waters, recorded: "I don't see how Mr. Harrison can help sending a fleet down here to teach these people manners."[58] The President fumed against "weaker powers" like Chile, but after American blustering and a change in the Chilean Cabinet in early 1892, the cautious South Americans expressed regret and paid an indemnity of $75,000 in gold.[59] The Chileans had been humbled by the North American giant, and Latin Americans had to wonder what Pan-Americanism really meant. Advocates of the expanding United States Navy cheered the "victory" over Chile, but as one critic put it: "We do not need a steam hammer to crack nuts."[60]

Senator George Shoup of Iowa drew a different lesson from the Chilean episode: "The American Republic will stand no more nonsense from any power, big or little."[61] Indeed, by the mid-1890s, the United States was far more self-confi-

STATE DEPARTMENT, WASHINGTON, D.C.

Punishment for Chile, 1891. An angry Uncle Sam is about to administer United States retribution to Chile after the exaggerated *Baltimore* affair. (*Harper's Weekly*, 1891)

dent and certainly cockier than it had been in 1865, and it was far more willing to exert the power it had built over the last few decades, especially in Latin America. The anti-imperialist sentiments that had spoiled earlier imperial ventures had weakened by the 1890s, undercut by chauvinistic nationalism, the seduction of international rivalry, the glut thesis, the depression of the 1890s, and the relentless United States expansion that had put Iowa farmers' cereals in England, missionaries in China, Singer sewing machines in the Caroline Islands, McCormick reapers in Russia, warships in Korea and Brazil, explorers in Africa, sugar growers in Hawaii and Cuba, mining companies in Mexico, and sailors in Chile—to mention only a few distant spots. Americans could only anticipate much more of the same in the future, even if it took war to complete the transformation of the United States from a regional to a global power.

FURTHER READING FOR THE PERIOD 1865–1895

General studies include Robert L. Beisner, *From the Old Diplomacy to the New* (1986); Charles S. Campbell, *The Transformation of American Foreign Relations, 1865–1900* (1976); Foster Rhea Dulles, *Prelude to World Power* (1968); James A. Field, Jr., "American Imperialism," *American Historical Review* (1978); John A. Garraty, *The New Commonwealth, 1877–1890* (1968); John A. S. Grenville and George B. Young, *Politics, Strategy, and American Diplomacy* (1967); Paul S. Holbo, "Economics, Emotion, and Expansion: An Emerging Foreign Policy," in H. Wayne Morgan, ed., *The Gilded Age* (1970); Walter LaFeber, *The New Empire* (1963); H. Wayne Morgan, *From Hayes to McKinley: National Party Politics, 1877–1896* (1969); Milton Plesur, *America's Outward Thrust* (1971); David M. Pletcher, *The Awkward Years: American Foreign Relations Under Garfield and Arthur* (1962); Emily S. Rosenberg, *Spreading the American Dream: American Economic and Cultural Expansion, 1890–1945* (1982); Robert Wiebe, *The Search for Order* (1967); and William A. Williams, *The Roots of the Modern American Empire* (1969).

Biographical studies include William M. Armstrong, *E. L. Godkin and American Foreign Policy* (1957); Michael Devine, *John W. Foster* (1980); David Donald, *Charles Sumner and the Rights of Man* (1970); Joseph A. Fry, *Henry S. Sanford* (1982); Allan Nevins, *Hamilton Fish* (1937); Ernest N. Paolino, *The Foundations of the American Empire* (1973) (Seward); Charles C. Tansill, *The Foreign Policy of Thomas F. Bayard, 1885–1897* (1940); Alice Felt Tyler, *The Foreign Policy of James G. Blaine* (1927); Glyndon C. Van Deusen, *William Henry Seward* (1967); and essays in Frank Merli and Theodore A. Wilson, eds., *Makers of American Diplomacy* (1974).

Economic foreign relations are treated in Beisner, Campbell, Holbo, LaFeber, and Williams above and in William H. Becker, *The Dynamics of Business-Government Relations: Industry and Exports, 1893–1921* (1982); Fred V. Carstensen, *American Enterprise in Foreign Markets* (1984); Robert B. Davies, *Peacefully Working to Conquer the World* (1976); David M. Pletcher, *Rails, Mines, and Progress: Seven American Promoters in Mexico, 1867–1911* (1958) and "Rhetoric and Results: A Pragmatic View of American Economic Expansionism, 1865–98," *Diplomatic History* (1981); Robert W. Rydell, *All the World's a Fair* (1985); Howard B. Schonberger, *Transportation to the Seaboard* (1971); Tom Terrill, *The Tariff, Politics, and American Foreign Policy, 1874–1901* (1973); and Mira Wilkins, *The Emergence of the Multinational Enterprise* (1970).

The American Navy is discussed in Benjamin F. Cooling, *Benjamin Franklin Tracy* (1973) and *Gray Steel and Blue Water Navy* (1979); Frederick C. Drake, *The Empire of the Seas* (1984) (Shufeldt); Kenneth J. Hagan, *American Gunboat Diplomacy and the Old Navy, 1877–1889* (1973) and "Alfred Thayer Mahan: Turning America Back to the Sea," in Merli and Wilson, eds., *Makers of American Diplomacy* (1974); Walter R. Herrick, *The American Naval Revolution*

(1966); Peter Karsten, *The Naval Aristocracy* (1972); Robert Seager, *Alfred Thayer Mahan* (1977); Harold and Margaret Sprout, *The Rise of American Naval Power, 1776–1918* (1966); and William N. Still, Jr., *American Sea Power in the Old World* (1980).

For relations with Great Britain and Canada, see Kenneth Bourne, *Britain and the Balance of Power in North America, 1815–1908* (1967); Robert C. Brown, *Canada's National Policy, 1883–1900* (1964); Charles S. Campbell, *From Revolution to Rapprochement: The United States and Great Britain, 1783–1900* (1974); Adrian Cook, *The Alabama Claims* (1975); Edward P. Crapol, *America for Americans: Economic Nationalism and Anglophobia in the Late Nineteenth Century* (1973); Brian Jenkins, *Fenians and Anglo-American Relations during Reconstruction* (1969); W. S. Neidhardt, *Fenianism in North America* (1975); Richard A. Preston, *The Defense of the Undefended Border* (1977); and Lester B. Shippee, *Canadian-American Relations, 1849–1874* (1939).

The interplay between the United States and Latin America is discussed in Richard H. Bradford, *The Virginius Affair* (1980); Jules Davids, *American Political and Economic Penetration of Mexico, 1877–1920* (1976); Joyce S. Goldberg, *The Baltimore Affair* (1986); Alfred J. Hanna and Kathryn A. Hanna, *Napoleon III and Mexico* (1971); Lester D. Langley, *Struggle for the American Mediterranean: United States-European Rivalry in the Gulf-Caribbean, 1776–1894* (1976); Dexter Perkins, *The Monroe Doctrine, 1867–1907* (1937); Frederick B. Pike, *Chile and the United States, 1880–1962* (1963); Karl M. Schmitt, *Mexico and the United States, 1821–1973* (1974); Thomas D. Schoonover, *Dollars over Dominion* (1978) (Mexico); Joseph Smith, *Illusions of Conflict: Anglo-American Diplomacy Toward Latin America, 1865–1896* (1979); Charles C. Tansill, *The United States and Santo Domingo, 1798–1873* (1938).

For Asian-American relations, see David L. Anderson, *Imperialism and Idealism* (1985); Gunther Barth, *Bitter Strength: A History of the Chinese in the United States, 1850–1870* (1964); Jerome Ch'en, *China and the West* (1979); Fred Harvey Harrington, *God, Mammon, and the Japanese: Horace N. Allen and Korean-American Relations, 1884–1905* (1944); Michael Hunt, *The Making of a Special Relationship* (1983) (China); Paul M. Kennedy, *The Samoan Tangle* (1974); Ralph S. Kuykendall, *The Hawaiian Kingdom, 1874–1893* (1953); Robert McClellan, *The Heathen Chinee: A Study of American Attitudes Toward China, 1890–1905* (1971); Stuart C. Miller, *The Unwelcome Immigrant* (1969) (Chinese); W. A. Russ, Jr., *The Hawaiian Revolution, 1893–94* (1959) and *The Hawaiian Republic, 1894–98* (1961); Merze Tate, *The United States and the Hawaiian Kingdom* (1965); Shih-shan Henry Tsai, *China and the Overseas Chinese in the United States, 1868–1911* (1983); and Marilyn Blatt Young, "American Expansion 1870–1900: The Far East," in Barton J. Bernstein, ed., *Toward a New Past* (1968).

Alaska and Russian-American relations are discussed in Paul S. Holbo, *Tarnished Expansion* (1983); Ronald J. Jensen, *The Alaska Purchase and Russian-American Relations* (1975); and Howard I. Kushner, *Conflict on the Northwest Coast* (1975).

United States interest in Africa can be followed in Edward W. Chester, *Clash of Titans* (1974); Clarence Clendenen, Robert Collins, and Peter Duignan, *Americans in Africa, 1865–1900* (1966); Sybil E. Crowe, *The Berlin West African Conference, 1884–1885* (1942); Edwin S. Redkey, *Black Exodus: Black Nationalist and Back-to-Africa Movements, 1890–1910* (1969); and Walter L. Williams, *Black Americans and the Evangelization of Africa, 1877–1900* (1982).

See also the General Bibliography and the following notes.

NOTES TO CHAPTER 5

1. Charles C. Tansill, *The United States and Santo Domingo, 1798–1873* (Baltimore: The Johns Hopkins Press, 1938), p. 134.

2. Quoted in David Donald, *Charles Sumner and the Rights of Man* (New York: Alfred A. Knopf, 1970), p. 443.

3. Rollo Ogden, ed., *Life and Letters of Edwin Lawrence Godkin* (New York: The Macmillan Company, 1907; 2 vols.), I, pp. 304–305.

4. Charles Francis Adams, *Before and After the Treaty of Washing-*

ton (New York: New York Historical Society, 1902), p. 76.

5. Quoted in Allan Nevins, *Hamilton Fish* (New York: Dodd, Mead, 1937), p. 372.

6. *The Works of Charles Sumner* (Boston: Lee and Shepard, 1870–1883; 15 vols.), XIV, pp. 94–124.

7. Quoted in Adrian Cook, *The Alabama Claims: American Politics and Anglo-American Relations, 1865–1872* (Ithaca, N.Y.: Cornell University Press, 1975), p. 132.

8. Quoted in Walter LaFeber, *The New Empire* (Ithaca, N.Y.: Cornell University Press, 1963), p. 106.

9. Quoted in Emily S. Rosenberg, *Spreading the American Dream: American Economic and Cultural Expansion, 1890–1945* (New York: Hill and Wang, 1982), p. 29.

10. Quoted in Milton Plesur, *America's Outward Thrust: Approaches to Foreign Affairs, 1865–1890* (DeKalb, Ill.: Northern Illinois University Press, 1971), p. 26.

11. Frederick J. Turner, "The Significance of the Frontier in American History," *Annual Report of the American Historical Association, 1893* (Washington, D.C.: Government Printing Office, 1894), p. 227.

12. Quoted in David M. Pletcher, "Economic Growth and Diplomatic Adjustment, 1861–1898," in William H. Becker and Samuel F. Wells, Jr., eds., *Economics and World Power* (New York: Columbia University Press, 1984), pp. 124–125.

13. Quoted in David M. Pletcher, "Rhetoric and Results: A Pragmatic View of American Economic Expansionism, 1865–98," *Diplomatic History*, V (Spring, 1981), p. 95.

14. Quoted in Plesur, *America's Outward Thrust*, p. 33.

15. Quoted in David Healy, *U.S. Expansionism: The Imperialist Urge in the 1890s* (Madison: University of Wisconsin Press, 1970), p. 44.

16. Quoted in Lance C. Buhl, "Maintaining 'An American Navy,' 1865–1889," in Kenneth J. Hagan, ed., *In Peace and War: Interpretations of American Naval History, 1775–1984* (Westport, Conn.: Greenwood Press, 1984; 2nd ed.), p. 167.

17. Quoted in Kenneth J. Hagan, *American Gunboat Diplomacy and the Old Navy, 1877–1889* (Westport, Conn.: Greenwood Press, 1973), p. 37.

18. Russell F. Weigley, *The American Way of War* (New York: Macmillan, 1973), p. 153.

19. Quoted in Jerry M. Cooper, "The Army's Search for a Mission, 1865–1890," in Kenneth J. Hagan and William R. Roberts, eds., *Against All Enemies: Interpretations of American Military History from Colonial Times to the Present* (Westport, Conn.: Greenwood Press, 1986), p. 188.

20. Peter Karsten, "Armed Progressives: The Military Reorganizes for the American Century," in Jerry Israel, ed., *Building the Organizational Society* (New York: The Free Press, 1972), pp. 196–232.

21. Quoted in Kenneth J. Hagan, "Alfred Thayer Mahan: Turning America Back to the Sea," in Frank Merli and Theodore A. Wilson, eds., *Makers of American Diplomacy* (New York: Charles Scribner's Sons, 1974), p. 290.

22. Quoted in Allen R. Millett and Peter Maslowski, *For the Common Defense: A Military History of the United States of America* (New York: The Free Press, 1984), p. 252.

23. LaFeber, *The New Empire*, p. 24.

24. Quoted in Oleh W. Gerus, "The Russian Withdrawal from Alaska: The Decision to Sell," *Revista de Historia de America*, LXXV–LXXVI (December, 1973), 162.

25. Quoted in Ronald J. Jensen, *The Alaska Purchase and Russian-American Relations* (Seattle: University of Washington Press, 1975), p. 55.

26. Quoted in Ernest N. Paolino, *The Foundations of the American Empire: William Henry Seward and U.S. Foreign Policy* (Ithaca, N.Y.: Cornell University Press, 1973), p. 207.

27. Quoted in Ted C. Hinckley, "William H. Seward Visits His Purchase," *Oregon Historical Quarterly*, LXXII (June, 1971), 146.

28. Quoted in Cook, *Alabama Claims*, p. 89.

29. Quoted in David P. Crook, *Diplomacy During the American Civil War* (New York: John Wiley & Sons, 1975), p. 131.

30. Quoted in Gerald M. Craig, *The United States and Canada* (Cambridge, Mass.: Harvard University Press, 1968), p. 149.

31. Quoted in Lawrence Martin, *The Presidents and the Prime Ministers* (Toronto: Doubleday Canada, 1982), p. 32.

32. Quoted in *ibid.*, p. 42.

33. Samuel Flagg Bemis, *A Diplomatic History of the United States* (New York: Holt, Rinehart and Winston, 1965; 5th ed.), p. 413.

34. Quoted in Michael H. Hunt, *The Making of a Special Relationship: The United States and China to 1914* (New York: Columbia University Press, 1983), p. 115.

35. Quoted in William A. Williams, *The Roots of the Modern American Empire* (New York: Random House, 1969), p. 219.

36. Quoted in Robert B. Davies, "Peacefully Working to Conquer the World: The Singer Manufacturing Company in Foreign Markets, 1854–1889, *Business History Review*, XLIII (Autumn, 1969), 323.

37. Quoted in David L. Anderson, *Imperialism and Idealism: American Diplomats in China, 1861–1898* (Bloomington, Ind.: Indiana University Press, 1985), pp. 3–4.

38. Quoted in Shih-shan Henry Tsai, *China and the Overseas Chinese in the United States, 1868–1911* (Fayetteville: University of Arkansas Press, 1983), p. 75.

39. Quoted in Frederick C. Drake, *The Empire of the Seas* (Honolulu: University of Hawaii Press, 1984), p. 105.

40. Quoted in Hunt, *The Making of a Special Relationship*, p. 128.

41. Quoted in David M. Pletcher, *The Awkward Years: American Foreign Relations Under Garfield and Arthur* (Columbia: University of Missouri Press, 1962), p. 70.

42. Quoted in Julius W. Pratt, *Expansionists of 1898* (Chicago: Quadrangle Paperbacks [c. 1936], 1964), p. 25.

43. Quoted in Merze Tate, *The United States and the Hawaiian Kingdom: A Political History* (New Haven: Yale University Press, 1965), p. 210.

44. Quoted in Gerald G. Eggert, *Richard Olney: Evolution of a Statesman* (University Park, Pa.: Pennsylvania State University Press, 1974), p. 183.

45. Quoted in Paul M. Kennedy, *The Samoan Tangle: A Study in Anglo-American Relations, 1878–1900* (New York: Barnes & Noble, 1974), p. 53.

46. Quoted in *ibid.*, p. 76.

47. Quoted in Healy, *U.S. Expansionism*, p. 118.

48. Quoted in Jon D. Holstine, "Vermonter in Paradise: Henry Clay Ide in Samoa," *Vermont History,* XLIII (Spring, 1975), 140.

49. Quoted in Drake, *Empire of the Seas,* p. 177.

50. Quoted in *ibid.,* p. 185.

51. Quoted in Pletcher, *Awkward Years,* p. 67.

52. Karl M. Schmitt, *Mexico and the United States, 1821–1973* (New York: John Wiley & Sons, 1974), p. 97.

53. T. Harry Williams, ed., *Hayes: The Diary of a President, 1875–1881* (New York: David McKay, 1964), p. 265.

54. Quoted in Richard W. Van Alstyne, *The Rising American Empire* (New York: W. W. Norton, [c. 1960], 1974), p. 163.

55. Quoted in Alice Felt Tyler, *The Foreign Policy of James G. Blaine* (Minneapolis: University of Minnesota Press, 1927), p. 178.

56. Quoted in Robert L. Beisner, *From the Old Diplomacy to the New, 1865–1900* (Arlington Heights, Ill.: Harlan Davidson, 1986; 2nd ed.), p. 102.

57. Quoted in Joyce S. Goldberg, "Consent to Ascent: The *Baltimore* Affair and the U.S. Rise to World Power Status," *Americas,* XLI (July, 1984), 22.

58. Robley D. Evans, *A Sailor's Log* (New York: D. Appleton, 1902), p. 265.

59. James D. Richardson, ed., *Messages of the Presidents* (Washington, D.C.: Government Printing Office, 1898; 10 vols.), IX, p. 225.

60. Quoted in H. Wayne Morgan, *From Hayes to McKinley: National Party Politics, 1877–1896* (Syracuse: Syracuse University Press, 1969), p. 362.

61. Quoted in Ernest R. May, *Imperial Democracy: The Emergence of America as a Great Power* (New York: Harper and Row, [1961], 1973), p. 10.

Chapter 6

Grover Cleveland (1837–1908). This caricature of the two-term President, overweight from frequenting saloons as a young man, captured the gruff American attitude toward Britain during the Venezuelan crisis. (Courtesy of The New York Historical Society, New York City)

Imperialist Thrust, 1895–1900

DIPLOMATIC CROSSROAD: THE VENEZUELAN CRISIS, 1895

Grover Cleveland was pleased. On July 7, 1895, the same day his third daughter was born at the family summer home on Cape Cod, Massachusetts, he wrote an enthusiastic note to Secretary of State Richard Olney. Just a few days before, Olney, who also escaped from the sweltering summer temperatures of Washington to a residence on the cape, had personally delivered a 12,000-word draft document to the President. The secretary had been on the job only a few weeks and this draft of a major message to London on the Venezuelan boundary dispute was one of his first efforts. Energetic Olney, a successful corporate lawyer and former attorney general, was naturally anxious. He knew that Cleveland wanted the dispute cleared up, and Olney himself liked to keep his desk tidy. The President's note arrived bearing laudatory words: "It's the best thing of the kind I ever read." Cleveland suggested some minor changes, "a little more softened verbiage here and there," and directed Olney to send the document to London, which he did on July 20, 1895. Cleveland later christened it Olney's "twenty-inch gun." It was as much Cleveland's weapon as Olney's.[1]

The gun was aimed at Great Britain, which for decades had haggled with Venezuela over the boundary line separating that country and British Guiana. A Britisher, Robert Schomburgk, had drawn a line in the 1840s, but nobody liked it. Both sides made claims which went deep into the other's territory. In the 1880s, the discovery of gold in the disputed region—the largest nugget ever found, 509 ounces, was unearthed there—heightened competition. At stake, too, was control of the mouth of the Orinoco River, gateway to the potential trade of northern South America. In the 1870s Venezuela had begun to appeal to the United States for help, arguing that the poaching British were violating the Monroe Doctrine. Washington repeatedly asked the British to submit the issue to arbitration, but met constant rebuff. In his annual message to Congress in December, 1894,

Cleveland renewed the call for arbitration. After another British refusal, the President grew impatient and ordered the State Department to prepare a report on the boundary question. The "twenty-inch gun" sounded Olney's memorable answer.

In retrospect it is easy to see why Cleveland and Olney were so agitated about the Venezuelan boundary question. First, the political dimension. William L. Scruggs, former American minister to Caracas, was hired in the early 1890s to propagandize Venezuela's case in the United States. He wrote a widely circulated pamphlet, *British Aggressions in Venezuela, or the Monroe Doctrine on Trial* (1895), which aroused considerable sympathy for the South American nation. Olney himself read it before preparing his blast of July 20. American sentiment soon congealed: the land-grabbing British were picking on a poor hemispheric friend of the United States. A unanimous congressional resolution of February, 1895, calling for arbitration, reflected the growing American concern. Cleveland listened attentively to such expressions, because his Democratic party had lost badly in the 1894 congressional elections and his Administration was being attacked, particularly by Republicans, as pusillanimous for not annexing Hawaii and for doing nothing when the British briefly landed troops in Nicaragua in April, 1895. Cleveland, it seemed, could deflect criticism and recoup Democratic losses by bold action. As one Democrat advised the President: "Turn this Venezuela question up or down, North, South, East or West, and it is a 'winner.'"[2]

The President did not need such political considerations to stimulate his interest. He was inclined toward action anyway because of momentous events in the 1890s. This was the golden age of European imperialism, when the powers were carving up territories in Asia, the Near East, and Africa. The British, already holding large stakes in Latin America, seemed intent upon enlarging them. Their intervention in Nicaragua was a fresh example. Nor was the French intervention in Mexico in the 1860s forgotten. Americans feared that new incursions could make Latin America another Africa. The boundary dispute in Venezuela seemed a symbol of the unwelcome European reach into the western hemisphere.

The American depression of the 1890s also helped fix attention on Venezuela. Many, including Cleveland, thought that overproduction was a major cause of the slump and that foreign trade expansion was a possible solution. Might the British close off the Orinoco River and hence the markets of the area? At that time, American economic involvement in Venezuela was ripening. For example, the National Association of Manufacturers, organized in 1895 to expand American exports, chose Caracas as the site for its first permanent overseas display of American products. In short, international competition and economic woes suggested that the national interest of the United States was tied to Venezuela's dispute with Britain.

Cleveland's own character and style colored his response. He did not like bullies pushing small fry around. He had already rejected Hawaiian annexation in part because he thought that Americans had bullied the Hawaiians against their will. It appeared to the President, exaggeration though it was, that America's perennial competitor Britain was arrogantly manhandling the Venezuelans. What he and the sometimes intemperate Olney needed was an intellectual peg upon which to hang the United States case. They found it in a refurbished Monroe Doctrine. Olney's "twenty-inch gun" of July 20, 1895, invoked that venerable principle in aggressive, bumptious, and unvarnished language that prejudged the issue against the British.

The brash message noted that the British claim had grown larger and larger,

"**The Real British Lion.**" A popular American depiction of the British global presence during the crisis over Venezuela. A few years later, President Cleveland himself recalled British behavior as "mean and hoggish." (*New York Evening World,* 1895)

cutting deeper and deeper into Venezuela. Further growth might lead to political control. It is conceivable, Olney stated, that the European struggle over the partition of Africa might be transferred to Latin America. The "safety," "honor," and "welfare" of the United States were at stake, and the Monroe Doctrine outlawed European intervention leading to control in the western hemisphere. Using history, Olney cited the successful application of the doctrine in the French-Mexican-American imbroglio of the 1860s. He quoted the doctrine at length and asserted that "any permanent political union between a European and an American state [was] unnatural and inexpedient."

Because its national interest was involved, the United States had to intervene in the dispute. "The states of America, South as well as North, by geographical proximity, by natural sympathy, by similarity of governmental constitutions, are friends and allies, commercially and politically, of the United States. To allow the subjugation of any one of them by a European power is, of course, to completely reverse that situation and signifies the loss of all the advantages incident to their natural relations with us." The forceful, overriding theme of Olney's proclamation was directed toward an international audience: "To-day the United States is practically sovereign on this continent, and its fiat is law upon the subjects to which it confines its interposition." And more: the United States' "infinite resources combined with its isolated position render it master of the situation and practically invulnerable as against any or all other powers."[3] Olney, finally, demanded arbitration, vaguely threatened United States intervention, and requested a British answer by the time of the President's annual message to Congress in December.

Ambassador to England Thomas Bayard delivered the document to the giant of European diplomats, Lord Salisbury, then doubling as the British prime minister and foreign secretary. The bearded sixty-five-year-old Salisbury struck an imposing figure—intelligent, aristocratic, cautious, and well read. He received the missive with some surprise and sent it to the Foreign Office for study. Through the summer months little was done, in part because vacations interrupted work. Salisbury saw no urgency, bothered as he was with crises elsewhere (especially in Africa). Anyway, in the late nineteenth century one expected American Anglophobic bombast. The issue, he thought, would probably fizzle out once American politics calmed down. Furthermore, he disliked arbitrating any question that might weaken the British Empire. Salisbury would never entrust British interests in the Orinoco area to the United States. Obviously, he did not appreciate how agitated the Cleveland Administration was. The British did not complete their reply until November 26, and it arrived in Washington after Cleveland's annual message (which was quite tame on the Venezuelan controversy). Salisbury's reply had a "ho-hum" quality. It discounted the applicability of the Monroe Doctrine and dismissed any United States interest in the dispute.

Cleveland, all 250 pounds of him, was duck-hunting in North Carolina when the British response reached Washington. Upon his return he read it and became "mad clean through."[4] Olney had already been working on a special congressional message. He had not counted on a flat British rejection. Now what? War? Retreat? Neither course would serve the national interest. Olney struggled for alternatives and finally selected one which left some maneuvering room, kept diplomacy in the hands of the executive branch, and avoided war or backstepping: an American study commission appointed by the President. Cleveland, although tired from his expedition among the ducks, stayed up all night to rewrite Olney's draft. He dispatched his special message to Congress on December 17 and it rang a bell of alarm. England must arbitrate; the United States would create an investigating

"If There Must Be War." Lord Salisbury and President Cleveland slug it out during the Venezuelan crisis as a substitute for full-scale war. (*Life,* 1896)

commission to set the true boundary line; and then American action would follow. Most observers labeled the message an ultimatum, with the possibility of war lurking throughout.

The nation buzzed over this verbal flexing of muscle. Congress appropriated funds for the investigating commission. Irish-Americans offered themselves as volunteers to fight the hated British; both Republicans and Democrats lined up behind the President, and Senator Henry Cabot Lodge noted with approval that "Jingoes are plenty enough now."[5] Theodore Roosevelt, always eager for a tussle, bubbled with enthusiasm: "Let the fight come if it must; I don't care whether our sea coast cities are bombarded or not; we would take Canada."[6] Many business-men rallied behind the Administration, with Whitelaw Reid, editor of the *New York Tribune*, hyperbolically declaring that "This is the golden opportunity of our merchants to extend our trade to every quarter of Central and South America."[7] British Ambassador Sir Julian Pauncefote detected "in Congress and among the Public a condition of mind which can only be described as hysterical."[8]

This high wave of emotionalism subsided rapidly in early 1896. Many bankers and businessmen became alarmed when the stock market plummeted, in large part because British investors were pulling out. On second thought, some Americans calculated that a war was unconscionable with Britain, a country so close in race, language, and culture. Critics like E. L. Godkin, editor of *The Nation*, and respected international law specialist John Bassett Moore pointed out how haughtily Cleve-land and Olney had acted. Ambassador Bayard was critical of the President's truculent stance: "I fear he has made a gross and great error of judgment and has been too *precipitate*, for I do not see why he should abandon suddenly his attitude of conservatism and go apparently into the camp of aggressiveness."[9] But Cleveland never wanted war. He wanted peace on American terms, even if it required aggressiveness.

AMERICAN FOREIGN POLICY AFTER VENEZUELA

What followed was anticlimactic. In a January 11, 1896 Cabinet meeting, Salisbury, still recommending delay, was overruled and instructed to begin negotiations with the United States. The British retreat was necessitated by a dispute with Germany over South Africa. England needed friends now, not enemies. Furthermore, Canada could not be defended and the Admiralty reported that the Royal Navy was inadequate in the North Atlantic and Caribbean. Formal talks ultimately began and dragged on until November, 1896, when Britain and the United States agreed to set up a five-person arbitral board to define the boundary, with each to name two members, who would in turn select the fifth. Finally, in October, 1899, the tribunal reached a decision that rejected the extreme claims of each party and generally followed the Schomburgk line. The pivotal Point Barima at the mouth of the Orinoco went to Venezuela, which came out of the dispute pretty well, considering the fact that neither the United States nor Great Britain cared much about what happened to *Venezuela's* national interest.

Indeed, a remarkable characteristic of this controversy was that the United States negotiated directly with Britain without consulting Venezuela. Venezuela had a duly accredited minister in Washington, but he was excluded from the talks. Olney never even gave the Venezuelans a copy of his "twenty-inch gun" (they eventually read it in the newspapers), and when they balked over the 1896

Anglo-American agreement he grew angry and simply told them what to do. He made one concession: Venezuela could name one of the five members of the arbitration board—so long as that person was not a Venezuelan. Scruggs complained that the United States was attempting to "over-awe and *bull-doze* Venezuela."[10] He was right, but Washington's vigorous diplomacy was directed at others besides that South American nation. The overweening theme of Olney's "twenty-inch gun" merits repeating: "To-day the United States is practically sovereign on this continent, and its fiat is law upon the subjects to which it confines its interposition."

The Venezuelan crisis, most scholars agree, was a significant event in American diplomatic history. Although Cleveland and Olney did not intend all the consequences which flowed from it, they did help move the United States toward world power status. As an example of forceful, even aggressive, American diplomacy, the Venezuelan controversy marked a time in history when the United States determined to demonstrate its weight in international affairs. Besides displaying a self-righteous disregard for the rights and sensibilities of small nations, it revealed a United States more sure of itself, more certain about the components of its "policy," and willing to lecture others. The episode stimulated American nationalism and pride, or what critics at the time called "jingoism." The Monroe Doctrine gained new stature as a warning to European nations to temper, if not abandon, their activities in the western hemisphere; the United States, nationalists were proud to relate, had humbled Great Britain and forced the olympian Salisbury to retreat. The executive branch kept the Venezuelan issue in *its* hands, thereby strengthening the foreign policy power of the President. Some congressmen and senators complained that Cleveland was committing the United States to possible war without appropriate consultation with the legislative branch.

Other ramifications became evident. Latin Americans learned once again that the United States intended to establish supremacy in the western hemisphere. They realized further that the United States would judge the national interests of other countries and intervene when it saw fit. The United States had always kept an eye on the Caribbean, but the Venezuelan crisis and the outbreak of revolution in Cuba in 1895 intensified American interest, a significant dimension of which was economic. The Venezuelan issue and the disposition of the Orinoco River also brought more attention to the theory of overproduction as a cause of depression, to be cured by exporting surplus goods. Commercial expansion, always a trend in American history, was given another boost.

The discord with Britain over Venezuela actually fostered Anglo-American rapprochement. Cooperation and mutual interest increasingly characterized relations between Washington and London. British diplomats sought United States friendship as a possible counterweight to growing German power, and one manifestation of the emerging détente was a self-conscious British decision to permit the United States to govern Caribbean affairs. One way, the chief way, the United States could manage events in that area was through naval power. The Venezuelan crisis, joined by crises in Asia and the belief that naval construction would employ those idled by depression, stimulated additional American naval expansion. The Navy Act of 1896, for example, provided for three new battleships and ten new torpedo boats. All told, the Venezuelan boundary dispute advanced the United States farther along the path of expansion.

That path, by the end of the decade, led to new United States colonies in the

"Either Caesar or Nothing!" Uncle Sam protests against imperialism, but refuses to return to his cramped log cabin now that he has taken up "sky-scraper" diplomacy, according to this German cartoon. (*Kladderadatsch,* 1899, Courtesy Dartmouth College Library)

Pacific, Far East, and the Caribbean, a decisive hold on Cuba, and Europe's recognition of the United States as the overlord of the Caribbean. By 1900, too, the United States had pledged itself to preserve the "Open Door" in China; it had built a navy that had just annihilated the Spanish fleet and ranked sixth in the world; and it had developed an export trade amounting to $1.5 billion. Its industrial might was symbolized by steel and iron production, which almost equaled that of Britain and Germany combined. American acquisition of new colonies after the Spanish-American War has led some observers to conclude that *only then,* about 1898, did the United States become an imperialist world power. But as we have seen, there was a continuity of expansionism and imperialism in nineteenth-century diplomacy. Seldom do major diplomatic squabbles or wars happen all of a sudden; they flow from cumulative events. Had William H. Seward lived in 1898, for example, he might have triumphantly emphasized the similarities between the 1890s and the 1860s. Had he been a good historian, he would have pointed out also that economic and political changes at home and increased competition with

European powers abroad had undermined anti-imperialist arguments and permitted his schemes for empire to be realized. Before the depression decade of the 1890s the United States had often taken halting steps toward a larger empire; in that decade it took the leap.

THE MAKING OF AMERICAN FOREIGN POLICY IN THE 1890s

Theodore Roosevelt described the anti-imperialists in 1897 as "men of a by-gone age" and "provincials."[11] Indeed, anti-imperialism waned through the late nineteenth century. Increasing numbers of educated, economically comfortable Americans made the case for formal empire (colonies or protectorates) or informal empire (commercial domination). Naval officers, diplomats, politicians, farmers, skilled artisans, businessmen, and clergymen made up what might be called the "foreign policy public." Better read than most Americans and having access to lecterns to disperse their ideas, this "elite" helped move America to war and empire. Recent scholarly research has shown, contrary to a long-standing assumption, that it was not "public opinion," the jingoistic "yellow press," or the "people" in the 1890s that compelled the United States to war, but rather two key elements: a McKinley Administration very much in charge of its diplomacy through skillful maneuvering, and a majoritarian view within the articulate "foreign policy public" in favor of a vigorous outward thrust.

The "hows," rather than the "whys," of decisionmaking can be explained by noting problems with the phrase "public opinion." One often hears that "public opinion" or "the man in the street" influenced a leader to follow a certain course of action. But "public opinion" was not a unified, identifiable group speaking with one voice. Furthermore, political leaders and other articulate, knowledgeable people often shaped the "public opinion" they wanted to hear by their very handling of events and their control over information. That is, they *led* in the true sense of the word. In trying to determine who the "people" are and what "public opinion" is, social science studies demonstrate that the people who counted, the people who were listened to, the people who expressed their opinion publicly in order to influence policy—these people in the 1890s numbered no more than 1.5 million to 3 million, or between 10 and 20 percent of the voting public. This percentage—upper- and middle-income groups, educated, active politically—constituted the "foreign policy public." As Secretary of State Walter Q. Gresham put it in 1893: "After all, public opinion is made and controlled by the thoughtful men of the country."[12] The "public opinion" the President heard in the 1890s was not that of some collection we loosely call the "people," but rather that of a small, articulate segment of the American population alert to foreign policy issues. Although they

Makers of American Foreign Policy from 1895 to 1900

Presidents	Secretaries of State
Grover Cleveland, 1893–1897	Richard Olney, 1895–1897
William McKinley, 1897–1901	John Sherman, 1897–1898
	William R. Day, 1898
	John Hay, 1898–1905

counted anti-imperialists in their numbers, the "foreign policy public" was heavily weighted on the side of imperialism.

The President, as a consummate politician and good tactician, is often the master of policymaking, even thwarting the advice of the "foreign policy public" itself. President Cleveland, for example, successfully resisted pressure to annex Hawaii and withdrew the treaty from the Senate. He never let Congress or influential public opinion set the terms of his policy toward the Venezuelan crisis. Nor was President William McKinley stampeded into decisions; he tried *his* diplomacy before trying the war that many leaders, especially in Congress, had been advocating for months and years. An imperialist-oriented "foreign policy public," rather than some immeasurable "public opinion," helped move the United States along a path to war and larger empire, but the administrations determined the speed of the movement. Pressures from jingoes in Congress and a sensationalist press were evident, but the initiative in foreign affairs, unlike the 1860s and 1870s, was largely in the hands of the executive branch. In most historical periods, the public *reacts* to *immediate* events; the executive *acts, manages,* with *long-term* policy considerations.

THE CUBAN REVOLUTION AND THE UNITED STATES, 1895–1897

Eighteen ninety-five was a year of momentous events. The Venezuelan crisis, Japan's defeat of China in the Sino-Japanese War, and the outbreak of revolution in Cuba—all carried profound meaning for American diplomacy. The sugar-rich island of Cuba, since the close of its unsuccessful war for independence (1868–1878), had stagnated in a state of political repression and glaring poverty. After that war Cuban nationalists prepared for a new assault upon their Spanish overlords. From 1881 to 1895, Cuban national hero José Martí plotted from exile in the United States. In 1892 he organized the Cuban Revolutionary party, using American territory to recruit men and money for a return to his homeland. Martí's opportunity came when Cuba's economic development was hurt in 1894 by a new American tariff, which raised duties on imported sugar and hence reduced Cuban sugar shipments to the United States. On February 24, 1895, with cries of *"Cuba Libre,"* the rebels opened their drive for independence. They kept a cautious eye on the United States, for they knew its historical interest in Cuba and feared ultimate American control. As Martí remarked, "I have lived in the bowels of the monster and I know it."[13]

Cuban and Spanish military strategies were calculated to produce destruction and death. Led by General Máximo Gómez, a veteran of the 1868–1878 war, the *insurrectos* burned cane fields, blew up mills, and disrupted railroads, with the goal of rendering Cuba an economic liability to Spain. "The chains of Cuba have been forged by her own richness," Gómez proclaimed, "and it is precisely this which I propose to do away with soon."[14] Although outnumbered (about 30,000 Cuban troops against 200,000 Spanish) and lacking adequate supplies (often their weapons and ammunition did not match), the insurgents, with the sympathy of the populace, wore the Spanish down through guerrilla tactics. By late 1896 they controlled about two-thirds of the island, with the Spanish concentrated in coastal and urban regions. That year, to break the rebel stronghold in the rural areas, Governor-General Valeriano y Nicolau Weyler instituted the brutal reconcentration program. He divided the island into districts and herded Cubans into fortified camps. A half million Cubans were driven from homes and livelihoods into these centers, where frightful sanitation conditions, poor food, and disease contributed to the death of perhaps 200,000 people. Cubans outside the camps were assumed to be rebels and targets for death. In the countryside Weyler's soldiers destroyed crops, killed livestock, and polluted water sources. This effort to starve the insurgents and deprive them of physical and moral support, combined with the rebels' destructive behavior, made a shambles of Cuba's society and economy.

The Cleveland Administration, keeping control of its diplomacy against congressional pressures, faced several alternatives. It could recognize Cuban belligerency. That was ruled out because such an act, Olney noted, would relieve Spain of any responsibility for paying claims filed by Americans for properties destroyed in Cuba. Cleveland and Olney found recognition of Cuban independence even less appetizing, for they believed the Cubans incapable of self-government and feared anarchy and even racial war. That course might also arouse a Spanish declaration of war or force American belligerency because, logically, a Spanish attempt to conquer an "independent" Cuba would constitute a violation of the Monroe Doctrine. War seemed out of the question, as did outright annexation, although apparently Olney toyed with buying the island at one point. The Cleveland Administration settled on a dual policy of hostility to the revolution and pressure on Spain to grant some autonomy. Diplomacy and lecturing to a foreign government seemed to be working in the Venezuelan crisis; perhaps it would work in the case of Cuba.

Stirred by a Republican Congress (it passed a resolution in April, 1896, urging the President to recognize Cuban belligerency), by continued evidence of wholesale destruction, and by Spanish obstinacy in refusing reforms and adhering to force, Olney sent a note to Spain in April, 1896. He told Spain it could not win by force, but said the United States preferred continued Spanish control of the island. The United States took an active interest in Cuban affairs, he went on, because the American people always supported freer political institutions, the war was being conducted inhumanely, commerce was being disrupted, and American property was going the way of the torch. Spain should initiate reforms short of independence. Olney was principally concerned with the interests of Americans, not with those of the Cubans. American property was estimated at $50 million and the decline in sugar production wrought disaster to Cuban-American trade relations. In 1892 Cuba had shipped to the United States goods worth $79 million; by 1898 that figure had slumped to $15 million.

When Spain rejected Olney's advice, the Cleveland Administration seemed stymied. It did not desire war, but it meant to protect American interests. Congress kept asking for firm action. And in Havana, hotheaded American Consul-General Fitzhugh Lee was openly clamoring for American annexation. Cleveland did not feel he could fire Lee, nephew of General Robert E. Lee, because the noisy fellow had some political clout at home, and Cleveland needed political friends at a time when the Democratic party was dumping the incumbent President in favor of William Jennings Bryan. Olney kept Lee at bay by bombarding him with endless requests for information. Cleveland and Olney were further bothered by the news that Spain was approaching the courts of Europe for diplomatic support, with the argument that the Monroe Doctrine threatened all European powers. Spain's appeal went unheeded, but the apprehension lingered in the minds of American leaders that European nations might intrude in Cuba.

British Ambassador to Spain H. Drummond Wolff believed "what the United States required for Cuba was 'peace with commerce.'"[15] Cleveland proved this estimate accurate when he sent his annual message to Congress in December, 1896. With a slight echo of Olney's "twenty-inch gun" about the United States' "fiat" in the western hemisphere, the President reported that neither the Spanish nor the Cuban rebels had established their authority over the island. Americans felt a humanitarian concern, he said, but their trade and investments ("pecuniary interest") were also jeopardized. Furthermore, to maintain its neutrality, the United States had to police the coastline to intercept unlawful expeditions. Spain must grant autonomy or "home rule," but not independence, to "fertile and rich" Cuba to end the bloodshed and devastation. If she did not, he warned, the United States, having thus far acted with "restraint," might abandon its "expectant attitude."[16]

But Cleveland was more bark than bite. Through Olney he successfully buried a Senate resolution urging recognition of Cuban independence and contented himself with some limited Spanish reforms of February, 1897. Thereafter he let the Cuban issue fester, bequeathing it to the incoming McKinley Administration. His legacy to the new Republican President was nevertheless significant; he had declared that American interests were at stake in Cuba and that the United States would continue to lecture Spain about its Cuban problem.

THE ROAD TO WAR: McKINLEY'S DIPLOMACY, 1897–1898

William McKinley, inaugurated in March of 1897, was a veteran Republican politician, a deft manager of men. The election of 1896 had been rough, but McKinley, pegged as the "Advance Agent of Prosperity," had beaten back William Jennings Bryan with a quiet campaign based upon the theme of a bright future for America. The teetotaling Ohioan was a stable, dignified figure in a time of crisis. He represented deep religious conviction, personal warmth, sincerity, commitment to economic development and the revival of business, party loyalty, and support for expansion abroad. Yet McKinley often gave the appearance of being an infantile follower, a mindless flunky of the political bosses, a spineless leader. One joke went: "Why is McKinley's mind like a bed?" Answer: "Because it has to be made up for him every time he wants to use it." Plucky Theodore Roosevelt allegedly remarked that McKinley had no more backbone than a chocolate éclair. Such an image was created in large part by bellicose imperialists who believed that McKinley was not moving fast enough and critics of domestic policy like Bryan who saw McKinley as clay in the hands of big business and party machines. McKinley certainly was a party regular and friend of large corporations, but he was no lackey. A manager of diplomacy, who wanted expansion and empire without war and a settlement of the Cuban question without American military intervention, McKinley was his own man.

McKinley shared America's image of itself as an expanding nation of superior institutions and as a major power in Latin America. He agreed that a large navy, overseas commerce, and foreign bases were essential to the United States. He believed strongly that America's surplus goods had to be exported. As a tariff specialist, he favored high tariffs on manufactured goods, low tariffs on raw materials, and reciprocity agreements. Although McKinley uttered almost nothing about foreign issues in the campaign of 1896, the Republican party platform overflowed with expansionist rhetoric and conviction worthy of William H. Seward

William McKinley (1843–1901). An Ohioan who studied at Allegheny College, fought in the Civil War, and served several terms as a congressman, the twenty-fifth President was a supreme politician and successful imperialist. He was assassinated in Buffalo, New York in 1901. (Library of Congress)

himself. Extolling a vigorous diplomacy, it urged American control of Hawaii, a Nicaraguan canal run by the United States, an enlarged navy, purchase of the Virgin Islands, and Cuban independence. Between election and inauguration, however, McKinley quietly joined Cleveland and Olney in successfully burying a Senate resolution for recognition of Cuba. He wanted a free hand, and he did not believe that Cubans could govern themselves. His appointment of the old and ailing Senator John Sherman as secretary of state suggested further that McKinley would take charge of his own diplomacy. His inaugural address vacuously urged peace, never mentioning the Cuban crisis.

McKinley's first tilt with Congress came in March, 1897, after he called a special session for revision of the tariff. Resolutions on Cuba sprang up repeatedly, but the President managed to kill them. He did satisfy imperialists by sending an Hawaiian annexation treaty to the Senate. The President was preparing for his own nonpublic diplomatic assault upon Spain. In June, Madrid received an American reprimand for Weyler's uncivilized warfare and for his disruption of the Cuban economy. "Capitalism and humanitarianism," historian Lester Langley has aptly noted, "had joined hands" in the American protest.[17] Spain, however, showed no signs of tempering its military response to the insurrection. American citizens suffered in Spanish jails; American property continued to be devastated. Fitzhugh Lee, who remained at his post in Havana, bellowed for American intervention. In July McKinley instructed the new American Minister to Spain, Stewart L. Woodford, to demand that the Spanish stop the fighting. Increasingly convinced that the Cuban insurrectos would not compromise, the President sought to persuade Spain to provide autonomy. A new Spanish government assumed power in October and soon moderated policy by offering Cuba a substantial degree of self-government or autonomy. Even more, it removed the hated Weyler and promised to end reconcentration. Yet these reforms were not fully implemented and did not bring an end to the warfare.

McKinley's December 6, 1897 annual message to Congress (which had not been in session from July to December, thus giving the President little trouble) discussed the Cuban insurrection at great length. The crisis caused Americans the "gravest apprehension." What were the alternatives for the United States? McKinley rejected annexation as "criminal aggression." He argued against recognition of belligerency, because the rebels hardly constituted a government worthy of recognition. And he ruled out intervention because it was premature at a time when the Spanish were traveling the "honorable paths" of reform. He asked for patient waiting to see if Spanish changes would work, but hinted that the United States would continue to consider all policy options, including intervention "with force."[18]

By mid-January evidence had poured into Washington proving that the reforms had not moderated the crisis; in fact, insurgents, conservatives, and the Spanish army all denounced them. Antireform Spaniards rioted in Havana. The United States ordered the warship *Maine* to Havana on January 24, 1898 to protect American citizens and demonstrate concern. On February 9, the State Department received a copy of a private letter written in late 1897 by Spanish Minister to the United States Enrique Dupuy de Lôme and sent to a senior Spanish politician touring Cuba. Intercepted in Cuba by a rebel sympathizer, the letter was forwarded to the Cuban junta in New York City. Not only did it reach the State Department; William Randolph Hearst's flamboyant *New York Journal* published it that day with the banner headline: "Worst Insult to the United States in its History." De Lôme labeled McKinley "weak," a "bidder for the admiration of the crowd," and a "would-be politician."[19] McKinley, along with most Americans, was infuriated by de Lôme's remarks. The Administration particularly resented another statement that suggested that Spain did not take its reform proposals seriously and would persist in fighting to defeat the rebels. Spain, it appeared, had been tricking the United States. De Lôme's hasty recall hardly salved the hurt.

Trying to avoid war, a restless McKinley nevertheless recognized the dangerous trend. On occasion in early 1898 he had to take drugs to sleep. His demeanor was not improved by the rapidity of critical events. Less than a week after the de Lôme episode, on February 15, explosions ripped through the *Maine*, anchored audaciously in Havana Harbor. Over 250 American sailors died as the 6,700-ton vessel sank quickly. With no evidence, but considerable emotion, some Americans hurried to conclude that Spain had committed the dastardly deed. Few asked why the *Maine* was there in the first place—in the troubled waters of a Spanish colony in open rebellion. McKinley ordered an official investigation, but said little publicly. Some decried his caution, but he decided to try diplomacy and

The U.S.S. *Maine* Before and After. Part of the battleship was raised in 1911, investigated, and sunk at sea with flag flying. The investigators concluded that the explosion that destroyed the vessel was external, but a 1976 Navy study by Admiral Hyman G. Rickover blamed the sinking on an internal accident. (Before—*Harper's Weekly*, 1888; after—National Archives)

threat again. In early March Woodford protested strongly to the Spanish government about the de Lôme incident and the *Maine*. The Cuban crisis was "grave" and had to be resolved. On March 6 the President met with Joe Cannon, chairman of the House Committee on Appropriations, and urged him to present a bill providing $50 million for arms. "I must have the money to get ready for war."[20] Congress enthusiastically obliged three days later. Spain, Woodford reported, was stunned by the appropriation.

In mid-March Senator Redfield Proctor of Vermont, a friend of McKinley considered to be against going to war, stirringly told his colleagues about his recent trip to Cuba. He recounted ugly stories about the concentration camps. "Torn from their homes, with foul earth, foul air, foul water, and foul food or none, what wonder that one-half died and that one-quarter of the living are so diseased that they cannot be saved?"[21] Shortly after this moving speech, which convinced many congressmen and businessmen that Spain could not bring order to Cuba, the American court of inquiry on the *Maine* concluded that the vessel was destroyed by an external mine. The board could not determine who placed it there. A Spanish commission at about the same time attributed the disaster to an internal explosion. We still do not know exactly what set off the forward powder magazine, but in 1898 vocal Americans pinned the crime squarely on Spain. "Remember the Maine, to hell with Spain" became the popular chant.

McKinley's options were certainly narrowed by these cumulative events and sentiments. After consultation with advisers and congressional leaders, the President decided on an ultimatum. On March 27 Washington cabled the American demands: an armistice, Cuban-Spanish negotiations to secure a peace, McKinley's arbitration of the conflict if there was no peace by October, termination of the reconcentration policy, and relief aid to the Cubans. Implicit was the demand that Spain grant Cuba its independence. As a last-ditch effort to avoid American military intervention, the ultimatum had little chance of success. Spain's national pride and interest would block acceptance; it could not accept surrender. Madrid's answer was soon forthcoming: it had terminated reconcentration, would launch reforms, and would accept an armistice if the rebels did so first. By rejecting McKinley's offer of mediation and Cuban independence, the Spanish reply did not satisfy the President or Congress. He began to write a war message in early April. On the ninth, probably in response to the entreaties of other European nations, Spain made a new concession, declaring a unilateral suspension of hostilities "for such length of time" as the Spanish commander "may think prudent."[22] The declaration seemed too qualified and fell far short of independence. Could the Spaniards be trusted?

WHY WAR: EXPLOITING OPPORTUNITY

On April 11 McKinley sent a message to Congress, asking for authority to use armed force to end the Cuban war. Since neither the Cubans nor the Spaniards could stem the flow of blood, America would do the job. The United States would do so because of the "cause of humanity" and the "very serious injury to the commerce, trade, and business of our people, and the wanton destruction of property." And, recalling the sinking of the *Maine*, McKinley described the conflict as "a constant menace to our peace." At the very end of the message the President noted that Spain had recently accepted an armistice. He asked Congress to give this new information "your just and careful attention."[23]

Congress gave little attention to a suspension of hostilities that the Cubans themselves rejected. McKinley beat back a Senate attempt to recognize the rebels, for he believed that Cuba needed American tutelage to prepare for self-government. Congress did endorse the seemingly selfless Teller Amendment, which disclaimed any United States intention of annexing the island. Some who voted for the amendment feared that annexation would commit the United States to assume Cuba's large bond debt. On April 19 Congress proclaimed Cuba's independence, demanded Spain's evacuation, and directed the President to use force to ensure these results. Spain, on April 21, broke diplomatic relations. On the twenty-second, American ships began to blockade Cuba; two days later Spain declared war. On the twenty-fifth, Congress declared that a state of war had existed from the twenty-first.

Because of the Teller Amendment, the decision for war seemed selfless and humanitarian, and for many Americans it undoubtedly was. But the decision was not motivated so simply. Different people called for or endorsed war for different reasons. McKinley himself cited humanitarian concern, property, commerce, and the removal of an annoyance. Republican leaders said that their party would lose the 1898 congressional elections if the President did not heed popular cries for war. Important businessmen, formerly hesitant, shifted in March and April to demand an end to the disruptive Cuban crisis. Farmers and businessmen interested in Asian and Latin American markets thought victory against Spain might open new trade doors by eliminating a colonial power. Many highly moralistic Americans simply felt compelled to end the bloodshed. Republican Senator George F. Hoar of Massachusetts, later an anti-imperialist, wrote that "we cannot look idly on while hundreds of thousands of innocent human beings. . . . die of hunger close to our doors. If there is ever to be a war it should be to prevent such things as that."[24] Religious leaders, both Protestant and Catholic, marched in the war parade. Lyman Abbott, well-known pastor of Plymouth Church in Brooklyn, thought war the "answer to America to the question of its own conscience: Am I my brother's keeper?"[25] Church missionaries dreamed of new opportunities to convert the "uncivilized." Imperialists hoped war would add new territories to the American empire and encourage the growth of a larger navy. But the "warriors" were not synonymous with the "imperialists." Some people opposed empire and sincerely thought war would halt the long conflict in Cuba, whereas the imperialists seized upon war as an opportunity to expand the American empire.

Emotional nationalism also figured in the American thirst for war. The de Lôme and *Maine* incidents stimulated a national anger already infused with notions of American superiority, racial and otherwise. Imperialist Senator Albert Beveridge was ebullient: "At last, God's hour has struck. The American people go forth in a warfare holier than liberty—holy as humanity."[26] Journalist Finley Peter Dunne's popular Irish-American characters always seemed to have the fitting summary: "'We're a gr-reat people,' said Mr. Hennessy, earnestly. 'We ar-re,' said Mr. Dooley. 'We ar-re that. An' th best iv it is, we know we ar-re.'"[27] Excited statements by people like Roosevelt, who looked upon war as he looked upon horseback riding and cowboying in the Dakotas—it was sport, a game, fun—aroused martial fevers. Newspapers of the "yellow press" variety, like Hearst's *New York Journal* and Joseph Pulitzer's *New York World*, sensationalized stories of Spanish atrocities. Others proudly compared the Cuban and American revolutions. The

"The Spanish Brute." Grant Hamilton's angry cartoon captured the American attitude toward Spain in the 1890s, but especially after the sinking of the *Maine*, which added "mutilation to murder." (*Judge*, 1898)

American people, already steeped in a brash nationalism and prepared by earlier aggressive diplomatic triumphs, were receptive to this hyperbole. There was something exhilarating, furthermore, about competing with the imperialist "Joneses."

Both Washington and Madrid had tried diplomacy, but their diplomatic paths never crossed. McKinley wanted "peace" and independence for Cuba. The first Spain could not deliver because the Cuban rebels were entrenched and bent on independence and Spanish forces were weak. The second Spain could not grant immediately because it had its own national pride. Spain said it would fight the war more humanely and grant autonomy, but McKinley and Congress wanted more, and they believed they had the right and duty to judge the affairs of Spain and Cuba.

Once McKinley insisted that Spain grant Cuba its independence, war seemed inevitable: here was one power, the United States, telling another power, Spain, how to manage its national interest. Critics said America might have been less haughty, letting the Cubans and Spaniards settle their own affairs. McKinley's actions in dispatching the *Maine* and asking Congress for $50 million probably encouraged the Cuban rebels to resist any compromise. He might have given Spain a bit more breathing space. Spain, after all, did fire Weyler, terminate re-concentration, and approve an armistice; most important, Madrid did grant partial autonomy, which ultimately might have led to independence. Some critics said the President should have recognized the Cuban insurgents and covertly aided them, and then American soldiers would not necessarily have had to fight in Cuba, the Philippines, and Puerto Rico. American materiel, not men, in other words, might have liberated Cuba from Spanish rule. "McKinley, of course, did not prefer war," the historian Robert L. Beisner has concluded. "But he did want what only war could provide—an end to violence in Cuba, which outraged his sense of decency, prolonged instability in the economy, smashed investment and trade with Cuba, created the spectacle of an America unable to master affairs close to home, threatened to incite a politically dangerous outburst of jingoism, and diverted policymakers' attention from historic events in China. . . . "[28] The United States, not for the first or last time, chose war to end war.

THE SPANISH-AMERICAN-CUBAN-FILIPINO WAR

Americans flocked to recruiting stations and enlisted in what they trumpeted as a glorious expedition to demonstrate United States right and might. They were cocky. Young author Sherwood Anderson joked that fighting Spain would be "like robbing an old gypsy woman in a vacant lot at night after a fair."[29] War almost seemed healthy. United States Ambassador to England John Hay called it a "splendid little war," and Theodore Roosevelt, who resigned as assistant secretary of the Navy to lead the flashy but overrated Rough Riders, remarked that "it wasn't much of a war, but it was the best war we had."[30] Yet the Spanish-American War, as a veteran recalled, was no "tin-foil" affair.[31] Much of the initial euphoria eroded in mosquito-infested camps, uncomfortable ships, and inadequate hospitals. It was a short war, ending August 12, but 5,462 Americans died in it—only 379 of them in combat. Most of the rest met death from malaria and yellow fever. The chief surgeon of the United States Volunteers witnessed the hundreds of disease-wracked men who came home to be quarantined on the tip of Long Island. "The pale faces, the sunken eyes, the staggering gait and the emaciated forms" marked some as "wrecks for life" and others as "candidates for a premature grave."[32]

That was not how it began. About 200,000 excited men entered army camps in April and May, 1898. Tampa, Florida became the busy base for the Cuban expedition. Camp life was tough. The amateur soldiers were plagued by poor food, including poisonous spoiled beef. They were issued heavy blue uniforms in a humid climate of rain and warm temperatures; most of the new brown tropical uniforms arrived at Tampa after the troops had left for Cuba. Sanitation earned low marks, diseases visited the camps early, and pungent body odors caused nausea. Black troops, in segregated units led by white officers, got no respite from the stings of racial insult and discrimination. Black resentment grew in the face of the epithet "nigger" and Jim Crow restrictions that barred them from "white only" public parks, bars, and cafes. A racial battle sparked by drunken whites rocked Tampa in early June; twenty-seven blacks and three whites had to be hospitalized. Although many blacks hoped to prove in war that they deserved white respect, others shared the views of a black chaplain: "Talk about fighting and freeing poor Cuba and of Spain's brutality; of Cuba's murdered thousands, and starving reconcentradoes. Is America any better than Spain?"[33]

Led by officers seasoned in the Civil War and campaigns against Native Americans, the new imperial fighters embarked from Florida in mid-June. The loading of ships was chaotic. Men rushed to the transports, fearful they would be left behind. Roosevelt's Rough Riders muscled out rivals competing for one vessel, but their horses were left behind for lack of space. Colonel Leonard Wood predicted that if the Americans did not fight the Spanish soon they would tear at one another. Seventeen thousand men, clutching their Krag-Jörgensen rifles, were stuffed into the flotilla for a week. They ate hardtack and tasteless canned beef, drank bitter coffee, waited anxiously, and got seasick. On the morning of June 22 they disembarked on Cuban soil, finding no Spanish resistance. Cuban insurgents met with American officers and agreed to help one another against Spanish forces.

Yet the big and surprising news had already arrived from the Philippine Islands, Spain's major colony in Asia. Only a few days after the American declaration of war, Commodore George Dewey sailed his Asiatic Squadron from Hong Kong to Manila Bay, where he smashed the Spanish fleet with the loss of one man. Every American ship in Manila Harbor, Senator Orville Platt of Connecticut proclaimed, was "a new *Mayflower* . . . the harbinger and agent of a new civilization."[34] Slipping by the strangely silent Spanish guns at Corregidor, Dewey had entered the bay at night. Early in the morning of May 1 his flagship *Olympia* began to demolish the ten incompetently handled Spanish ships. With his laconic order, "You may fire when ready, Gridley," Dewey quickly became a first-line hero. Some people, ignorant of American interests in the Pacific, the beckoning China market, and the feebleness of Spanish rule over the Philippines, wondered how a war to liberate Cuba saw its first action in Asia. Although probably few Americans knew the location of the Philippines, naval officials had pinpointed them in contingency plans as early as 1896 and were ready for the attack when war erupted. Often credited alone with ordering Dewey on February 25, 1898 to sail for Manila if war broke out, Assistant Secretary of the Navy Theodore Roosevelt was really a McKinley Administration functionary fulfilling policy that the President endorsed.

By late June, the American troops in Cuba were moving toward Santiago, where ill-equipped and disspirited Spanish soldiers manned antique guns. Joined by experienced Cuban rebels, the Americans approached the city, and on July 1 battled for San Juan Hill. Having given away their position by sending up an observation balloon, the American troops, spearheaded by the Rough Riders and the black soldiers of the Ninth Cavalry, finally captured the strategic promontory overlooking Santiago. It was a near defeat with heavy casualties, but an important victory. Two days later the Spanish fleet, which had been locked into Santiago Harbor for weeks by American warships, made a desperate, fatalistic daylight break for open sea. American officers were dumbfounded, having expected that the Spanish ships would attempt to sneak out at night. Some American vessels nearly collided as they hurried to sink the helpless Spanish craft, which went down with 323 dead. Its fleet destroyed, Spain entered its imperial death throes. Santiago soon fell, and the Americans easily occupied another Spanish colony, Puerto Rico. Manila collapsed in mid-August, after the Spanish put up token resistance in a deal with Dewey that salvaged Spanish pride and kept insurgent Emilio Aguinaldo from the walled city. Washington soon ordered Aguinaldo and the Filipino rebels, who had been fighting openly against the Spanish for independence since 1896 and had surrounded Manila for weeks, to remain outside the capital and to recognize the authority of the United States.

In July, to insure uninterrupted reinforcement of Dewey, the United States officially absorbed Hawaii, where ships touched en route to Manila. From 1893 to 1897, when Cleveland refused annexation, politics in Hawaii had changed little. The white revolutionaries would not give up power, especially after the Queen promised to behead them upon her return to the throne. McKinley's election removed the uncertainty. Committed to annexation, he negotiated a new agreement with the provisional Hawaiian government. But, fearful that the Senate would not give him the two-thirds vote needed for a treaty, the President decided to ask for a joint resolution. On July 7, 1898 Congress passed the resolution for annexation by a majority vote (290–91 in the House and 42–21 in the Senate), thereby formally attaching the strategically and commercially important islands to the United States.

PEACE AND EMPIRE: THE DEBATE IN THE UNITED STATES

Spain sued for peace, and on August 12 the belligerents proclaimed an armistice. To negotiate with the Spanish in Paris, McKinley appointed a "peace commission" loaded with imperialists and headed by Secretary of State William R. Day, friend and follower of the President's wishes. As the talks dragged on into the autumn, McKinley, who had made a political tour and recognized that the British would acquiesce in American imperialism, instructed the commissioners to demand all of the Philippines and Puerto Rico, as well as to make Cuba independent. Articulate Filipinos pleaded for their country's freedom but were rebuffed. Spanish diplomats were aghast at this American land grab, but they accepted it after the United States offered $20 million in salve. By early December the treaty was signed, and the American delegates walked out of the elegant French conference room with the Philippines, Puerto Rico, and Guam.

Anti-imperialists howled in protest against the treaty. They had organized the Anti-Imperialist League in Boston in November, 1898, but they were never truly united. They counted among their number such unlikely bedfellows as steel magnate Andrew Carnegie, labor leader Samuel Gompers, agrarian spokesman William Jennings Bryan, Massachusetts Senator George Hoar, President Charles W. Eliot of Harvard, and Mark Twain—people who had often been opponents

"**Hurrah for Imperialism.**" This anti-imperialist cartoon suggested the fear that the United States was walking blindly along a disastrous path of empire. Anti-imperialists lost the debate in large part because Uncle Sam knew quite well where he was going in adding new territories to the American domain. (*Life,* 1898)

George F. Hoar (1826–1904). Graduate of Harvard, this Republican became a United States senator in 1877. He urged Cuban independence, but he sounded a strong anti-imperialist call in his opposition to the annexation of the Philippines. He praised the Filipinos for their written constitution and demonstrated ability to govern themselves. He compared the lynching of Southern black Americans to the "lynching" of the Filipino people. (Library of Congress)

on domestic issues. Many of the anti-imperialists were inconsistent. Hoar, the most outspoken senator against the treaty, had voted for war and for the resolution to annex Hawaii. An expansionist, Carnegie apparently would accept colonies if they could be taken without force. "I am no little American," he asserted. "The day is coming when we shall own all these West Indian islands. They will gravitate to us of their own accord."[35] He even offered to write a personal check for $20 million to buy the independence of the Philippines. And the anti-imperialists were hampered by the *fait accompli*, possession and occupation of territory, handed them by McKinley. After all, argued the President, could America really let loose of this real estate so nobly taken in battle? The anti-imperialists, rejecting immediacy in favor of principle, denounced the thesis that greatness lay in colonies. They wanted trade too, but not at the cost of subjugating other peoples. Anti-imperialist David Starr Jordan, president of Stanford University, spoke of the "peaceful conquest" of Mexico by trade rather than by annexation.[36] Quoting the Declaration of Independence and Washington's Farewell Address as lessons from the past, these critics recalled America's tradition of self-government and *continental* expansion. Furthermore, the imposition of a government by force on another people was inhumane and immoral. Mark Twain wrote *The War Prayer* to mock statements that God was on America's side: "O Lord our God, help us to tear their soldiers to bloody shreds with our shells . . . , blast their hopes, blight their lives, protract their bitter pilgrimage."[37] Social reformer Jane Addams saw children playing war games in the streets of Chicago. The kids were *not freeing Cubans,* she protested, but rather *slaying Spaniards* in their not-so-innocent play. Some anti-imperialists insisted that the United States had serious domestic problems that demanded attention and resources first; others were racists who predicted that Filipinos and Puerto Ricans would ultimately corrupt Anglo-Saxon blood.

The imperialists, led by Senators Henry Cabot Lodge and Nelson Aldrich, Roosevelt, and McKinley, and backed strongly by articulate business leaders, engaged their opponents in vigorous debate in early 1899. They concentrated on pragmatic considerations, although they expressed common ideas of racial superiority and national destiny to civilize the savage world—to take up "the white man's burden." Social Darwinist philosophy was cited: that some were more fit than others to survive. The Philippines provided steppingstones to the rich China market and strategic ports for the expanding Navy that protected American commerce and demonstrated American prestige. International competition also dictated that the United States keep the fruits of victory, argued the imperialists; otherwise, a menacing Germany or expansionist Japan might pick up what America discarded. It was inconceivable to large numbers of Americans that the United States would relinquish territory it had acquired through blood. It became a question of national honor. Roosevelt, countering the protest that the Filipinos had never been asked if they wanted to be annexed to the United States, cited historical precedent. Jefferson, he delighted in telling Democratic anti-imperialists, took Louisiana without a vote by its inhabitants. Furthermore, said Richard Olney, Washington's Farewell Address had outlived its usefulness; there could be no more American isolation. Duty, destiny, defense, and dollars was the alliterative imperialist litany.

Pro-imperialist Senator Lodge described the treaty fight as the "closest, most bitter, and most exciting struggle I have ever known, or ever expect to see in the Senate."[38] Shortly before the upper house took action, word reached Washington that Filipino insurrectionists and American soldiers had begun to fight. The news apparently stimulated support for the Treaty of Paris. Democrats tended to be anti-imperialists and Republicans imperialists, yet enough of the former endorsed the treaty on February 6, 1899 to pass it, just barely, by the necessary two-thirds vote, 57 to 27. William Jennings Bryan, believing that a rejection of the treaty would mean continued war, that a majority should rule in a democracy, and that the Philippines could be freed after terminating the hostilities with Spain, urged an "aye" vote upon his anti-imperialist friends. The Republicans probably had enough votes in reserve to pass the treaty even if Bryan had opposed it. Eight days later, the tie-breaking vote of the vice-president killed a Senate resolution providing for Philippine independence as soon as the Filipinos established a stable government.

ASIAN CHALLENGES: THE PHILIPPINE INSURRECTION AND THE OPEN DOOR IN CHINA

Controlling, protecting, and expanding the enlarged empire became a major chore. The Filipinos proved to be the most obstinate. By the end of the war, Aguinaldo and rebel warriors held control over most of the islands, having routed the Spanish and driven them into Manila. Aguinaldo had been brought from exile in an American warship and believed that American leaders, including Dewey, had promised his country independence if he joined American forces in defeating the Spanish. After the Spanish-American armistice, he grew resentful of Ameri-

Emilio Aguinaldo (1869–1964). Of mixed Chinese and Tagalog ancestry, this Filipino nationalist was exiled by the Spanish from his country in 1897. He returned with American forces and later clashed with them when he declared independence for the Philippines. He was captured in 1901 and then declared allegiance to the United States. During World War II, however, he favored the Japanese, who occupied the islands, and he was briefly imprisoned by American authorities in 1945 when they re-established United States power over Manila. (U.S. Signal Corps, National Archives)

can behavior. He and his men were ordered to stay out of the city, were gradually isolated from decisions, and were insulted by racial slurs, including "nigger" and "goo goo." American soldiers occupying the Manila area considered the Filipinos inferior, the equivalent of Indians and blacks at home. Imperialism, said critics, exported the worst in American life. In the fall and winter of 1898 American officers barred insurgent vessels from Manila Bay and showed no appreciation for the profound Filipino sentiment for independence. The Treaty of Paris angered the Filipinos, as did McKinley's dictate that the authority of the United States was supreme in the Philippines. In open defiance of Washington, Aguinaldo and other prominent Filipinos organized a government at Malolos, wrote a constitution, and proclaimed the Philippine Republic in late January, 1899.

Although American anti-imperialist critics were probably correct when they said that the Filipino government was as virtuous as that of Chicago, McKinley believed his new colonials to be ill-fitted for self-government. In February, 1899 the Filipinos began fighting better-armed American troops. After bloody struggles, Aguinaldo was captured in March, 1901. Before the insurrection collapsed in 1902, over 5,000 Americans and 200,000 Filipinos died. One hundred and twenty-five thousand American troops had to be used to quell the insurrection, which cost the United States at least $160 million. Anti-imperialist William James, distinguished Harvard University philosopher, poignantly summarized the impact on the Philippines:[39]

> Here were the precious beginnings of an indigenous national life, with which, if we had any responsibility to these islands at all, it was our first duty to have squared ourselves. . . . We are destroying the lives of these islanders by the thousands, their villages and their cities. . . . We are destroying down to the root every germ of a healthy national life in these unfortunate people. . . . No life shall you have, we say, except as a gift from our philanthropy after your unconditional surrender to our will. . . . Could there be a more damning indictment of that whole bloated ideal termed "modern civilization" than this amounts to? Civilization is, then, the big, hollow, resounding, corrupting, sophisticating, confusing torrent of mere brutal momentum and irrationality that brings forth fruits like this!

Indeed, it was one of the ugliest wars in American history and both sides committed atrocities. Insurgents chopped off the ears of American prisoners. Americans burned *barrios* to the ground, placing villagers in reconcentration camps like those so detested in Cuba. To get information, Americans administered the "water cure" by forcing prisoners to swallow gallons of water and then stepping on or punching the swollen stomach to empty it quickly. American soldiers were tired, mosquito-bitten, and poorly fed, and their patience wore thin. Filipino guerrilla fighters harassed them. Racism and notions of white superiority surfaced. An American correspondent explained that "it is not civilized warfare, but we are not dealing with a civilized people. The only thing they know and fear is force, violence, and brutality; and we give it to them."[40] The civil governor of the Philippines from 1901 to 1904, William Howard Taft, put the question less crudely when he described the American mission as the creation of a Filipino government "which shall teach those people individual liberty, which shall lift them up to a point of civilization . . . , and which shall make them rise to call the name of the United States blessed."[41] Charles Francis Adams, Jr., a critic of the American

"A Fair Field and No Favor." Holding back the militant-minded imperialists of Europe, the United States permits China to inspect American wares. "I'm out for commerce, not conquest," asserts Uncle Sam. (*Harper's Weekly*, 1899)

American Cigarettes in China. An American soldier stationed in China at the turn of the century peddles some American-made cigarettes in a singular instance of private enterprise abroad. (Edward J. Parrish Papers, Duke University Library)

acquisition of the Philippines, ridiculed such thinking: "We are going to make them a self-governing community by forbidding them absolutely to discuss the principle of self-government. We are going to make them an independent people by putting them in jail if they mention the word 'independence.'"[42]

One of the prime attractions the Philippines held for the United States was their proximity to China, where American leaders predicted lucrative markets for American products. In early 1898 American businessmen organized the American Asiatic Association to stimulate public and governmental concern to protect and enlarge United States interests in China. Assistant Secretary of the Treasury Frank Vanderlip typically lauded the Philippines as the "pickets of the Pacific, standing guard at the entrances to trade with the millions of China and Korea, French Indo-China, the Malay Peninsula, and the islands of Indonesia."[43] American traders had long dreamed of an unbounded China market, and missionaries romanticized a Christian kingdom. These ambitions remained dreams more than reality. Yet dreams became a rationale for action, and during the 1890s the United States, despite limited power, began to speak in defense of its Asian interests, real and imagined. In that decade the European powers and Japan were dividing China, rendered helpless in 1895 after its disastrous defeat in the Sino-Japanese War, into spheres of influence and establishing discriminatory trading privileges in their zones. The McKinley Administration in early 1898 watched anxiously as Germany grabbed Jiaozhou (Kiaochow) and Russia demanded and got a lease at Port Arthur on the Liaodong Peninsula. France, already ensconced in Indochina, leased

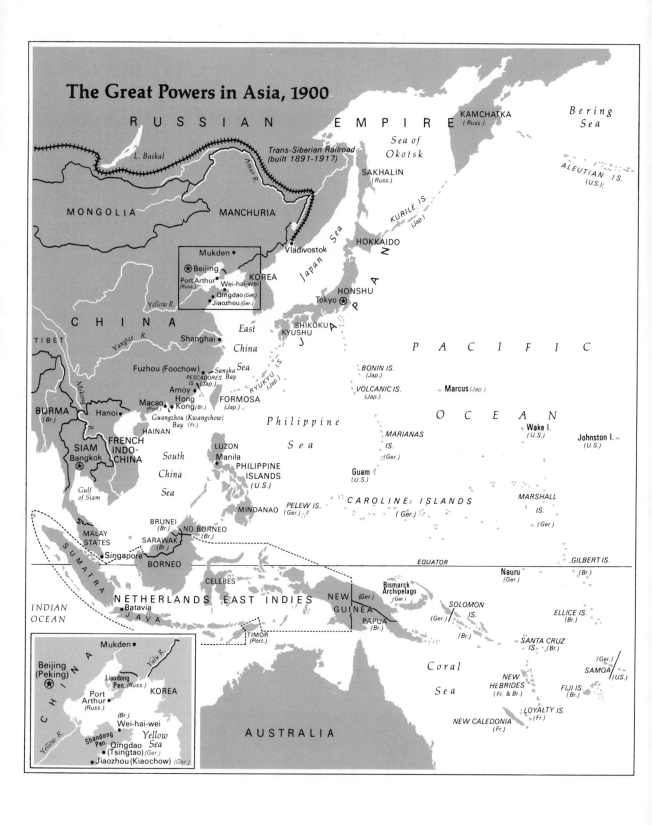

The Great Powers in Asia, 1900

RUSSIAN EMPIRE

KAMCHATKA *(Russ.)*

Bering Sea

Sea of Okotsk

L. Baikal

Trans-Siberian Railroad (built 1891–1917)

Amur R.

SAKHALIN *(Russ.)*

ALEUTIAN IS. *(U.S.)*

MONGOLIA

MANCHURIA

KURILE IS. *(Jap.)*

Mukden

Vladivostok

HOKKAIDO

⊛ Beijing
Port Arthur *(Russ.)*
Wei-hai-wei
KOREA

Japan Sea

CHINA

Qingdao *(Ger.)*
Jiaozhou *(Ger.)*

HONSHU
Tokyo ⊛

Yellow R.

J A P A N

TIBET

Yangtze R.

Shanghai

East China Sea

SHIKOKU
KYUSHU

BONIN IS. *(Jap.)*

Fuzhou (Foochow)
Sansha Bay
PESCADORES IS. *(Jap.)*
RYUKYU IS. *(Jap.)*

VOLCANIC IS. *(Jap.)*

Marcus *(Jap.)*

P A C I F I C

Amoy
Macao *(Port.)*
Hong Kong *(Br.)*
FORMOSA *(Jap.)*

Philippine Sea

MARIANAS IS. *(Ger.)*

Wake I. *(U.S.)*

Johnston I. *(U.S.)*

O C E A N

BURMA *(Br.)*
Hanoi
Guangzhou (Kwangchow) Bay *(Fr.)*
HAINAN

FRENCH INDO-CHINA
SIAM
Bangkok ⊛

South China Sea

LUZON
Manila
PHILIPPINE ISLANDS *(U.S.)*

Guam *(U.S.)*

Gulf of Siam

MINDANAO

PELEW IS. *(Ger.)*

C A R O L I N E   I S L A N D S *(Ger.)*

MARSHALL IS. *(Ger.)*

MALAY STATES
Singapore
BRUNEI *(Br.)*
SARAWAK *(Br.)*
NO. BORNEO *(Br.)*
BORNEO

EQUATOR

GILBERT IS. *(Br.)*

SUMATRA

INDIAN OCEAN

NETHERLANDS EAST INDIES
Batavia
JAVA

CELEBES

NEW GUINEA *(Ger.)*
PAPUA *(Br.)*

Bismarck Archipelago *(Ger.)*

Nauru *(Ger.)*

SOLOMON IS. *(Ger.)*

ELLICE IS. *(Br.)*

TIMOR *(Port.)*

SANTA CRUZ IS. *(Br.)*

(Ger.)
SAMOA *(U.S.)*

AUSTRALIA

Coral Sea

NEW HEBRIDES *(Fr. & Br.)*
FIJI IS. *(Br.)*

LOYALTY IS. *(Fr.)*

NEW CALEDONIA *(Fr.)*

Inset map

CHINA

Mukden

Yalu R.

Beijing (Peking) ⊛

Liaodong Pen. *(Russ.)*

KOREA

Port Arthur *(Russ.)*

(Br.)
Wei-hai-wei

Shandong Pen.

Yellow Sea

Qingdao (Tsingtao) *(Ger.)*

Jiaozhou (Kiaochow) *(Ger.)*

Yellow R.

Guangzhou Bay in southern China in April of that year. Japan already had footholds in Formosa and Korea. Britain approached Washington in March, 1898 and suggested a joint Anglo-American declaration on behalf of equal commercial opportunity in China. In the midst of the Cuban crisis, the United States gave little attention to the request. Britain then forced China to give up part of the Shandong Peninsula. China had become "the Sick Man of Asia."

American economic and religious interests in China seemed threatened. Businessmen from the American Asiatic Association and missionaries appealed to Washington for help. Drawing upon recommendations from William W. Rockhill, adviser on Asian policy, who in turn drew upon advice from his British friend and an officer of the Chinese customs service, Alfred Hippisley, Secretary of State John Hay tried words. On September 6, 1899, Hay sent an "Open Door" Note to Japan, Germany, Russia, Britain, France, and Italy, asking them to respect equal trade opportunity for all nations in their spheres. It was, of course, a traditional American principle, and given minimal military power in the Far East, it was the best the United States could do. Noncommittal replies trickled back, but Hay read into them what he wanted and proclaimed the definitive acceptance of the "Open Door" proposal.

Although frail, the Open Door policy carried meaning. Americans knew they were weaker than the other imperialists in Asia, but they also noted that a delicate balance of power existed there that the United States could unbalance. The European powers and Japan might be wary of excluding American commerce altogether from China, for fear that the United States would tip that balance by joining one of the powers against the others. They also feared that a world war might erupt from the competition in Asia. Americans hoped the Open Door policy would serve their goals in an area where American military power was feeble. The United States wanted the commercial advantages without having to employ military force, as it did in Latin America. The policy did not always work, but it fixed itself in the American mind as a guiding principle for Chinese affairs.

The Open Door Note notwithstanding, the Manchu dynasty (1644–1912) was near death and unable to cope with the foreign intruders. Resentful nationalistic Chinese, led by a secret society called *Yihequan* ("Righteous and Harmonious Fists," or the "Boxers"), undertook in 1900 to throw out the imperialist aggressors. The Boxers murdered hundreds of Christian missionaries and their Chinese converts, and laid siege to the foreign legations in Peking. To head off a complete gouging of China by vengeful Europeans and Japanese, Washington took two steps. It sent 2,500 American troops to Peking from the Philippines to join 15,500 soldiers from other nations to lift the siege. And Hay, without consulting the Chinese government, issued another Open Door Note on July 3, 1900. He defined United States policy as the protection of American life and property, the safeguarding of "equal and impartial trade," and the preservation of China's "territorial and administrative entity."[44] In short, keep the trade door open by keeping China intact. Certainly these actions did not save China from continued incursion (it was, for example, assessed over $300 million to pay for the Boxers' damages). The United States itself even asked for a territorial concession in late 1900 at Sansha Bay, Fujian Province. The Japanese, catching Hay redhanded, politely reminded him of his notes and he shelved the request. The United States continued to attempt to gain recognition for the Open Door and thereby immersed itself more and more in the boiling Asian cauldron. As historian Marilyn Blatt Young

John M. Hay (1838–1905). The author of the Open Door Notes graduated from Brown University and served as one of President Abraham Lincoln's secretaries during the Civil War. He became a newspaper editor and diplomat, and in 1897 he was appointed ambassador to Great Britain. The following year McKinley named him secretary of state, a post he held until his death. One historian, Christopher Thorne, has described the Open Door policy as a "singular blend of evangelicalism, political calculation, benevolent imperialism, and crude self-interest." (National Portrait Gallery, Smithsonian Institution)

has concluded: "In the late nineteenth century Americans came to feel that having influence in Asia was a categorical imperative for a world power. America, after the Spanish-American War, was a world power, *ergo* it must take a key part in Far Eastern Affairs."[45]

TOWARD WORLD POWER, 1895–1900

Venezuela, Cuba, Hawaii, the Philippines, Open Door Notes—together they meant an unprecedented set of commitments and responsibilities for the United States. Symbolic of this thrust to world power status was the ascendancy of the imperialist's imperialist, Theodore Roosevelt, to the office of the President in 1901. Peering into the twentieth century, Roosevelt warned Americans to avoid "slothful ease and ignoble peace." Never "shrink from the hard contests"; "let us therefore boldly face the life of strife."[46] Indeed, many diplomats looked back upon the triumphs of the 1890s as a testing time when the United States met the international challenge and rightfully asserted its place as a major world power. Europeans watched anxiously. Some, especially Germans, spoke of the "American peril" or "American menace." Italians worried that the United States would grab their poorly defended colonies. With its industrial and naval strength and its string of colonies, the United States, European leaders pointed out, was now a factor in the "balance of power." With whom, they asked in some trepidation, would the nation ally itself?

The odds seemed to favor Great Britain, although the Anglo-American courtship would be prolonged and marriage something for the future. Ever since the eye-opening Venezuelan crisis, London and Washington had been moving closer together in what has been called the "great rapprochement." Looking for support against an expansionist Germany, John Bull thought Uncle Sam a fit partner. During the Spanish-American War the British were noticeably friendly to the American side and to the subsequent absorption of Spanish colonies. Americans, in turn, sympathized with the British repression of the Boer Republics in South Africa, comparing that struggle to their own war with the Filipinos. Articulate Americans welcomed Britain's implicit acceptance of their imperialism. Germany seemed to replace Britain as the major power hostile to America. Vague Anglo-Saxonism and cultural ties joined British recognition of the power of the United States to forge more amicable relations. As the British Admiralty informed the Cabinet in December of 1899, "our squadron [West Indies], which in 1889 was superior to that of the United States, is now in 1899 completely outclassed by them."[47] Anglophobes continued to twist the lion's tail and Anglo-American commercial competition was intense, but the strands connecting the two powers grew tighter as they entered the twentieth century.

Britain still ranked first in naval power, but in the late 1890s the United States was growing, standing sixth by 1900. In 1898 alone, spurred by the war with Spain, the United States added 128 vessels to its Navy, at a cost of $18 million. At the 1898 American Historical Association meeting, Professor Edwin A. Grosvenor of Amherst College caught the new times in his address: "Barriers of national seclusion are everywhere tumbling like the great wall of China. Every nation elbows other nations to-day. . . . What was whispered at evening in the conclave of envoys and ambassadors is shouted the next morning by newsboys thousands of miles distant."[48] Many commentators reported that the United States, although

Pears' Soap Advertisement. This unusual mixture of commercial and diplomatic advertising salutes the Anglo-American rapprochement. (*Life,* 1898)

still divided North and South on many issues, was united as never before. Southern racists and Northern imperialists now had something in common: the need to
keep inferior peoples in their place. Senator Benjamin Tillman of South Carolina,
in noting the Filipino insurrection, put it this way: "No Republican leader . . . will
now dare to wave the bloody shirt and preach a crusade against the South's
treatment of the negro. The North has a bloody shirt of its own. Many thousands
of them have been made into shrouds for murdered Filipinos."[49]

The events of the 1895–1900 period meant further changes in the process of
decisionmaking. Both Cleveland and McKinley conducted their own foreign
policies, often thwarting or directing Congress. They helped establish the authority
of the President over foreign policy. In 1907, looking back upon the days of 1898
and citing the past, Woodrow Wilson, then president of Princeton University,
recorded the historical impact: "The war with Spain again changed the balance of
powers. Foreign questions became leading questions again, as they had been in the
first days of the government, and in them the President was of necessity leader.
Our new place in the affairs of the world has since that year of transformation kept
him at the front of our government, where his own thoughts and the attention of
men everywhere is centered on him. . . . The nation has risen to the first rank in
power and resources. . . . Our President must always, henceforth, be one of the
great powers of the world."[50] Wilson exaggerated America's power, for that
strength was still largely centered in the western hemisphere, but for the United
States, as the *Washington Post* editorialized in 1898, "the policy of isolation is
dead. . . . A new consciousness seems to have come upon us—the consciousness
of strength, and with it a new appetite, a yearning to show our strength. . . .
Ambition, interest, land-hunger, pride, the mere joy of fighting, whatever it may
be, we are animated by a new sensation. . . . The taste of empire is in the mouth of
the people, even as the taste of blood in the jungle."[51] After 1900 the task became
the translation of this consciousness into the actual management of the empire.

FURTHER READING FOR THE PERIOD 1895–1900

For events and attitudes in the 1890s and America's path to empire, see some of the works
cited in Chapter 5 and the following: Robert L. Beisner, *From the Old Diplomacy to the New*
(1986); Richard D. Challener, *Admirals, Generals, and American Foreign Policy, 1898–1914*
(1973); John A. S. Grenville and George B. Young, *Politics, Strategy, and American Diplomacy*
(1967); David Healy, *U.S. Expansionism: The Imperialist Urge in the 1890s* (1970); Richard
Hofstadter, *Social Darwinism in American Thought* (1955) and "Manifest Destiny and the
Philippines," in Daniel Aaron, ed., *America in Crisis* (1952); Walter LaFeber, *The New Empire*
(1963); Ernest R. May, *Imperial Democracy* (1961); H. Wayne Morgan, *America's Road to
Empire* (1965); Goran Rystad, *Ambiguous Imperialism: American Foreign Policy and Domestic
Politics at the Turn of the Century* (1981); R. Hal Williams, *Years of Decision: American Politics in
the 1890s* (1978); William A. Williams, *The Roots of the Modern American Empire* (1969) and
The Tragedy of American Diplomacy (1962).

For the coming of the Spanish-American-Cuban-Filipino War, see the works above and
Philip S. Foner, *The Spanish-Cuban-American War and the Birth of American Imperialism*
(1972); Julius Pratt, *Expansionists of 1898* (1938); Hyman G. Rickover, *How the Battleship
Maine Was Destroyed* (1976); and Joseph E. Wisan, *The Cuban Crisis as Reported in the New
York Press, 1895–1898* (1934).

For studies of the Spanish-American War, consult Charles H. Brown, *The Correspondent's
War: Journalists in the Spanish-American War* (1967); Graham A. Cosmas, *An Army for Empire:*

The United States Army in the Spanish-American War (1971); Willard B. Gatewood, Jr., *Black Americans and the White Man's Burden, 1898–1903* (1975); Gerald F. Linderman, *The Mirror of War: American Society and the Spanish-American War* (1974); and David F. Trask, *The War with Spain in 1898* (1981).

For American imperialist leaders and their case for empire, see H. K. Beale, *Theodore Roosevelt and the Rise of America to World Power* (1956); John Braeman, *Albert J. Beveridge* (1971); Kenton Clymer, *John Hay* (1975); Gerald Eggert, *Richard Olney* (1973); Lewis L. Gould, *The Presidency of William McKinley* (1980); Margaret Leech, *In the Days of McKinley* (1959); H. Wayne Morgan, *William McKinley and His America* (1963); Edmund Morris, *The Rise of Theodore Roosevelt* (1979); Ronald Spector, *Admiral of the New Empire* (1974) (on Dewey); and William C. Widenor, *Henry Cabot Lodge and the Search for an American Foreign Policy* (1980).

Anti-imperialists and anti-imperialism are treated in William N. Armstrong, *E. L. Godkin and American Foreign Policy* (1957); Robert L. Beisner, *Twelve Against Empire* (1968); Kendrick A. Clements, *William Jennings Bryan, Missionary Isolationist* (1983); Paolo E. Coletta, *William Jennings Bryan* (1964–1969); John C. Farrell, *Beloved Lady: A History of Jane Addams' Ideas on Reform and Peace* (1967); Thomas J. Osborne, *"Empire Can Wait": American Opposition to Hawaiian Annexation, 1893–1898* (1981); E. Berkeley Tompkins, *Anti-Imperialism in the United States* (1970); Hans L. Trefousse, *Carl Schurz* (1982); and Joseph F. Wall, *Andrew Carnegie* (1970).

The Open Door policy and Asian events are discussed in Thomas A. Breslin, *China, American Catholicism, and the Missionary* (1980); Charles S. Campbell, *Special Business Interests and the Open Door Policy* (1951); Michael Hunt, *Frontier Defense and the Open Door: Manchuria in Chinese-American Relations, 1895–1911* (1973) and *The Making of a Special Relationship* (1983); Akira Iriye, *Across the Pacific* (1967); Robert McClellan, *The Heathen Chinee: A Study of American Attitudes Toward China, 1890–1905* (1971); Thomas McCormick, *China Market* (1967); Valentin H. Rabe, *The Home Base of American China Missions, 1880–1920* (1978); Merze Tate, *Hawaii: Reciprocity or Annexation* (1968); Paul A. Varg, *The Making of a Myth* (1968); and Marilyn Blatt Young, *The Rhetoric of Empire* (1968).

The Philippine rebellion and the American debate about it receive scrutiny in Teodoro Agoncillo, *Malolos* (1960); John M. Gates, *Schoolbooks and Krags: The United States Army in the Philippines, 1898–1902* (1973); Stuart C. Miller, *"Benevolent Assimilation"* (1982); Daniel B. Schirmer, *Republic or Empire* (1972); David R. Sturtevant, *Popular Uprisings in the Philippines* (1976); and Richard E. Welch, *Response to Imperialism: American Resistance to the Philippine War* (1979). See also "American Empire, 1898–1903," *Pacific Historical Review* (1979) (entire issue) and Edward J. Berbusse, *The United States in Puerto Rico, 1898–1900* (1966).

For Anglo-American relations, including the Venezuelan crisis, see Stuart Anderson, *Race and Rapprochement: Anglo-Saxonism and Anglo-American Relations, 1815–1904* (1981); Alexander E. Campbell, *Great Britain and the United States, 1895–1903* (1960); Charles S. Campbell, *Anglo-American Understanding* (1957) and *From Revolution to Rapprochement* (1974); R. G. Neale, *Great Britain and United States Expansion, 1800–1900* (1966); and Bradford Perkins, *The Great Rapprochement* (1968).

See also the General Bibliography and the following notes.

NOTES TO CHAPTER 6

1. Quoted in Gerald G. Eggert, *Richard Olney: Evolution of a Statesman* (University Park: Pennsylvania State University Press, 1974), p. 208.
2. Quoted in Ernest R. May, *Imperial Democracy: The Emergence of America as a Great Power* (New York: Harper & Row, [1961], 1973), p. 33.
3. *Papers Relating to the Foreign Relations of the United States, 1895,* Part I (Washington: Government Printing Office, 1896), pp. 545–562.
4. Quoted in Robert L. Beisner, *From the Old Diplomacy to the New, 1865–1900* (Arlington Heights, Ill.: Harlan Davidson, 1986; 2nd ed.) p.111.

5. Quoted in Howard K. Beale, *Theodore Roosevelt and the Rise of America to World Power* (New York: Collier Books, [1956], 1962), p. 60.
6. *Ibid.,* p. 61.
7. Quoted in Eggert, *Olney,* p. 223.
8. Quoted in Charles S. Campbell, *From Revolution to Rapprochement* (New York: John Wiley & Sons, 1974), p. 182.
9. Memorandum of January 10, 1896, quoted in Allan Nevins, *Grover Cleveland: A Study in Courage* (New York: Dodd, Mead, 1932), p. 644.
10. Quoted in George B. Young, "Intervention Under the Monroe Doctrine: The Olney Corollary," *Political Science Quarterly,* LVII (June, 1942), p. 277.
11. Quoted in Richard E. Welch, Jr., *George Frisbie Hoar and the Half-Breed Republicans* (Cambridge, Mass.: Harvard University Press, 1971), p. 209.
12. Walter Q. Gresham to Carl Schurz, October 6, 1893, Walter Q. Gresham Papers, Library of Congress.
13. Quoted in Ramon Ruiz, *Cuba: The Making of a Revolution* (New York: W. W. Norton, [c. 1968], 1970), p. 73.
14. Quoted in Philip S. Foner, *The Spanish-Cuban-American War and the Birth of American Imperialism* (New York: Monthly Review Press, 1972; 2 vols.), I, 21.
15. Quoted in Eggert, *Olney,* p. 265 (August 14, 1896).
16. James D. Richardson, ed., *A Compilation of the Messages and Papers of the Presidents, 1789–1897* (Washington, D.C.: Government Printing Office, 1896–1899; 10 vols.), IX, 716–722.
17. Lester D. Langley, *The Cuban Policy of the United States: A Brief History* (New York: John Wiley and Sons, 1968), p. 97.
18. *Congressional Record,* 55th Cong., 2nd Sess., XXXI, 3–5.
19. *Papers Relating to the Foreign Relations of the United States, 1898* (Washington, D.C.: Government Printing Office, 1901), pp. 1007–08.
20. Quoted in Walter LaFeber, *The New Empire: An Interpretation of American Expansion, 1860–1898* (Ithaca, N.Y.: Cornell University Press, 1963), p. 349.
21. *Congressional Record,* 55th Cong., 2nd Sess., XXXI, 2916–19.
22. *Foreign Relations, 1898,* p. 746.
23. *Congressional Record,* 55th Cong., 2nd Sess., XXXI, 3699–3702.
24. Quoted in H. Wayne Morgan, *America's Road to Empire: The War with Spain and Overseas Expansion* (New York: John Wiley and Sons, 1965), p. 63.
25. May 7, 1898, quoted in Winthrop S. Hudson, "Protestant Clergy Debate the Nation's Vocation, 1898–1899" (unpublished manuscript, 1974).
26. Quoted in John Braeman, *Albert J. Beveridge: American Nationalist* (Chicago: University of Chicago Press, 1971), p. 23.
27. Finley Peter Dunne, *Mr. Dooley in Peace and War* (Boston: Small, Maynard, 1899), p. 9.
28. Beisner, *From the Old Diplomacy to the New,* p. 129.
29. Quoted in Gerald F. Linderman, *The Mirror of War: American Society and the Spanish-American War* (Ann Arbor: University of Michigan Press, 1974), p. 125.
30. Quoted in Ruiz, *Cuba,* p. 21.
31. Quoted in Frank Freidel, *The Splendid Little War* (Boston: Little, Brown, 1958), p. 306.
32. *Ibid.,* p. 295.
33. Quoted in Willard B. Gatewood, Jr., *"Smoked Yankees" and the Struggle for Empire: Letters from Negro Soldiers, 1898–1902* (Urbana, Ill.: University of Illinois Press, 1971), p. 28.
34. Quoted in Paul C. Nagel, *This Sacred Trust: American Nationality, 1798–1898* (New York: Oxford University Press, 1971), p. 252.
35. Quoted in David Healy, *U.S. Expansionism: The Imperialist Urge in the 1890s* (Madison: University of Wisconsin Press, 1970), p. 55.
36. Quoted in Robert L. Beisner, "1898 and 1968: The Anti-Imperialists and the Doves," *Political Science Quarterly,* LXXV (June, 1970), 200.
37. Mark Twain, *The War Prayer* (New York: Harper and Row, [1923], 1970).
38. Quoted in H. Wayne Morgan, *William McKinley and His America* (Syracuse: Syracuse University Press, 1963), p. 422.
39. From the *Boston Evening Transcript,* March 1, 1899, reprinted in Ray Ginger, ed., *The Nationalizing of American Life, 1877–1900* (New York: The Free Press, 1965), pp. 310–315.
40. Quoted in Stuart C. Miller, "Our Mylai of 1900: Americans in the Philippine Insurrection," *Transaction,* VII (September, 1970), 24.
41. Henry F. Graff, ed., *American Imperialism and the Philippine Insurrection* (Boston: Little, Brown, 1969), p. 36.
42. Charles Francis Adams to Moorfield Storey, February 24, 1902, Moorfield Storey Papers, Massachusetts Historical Society, Boston.
43. Quoted in Thomas J. McCormick, *China Market: America's Quest for Informal Empire, 1893–1901* (Chicago: Quadrangle Books, 1967), p. 119.
44. *Foreign Relations of the United States, 1901,* Appendix: "Affairs in China" (Washington: Government Printing Office, 1902), p. 12.
45. Marilyn Blatt Young, "American Expansion, 1870–1900: The Far East," in Barton J. Bernstein, ed., *Towards a New Past: Dissenting Essays in American History* (New York: Pantheon Books, 1968), p. 196.
46. Quoted in Beale, *Theodore Roosevelt,* p. 84.
47. Quoted in Alexander E. Campbell, *Great Britain and the United States, 1895–1903* (London: Longmans, 1960), p. 31.
48. American Historical Association, *Annual Report, 1898* (Washington: Government Printing Office, 1899), p. 288.
49. Quoted in C. Vann Woodward, *The Strange Career of Jim Crow* (New York: Oxford University Press, 1974; 3rd rev. ed.), p. 73.
50. Quoted in Arthur Link's essay in *Wilson's Diplomacy: An International Symposium* (Cambridge, Mass.: Schenkman, 1973), p. 6.
51. *Washington Post,* June 2, 1898.

Chapter 7

Theodore Roosevelt (1858–1919). Graduate of Harvard, historian, Rough Rider, and New York governor, Republican Roosevelt became President in 1901 after William McKinley was assassinated. TR's famed impetuosity notwithstanding, biographer Frederick W. Marks has written that the President "stands in a class by himself for that blend of statesmanlike qualities which might best be described as velvet on iron." (Library of Congress)

Managing and Extending the American Empire, 1900–1914

DIPLOMATIC CROSSROAD:
TAKING PANAMA, 1903

"Revolution imminent," read the cable from the American consul at Colón, a normally sleepy Colombian seaport on the Atlantic side of the Isthmus of Panama. Acting Secretary of State Francis B. Loomis bridled his curiosity for an hour and five minutes. Then he fired off an inquiry to the United States consul at Panama City, on the Pacific slope: "Uprising on Isthmus reported. Keep Department promptly and fully informed." The response came back in four hours: "No uprising yet. Reported will be in the night. Situation is critical." Loomis' anxiety, already intense, increased sharply five minutes later when he learned that an "important message" intended for the U.S.S. *Nashville* anchored at Colón had miscarried, and troops of the Colombian government had landed in the city.

At the Department of State it was now 8:20 P.M., November 3, 1903. As far as Loomis knew, a revolution had not yet broken out on the isthmus. Nonetheless, he hurriedly drafted instructions for the consuls at Panama and Colón. "Act promptly," he directed in near desperation. Somehow convey to the commanding officer of the *Nashville* this order: "In the interests of peace make every effort to prevent [Colombian] Government troops at Colón from proceeding to Panama." Having ordered intervention against a friendly government during a revolution that to his knowledge had not yet begun, Loomis was left to agonize for another hour. Finally, a new cable arrived: "Uprising occurred to-night . . . no bloodshed. . . . Government will be organized to-night." Loomis no doubt sighed in relief. He had done his part to insure success in the reckless gamble for a canal controlled by the United States.

If November third was a busy day for Francis Loomis, it was far more hectic for José Augustín Arango and his fellow conspirators in Panama. The tiny mixed band of Panamanians and Americans living on the isthmus had been actively plotting revolution since August, when the Colombian Congress dashed their hopes for prosperity by defeating the treaty that would have permitted the United

States to construct an isthmian canal. By the end of October, they had become convinced that the North American colossus, frustrated in its overtures to Colombia, would lend them moral and physical support. Confident that American naval vessels would be at hand, they selected November fourth as the date of their coup d'état. To their dismay, however, the Colombian steamer *Cartagena* disembarked about 400 troops at Colón early in the morning of November 3. Because the "important message" directing him to prevent the "landing of any armed force . . . either Government or insurgent at Colón" had been delayed in transmission, Commander John Hubbard of the *Nashville* did not interfere with the landing.

Forced to rely on their own wits, the conspirators made good use of the transisthmian railroad. They deviously separated the Colombian commanding general from his troops, lured him aboard a train, and sped him ceremoniously across the isthmus to Panama City. At 6:00 P.M. on the third, the revolutionaries arrested their guest, formed a provisional government, and paraded before a cheering crowd at the Cathedral Plaza. But the revolution would remain perilously unfinished so long as armed Colombian soldiers occupied Colón. Too weak to expel the soldiers by force, the insurgents gave the colonel in charge $8000 in gold, whereupon he ordered his troops aboard a departing steamer. The American consul at Panama City cabled: "Quiet prevails." At noon the next day, Secretary of State John Hay recognized the sovereign Republic of Panama.

The frantic pace of American isthmian diplomacy continued. The new Panamanian government appointed as its minister plenipotentiary a Frenchman, Philippe Bunau-Varilla, who had long agitated for a Panama canal and who recently had conspired for Panamanian independence from Colombia. With Gallic flourish Bunau-Varilla descended upon Secretary Hay. He extolled the United States for rescuing Panama "from the barbarism of unnecessary and wasteful civil wars to consecrate it to the destiny assigned to it by Providence, the service of humanity, and the progress of civilization."[1] John Hay thoroughly understood the meaning of Bunau-Varilla's rhetoric and eagerly negotiated the treaty both men wanted. On November 18, 1903, less than two weeks after American recognition of Panama, they signed the Hay–Bunau-Varilla Treaty, by which the United States government would build, fortify, and operate a canal linking the Atlantic and Pacific oceans.

Hay had at last achieved a goal set by his chief, President Theodore Roosevelt, several years earlier. "I do not see why we should dig the canal if we are not to fortify it," Roosevelt had explained to navalist Alfred Thayer Mahan early in 1900. If an unfortified, neutral canal had existed in Central America during the recent war with Spain, Roosevelt argued in another letter, "we could have got the *Oregon* around in time," but the United States would have spent most of the war in "wild panic," fearful that the Spanish fleet would slip through the waterway and rush to the Philippines to attack Commodore Dewey. The lesson was manifest. Enemy fleets of the future must not be allowed to steam through an isthmian canal to strike the United States at exposed and vulnerable places. "Better to have no canal at all, than not give us the power to control it in time of war," Roosevelt expostulated.[2] What he really wanted, of course, was a canal run by Americans for the benefit of the United States.

The major barrier to that goal was the Clayton-Bulwer Treaty of 1850, stipulating joint Anglo-American construction and operation of any Central American canal. In December, 1898, flushed with victory over Spain, President William McKinley had directed Secretary Hay to discuss modification of that agreement

Teddy Roosevelt the Pirate. The Colombian minister called the United States a "pirate" that had "mutilated" his nation by severing Panama. Cartoonist Frank Nankivell's rendering of the strong-willed President captured the Colombian viewpoint. (Swann Collection of Caricature and Cartoon)

with the British Ambassador, Sir Julian Pauncefote. The Hay-Pauncefote Treaty of February, 1900 permitted the United States to build a canal but forbade its fortification, much to the chagrin of Theodore Roosevelt, then governor of New York. He spearheaded an attack that defeated the treaty in the Senate, forcing renegotiation. On November 18, 1901, with Roosevelt now President, Hay and Pauncefote signed a pact satisfactory to the Rough Rider.

Then began the complex process of determining the route. In November, 1901, after an investigation lasting two years, the Walker Isthmian Canal Commission reported in favor of Nicaragua. The decisive criterion was cost, which in the case of Panama was made incalculable by the obduracy of the New Panama Canal Company, a French-chartered firm that held the Colombian concession for canal rights. The company estimated its assets on the isthmus at $109 million—

machinery, property, and excavated soil left by the defunct de Lesseps organization after its failure to cut through Panama in 1888. When coupled with the engineering costs, purchase of the New Panama Canal Company's rights and holdings would make construction through Panama prohibitively expensive, even though technologically easier. For these reasons, the House of Representatives on January 8, 1902 passed the Hepburn Bill authorizing a canal through Nicaragua.

The New Panama Canal Company's American lawyer, William Nelson Cromwell, described by one irritated congressman as "the most dangerous man this country has produced since the days of Aaron Burr—a professional revolutionist," swung into action.[3] Cromwell was a partner in the prestigious New York law firm of Sullivan and Cromwell, and his fixed purpose in 1902–1903 was to sell the assets of his French client for the highest possible price. The Walker Commission had estimated the company's worth at $40 million, a figure Cromwell reluctantly accepted in face of the passage of the Hepburn Bill. The attorney began an intense

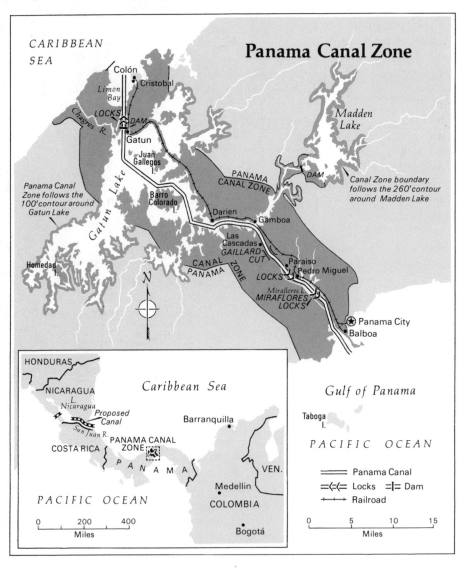

lobbying campaign directed principally at President Roosevelt, Republican senators Mark Hanna and John C. Spooner, and members of the Walker Commission.
Cromwell was joined by Bunau-Varilla, formerly chief engineer for de Lesseps, in
what has been described as one of the "masterpieces of the lobbyist's art."[4]

On January 18, 1902, the Walker Commission reversed itself and decided for the
technologically preferable Panama passage, citing the company's willingness to sell
out for the reduced sum of $40 million. Guided by Roosevelt, Spooner, and
Cromwell, Congress five months later passed the Spooner Act, approving the
Panama route. The State Department soon opened negotiations with Colombia.
The price of the annual rental became a stumbling block, which Hay removed only
by delivering an ultimatum to the Colombian chargé d'affaires, Tomás Herrán, in
January, 1903. On January 22 he and Hay signed a treaty granting Colombia an
initial payment of $10 million and $250,000 annually. The United States reaped
control over the six-mile wide canal zone for 100 years, a privilege renewable at the
"sole and absolute option" of the North American republic.[5]

The United States Senate approved the Hay-Herrán Treaty on March 17, 1903,
but the Colombian government, although genuinely desiring American construction of a canal, moved slowly. Faced with a treasury drained by a long and costly
civil war, Bogotá attempted to extract a $10 million payment from the New Panama
Canal Company for permitting the transfer of its assets to the American government. At this juncture Hay succumbed to the blandishments of William Nelson
Cromwell. After meeting with the lawyer in April, the secretary bluntly announced
that any discussion of a payment by the new Panama Canal Company to Colombia
"would be in violation of the Spooner law and not permissible."[6]

As a second stratagem, the Colombian government attempted to raise the initial
American cash payment from $10 to $15 million. Roosevelt waxed indignant,
snapping to Hay that "those contemptible little creatures in Bogotá ought to
understand how much they are jeopardizing things and imperilling their own
future."[7] The President came to believe that "you could no more make an agreement with the Colombian rulers than you could nail currant jelly to the wall."[8]
TR's intransigence and Hay's extraordinary intercession on behalf of a privately
owned foreign corporation increased the anxiety felt by many Colombian congressmen about the Hay-Herrán Treaty's severe infringement upon Colombia's
sovereignty over Panama. They unanimously defeated the treaty on August 12,
1903.

Bogotá's rejection did not catch Roosevelt napping. As early as March 30, Minister Arthur N. Beaupré had cautioned Washington that "without question public
opinion is strongly against its ratification," and Roosevelt had begun to ponder
undiplomatic alternatives.[9] On June 13 the ubiquitous Cromwell had met with
Roosevelt and then planted a story in the *New York World* reporting that, if Colombia rejected the treaty, Panama would secede and grant to the United States "the
equivalent of absolute sovereignty over the Canal Zone." Moreover, alleged the
World, "President Roosevelt is said to strongly favor this plan."[10] As it became
increasingly likely that Colombia would repudiate the Hay-Herrán pact, Roosevelt's contempt for the Colombian people mounted. In private letters to Hay and
others he denounced them as "jack rabbits," "foolish and homicidal corruption-
ists," and "cat-rabbits."[11] Hay, usually urbane and restrained, uttered a diatribe
against "the government of folly and graft that now rules at Bogotá."[12]

Roosevelt and Hay now considered two options: seizure of Panama by force, or extension of instant recognition and support to any revolutionary regime in Panama. The President inclined sharply toward the latter course after a meeting with Bunau-Varilla on October 10, during which the Frenchman predicted an uprising. Although TR was guarded in his reply, he later admitted that Bunau-Varilla "would have been a very dull man" if unable to "guess" that the United States would respond favorably to a revolution.[13] One week later, on October 16, Secretary Hay informed Bunau-Varilla that American naval vessels were heading toward the isthmus. Bunau-Varilla shrewdly calculated the steaming time and cabled the revolutionaries waiting on the isthmus that American warships would arrive by November 2. Early that evening the U.S.S. *Nashville* dropped anchor at Colón as predicted.

In his annual message to Congress after the Panamanian revolution, Roosevelt urged swift ratification of the Hay-Bunau-Varilla Treaty, saying that the colossal canal project would benefit the United States and the rest of mankind as well. When Democrats in the Senate questioned the President's role in the insurrection, Roosevelt disingenuously replied: "No one connected with this Government had any part in preparing, inciting, or encouraging the late revolution."[14] Apparently mollified, on February 23, 1904, the Senate approved the treaty by a vote of 66 to 14. The treaty granted the United States "power and authority" within the zone as "if it were the sovereign of the territory. . . ."[15] Later, in 1911, TR was widely reported as boasting that "I took the Canal Zone and let Congress debate; and while the debate goes on the Canal does also."[16]

Construction began in mid-1904, and the fifty-mile-long canal opened to traffic on August 15, 1914. During the first year of operation alone, 1,058 merchant vessels slid through the locks, while the Atlantic and Pacific fleets of the United

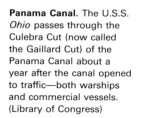

Panama Canal. The U.S.S. *Ohio* passes through the Culebra Cut (now called the Gaillard Cut) of the Panama Canal about a year after the canal opened to traffic—both warships and commercial vessels. (Library of Congress)

States Navy freely exchanged ships. In 1922 the United States paid "conscience money" or "canalimony" of $25 million to Colombia but did not formally apologize for having taken the canal zone. Although Roosevelt's handling of the Panama issue, according to historian William Harbaugh, constitutes "one of the ineradicable blots on his record," most Americans have applauded his bold meddling in the internal affairs of the sovereign nation of Colombia.[17] Roosevelt himself ranked his accomplishment alongside the Louisiana Purchase and the acquisition of Texas.

THE CONSERVATIVE SHAPERS OF THE AMERICAN EMPIRE

The taking of Panama symbolized the new activism characteristic of American foreign policy after the Spanish-American War, and construction of the canal placed the United States in a physical position of undisputed domination over Latin America. Great Britain, the only Old World power that might have contested America's new pre-eminence, faced a stiff political and naval challenge from Germany. In a series of remarkable retreats beginning with the first Hay-Pauncefote Treaty, London diplomatically recognized the shifting balance of power in Europe and the Americas and acquiesced in United States hegemony over Latin America. President Roosevelt perceived more clearly than most Americans an opportunity to capitalize on this historic transformation. The Panama Canal marked one result.

In the late nineteenth century, Roosevelt had associated closely with the most vocal pressure group agitating for an American canal, the uniformed "professors of war" at the Naval War College.[18] He corresponded regularly with one of those officers, Alfred Thayer Mahan, the navalist who tirelessly explained the strategic advantages of a canal in the idiom of the 1890s. "Wherever situated, whether at Panama or Nicaragua," Mahan preached, "the fundamental meaning of the canal will be that it advances by thousands of miles the frontiers . . . of the United States."[19] In the course of expanding those frontiers during the "splendid little war" of 1898, the cruiser *Oregon* dashed at full speed from San Francisco to the tip of South America and through the Strait of Magellan to Cuba in time to help destroy the Spanish fleet off Santiago. The race of over 14,000 miles fired American imaginations, but it also consumed sixty-eight days and dramatically underscored the need for an interoceanic canal across Central America.

Roosevelt's sense of isthmian strategic necessity reflected a broad world view he shared with many "progressives" in the reform era of the early twentieth century. A conservative patrician reformer motivated by noblesse oblige, he "feared that unrest caused by social and economic inequities would impair the nation's strength and efficiency."[20] He saw a similar danger to American interests in unrest abroad, and he sought to exert United States influence to create order on a global scale. "More and more," Roosevelt told Congress in 1902, "the increasing interdependence and complexity of international political and economic relations render it incumbent on all civilized and orderly powers to insist on the proper policing of the world."[21] A quintessential chauvinist, Roosevelt talked about doing the "rough work of the world" and about the need to "speak softly and carry a big stick."[22] Like his contemporaries, TR had imbibed the Social Darwinist doctrines of "natural selection" and the "survival of the fittest," and he articulated racist notions about Anglo-Saxon superiority and the "white man's burden" to tutor "backward" peoples. For Roosevelt in particular, that superiority was best ex-

Makers of American Foreign Policy from 1900 to 1914

Presidents	Secretaries of State
Theodore Roosevelt, 1901–1909	John Hay, 1898–1905
	Elihu Root, 1905–1909
	Robert Bacon, 1909
William Howard Taft, 1909–1913	Philander C. Knox, 1909–1913
Woodrow Wilson, 1913–1921	William Jennings Bryan, 1913–1915

pressed in war. "All the great masterful races have been fighting races," he lectured an audience at the Naval War College.[23] Progressive politicians, however, were decidedly split over foreign policy questions. Some joined Roosevelt in advocating a vigorous activism abroad. Others, like Wisconsin's Senator Robert M. LaFollette, were anti-imperialists and critics of war who believed that the corporate monopolies they were battling at home were dragging the United States into perpetual interventionism abroad.

Roosevelt always vigorously debated his critics and added his unique personal characteristics to American foreign policy. Exuberant and calculating, having the instinct for the jugular, he centralized and personalized foreign policy decision-making, frequently bypassed Congress, and believed "the people" so ignorant about foreign affairs that they should not direct an informed President like himself. In the search for a stable world order and a balance of power, Roosevelt could assume the garb of the peacemaker trying to reconcile competing national interests. For example, he won the Nobel Peace Prize in 1906 for his mediating effort at the Portsmouth Conference (see p. 239). The candid President disliked the pomp and ceremony of traditional diplomacy and on occasion disrupted protocol with a memorable incident: he once broke up a luncheon by demonstrating jujitsu holds on the Swiss minister. "The biggest matters," this progenitor of the imperial presidency later wrote, "such as the Portsmouth peace, the acquisition of Panama, and sending the fleet around the world, I managed without consultation with anyone; for when a matter is of capital importance, it is well to have it handled by one man only."[24]

Roosevelt and other shapers of American foreign policy between the Spanish-American War and the First World War were members of an American quasi-aristocracy and sure-footed devotees of "order." Most had graduated from prestigious eastern colleges and distinguished themselves in high political office or in the professions. They moved comfortably in the affluent, cosmopolitan, upper-class society of the Atlantic seaboard. Roosevelt, a graduate of Harvard College, had been assistant secretary of the Navy and governor of New York and was a prolific author. His successor, Ohioan William Howard Taft, a graduate of Yale, had served as a federal circuit court judge, governor of the Philippines (1901–1904), and secretary of war (1904–1908). Woodrow Wilson earned a Ph.D. from Johns Hopkins, wrote books on history, presided over Princeton, and governed New Jersey before entering the White House.

Their secretaries of state, with one exception, were members of the same elite. John Hay, secretary for 1898–1905, was born in Indiana and educated at Brown

University. Wealthy and recognized as a poet, novelist, biographer, and editor of the *New York Tribune,* he had served as Lincoln's personal secretary during the Civil War and later as McKinley's ambassador to Great Britain. He thought the "indispensable feature of our foreign policy should be a firm understanding with England," and he was one of the chief architects of the Anglo-American rapprochement of the early twentieth century.[25] His successor Elihu Root (1905–1909), a cautious conservative who praised Theodore Roosevelt as "the greatest conservative force for the protection of property and capital," was born in upstate New York, graduated from Hamilton College, took a law degree at New York University, and became one of America's most successful corporation lawyers.[26] As secretary of war from 1899 to 1904, he created mechanisms, such as the Platt Amendment for Cuba, for managing the American empire. Like TR, he believed that the "main object of diplomacy is to keep the country out of trouble" and maintain order abroad.[27] Philander C. Knox (1909–1913) followed Root. A corporation lawyer born in Pennsylvania, he had helped form the giant United States Steel Corporation. He served as attorney general and United States senator before entering the State Department. Habitually seeking leisure, Knox liked to play golf at Chevy Chase, spend summers with his trotters at his Valley Forge Farms estate, vacation in Florida in the winter, and delegate departmental work to subordinates. He advocated "dollar diplomacy" as a means of creating order in revolution-prone areas—that is, the use of private financiers and businessmen to promote foreign policy, and vice versa. The second man to serve under President Wilson was New Yorker Robert Lansing (1915–1920), a graduate of Amherst College, son-in-law of a former secretary of state, and practitioner of international law. Reserved and conservative, Lansing also would not tolerate disorder in the United States sphere of Latin America.

William Jennings Bryan, Wilson's first appointment (1913–1915), did not conform to the conservative elite status of most makers of foreign policy. The "boy orator" of Nebraska could mesmerize crowds by decrying the "cross of gold" upon which eastern capitalists were crucifying western and southern farmers, but he could not win a presidential election (he ran in 1896, 1900, and 1908). The "Great Commoner" languished for years as the most prominent has-been of the Democratic party, until Wilson appointed him secretary of state out of deference to his long service to the partisan cause and as a reward for support at the convention of 1912. The President let Bryan appoint "deserving Democrats" to diplomatic posts and indulge his fascination with peace or "cooling off" treaties, but Wilson bypassed him in most important diplomatic decisions, even to the point of composing overseas cables on his own White House typewriter. In 1915, during World War I, Bryan resigned to protest Wilson's pro-British leanings.

These conservative managers of American foreign policy believed that a major component of national power was a prosperous, expanding economy invigorated by a healthy foreign trade. The principle of the "Open Door"—to keep open trade and investment opportunities—became a governing tenet voiced globally, although often tarnished in application. Mahan believed that commerce was the "energizer of material civilization," and Roosevelt declared to Congress in his annual message of 1901 that "America has only just begun to assume that commanding position in the international business world which we believe will more and more be hers."[28] In 1900 the United States exported goods valued at $1.5 billion. By 1914, at the start of World War I, that figure stood at $2.5 billion.

Exports to Latin America increased markedly from $132 million at the turn of the century to $309 million in 1914. Investments there in sugar, transportation, and banking shot up. By 1913 the United Fruit Company, the banana empire, had some 130,000 acres in cultivation in Central America, a fleet of freighters, and political influence as well. By 1914 the United States dominated nickel mining in Canada and sugar production in Cuba, and total American investments abroad equaled $3.5 billion.

But those statistics were not important solely as contributions to pocketbooks. Americans believed that economic expansion also meant that the best of "Americanism," the values of industriousness, honesty, morality, and private initiative, were carried abroad. Thus Yale University-in-China and the Young Men's Christian Association (YMCA) joined the Standard Oil Company and Singer Sewing in China as advance agents of civilization. And, as Secretary of War Taft said about the Chinese in 1908, "The more civilized they become the more active their industries, the wealthier they become, and the better market they will become for us."[29] President Wilson, who added a conspicuous tinge of missionary paternalism to the quest for order, said simply that he would "teach the South American Republics to elect good men."[30] As historian Jerry Israel has noted, "reforming cultures, making profits, and saving souls were not incompatible goals."[31] All were intertwined in the American compulsion to shape the lives of other people while denying any intention of dominating them.

THE CUBAN PROTECTORATE

President William McKinley faced a dilemma in 1898. The Teller Amendment, which he had unsuccessfully opposed, forbade the annexation of Cuba. Yet, in negotiating the preliminary protocol of peace he had insisted that Spain relinquish sovereignty over the island. Cuba lay athwart the approaches to the Gulf of Mexico and Caribbean Sea. Unless brought firmly within the American orbit, it could threaten the security of the Gulf states and United States hegemony over Central America. The President understandably equivocated. In his annual message of December, 1898, he promised to help the Cubans build a "free and independent" government, but he also warned that American military rule would continue until "complete tranquillity" and a "stable government" existed on the island.[32]

Two months later the Philippine insurrection erupted, sending shock waves through America's policy-makers. Secretary of War Elihu Root, charged with the formulation of Cuban occupation policy, feared that in Cuba the United States was "on the verge daily of the same sort of thing that happened to us in the Philippines."[33] To accelerate the evolution of Cuban democracy and stability, Root appointed General Leonard Wood the military governor of the island. A Harvard graduate with a degree in medicine, Wood had entered the Army for excitement. A spiritual relative and a friend of the adventurous Roosevelt, Wood favored outright annexation of Cuba, but he loyally subordinated his own preferences to the Administration's policy of patrician tutelage in the ways of progress and freedom. During his tenure as military governor (1899–1902), he worked to eradicate yellow fever, Americanize education, construct highways, and formulate an electoral law guaranteeing order. The general defined his objectives in a conservative manner: "When money can be borrowed at a reasonable rate of interest and when capital is willing to invest in the Island, a condition of stability will have been reached."[34] Senator Joseph B. Foraker, an old Ohio rival of McKinley, viewed overseas investments in a less friendly light and sought to retard the annexationist tendencies that followed the flow of capital abroad. In February of 1899 he successfully attached an amendment to the Army Appropriation Bill that prohibited the American military government of Cuba from granting permanent economic concessions. However, Secretary of War Root outflanked the senator by granting revocable permits, beginning with a railroad franchise in 1901.

With the economic foundation of his policy safely laid, Root began construction of a Cuban-American political relationship designed to weather the storms of independence. Working closely with Senator Orville Platt, an Administration spokesman, Root fashioned the so-called Platt Amendment to the Army Appropriation Bill of 1901. By the Platt Amendment's terms, Cuba could not make a treaty with any nation that might impair its independence. Should Cuban independence ever be threatened, or should it fail to protect adequately "life, property, and individual liberty," the United States had the right to intervene. For these purposes, Cuba would cede to the United States "lands necessary for coaling or naval stations." The Platt Amendment also stipulated that "by way of further assurance" Cuba and the United States would "embody the foregoing provisions in a permanent treaty."[35]

Cubans howled. On Good Friday, 1901, the front page of Havana's *La Discusión* carried a cartoon of "The Cuban Calvary" depicting the Cuban people as Christ and Senator Platt as a Roman soldier. Many Americans agreed that the amendment

"If General Wood Is Unpopular with Cuba, We Can Guess the Reason." General Leonard Wood (1860–1927), before he served as military governor of Cuba (1899–1903), was a surgeon from Boston who entered the Army in 1886 and earned a promotion for his role in capturing Indian leader Geronimo. He also commanded the Rough Riders at San Juan Hill during the Spanish-American War. Later he helped govern the Philippines. (*Minneapolis Tribune* in *Literary Digest,* 1901)

relegated Cuba to the status of a protectorate. Theodore Roosevelt retorted that the critics were "unhung traitors . . . liars, slanderers and scandal mongers."[36] Root ingeniously informed Wood that intervention was not "synonymous with inter-meddling or interference with the affairs of a Cuban government," but the more straightforward general privately conceded that there was, "of course, little or no independence left Cuba under the Platt Amendment."[37] Wood himself forced a resistant Cuban convention to adopt the measure as an amendment to the new constitution on June 12, 1901, and the two governments signed a treaty embodying the provisions of the Platt Amendment on May 22, 1903. In 1903 the United States Navy constructed a naval base at Guantánamo Bay; "Gitmo," as the Marines christened it, was leased to the United States in perpetuity. A Reciprocity Treaty of 1902 permitted Cuban products to enter the United States at specially reduced tariff rates, thereby interlocking the economies of the two countries.

The first President of the Republic of Cuba, Tomás Estrada Palma, has been described as "more plattish than Platt himself."[38] Following his rigged re-election and second inauguration, discontented Cuban nationalists revolted. In a cable of September 8, 1906, the American consul-general in Havana reported Estrada Palma's inability to quell the rebellion or "protect life and property."[39] He pleaded for warships. President Roosevelt immediately ordered the cruiser *Denver* to Havana, but his tardy instructions failed to leash the ship's commanding officer, who landed a battalion of sailors at Estrada Palma's request. Roosevelt summarily ordered the men back aboard ship, adding further to the political chaos. "Just at the moment I am so angry with that infernal little Cuban republic," exploded the Rough Rider, "that I would like to wipe its people off the face of the earth." All he wanted from the Cubans, he said, was that "they should behave them-selves."[40]

Into this turmoil stepped the portly Secretary of War, William Howard Taft, whom Roosevelt ordered to Cuba on a peace mission. Groping for a solution that would "put an end to anarchy without necessitating a reoccupation of the island by our troops," Roosevelt instructed Taft to mediate between the warring factions.[41] The Teller Amendment weighed upon the President's mind, as did memory of the bloody crushing of insurgent Emilio Aguinaldo in the Philippines. Army officers predicted that American suppression of the Cuban revolution would necessitate drastic reconcentration of the Cuban population, making political annexation inevitable. Estrada Palma resigned, permitting Taft to establish a new provisional government. Taft, the American secretary of war, thus became the provisional governor of Cuba on September 29, 1906. He soon lectured students of the National University of Havana that Cubans needed a "mercantile spirit," a "desire to make money, to found great enterprises."[42] Taft returned home in mid-October, leaving behind a government headed by an American civilian, administered by United States Army officers, and supported by over 5,000 American soldiers. For twenty-eight months Governor Charles E. Magoon attempted to reinstate Leonard Wood's electoral and humanitarian reforms, while Roosevelt publicly scolded the Cubans that if their "insurrectionary habit" persisted it was "absolutely out of the question that the Island should continue independent."[43] Privately he mused, "it is not our fault if things go badly there."[44]

Under his successor Taft, and under Taft's successor Woodrow Wilson, Ameri-can policy toward Cuba consisted of reflexive support for existing governments, by means of force if necessary. Taft and Wilson made no serious effort to reform

Cuba in the American image. In what has been called both "a preventive policy" and "Dollar Diplomacy," the United States sought order in Cuban politics and security for American investments and commerce, particularly in sugar.[45] The $50 million invested by Americans in 1896 jumped to $220 million in 1913. By 1920 American-owned mills produced about half of Cuba's sugar. Cuban exports to the United States in 1900 equaled $31 million, by 1914 $131 million, and by 1920 $722 million. When these interests were threatened by revolution, as in May of 1912 and February of 1917, the Marines went ashore. After Havana followed Washington's lead and declared war against Germany in April, 1917, some 2,500 American troops were sent to Cuba for the protection of the sugar plantations that helped feed the Allied armies. Cuba, under the yoke of the Platt Amendment, the American military, and American economic interests, remained a protectorate of the United States. The island's "independence" was a myth, but its frustrated nationalism was a reality with which Americans always had to contend.

POLICING THE CARIBBEAN: VENEZUELA, THE DOMINICAN REPUBLIC, AND THE ROOSEVELT COROLLARY

President Theodore Roosevelt devoted a great deal of thought to Latin America in the winter of 1901–1902. He guided the second Hay-Pauncefote Treaty through the Senate, fretted over the route of his isthmian canal, and helped Elihu Root shape the terms of the occupation of Cuba. He also turned his mind toward the most hallowed of American doctrines, that propounded by James Monroe in 1823. In his first annual message, on December 3, 1901, Roosevelt emphasized the economic aspect of the doctrine: "It is really a guarantee of the commercial independence of the Americas." The United States, however, as protector of that independence, would "not guarantee any state against punishment if it misconducts itself, provided that punishment does not take the form of the acquisition of territory by any non-American power."[46] If a South American country misbehaved in its relations with a European nation, Roosevelt would "let the European country spank it."[47]

The President was thinking principally of Germany and Venezuela. Under the rule of Cipriano Castro, an unsavory dictator whom Roosevelt once characterized as an "unspeakable villainous monkey," Venezuela perpetually deferred payment on bonds worth more than $12.5 million and held by German investors.[48] Berlin became understandably impatient. Great Britain felt equally irritated by Venezuela's failure to meet its debts to British subjects. In December, 1902, after clearing the way with Washington, Germany and Britain delivered an ultimatum demanding immediate settlement of their claims, seized several Venezuelan vessels, bombarded two forts, and proclaimed a blockade closing Venezuela to commerce. To all of this Theodore Roosevelt acquiesced, but American congressional and editorial opinion reacted adversely. The *Literary Digest* of December 20 worried "that England and Germany will overstep the limits prescribed by the Monroe Doctrine" and concluded that many newspapers "think that the allies have already gone too far."[49]

In mid-January, 1903, the German Navy bombarded two more forts. Popular criticism of the intervention sharpened in the United States, and TR privately mused: "The only power which may be a menace to us in anything like the immediate future is Germany."[50] Shaken by the American reaction, Kaiser Wilhelm II

Roosevelt at Work. TR was, according to biographer William Harbaugh, "a man of surpassing charm, extraordinary charisma, and broad intellectual interests . . . a curious compound of realist and idealist, pragmatist and moral absolutist." A lover of power, he knew that one way to achieve it was through vigorous oratory. (*Kladderadatsch*, Berlin)

replaced his ill-informed ambassador with Hermann Speck von Sternburg, an old friend of Roosevelt. The President received Speck on the day of his arrival in Washington and urged a quick settlement to quell the clamor in Britain and the United States. Under this mounting criticism and pressure from Roosevelt, Britain and Germany in early February lifted the blockade and submitted the dispute to the Permanent Court at the Hague. Prime Minister Arthur Balfour calmed troubled Anglo-American waters by publicly denying any intention of acquiring additional territory in the western hemisphere and welcoming an "increase of the influence of the United States" in Latin America.[51] Even more, he accepted the Monroe Doctrine as international law. On February 22, 1904, the Hague Tribunal awarded preferential treatment to the claims of the two nations that had used force against Venezuela. A prominent State Department official complained that this decision put "a premium on violence" and made likely similar European interventions in the future.[52]

Theodore Roosevelt also worried increasingly about the chronic disorder and fiscal insolvency of the Dominican Republic, which had been torn continually by revolution since 1899. "I have about the same desire to annex it," Roosevelt said privately, "as a gorged boa constrictor might have to swallow a porcupine wrong-end to."[53] An American firm that formerly handled the country's tariff collections (customs) claimed damages of several million dollars, and European creditors demanded action by their governments. The President had been "hoping and praying . . . that the Santo Dominigans would behave so that I would not have to act in any way." By the spring of 1904 he thought he might have "to do nothing but what a policeman has to do."[54] He preferred to do it after the presidential election of 1904.

After the electorate resoundingly endorsed his presidency, he described to Congress his conception of the United States as policeman of the western hemisphere. "Chronic wrongdoing, or an impotence which results in a general loosening of the ties of civilized society," he proclaimed, "may in America, as elsewhere, ultimately require intervention by some civilized nation, and in the Western Hemisphere the adherence of the United States to the Monroe Doctrine may force the United States, however reluctantly, in flagrant cases of such wrongdoing or impotence, to the exercise of an international police power."[55] With this statement of December 6, 1904, the twenty-sixth President of the United States added to the Monroe Doctrine his corollary, which fundamentally transformed that prohibition upon European meddling into a brash promise of United States regulation of the Americas.

The Rough Rider acted accordingly. In December the State Department initiated discussions with the Dominican Republic aimed at American collection and distribution of the Latin republic's customs revenues. A protocol to this effect was signed on February 7, 1905, but it ran into determined Democratic opposition in the Senate. Roosevelt, however, would not be deterred. He arranged a modus vivendi, assigning an American collector of the Dominican customs, an arrangement finally sanctified in a treaty negotiated by Secretary of State Root and approved by the Senate on February 25, 1907. While easing the new Dominican customs treaty through the Senate, Root explained the interrelationship between Latin American political stability and the security of the Panama Canal. The "inevitable effect of our building the Canal," he wrote, "must be to require us to police the surrounding premises."[56] The United States would reap "trade and control, and the obligation to keep order" and would simultaneously draw Latin America "up out of the discord and turmoil of continual revolution into a general public sense of justice and determination to maintain order."[57]

Taft's Secretary of State, Philander C. Knox, applauded Root's customs receivership in the Dominican Republic because it denied to rebels the funds they so eagerly "collected" through the capture of customs houses. Knox credited the receivership with curing "century-old evils."[58] The assassination of the Dominican President the following November, 1911, demonstrated that Knox spoke somewhat prematurely. And in 1912 revolutionaries operating from the contiguous country of Haiti marauded throughout the Dominican Republic. Their forays forced the closure of several customs houses that the United States had protected under the Treaty of 1907. To restore order, Taft in September, 1912, sent a commission backed by 750 Marines. The commissioners redefined the Haiti–Dominican Republic border, forced the corrupt Dominican president to resign by stopping his revenues from the customs service, avoided direct interference in a new election, and returned to Washington in December.

President Wilson and Secretary Bryan eloquently disparaged the evils of "dollar diplomacy" and promised that the United States would "never again seek one additional foot of territory by conquest."[59] That sounded new, but Roosevelt and Taft had already repudiated further American territorial acquisitions. Moreover, Wilson's search for stability in Latin America retraced familiar steps. When, in September, 1913, revolution again threatened the Dominican government, Bryan warned "that this Government will employ every legitimate means to assist in the restoration of order and the prevention of further insurrections."[60] The Navy Department sent a cruiser to the island, and Wilson urged political and economic reforms. Discouraged by a new revolutionary outburst in May of 1916, the Administration sent two warships, landed men, and permitted the admiral in command to threaten bombardment of the city of Santo Domingo if the leading revolutionary did not surrender. The Dominican and American governments thereupon debated terms of a treaty giving the United States full control over Dominican finances, while the United States Navy tightened its grip on the island. In November, as American involvement in the European war became increasingly probable, President Wilson proclaimed the formal military occupation of the Dominican Republic, ostensibly to curtail the activities of revolutionaries suspected of a pro-German bias. The American Navy governed the Dominican Republic until 1922.

THE QUEST FOR STABILITY IN HAITI AND NICARAGUA

The Dominican Republic shares the island of Hispaniola with Haiti, where revolution became an increasingly popular mode of changing governments after 1911. American investments in the country were limited to ownership of a small railroad and a one-third share in the Haitian National Bank. Nationals of France and Germany controlled the bank, and disorder thus could give either European nation a pretext for intervention. After the outbreak of World War I, the Wilson Administration worried about "the ever present danger of German control" of Haiti.[61] At stake was the security of the Panama Canal, along the approaches to which lay Haiti's deep water harbor of Môle Saint Nicolas. The Navy Department, content with bases in Cuba and Puerto Rico, no longer desired a station in Haiti, but

Wilson could not let Môle Saint Nicolas fall into the unfriendly hands of Germany. Moreover, the President realized that Haitian instability fueled the revolution in the Dominican Republic, which he was also combatting. He therefore pressed for an American customs receivership on the Dominican model.

The Haitians resisted successfully until July, 1915, when the regime of Guillaume Sam fell in an orgy of grisly political murders. Wilson could stomach no more, and he ordered the Navy to Haiti. While 2,000 Marines imposed martial law, Secretary of State Robert Lansing explained to the Haitians that his government expected "to be entrusted with the practical control of the customs, and such financial control over the affairs of the Republic of Haiti as the United States may deem necessary for an efficient administration."[62] Lansing drafted a treaty putting Americans in charge of all aspects of Haiti's finances, privately admitting to Wilson that "this method of negotiation, with our marines policing the Haytian Capital, is high handed."[63] The United States naval and diplomatic vise meant that Haiti would be ruled until 1934 by what historian David Healy has called "an American military regime which acted, when it pleased, through the [Haitian] president."[64]

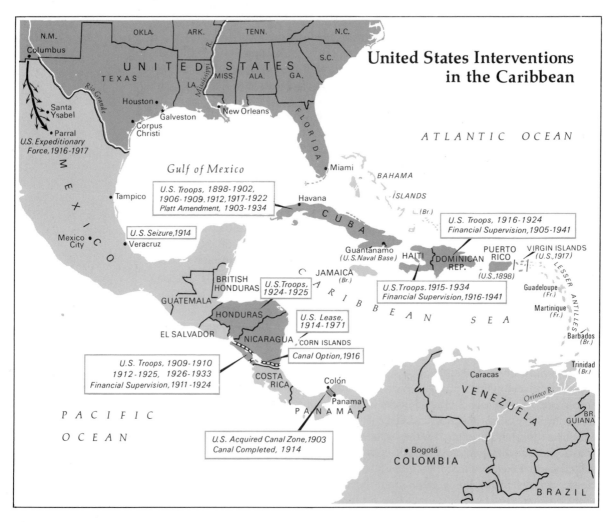

United States Interventions in the Caribbean

The United States also intervened, virtually at will, in hapless Nicaragua. For Theodore Roosevelt, Nicaragua had been important primarily as a potential canal route, a rivalry decided in Panama's favor in 1903. Subsequently, he manifested interest in Nicaragua only briefly, during 1907, when he and the President of Mexico jointly proposed a peace conference to end the incessant warfare among Central American states. Secretary Root explained that the conduct of those countries was "important to us," because the Panama Canal put them "in the front yard of the United States."[65] Philander C. Knox continued the search for stability in Central America, but an abiding antipathy "to all Spanish-American modes of thought" made him more ready to countenance the use of force.[66] Thus, when José Santo Zelaya's Nicaraguan government executed two Americans for joining a revolutionary army in 1909, Knox broke diplomatic relations, gave "the revolution strong moral support," and tolerated an American naval interposition favoring the rebels in a decisive battle.[67] He then negotiated a treaty with the victorious revolutionaries led by Adolfo Díaz, providing for American control of the customs service and an American loan. The United States Senate refused ratification, but Knox and a group of bankers simply acted ad interim without the authorization of a treaty. In September, 1912, the Administration ordered the Marines into battle alongside Díaz's troops. After tipping the scales against the newest revolutionary army, the leathernecks returned home, leaving one hundred behind as a legation guard in Managua.

The Marines could prevent a coup d'état, but they could not easily put Díaz's house in fiscal order. Although critical of Taft's "dollar diplomacy," Bryan in the spring of 1913 dusted off a shelved draft treaty granting the United States a canal option in Nicaragua in exchange for three million dollars. Bryan hoped that this monetary prospect would "give sufficient encouragement" to American bankers to lend Díaz more money.[68] The secretary also added a clause similar to the Platt Amendment before sending the Bryan-Chamorro Treaty to the Senate. The upper house balked at this extension of American commitments and, to gain approval, the Wilson Administration had to delete the right of intervention. Ratification in February, 1916, did help to shore up Nicaragua's finances. The treaty also insured that European powers could not gain naval bases in the Gulf of Fonseca, and to make that point stick, Wilson ordered United States warships to cruise offshore during the 1916 Nicaraguan presidential campaign. Although nominally independent, Nicaragua remained a United States protectorate until 1933.

MEDDLING IN MEXICO

Mexico changed governments with uncharacteristic frequency after the outbreak of revolution in 1910. In 1911 Francisco I. Madero toppled Porfirio Díaz, the aged dictator who had maintained order, personal power, and a healthy environment for American investments since the late 1870s. United States citizens owned over 40 percent of Mexico's property and thus the Mexican Revolution was tinged with an anti-American bias. President Taft grew angry with the chaos that threatened American lives and property, but he determined to "sit tight on the lid and it will take a good deal to pry me off."[69] In February, 1913, United States Ambassador Henry Lane Wilson encouraged one of Madero's trusted generals, Victoriano Huerta, to overthrow the revolutionary nationalist. Indeed, Huerta had Madero shot and then set about to consolidate his own power. The Taft Administration prepared to recognize Huerta's government in return for a settlement of claims against Mexico. But after Huerta requested formal oaths of allegiance from Mexican state governors, one of them, Venustiano Carranza, took up arms and led the "Constitutionalist" revolt on February 26. Americans and their property were caught in the crossfire. Just before leaving office, Taft recoiled from recognition of Huerta's government, insisting that it first punish the "murderers of American citizens" and "put an end to the discriminations against American interests."[70]

Woodrow Wilson seemed to worry less about the large private American investment of one billion dollars. He redefined American recognition policy, requiring governments to meet a test of morality. Referring to Mexico, he said he would not recognize a "government of butchers."[71] Despising Huerta's treachery, Wilson denounced the Mexican as a "diverting brute! . . . seldom sober and always impossible."[72] Unlike Ambassador Wilson, who advocated recognition of Huerta to protect American financial and commercial interests, the President remarked that he himself was "not the servant of those who wish to enhance the value of their Mexican investments."[73] In July, 1913, he had the ambassador recalled; a month later Henry Lane Wilson was dismissed from the diplomatic corps. Thereafter the President treated with Mexico through special emissaries, only one of whom spoke fluent Spanish. None was intimately familiar with Mexico and all were chosen because of earlier friendships with the President or Secretary Bryan.

On August 8, 1913, one of these representatives, John Lind, arrived in Mexico City, after landing on Mexican soil from an American warship. A rabid anti-Catholic and former governor of Minnesota without diplomatic experience, Lind delivered Wilson's plan of "counsel and assistance." The American President wanted an armistice between Huerta's federalist troops and all revolutionary groups, "an early and free election," and Huerta's promise not to run for president. In exchange, the United States pledged recognition and aid to "the administration chosen and set up . . . in the way and on the conditions suggested." With sublime arrogance, Woodrow Wilson wondered, "can Mexico give the civilized world a satisfactory reason for rejecting our good offices?"[74] The Mexican minister of foreign relations thought he could. Already annoyed that Lind had arrived on a warship and held no formal diplomatic rank, Federico Gamboa issued a scathing reply on August 26, excoriating Wilson's "counsels and advice (let us call them thus)." Adherence to American dictates would mean that "all the future elections for president would be submitted to the veto of any President of the United States of America," and no government of Mexico would ever perpetrate "such an enormity" upon its people.[75] After this snub, Woodrow Wilson announced a restrained policy of "watchful waiting," clamped an embargo on arms to Mexico, and advised Americans to leave that country.[76]

Undeterred, Huerta in October dissolved an unruly legislature, arrested its members, and held a special election, which returned an entirely submissive congress ready to extend his presidency indefinitely. Wilson then turned to Carranza. He sent a personal representative to the revolutionary chief's headquarters in northern Mexico with the same proposal Huerta's foreign minister had rejected in August. Carranza proved ardently nationalistic as well as revolutionary. He contemptuously rejected Wilsonian mediation in the civil war and refused any solution short of his own triumph. Thoroughly isolated himself, Wilson on November 24 issued a circular note to the other powers informing them of his

Woodrow Wilson (1856–1924). The twenty-eighth President was proud of his "missionary diplomacy" because he believed that "every nation needs to be drawn into the tutelage of America." Latin Americans, however, resisted his paternalism, just as they had resisted Roosevelt's "big stick" and Taft's "dollar diplomacy." (U.S. Signal Corps, National Archives)

policy "to isolate General Huerta entirely; to cut him off from foreign sympathy . . . and so to force him out." But if political and economic pressure failed to induce Huerta's retirement, "it will become the duty of the United States to use less peaceful means to put him out."[77]

Most European powers had recognized Huerta and disapproved of Wilson's indignant opposition to him. The nation most deeply affected was Great Britain, whose capital investments in Mexico were second only to those of the United States. Also, the Royal Navy relied on Mexican oil as a backup to Middle Eastern sources. It took the British Foreign Office several months to realize that Wilson was serious about deposing Huerta. One senior official concluded darkly, "the United States cherish very sinister designs toward Mexico and desire that a condition of complete anarchy should supervene."[78] For London, however, the growing menace of Germany made American goodwill absolutely essential. In the event of conflict, England would need American war materiel. The Foreign Office therefore notified Huerta that it could not support him against the United States, advised him to retire as president, and recalled the British minister because of American antipathy toward him—all the while believing American views were "most impractical and unreasonable."[79]

With British compliance assured, Wilson acted. On February 1, 1914, he lifted the arms embargo, permitting large quantities of arms to flow to both factions. As Carranza's resupplied forces pushed south, the President sent American naval vessels to the busy port of Veracruz and the oil-producing town of Tampico, both on the Gulf of Mexico. On April 9, at Tampico, Huerta's inexperienced federal troops arrested several American sailors loading gasoline aboard a whaleboat docked provocatively near their forward outpost. The Mexican colonel in charge quickly disavowed the arrest, freed the sailors, and apologized orally. This redress failed to appease the hotheaded commander of the American squadron at Tampico, Rear Admiral Henry T. Mayo. He demanded a formal written apology and a twenty-one-gun salute to the American flag, because "taking men from a boat flying the American flag is a hostile act, not to be excused."[80] Wilson immediately warned the Mexican government "that unless the guilty persons are promptly punished consequences of [the] gravest sort might ensue." To reporters he bluntly said, "the salute will be fired."[81] He soon decided to use Huerta's rejection of the Mayo ultimatum as justification for military intervention designed to humiliate the Mexican leader and drive him from power. In the early afternoon of April 20 Wilson requested congressional approval to use armed force "to obtain from General Huerta and his adherents the fullest recognition of the rights and dignity of the United States."[82] Meanwhile, Secretary of the Navy Josephus Daniels had learned of the imminent arrival at Veracruz of a German-owned steamer, the *Ypiranga,* carrying two hundred machine guns and over fifteen million cartridges. The United States could not allow these arms to reach Huerta on the eve of American military intervention. Thus Daniels ordered the Navy to interdict the shipment by seizing the customs house at Veracruz.

On April 21, 1914, eight hundred American sailors and Marines landed. Although most of Huerta's federal troops withdrew under orders from the Ministry of War, a local federalist liberated prisoners from city jails and armed them to resist the Americans. These desperadoes and other irregulars fought in the streets and sniped from hiding places so tenaciously that four Americans were killed and twenty were wounded on the first day alone. Nineteen Americans and several hundred Mexicans died before the fighting stopped. Wilson was stunned by the bloody turn of events. To one observer, the shaken President appeared "preternaturally pale, almost parchmenty," and to his personal physician Wilson moaned, "the thought haunts me that it was I who ordered those young men to their deaths."[83] Although the invasion was designed to undermine Huerta, historian Ramón E. Ruíz has written, "The capture of Veracruz nearly united Mexicans behind him . . . [because] Mexicans, believing their independence endangered, rushed to enlist in Huerta's army."[84] Apparently chastened, Wilson accepted mediation when proposed by Argentina, Brazil, and Chile (the ABC powers) on April 25.

A month later, representatives of the United States, Huerta, and the ABC powers met on the Canadian side of Niagara Falls. From the outset, Wilson and Carranza doomed the mediation by their intransigence. The American President refused to allow his delegates to discuss the evacuation of Veracruz or Tampico, a major reason for convening the conference. He sought instead "the entire elimination of General Huerta" and creation of a provisional government under the Constitutionalists.[85] But Carranza indignantly refused to attend any foreign meeting dealing with Mexico's internal affairs. By early June the deadlock was complete, and one newspaper editor sarcastically proposed: "Why should not Abyssinia, Servia, and Senegabia—the A.S.S. powers—tender their good offices? Send out the SOS for the A.S.S."[86] On July 2 the hapless mediators adjourned; two weeks later Huerta fled to Europe, and on August 20 a triumphant Carranza paraded before enthusiastic throngs in Mexico City.

The Constitutionalist triumph was short-lived. One of Carranza's northern generals, Francisco (Pancho) Villa, soon broke from the ranks, marched south, and in December occupied Mexico City. Villa, an intelligent and dedicated revolutionary nationalist, initially showed restraint toward Americans and seemed to approve President Wilson's Mexican policies, including the intervention at Veracruz. Wilson persuaded himself that "General Villa certainly seems capable of some good things and often shows susceptibility of the best influences," and encouraged him by refusing to recognize Carranza's government.[87] To avoid danger of a military clash with any Mexican faction, Wilson withdrew all American troops from Veracruz on November 23, 1914. Once again, Wilson watched and waited, thereby stimulating continued disorder in Mexico with his refusal to recognize the legitimacy of its government.

Mexican-American relations remained tense during the first months of 1915. Carranza's forces gradually drove Villa north, but in the process Mexico City became a no-man's-land, with bread riots and starvation threatening its inhabitants, including 2,500 Americans and 23,000 other foreign residents. Wilson gave some thought to relieving the city by force, perhaps with Pan American cooperation, but deteriorating German-American relations preoccupied him, especially after a German U-boat torpedoed the *Lusitania* in May. Resigned to failure in Mexico, Wilson seemed to repudiate all further interference in Mexican affairs: "Carranza will somehow have to be digested."[88] Two months later the United States extended partial, or de facto, recognition to the Constitutionalist government and permitted munitions exports, while embargoing arms to the Constitutionalists' enemies.

Convinced that Wilson and Carranza planned to make Mexico a protectorate of the United States, Villa denounced *Carranzistas* as "vassals" and prepared to show Americans that "Mexico is a land for the free and a tomb for thrones, crowns, and

Pancho Villa (1878–1923). The colorful Mexican rebel bedeviled both Mexico and the United States. His daring raid on an American town was calculated to outrage President Wilson, whom he mocked as "an evangelizing professor of philosophy who is destroying the independence of a friendly people." (Library of Congress)

**Uncle Sam Shooting
Dice with Carranza.** The
Mexican leader tells a
grudging Uncle Sam in
1917 to put his dice
(army) back in the box.
(*Washington Evening Star*,
Library of Congress)

traitors."[89] In the predawn hours of March 9, 1916, Villa led a band of *Villistas*
across the border and tore into Columbus, New Mexico, initiating a bloody battle
that left seventeen Americans and more than a hundred Mexicans dead. Within
hours of the tragedy, Wilson unleashed the United States Army against Villa.
General John J. "Black Jack" Pershing commanded a Punitive Expedition, eventually totaling almost 7,000 men, which reached 350 miles into Mexico in a vain
search for Pancho Villa. A clash with Carranza's forces in August occurred
instead.

Carranza kept up drumfire pressure for American withdrawal, but Wilson
hesitated for fear of appearing weak during a presidential election year. When
United States participation in the European war finally became inescapable,
Wilson disengaged from Mexico. On January 28, 1917, three days before Ambassador Johann von Bernstorff notified Secretary of State Lansing of Germany's
resumption of unrestricted submarine warfare, Secretary of War Newton D. Baker
announced that Pershing's troops were marching home. The last American soldier
left Mexico on February 5. In late February, the secret Zimmermann telegram
proposing an anti-American alliance between Germany, Japan, and Mexico came
into the hands of the State Department, courtesy of British intelligence. This dire
German ploy accelerated Wilson's movement toward full diplomatic relations with
Carranza's government. The United States extended de jure recognition on August 31, 1917, in order to insure Mexican neutrality during the fight against

Germany. Thus, after four futile years, Wilson had given up on his haughty attempt to tell the Mexicans how to run their own affairs.

THE OPEN DOOR AND DOLLAR DIPLOMACY IN EAST ASIA

Telling Asians how to run their affairs proved even more difficult. Secretary of State John Hay's endorsement of Chinese political and administrative integrity in the Open Door Note of July, 1900, did not prevent the further emasculation of China. During the Boxer Rebellion Russia stationed 175,000 troops in Manchuria and demanded exclusive rights from China, including a commercial monopoly. President Roosevelt and Hay could do little to stop this infringement of China's sovereignty. The United States, they said, had "always recognized the exceptional position of Russia" in Manchuria and had merely sought the commercial freedom "guaranteed to us by . . . the whole civilized world."[90] Washington retreated from the Open Door Circular of 1900 because Roosevelt realized that the American people would not fight for nebulous principles of Chinese integrity in Manchuria, an area considered strategically remote and economically inconsequential. He understood the futility of trying, in historian Akira Iriye's words, "to play the role of an Asian power without military power."[91]

Japan viewed the question quite differently. Russia blocked Japanese economic expansion into Manchuria, posed a potential naval menace, and endangered the Japanese position in Korea. Tokyo covered its flanks with an Anglo-Japanese Alliance in 1902, opened negotiations aimed at explicit Russian recognition of nominal Chinese governance over Manchuria, and prepared for war. On February 8, 1904, the Japanese Navy suddenly captured headlines when it destroyed Russia's Far Eastern Fleet in a surprise attack at Port Arthur. At first Roosevelt cheered privately, "for Japan is playing our game," but as the enormity of Japanese victories became apparent he began to hope for peace "on terms which will not mean the creation of either a yellow peril or a Slav peril."[92] By the spring of 1905 Japanese soldiers had triumphed at Mukden, where Russia lost 97,000 men, and the navy had sunk the Russian Baltic Fleet in the straits of Tsushima. Still, the imperial treasury was drained and the army stretched thin. On May 31, Minister Kogoro Takahira requested Roosevelt, "on his own motion and initiative," to invite Russia and Japan to negotiate a peace treaty.[93]

Seizing the opportunity to balance the powers in order to protect America's territorial and commercial interests in the Pacific and Asia, the President invited Japanese and Russian representatives to meet at Portsmouth, New Hampshire on August 9, 1905. The Japanese delegates demanded Russia's leasehold on the Liaodong Peninsula and the railroad running from Harbin to Port Arthur, evacuation of Russian troops from Manchuria, and complete freedom of action for Japan in Korea. The Russians quickly conceded these points, but rejected additional Japanese requests for a monetary indemnity and cession of the island of Sakhalin. With negotiations deadlocked, Roosevelt telegraphed Tsar Nicholas II proposing division of Sakhalin between the belligerents and agreement "in principle" upon an indemnity. The Tsar agreed to partition the island but refused any payment. Needing peace more than money, Japan yielded on August 29.

The Roosevelt Administration's search for equipoise in East Asia neither began nor ended at Portsmouth. As early as March, 1904, TR had conceded to Japan a relationship with Korea "just like we have with Cuba."[94] Secretary of War Taft reaffirmed the concession during a discussion with Prime Minister Taro Katsura on July 27, 1905. In the Taft-Katsura "agreed memorandum of conversation," the Prime Minister denied Japanese designs on the Philippines, and Taft, in the words of historian John Wilz, put an American "seal on the death warrant of an independent Korea."[95] A year later the Japanese reopened southern Manchuria to foreign and American trade, but discouraged foreign capital investments. In 1910 Japan formally annexed Korea.

This artful balancing of interests augured well for a continuation of traditional Japanese-American cordiality, until a local dispute in California abruptly undercut Rooseveltian diplomacy. On October 11, 1906, the San Francisco School Board created a special "Oriental Public School" for all Japanese, Chinese and Korean children. Japan immediately protested this racial discrimination against its citizens, and Theodore Roosevelt denounced the "infernal fools in California" whose exclusion of Japanese from all other public schools constituted "a confession of inferiority in our civilization."[96] At one point he wrote that the "feeling on the Pacific slope . . . is as foolish as if conceived by the mind of a Hottentot."[97] Yet there was little he constitutionally could do, other than rail against the recalcitrant school board, apply political pressure to the California legislature to prevent statewide discriminatory measures, and propose congressional legislation to naturalize Japanese residing permanently in the United States. The public outburst against naturalization finally convinced Roosevelt that he had seriously underestimated the depth of "genuine race feeling" throughout the United States, especially in California.[98] Always the political realist, Roosevelt accepted what he personally disliked and sought accommodation with Japan. By March, 1907, he had contrived a "Gentlemen's Agreement" with Tokyo sharply restricting Japanese immigration.

Two months later anti-Japanese riots and yellow journalistic agitation by what Secretary Root called the "leprous vampires" of San Francisco confirmed Roosevelt's apprehensions that local disturbances in California would create further crises with Japan.[99] The President shrewdly pressed for more battleships and fortification of Hawaii and the vulnerable Philippines, now America's "heel of Achilles," so that the United States would "be ready for anything that comes."[100] He also dramatized the importance of a strong navy to Congress and Japan by ordering the battle fleet on a voyage to the Pacific and around the world. This "good will cruise" by the "sixteen messengers of peace" netted two goals for Roosevelt.[101] In the spring of 1908 Congress endorsed a policy of building two battleships per year, and Ambassador Takahira invited the "Great White Fleet" to Tokyo, where it received a rousing popular reception. On the day the ships sailed from Tokyo Bay, Takahira received instructions to seek an agreement with the United States recognizing the Pacific Ocean as an open avenue of trade, pledging the integrity of Japanese and American insular possessions in the Pacific, supporting the status quo, and promising equal opportunity in China. After extensive refinement of rhetoric, these concepts were promulgated as the Root-Takahira declaration of policy on November 30, 1908. Japanese-American relations appeared ready for a period of mature harmony premised on mutual understanding of one another's national interests.

The new epoch did not materialize. William Howard Taft and Philander C. Knox chose to champion the "Open Door" and Chinese nationalism, thereby threatening

Japan. The first explosion of twentieth-century Chinese nationalism had occurred in 1900, when the Boxers challenged both the Manchus and the Western powers exploiting the old dynasty. Angry Chinese patriots thereafter decried American participation in the suppression of the uprising, the concurrent bloody extirpation of Aguinaldo's Filipino partisans, and a racist 1904 act of Congress permanently barring Chinese immigration into the United States and its territories. Chinese nationalists inspired a short-lived boycott of American goods in 1905 and official revocation of a railroad franchise held by financier J. P. Morgan. Roosevelt explained to the financial baron his interest in seeing American commercial interests prosper in the Orient, but he restricted his diplomatic initiatives in East Asia to matters directly touching Japan.

Not everyone shared Roosevelt's fixation on Japan. As early as 1905 Secretary of War Taft dreamed about the American share of "one of the greatest commercial prizes of the world," the China market.[102] During a trip to East Asia in 1905, Taft met the impressive, intensely anti-Japanese American Consul General in Mukden, Willard Straight. Two years later Straight proposed the creation of a Manchurian bank, to be financed by the American railroad magnate E. H. Harriman, only to have the economic panic of 1907 dash all hopes for subsidizing the Chinese administration of Manchuria. When Wall Street revived in 1908, Straight was

"Spread-eagleism" in China. The missionary teacher Grace Roberts teaches a Bible class in 1903 in Kalgan, Manchuria. Americanism and religious work, flag and missionary, became partners abroad. The mission force was feminized—the great majority of missionaries were women. (By permission of the Houghton Library, Harvard University)

recalled to advise New York financiers on the exploitation of Manchuria. He arrived in time to condemn the Root-Takahira agreement as "a terrible diplomatic blunder," because it seemed to recognize Japan's exploitative position in Manchuria.[103] Under Taft, Straight and the State Department quickly inspired several New York banks to form a combination, headed by J. P. Morgan, to serve as the official agency of American railroad investment in China. As acting chief of the department's new Far Eastern Division, Straight instructed Minister William W. Rockhill in Beijing to demand admission of the American bankers into a European banking consortium undertaking construction of the Huguang Railway running southwest from Hankou. Having thus set up an American financial challenge in both Manchuria and China proper, Straight resigned from the State Department to become the Morgan group's roving representative.

Secretary of State Knox continued Straight's policy of injecting American capital into China and Manchuria. In November, 1909, Knox proposed to Britain the neutralization of Manchurian railroads through a large international loan to China for the purchase of the lines. Britain, however, joined both Japan and Russia to reject the neutralization proposal in January, 1910. "Instead of dividing Russia and Japan, and opening the door to American financial exploitation of Manchuria," historian A. Whitney Griswold has observed of Knox, "he had, as it were, nailed that door closed with himself on the outside."[104]

Although international resistance had shattered their Manchurian policy, Knox and Taft continued to seek American entrée to the British, French, and German consortium negotiating the Huguang loan. They made persistent representations at the Court of St. James's, and Taft sent an extraordinary personal message to the Regent of China insisting upon "equal participation by American capital in the present railway loan."[105] At length, on November 10, 1910, a quadruple agreement expanded the consortium to include the American bankers, and the loan was floated the following June. But the Chinese Revolution of 1911, sparked in part by this new intrusion upon China's autonomy, delayed any actual railroad construction until 1913. "'Dollar' diplomacy," Willard Straight ruefully admitted, "made no friends in the Hukuang matter."[106]

This stringent assessment by one of dollar diplomacy's earliest advocates failed to dissuade Knox from coming to the financial aid of Yuan Shikai, the dominant leader of the 1911 revolution. Yüan asserted his power ruthlessly, but American missionaries overlooked his faults because he promised religious toleration. They saw in his new republic "the coming of the larger civilization of men which draws no national boundaries and which is controlled by good will. Jesus called it the Kingdom of God."[107] This "Missionary Mind," as James Reed describes it, reinforced the Taft Administration's pro-China orientation.[108] When Yüan sought dollars to bolster his nascent republic, Knox urged expansion of the four-power consortium to include Japan and Russia, whom he now thought might be restrained or co-opted by the others. Instead, Tokyo and St. Petersburg stipulated further erosion of Chinese sovereignty over Manchuria and Mongolia as the price for their participation. London and Paris backed them, but Beijing resisted. Britain, France, Germany, and the United States then attempted to extort concessions from stubborn China by withholding diplomatic recognition throughout 1912.

Within days of Woodrow Wilson's inauguration, Straight and other representatives of the American banking group called the new President's attention to the convoluted result of dollar diplomacy in China. Wilson and Secretary Bryan at

William Howard Taft (1857–1930) and Elihu Root (1845–1937). Under President Theodore Roosevelt, Taft served as secretary of war (1904–1908) and Root served as secretary of state (1905–1909). Both helped devise methods for managing the American empire. Taft, who became President for one term beginning in 1909, characterized his administration's policy "as substituting dollars for bullets," a pithy explanation of dollar diplomacy. (Library of Congress)

once perceived the infringement on Chinese sovereignty inherent in the proposed six-power loan, and the President repudiated American participation in the international consortium on March 18, 1913. Failure to cancel the loan, Wilson believed, would have cost the United States "the proud position . . . secured when Secretary Hay stood for the open door in China after the Boxer Uprising." Because he felt "so keenly the desire to help China," he extended diplomatic recognition to the struggling republic on May 2.[109] After less than two months in office Wilson had renewed America's commitment to the political integrity of China, a goal pragmatically abandoned by Roosevelt, unsuccessfully resuscitated by Taft, and consistently opposed by Japan.

Events in California shortly proved that, despite his moralistic disdain for dollar diplomacy, Wilson's disregard for Japan's sensibilities made his Far Eastern policy resemble Taft's more than Roosevelt's. In April, 1913, Democratic and Progressive politicians placed before the California legislature a bill denying residents "ineligible to citizenship" the right to own land. The measure struck directly at the 50,000 Japanese living in California, whose exceptional agricultural productivity had raised fears that they were, in the words of Governor Hiram Johnson, "driving the root of their civilization deep into California soil."[110] Racist passion erupted in California. One farmer pointed out that his neighbors were actually a Japanese man and a white woman with an interracial baby: "What is that baby? It isn't a Japanese. It isn't white. It is a germ of the mightiest problem that ever faced this state; a problem that will make the black problem of the South look white."[111] Basically sharing the Californians' anti-Japanese prejudices, and philosophically sensitive to states' rights, Wilson reacted cautiously. He urged restraint upon the California government, sent Bryan to Sacramento to beg for a euphemistic statute, and publicly discounted the "criminal possibility" of war when jingoes in Japan and the United States beat the drums.[112] But the California legislature passed the offensive bill on May 3, 1913, and when Japan protested strongly against the "unfair and intentionally racially discriminatory" measure, Wilson and Bryan took refuge in the legalistic defense that one state's legislation did not constitute a "national discriminatory policy."[113]

Wilson's antipathy toward Japan reappeared during the First World War. In the fall of 1914 Japan declared war on Germany, seized the German Pacific islands north of the equator, and swept across China's Shandong Peninsula to capture the German leasehold of Jiaozhou. Tokyo immediately followed this grab with the Twenty-One Demands of January 18, 1915, by which it insisted upon a virtual protectorate over all of China. Stout resistance by Beijing resulted in amelioration of the harshest exactions, but Japan emerged with extensive new political and economic rights in Shandong, southern Manchuria, and Mongolia. Preoccupied with Mexico, the British blockade, and the *Lusitania* crisis, the Wilson Administration limited its reaction to Secretary Bryan's caveat of May 11, 1915, refusing to recognize "any agreement . . . impairing the treaty rights of the United States and its citizens in China, the political or territorial integrity of the Republic of China, or . . . the open door policy."[114]

Wilson's nonrecognition policy was undermined, however, by secret treaties in which the European Allies promised to support Japan's conquests at the peace conference. Diplomatically isolated, the United States sought recourse in ambiguity. In an agreement with Viscount Kikujiro Ishii, signed November 2, 1917, Secretary Lansing admitted that "territorial propinquity creates special relationships between countries, and consequently . . . Japan has special interests in China," while Ishii pledged his nation's dedication to the Open Door and integrity of China.[115] Simultaneously, the Wilson Administration revived the international banking consortium as a means of checking further unilateral Japanese economic penetration of China proper. Once again, however, as in 1912, Britain, France, and the United States ultimately had to exclude the consortium from Manchuria as the price of Japanese participation. The wheel had turned full circle for Wilson. Like Taft before him, his attempt to succor Chinese independence had been thwarted by Japan.

THE ANGLO-AMERICAN RAPPROCHEMENT

After the Venezuelan crisis of 1895, London and Washington sought closer relations, encouraging Theodore Roosevelt to conclude that "together . . . the two branches of the Anglo-Saxon race . . . can whip the world." Indeed, "I think the twentieth century will still be the century of the men who speak English."[116] But

TR's chauvinistic prediction first had to overcome serious strains in Anglo-American relations. Control of the isthmian canal ranked high as a point of contention. In December, 1898, President McKinley directed Secretary Hay to negotiate modification of the Clayton-Bulwer Treaty (1850), which forbade unilateral construction, operation, or fortification of a canal in Central America. For almost a year negotiations foundered on Ambassador Pauncefote's insistence that the United States make concessions along the ill-defined boundary of the Alaskan panhandle, in exchange for British compromises on the canal. At length, made painfully aware of their diplomatic isolation during the Boer War, and apprehensive of unilateral congressional abrogation of the Clayton-Bulwer Treaty, the British yielded and signed the first Hay-Pauncefote Treaty on February 5, 1900. The United States would now be permitted to construct and operate a canal, but one that was neutralized and not fortified.

Overcoming a self-proclaimed, if dubious, reluctance "to meddle in National Affairs," then New York Governor Theodore Roosevelt campaigned against the Hay-Pauncefote Treaty from the governor's mansion in Albany. Only a week after the agreement had been signed, Roosevelt argued publicly that complete American control of the canal was "vital, from the standpoint of our sea power, no less than from the standpoint of the Monroe Doctrine."[117] When the aggrieved Hay protested, Roosevelt praised him as "the greatest Secretary of State I have seen in my time," but advised him to "drop the treaty and push through a bill to build *and fortify* our own canal."[118] He then urged Senator Henry Cabot Lodge and other exponents of a "large policy" to amend the treaty so as to allow fortification and exclusive United States regulation of a canal.

Lodge and his allies succeeded in amending the Hay-Pauncefote Treaty as Roosevelt urged, but in March of 1901 Great Britain understandably rejected the butchered pact, forcing Pauncefote and Hay to reopen negotiations. This time the secretary of state worked closely with Lodge to forestall further embarrassing senatorial opposition, while Roosevelt, first as vice-president and then as president, lectured the British on the firm American resolve to build, fortify, and control the canal. Britain conceded every point in order to win American friendship, and a second Hay-Pauncefote Treaty was signed on November 18, 1901. President Roosevelt and his sympathizers in the Senate rushed it to ratification a month later. This British capitulation constituted a very significant element of what one historian has called the "great rapprochement" marking Anglo-American relations between 1895 and 1914.[119]

Another obstacle to entente was overcome almost simultaneously and for the same reasons. After the discovery of gold along the Klondike in 1896, Canadian politicians revived an old boundary dispute with the Americans. The Anglo-Russian Treaty of 1825, which the United States inherited with Alaska in 1867, had left vague the territorial demarcation between the Alaskan panhandle and British North America. Advancing a maximum claim, Canada sought to run the line along the mouths of the numerous inlets reaching inland from the Pacific Ocean. The United States stood for a more easterly isogram at the water's high tide. Ottawa's interpretation would figuratively drive Americans into the sea, and Washington's claim would literally set the United States astride the avenues of approach to a suddenly valuable part of Canada. London initially supported the extreme Canadian claim by linking this issue to abrogation of the Clayton-Bulwer Treaty, hoping that the United States would sacrifice Alaskan territory in exchange for enlarged rights in Central America. Shrill European denunciations of Britain's painful suppression of the Boers in South Africa, coupled with benevolent American silence on the same topic, persuaded Sir Julian Pauncefote to advocate separation of the two disputes in early 1900. "America seems to be our only friend just now," he commented to Foreign Secretary Lord Lansdowne, "and it would be unfortunate to quarrel with her."[120] Disentanglement followed, but the Alaskan boundary dispute remained unresolved when Theodore Roosevelt entered the White House.

Declining arbitration by a third party on the grounds that the "manifestly clear and unanswerable" claim of the United States constituted a case where the "nation had no business to arbitrate," the President sent 800 soldiers to Alaska to impress England.[121] London hesitated, but Washington's criticism of British collaboration

John Bull in Need of Friends. Battered by criticism over its war against the Boers in South Africa and challenged by a rising Germany, Great Britain found a new friend in the United States. According to historian Thomas Noer: "forced to decide between support of continued Boer independence or a unified South Africa under direct British control, American leaders gradually became convinced of the advantages of British imperialism. . . . They decided that British control was necessary for the economic development, social changes, and racial policies the United States desired in the area." (*Des Moines Leader* in *Literary Digest,* 1901)

with Germany in chastising Venezuela soon impelled the Foreign Office to eliminate all Anglo-American irritants. On January 24, 1903, Britain agreed to an
American proposal for a mixed boundary commission composed of six "impartial
jurists of repute," three from each side.[122] Roosevelt took no chances. He appointed Senator Lodge and Secretary Root, hardly disinterested judges, to the
commission. He informed them that the 1825 treaty "was undoubtedly intended to
cut off England, which owned the Hinterland, from access to the sea," and
informally warned London he would run the line himself if the commissioners
failed to agree.[123] After persuasion by Prime Minister Balfour, the British commissioner, Lord Chief Justice Alverstone, sided with the Americans, and on
October 20, 1903, by a vote of four to two, the commission officially decided for
the United States. Canada's claims had not been defeated because they lacked
historical foundation. They had been sacrificed as unworthy impediments to
improved Anglo-American relations.

Theodore Roosevelt later commented that the final definition "of the Alaskan
boundary settled the last serious trouble between the British Empire and ourselves," an observation especially pertinent to Anglo-American policies in the
western hemisphere.[124] In February, 1903, shortly after agreeing to the Alaskan
commission, British leaders silenced trans-Atlantic criticism of the intervention in
Venezuela by accepting international adjudication of the Anglo-German claims
and publicly praising the Monroe Doctrine. A month later the British Ambassador,
Sir Michael Herbert, half-jocularly admonished President Roosevelt to "be ready
to police the whole American Continent" since the United States no longer would
permit European nations to collect debts by force.[125] The Roosevelt Corollary
therefore neither surprised nor displeased Great Britain, and the same was true of
the denouement in Panama in 1903. London declined diplomatic assistance to
embattled Colombia prior to its rejection of the Hay-Herrán Treaty, and British
observers complacently watched the subsequent revolution lead to the Hay-
Bunau-Varilla Treaty.

English acquiescence also characterized another Anglo-American settlement of
Roosevelt's presidency, the North Atlantic fisheries dispute. Since 1782 American
fishermen, especially those from Massachusetts, had insisted on retaining their
pre-Revolutionary privileges along the coasts of Newfoundland. The modus
vivendi of 1888, by which they had fished for several years, collapsed in 1905 when
Newfoundland's Parliament placed restrictions on American fishing vessels.
Senator Lodge cried for warships to protect his constituents' livelihood. To avoid a
heated quarrel with Britain over a matter important largely to one state, Roosevelt
proposed, and London accepted, arbitration at the Hague Tribunal. In 1910 the
tribunal ruled that Britain could oversee fishing off Newfoundland if it established
reasonable regulations, that a fisheries commission would hear cases disputing the
definition of reasonableness, and that Americans could fish in large bays if they
remained three miles from shore. This compromise defused the oldest dispute in
American foreign relations and symbolized London's political withdrawal from
the western hemisphere.

The naval retreat had occurred earlier, when the Admiralty abolished the North
Atlantic station based at Halifax. After 1902 the Royal Navy patrolled the Carib-
bean only with an annual visit by a token squadron of cruisers. Admiral Sir John
Fisher, who oversaw this historic retrenchment, wanted to concentrate his heavy

ships in the English Channel and North Sea as monitors of the growing German Navy, but he acted on the dual premise that the United States was "a kindred state with whom we shall never have a parricidal war."[126]

Even the aggressive hemispheric diplomacy of Taft and Wilson did not undermine the Anglo-American rapprochement. Although Britain criticized dollar diplomacy in Latin America, the complaints, in the words of historian Bradford Perkins, "were sporadic and carping rather than a rising crescendo of calls for positive action."[127] Wilson's quixotic efforts to dislodge Huerta from the presidency of Mexico met with little, if any, sympathy in England, but Foreign Secretary Sir Edward Grey tersely laid to rest all talk of a challenge: "His Majesty's Government cannot with any prospect of success embark upon an active counter-policy to that of the United States, or constitute themselves the champions of Mexico or any of these republics against the United States."[128] In reciprocation, Wilson eliminated the one potentially dangerous British grievance inherited from his predecessor. Late in the Taft Administration, Congress had enacted a measure exempting American intercoastal shippers from payment of tolls at the Panama Canal. British opinion unanimously condemned this shifting of canal maintenance costs to other users. Wilson soon decided that the law unjustly discriminated against foreign shipping, and in June, 1914, Congress revoked the preferential treatment.

In the geographic area of secondary interest to the United States, the Far East, the Anglo-American rapprochement proved less fruitful. London negotiated the alliance with Tokyo in 1902 as a makeweight against Russian pressure upon China and as a means of concentrating more British battleships in home waters. Japan's defeat of Russia in 1904–1905 eliminated the alliance's principal theoretical opponent and removed any serious barriers to Japanese expansionism. The British faced a dilemma. They tried to maintain an alliance now valuable against the mounting German threat without sacrificing the equally vital harmony with the United States, the major power alternately accepting and resisting Japanese expansion. The Taft-Katsura and Root-Takahira exchanges, seemingly exhibiting Washington's acceptance, therefore elicited favorable comment from the British Foreign Office. Secretary of State Knox's neutralization and loan schemes, on the other hand, encountered a mixture of polite discouragement and firm disapproval.

The First World War simply accentuated Anglo-American differences over Japan and China. Britain welcomed Japanese expulsion of Germany from its insular positions in the Pacific and on the Shandong Peninsula of China, and British imperial forces seized all German islands south of the equator. On February 16, 1917, the two allies signed an additional, and secret, treaty pledging reciprocal support for their new territorial claims at the postwar peace conference. This rock lay beneath the deceptively tranquil surface of the Anglo-American wartime coalition, ready to surface when the tides of war receded.

AMERICAN FOREIGN POLICY ON THE EVE OF THE "GREAT WAR"

Prior to the outbreak of the First World War, American policymakers largely adhered to the tradition of aloofness from continental European political and military affairs, as prescribed in Washington's Farewell Address and Jefferson's

Naval Arms Race. The vigorous international competition for large navies in the early twentieth century was foreboding. Disarmament talks at The Hague Conferences and arbitration treaties did not curb the arms buildup. Theodore Roosevelt's decision to send the "Great White Fleet" around the world in 1907–1908 may have encouraged both Japan and Germany to speed up their naval programs. (*Detroit News* in *Literary Digest*, 1904)

First Inaugural. Even Theodore Roosevelt, who appeared so impetuous, tampered only once with Europe's balance of power. In 1904 France acquiesced in British control of Egypt, in exchange for primacy in semi-independent Morocco. A year later, Germany decided to test the solidity of the new Anglo-French entente by challenging France's extension of power in Morocco. Speaking at Tangier, the Kaiser belligerently demanded a German political role in Morocco, which France at once refused. After a brief European war scare, in which Britain stood by her ally, Germany asked Roosevelt to induce France and England to convene a conference to settle Morocco's future. On the grounds that world peace was threatened, Roosevelt accepted the personal invitation only after assuring Paris that he was not acting on Berlin's behalf. During the conference, held in early 1906 at Algeciras, Spain, Roosevelt devised a compromise substantively favorable to Paris and persuaded the Kaiser to accept it. This political intervention isolated Germany and reinforced the Anglo-French entente, but it generated criticism at home. Roosevelt's successors made sure they did not violate the American policy of nonentanglement with Europe during the more ominous second Moroccan and Balkan crises preceding the "Great War."

Nonentanglement also doomed the sweeping arbitration treaties that Secretary of State Hay negotiated with several world powers. The Senate, always the jealous guardian of prerogative and aloofness, attached emasculating amendments, leading Roosevelt to withdraw the treaties because they now did "not in the smallest degree facilitate settlements by arbitration, [and] to make them would in no way further the cause of international peace."[129] After 1905 Secretary Root persuaded Roosevelt to accept watered-down bilateral arbitration treaties, and Secretary Bryan later negotiated a series of supplementary "cooling-off" treaties by which nations pledged to refrain from war during international investigations of serious disputes. None of these arrangements, however, effectively bound any of the signatories, and like the Permanent Court of Arbitration at The Hague, they represented a backwater in international diplomacy.

The mainstream of American foreign policy between 1900 and 1914 flowed through the Panama Canal. That momentous political, military, and technological achievement drew the United States physically into the Caribbean and Gulf of Mexico with unprecedented force. After ratification of the Hay–Bunau-Varilla Treaty, the United States became the unchallenged policeman of Central America. For Taft, the treaty "permits us to prevent revolutions" so that "we'll have no more."[130] In East Asia, American power was pale in comparison. The United States was in no position to challenge Japan or England, especially after the formation of the Anglo-Japanese Alliance in 1902 and the defeat of Russia in 1904–1905. As Roosevelt wrote Taft in 1910, the Open Door "completely disappears as soon as a powerful nation determines to disregard it."[131] Nor were American interests in Asia clearly discernible. The vulnerable Philippines needed protection, but diplomatic agreements were the only safeguards that even Theodore Roosevelt could devise, given the remoteness of the islands and congressional distaste for military spending. Beyond the Philippines, many Americans believed in what historian Paul Varg has called "the myth of the China market."[132] Straight, Taft, and Knox conceived of dollar diplomacy as a means of blocking Japanese expansion, sustaining Chinese independence, and stimulating American overseas investments and trade. Wilson's futile revival of the ill-fated consortium was largely a political act aimed at Japan. This persistent but ineffectual opposition to Japanese expansion constituted a most deleterious legacy. To the next generation it bequeathed war in the Pacific.

Another legacy of the 1900–1914 period was less measurable, but nevertheless a long-term consequence: American insensitivity to the nationalism of other peoples. The violent Filipino resistance to American domination, Cuban anger over the interventionist Platt Amendment, Colombian outrage over the "rape" of Panama, and Mexican rejection of Wilsonian meddling, bore witness to the depth of nationalistic sentiments. Like the European powers who were carving up Asia, Africa, and the Middle East, the United States was developing its empire and subjugating peoples and trampling on their sovereignty, especially in Latin

America. With the exception of the Virgin Islands, purchased from Denmark for $25 million in 1917 to forestall any wartime German seizure, the empire of the United States grew little from outright territorial gains. It was, instead, an informal empire administered by Marines, financial advisers, and reformers who showed contempt for native peoples' culture, politics, and economies through a paternalistic demeanor. "There is something pathetic and childlike about the people," Roosevelt wrote condescendingly of the Puerto Ricans, who did not gain citizenship status until 1917 and whose country has remained a colony to this day.[133] North American chauvinism was equally characteristic of Roosevelt's "big stick," Taft's "dollar diplomacy," and Wilson's missionary zeal to remake other societies.

The much heralded rapprochement between Britain and the United States also meant mutual respect for each other's empires. Roosevelt, for example, encouraged London to frustrate native aspirations for independence in India, while the British accepted the American suppression of the Filipinos and United States hegemony in Latin America. American leaders usually spoke favorably of independence for colonial peoples, but independence only after long-term education to make them "fit" and "civilized" enough to govern. In 1910 in Egypt, where Roosevelt applauded Britain's "great work for civilization," the ex-President even lectured restless Moslem nationalists about Christian respect for womanhood.[134]

This United States insensitivity to nationalism in the colonial world was evident especially in the new imperial possession of the Philippines. Although Aguinaldo was captured, Filipino resistance continued for years thereafter. From 1903 to 1914, for example, Artemio Ricarte harassed American military authorities with his hit-and-run tactics. Deported several times, he consistently refused to take an oath of allegiance to the United States. To silence less violent dissenters, the American colonial government imposed the Sedition Act of 1901, which made it unlawful to express any "scurrilous libels" against America. Newspapers were censored and sometimes shut down. Recalcitrant dissidents were jailed. American efforts at what historian Glenn May has called "social engineering" did produce some economic benefits, improvements in transportation and sanitation, and new educational facilities like the University of the Philippines (1908), but such tutelage also helped create an English-speaking, educated elite far removed from the mass of lower-class people.[135] With American rule came a misplaced pride in things "stateside"—a colonial mentality. Filipino history became "American" history. One Filipino critic wrote that "the history of our ancestors was taken up as if they were strange and foreign peoples who settled in these shores, with whom we had the most tenuous ties. We read about them as if we were tourists in a foreign land."[136]

In 1916, after years of Democratic party pledges, Congress passed and Wilson signed the Jones Act, promising Philippine independence, but setting no date. Thirty years later the United States would in fact relinquish the Philippines, gaining for itself the accolade from apologists of being a "good" imperialist, or—as historian Dexter Perkins has put it—an imperialist with an "uneasy conscience."[137] "Uneasy conscience" or not, Americans as imperialists behaved not unlike the European imperial warriors they so roundly condemned. Indeed, that phrase might better be applied to the American decision to intervene in the "Great War" of 1914–1919—an intervention which permitted the United States to extend further the foreign interests it had cultivated in the previous two decades.

FURTHER READING FOR THE PERIOD 1900–1914

For general studies, see "American Empire, 1898–1903," *Pacific Historical Review* (1979); William H. Becker, *The Dynamics of Business-Government Relations: Industry and Exports, 1893–1921* (1982); Barton J. Bernstein and Franklin A. Leib, "Progressive Republican Senators and American Imperialism, 1898–1916: A Reappraisal," *Mid-America* (1968); Lester H. Brune, *The Origins of American Security Policy: Sea Power, Air Power, and Foreign Policy, 1900–1941* (1981); Frederick S. Calhoun, *Power and Principle: Armed Intervention in Wilsonian Foreign Policy* (1986); Kendrick A. Clements, *William Jennings Bryan, Missionary Isolationist* (1982); Paolo E. Coletta, *The Presidency of William Howard Taft* (1973) and *William Jennings Bryan* (1964–1969); John M. Cooper, Jr., "Progressivism and American Foreign Policy," *Mid-America* (1969) and *The Warrior and the Priest: Woodrow Wilson and Theodore Roosevelt* (1983); Norman A. Graebner, ed., *An Uncertain Tradition: American Secretaries of State in the Twentieth Century* (1961); Robert C. Hilderbrand, *Power and the People: Executive Management of Public Opinion in Foreign Affairs, 1897–1921* (1981); Philip C. Jessup, *Elihu Root* (1938); William Leuchtenburg, "Progressivism and Imperialism," *Mississippi Valley Historical Review* (1952); Ralph E. Minger, *William Howard Taft and United States Foreign Policy: The Apprenticeship Years, 1900–1908* (1975); John M. Mulder, *Woodrow Wilson: The Years of Preparation* (1978); Julius W. Pratt, *America's Colonial Experiment* (1950) and *Challenge and Reaction* (1967); Henry F. Pringle, *The Life and Times of William Howard Taft* (1939); Emily S. Rosenberg, *Spreading the American Dream: American Economic and Cultural Expansion, 1890–1945* (1982); Walter V. and Marie V. Scholes, *The Foreign Policies of the Taft Administration* (1970); E. Berkeley Tompkins, *Anti-Imperialism in the United States* (1970); Richard H. Werking, *The Master Architects: Building the United States Foreign Service, 1890–1913* (1977); Rachel West, *The Department of State on the Eve of the First World War* (1978); and William C. Widenor, *Henry Cabot Lodge and the Search for an American Foreign Policy* (1980).

Theodore Roosevelt and his foreign policy are the subject of Howard K. Beale, *Theodore Roosevelt and the Rise of America to World Power* (1956); John M. Blum, *The Republican Roosevelt* (1954); David H. Burton, *Theodore Roosevelt: Confident Imperialist* (1968); Richard H. Collin, *Theodore Roosevelt, Culture, Diplomacy, and Expansion* (1985); Thomas G. Dyer, *Theodore Roosevelt and the Idea of Race* (1980); Raymond A. Esthus, *Theodore Roosevelt and the International Rivalries* (1970); William H. Harbaugh, *The Life and Times of Theodore Roosevelt* (1975); Frederick W. Marks, *Velvet on Iron: The Diplomacy of Theodore Roosevelt* (1979); and Henry F. Pringle, *Theodore Roosevelt* (1956).

United States relations with Latin America are examined in Jose A. Cabranes, *Citizenship and the American Empire* (1979) (on Puerto Rico); Raymond A. Carr, *Puerto Rico* (1984); Arturo M. Carrión, *Puerto Rico* (1983); David Healy, *Gunboat Diplomacy in the Wilson Era: The U.S. Navy in Haiti. 1915–1916* (1976) and *The United States in Cuba, 1898–1902* (1963); James H. Hitchman, *Leonard Wood and Cuban Independence, 1898–1902* (1971); Warren G. Kneer, *Great Britain and the Caribbean, 1901–1913* (1975); Walter LaFeber, *The Panama Canal* (1978) and *Inevitable Revolutions* (1983); Lester D. Langley, *Struggle for the American Mediterranean: United States–European Rivalry in the Gulf-Caribbean, 1776–1904* (1976), *The United States and the Caribbean, 1900–1970* (1980) and *The Banana Wars: An Inner History of American Empire, 1900–1934* (1983); David McCullough, *The Path Between the Seas: The Creation of the Panama Canal, 1870–1914* (1977); Allan R. Millett, *The Politics of Intervention: The Military Occupation of Cuba, 1906–1909* (1968); Dwight C. Miner, *The Fight for the Panama Route* (1940); Dana Munro, *Intervention and Dollar Diplomacy* (1964); Dexter Perkins, *The Monroe Doctrine, 1867–1907* (1937); and Hans Schmidt, *The United States Occupation of Haiti, 1915–1934* (1971).

Relations with Mexico are treated in Peter Calvert, *The Mexican Revolution, 1910–1914* (1968); Clarence C. Clendenen, *Blood on the Border: The United States Army and the Mexican Irregulars* (1969); Howard F. Cline, *The United States and Mexico* (1963); Jules Davids, *American Political and Economic Penetration of Mexico, 1877–1920* (1976); Mark T. Gilderhus, *Diplomacy and Revolution: U.S.–Mexican Relations Under Wilson and Carranza* (1977); Kenneth J. Grieb, *The United States and Huerta* (1969); Larry D. Hill, *Emissaries to a Revolution: Woodrow*

Wilson's Executive Agents in Mexico (1973); Friedrich Katz, *The Secret War in Mexico: Europe, the United States, and the Mexican Revolution* (1981); Robert E. Quirk, *An Affair of Honor: Woodrow Wilson and the Occupation of Veracruz* (1962); Ramon E. Ruiz, *The Great Rebellion: Mexico, 1905–1924* (1980); Karl M. Schmitt, *Mexico and the United States, 1821–1973* (1974); and Josefina Vazquez and Lorenzo Meyer, *The United States and Mexico* (1985).

America's interaction with China and Asia in general is the subject of William R. Braisted, *The United States Navy in the Pacific, 1897–1909* (1958) and *1909–1922* (1971); Warren I. Cohen, *America's Response to China* (1980); Daniel M. Crane and Thomas A. Breslin, *An Ordinary Relationship: American Opposition to Republican Revolution in China* (1986); Roy W. Curry, *Woodrow Wilson and Far Eastern Policy, 1913–1921* (1957); A. Whitney Griswold, *The Far Eastern Policy of the United States* (1938); Robert A. Hart, *The Great White Fleet* (1965); Akira Iriye, *Across the Pacific* (1967); Jerry Israel, *Progressivism and the Open Door: America and China, 1905–1921* (1971); Delber L. McKee, *Chinese Exclusion versus the Open Door Policy, 1900–1906* (1976); Noel H. Pugach, *Paul S. Reinsch: Open Door Diplomat in Action* (1979); Paul A. Varg, *The Making of a Myth: The United States and China, 1897–1912* (1968); and Charles Vevier, *The United States and China, 1906–1913* (1955).

Japanese-American relations can be studied in Burton F. Beers, *Vain Endeavor: Robert Lansing's Attempt to End the American-Japanese Rivalry* (1962); Raymond A. Esthus, *Theodore Roosevelt and Japan* (1966); Akira Iriye, *Pacific Estrangement: Japanese and American Expansion, 1897–1911* (1972); Charles E. Neu, *An Uncertain Friendship: Theodore Roosevelt and Japan, 1906–1909* (1967) and *The Troubled Encounter* (1975); and E. P. Trani, *The Treaty of Portsmouth* (1969).

For Americans in the Philippines, see David H. Bain, *Sitting in Darkness* (1985); Glenn A. May, *Social Engineering in the Philippines* (1980); William J. Pomeroy, *American Neo-Colonialism: Its Emergence in the Philippines and Asia* (1970); Bonifacio S. Salamanca, *The Filipino Reaction to American Rule, 1901–1913* (1968); and Peter Stanley, *A Nation in the Making: The Philippines and the United States, 1899–1921* (1974) and ed., *Reappraising an Empire* (1984). See also works cited in Chapter 6.

The work of American missionaries, especially in Asia, is discussed in Kenton J. Clymer, *Protestant Missionaries in the Philippines, 1898–1916* (1986); Patricia R. Hill, *The World Their Household: The American Woman's Foreign Mission Movement and Cultural Transformation, 1870–1920* (1985); Jane Hunter, *The Gospel of Gentility: American Women Missionaries in Turn-of-the-Century China* (1984); and James Reed, *The Missionary Mind and American East Asia Policy, 1911–1915* (1983).

The history of United States relations with Europe and Great Britain is discussed in A. E. Campbell, *Great Britain and the United States, 1895–1903* (1960); Charles S. Campbell, *Anglo-American Understanding, 1898–1903* (1957); Thomas J. Noer, *Britain, Boer, and Yankee* (1978); and Bradford Perkins, *The Great Rapprochement: England and the United States, 1895–1914* (1968).

Economic, racial, and military ingredients in American foreign policy are described in Paul P. Abrahams, *The Foreign Expansion of American Finance . . . , 1907–1921* (1976); Richard D. Challener, *Admirals, Generals, and American Foreign Policy, 1898–1914* (1973); Roger Daniels, *The Politics of Prejudice: The Anti-Japanese Movement in California and the Struggle for Japanese Exclusion* (1962); Rubin F. Weston, *Racism in United States Imperialism* (1972); and Mira Wilkins, *The Emergence of Multinational Enterprise: American Business Abroad from the Colonial Era to 1914* (1970).

The peace movement and the role of the Hague are discussed in Peter Brock, *Pacifism in the United States* (1968); Merle E. Curti, *Peace or War* (1936); Calvin Davis, *The United States and the First Hague Conference* (1962) and *The United States and the Second Hague Peace Conference* (1976); Charles DeBenedetti, *The Peace Reform in American History* (1980); Sondra R. Herman, *Eleven Against War* (1969); Charles F. Howlett and Glen Zeitzer, *The American Peace Movement* (1985); C. Roland Marchand, *The American Peace Movement and Social Reform, 1898–1918* (1973); and David S. Patterson, *Toward a Warless World: The Travail of the American Peace Movement, 1887–1914* (1976).

See also the General Bibliography and the following notes.

NOTES TO CHAPTER 7

1. This and previous quotations from U.S. Congress, *Diplomatic History of the Panama Canal*, Senate Document 474 (1914), pp. 345–363.
2. Elting E. Morison, ed., *The Letters of Theodore Roosevelt* (Cambridge: Harvard University Press, 1951–1954; 8 vols.), II, 1185–1187.
3. Quoted in Gerstle Mack, *The Land Divided* (New York: Alfred A. Knopf, 1944), p. 417.
4. Dwight C. Miner, *The Fight for the Panama Route* (New York: Columbia University Press, 1940), p. 75.
5. *Diplomatic History of the Canal*, p. 261.
6. Quoted in Miner, *Fight for the Panama Route*, p. 275.
7. Quoted in Henry F. Pringle, *Theodore Roosevelt* (New York: Harcourt, Brace, 1931), p. 311.
8. Quoted in Howard K. Beale, *Theodore Roosevelt and the Rise of America to World Power* (Baltimore: The Johns Hopkins Press, 1956), p. 33.
9. Quoted in David McCullough, *The Path Between the Seas* (New York: Simon and Schuster, 1977), p. 333.
10. *New York World*, June 14, 1903.
11. Quoted in Pringle, *Roosevelt*, p. 311.
12. Quoted in Tyler Dennett, *John Hay* (New York: Dodd, Mead, 1933), p. 377.
13. Quoted in Walter LaFeber, *The Panama Canal* (New York: Oxford University Press, 1978), p. 30.
14. James D. Richardson, ed., *A Compilation of the Messages and Papers of the Presidents, 1789–1897* (Washington, D.C.: Government Printing Office, 1896–1899; 10 vols.), IX, 6919–6923.
15. Quoted in LaFeber, *The Panama Canal*, p. 38.
16. *New York Times*, March 25, 1911.
17. William H. Harbaugh, *The Life and Times of Theodore Roosevelt* (New York: Oxford University Press, 1975; rev. ed.), p. 197.
18. Ronald H. Spector, *Professors of War: The Naval War College and the Development of the Naval Profession* (Newport, R.I.: Naval War College Press, 1977).
19. Quoted in Kenneth J. Hagan, "Alfred Thayer Mahan: Turning America Back to the Sea," in Frank Merli and Theodore Wilson, eds., *Makers of American Diplomacy* (New York: Charles Scribner's Sons, 1974), p. 298.
20. John M. Cooper, Jr., "Progressivism and American Foreign Policy: A Reconsideration," *Mid-America*, LI (October, 1969), 261.
21. Quoted in John Morton Blum, *The Republican Roosevelt* (New York: Atheneum, 1973 [1954]), p. 127.
22. Quoted in Beale, *Theodore Roosevelt*, p. 77 and G. Wallace Chessman, *Theodore Roosevelt and the Politics of Power* (Boston: Little, Brown, 1969), p. 70.
23. Quoted in Beale, *Theodore Roosevelt*, p. 140.
24. Quoted in John Milton Cooper, Jr., *The Warrior and the Priest* (Cambridge: Harvard University Press, 1983), p. 75.
25. Quoted in Foster Rhea Dulles, "John Hay," in Norman A. Graebner, ed., *An Uncertain Tradition* (New York: McGraw-Hill, 1961), p. 24.
28. Quoted in David H. Burton, *Theodore Roosevelt: Confident Imperialist* (Philadelphia: University of Pennsylvania Press, 1968), p. 97, and *Congressional Record, XXXV* (December 3, 1901), 82–83.
29. Quoted in Ralph E. Minger, *William Howard Taft and United States Foreign Policy: The Apprenticeship Years, 1900–1908* (Urbana: University of Illinois Press, 1975), p. 179.
30. Quoted in Ray S. Baker, *Woodrow Wilson: Life and Letters* (Garden City, N.Y.: Doubleday, Doran, 1927–1939; 8 vols.), IV, 289.
31. Jerry Israel, "'For God, for China and for Yale'—The Open Door in Action," *American Historical Review, LXXV* (February, 1970), 807.
32. *Foreign Relations of the United States, 1898* (Washington, D.C.: Government Printing Office, 1901), pp. lxvi–lxvii.
33. Quoted in Philip C. Jessup, *Elihu Root* (New York: Dodd, Mead, 1938; 2 vols.), I, 286–287.
34. Quoted in David F. Healy, *The United States in Cuba, 1898–1902* (Madison: University of Wisconsin Press, 1963), p. 133.
35. *Congressional Record, XXXIV* (February 26, 1901), 3036.
36. Quoted in Healy, *United States in Cuba*, p. 177.
37. Quoted in H. Hagedorn, *Leonard Wood* (New York: Harper, 1931; 2 vols.), I, 362; Healy, *United States in Cuba*, p. 178.
38. Quoted in R. H. Fitzgibbon, *Cuba and the United States, 1900–1935* (New York: Russell & Russell, 1964), p. 112.
39. Quoted in Allan R. Millett, *The Politics of Intervention* (Columbus: Ohio State University Press, 1968), p. 72.
40. Quoted in Burton, *Theodore Roosevelt*, p. 106.
41. Quoted in Millett, *Politics of Intervention*, p. 78.
42. Richardson, *Messages of the Presidents*, X, 7436–7437.
43. Quoted in Minger, *William Howard Taft*, p. 136.
44. Lawrence F. Abbott, ed., *The Letters of Archie Butt* (Garden City, N.Y.: Doubleday, Page, 1924), p. 325.
45. Fitzgibbon, *Cuba and the United States*, p. 145 and Millett, *Politics of Intervention*, p. 267.
46. Fred L. Israel, ed., *The State of the Union Messages of the Presidents, 1790–1966* (New York: Chelsea House, 1967; 3 vols.), II, 2038.
47. Morison, *Letters of Roosevelt*, III, 116.
48. *Ibid.*, IV, 1156.
49. *Literary Digest, XXV* (December 20, 1902), 823–824.
50. Quoted in Manfred Jonas, *The United States and Germany* (Ithaca: Cornell University Press, 1984), pp. 68–69.
51. Quoted in Dexter Perkins, *The Monroe Doctrine, 1867–1907* (Baltimore: The Johns Hopkins Press, 1937), p. 360.
52. Quoted *ibid.*, p. 420.
53. Quoted in Lloyd Gardner, "A Progressive Foreign Policy, 1900–1921," in William A. Williams, ed., *From Colony to Empire* (New York: John Wiley and Sons, 1972), p. 218.
54. Quoted in Perkins, *Monroe Doctrine*, p. 420.
55. Israel, *State of the Union Messages*, II, 2134.
56. Quoted in Jessup, *Root*, I, 471.
57. Elihu Root, *Latin America and the United States* (Cambridge: Harvard University Press, 1917), p. 275.
58. *Foreign Relations, 1912* (Washington, D.C.: Government Printing Office, 1919), p. 1091.
59. *Congressional Record, L* (November 3, 1913), 5845.
60. *Foreign Relations, 1913* (Washington, D.C.: Government Printing Office, 1920), p. 426.
61. Quoted in D. G. Munro, *Intervention and Dollar Diplomacy in the Caribbean* (Princeton: Princeton Univ. Press, 1964), p. 336.
62. Quoted in David F. Healy, *Gunboat Diplomacy in the Wilson Era* (Madison: University of Wisconsin Press, 1976), p. 109.

63. Quoted *ibid.*, p. 131.

64. *Ibid.*, p. 205.

65. Quoted in Munro, *Intervention and Dollar Diplomacy*, p. 155.

66. *Ibid.*, p. 160.

67. *Ibid.*, p. 181.

68. Quoted in Baker, *Wilson*, IV, 436.

69. Quoted in Paolo E. Coletta, *The Presidency of William Howard Taft* (Lawrence: University Press of Kansas, 1973), p. 176.

70. *Foreign Relations, 1912*, p. 846.

71. Quoted in Howard F. Cline, *The United States and Mexico* (New York: Atheneum, 1963; rev. ed.), p. 144.

72. Quoted in Arthur S. Link, *Wilson: The New Freedom* (Princeton: Princeton University Press, 1956), p. 360.

73. Quoted in Arthur S. Link, *Wilson: Confusions and Crises, 1915–1916* (Princeton: Princeton University Press, 1964), p. 317.

74. Quoted in Link, *Wilson: New Freedom*, p. 358.

75. Quoted *ibid.*, p. 360.

76. Quoted in Kenneth J. Grieb, *The United States and Huerta* (Lincoln: University of Nebraska Press, 1969), p. 137.

77. Quoted in Link, *Wilson: New Freedom*, pp. 386–387.

78. Quoted in Grieb, *United States and Huerta*, p. 137.

79. Quoted *ibid.*, p. 135.

80. Quoted in Robert E. Quirk, *An Affair of Honor* (Lexington: University of Kentucky Press, 1962), p. 26.

81. Quoted *ibid.*, pp. 32, 49.

82. Quoted in Mark T. Gilderhus, *Diplomacy and Revolution* (Tucson: University of Arizona Press, 1977), p. 11.

83. Quoted in Henry C. Lodge, *The Senate and the League of Nations* (New York: Charles Scribner's Sons, 1925), p. 18 and Cary T. Grayson, *Woodrow Wilson: An Intimate Memoir* (New York: Holt, Rinehart and Winston, 1960), p. 30.

84. Ramón Eduardo Ruíz, *The Great Rebellion: Mexico, 1905–1924* (New York: W. W. Norton, 1980), p. 395.

85. Quoted in Grieb, *United States and Huerta*, p. 160.

86. *Washington Post*, June 3, 1914.

87. Quoted in A. S. Link, *Wilson: The Struggle for Neutrality, 1914–1915* (Princeton: Princeton University Press, 1960), p. 239.

88. Quoted *ibid.*, p. 491.

89. Quoted in F. Katz, "Pancho Villa and the Attack on Columbus, New Mexico," *American Hist. Rev. LXXXIII*, 111, 114.

90. Morison, *Letters of Roosevelt*, III, 497–498.

91. Akira Iriye, *The Cold War in Asia* (Englewood Cliffs, N.J.: Prentice Hall, 1974), p. 35.

92. Morison, *Letters of Roosevelt*, IV, 724, 761.

93. *Ibid.*, p. 1222.

94. Quoted in Raymond A. Esthus, *Theodore Roosevelt and Japan* (Seattle: University of Washington Press, 1966), p. 101.

95. John Edward Wilz, "Did the United States Betray Korea in 1905?" *Pacific Historical Review*, LIV (August, 1985), 252.

96. Quoted in Charles E. Neu, *An Uncertain Friendship* (Cambridge: Harvard University Press, 1967), pp. 36, 47.

97. Quoted in Akira Iriye, *Across the Pacific* (New York: Harcourt, Brace & World, 1967), p. 107.

98. Quoted in Esthus, *Roosevelt and Japan*, p. 149.

99. Quoted *ibid.*, p. 173.

100. Morison, *Letters of Roosevelt*, V, 729–730, 761–762.

101. Quoted in Frederick W. Marks, *Velvet on Iron: The Diplomacy of Theodore Roosevelt* (Lincoln: University of Nebraska Press, 1979), p. 57.

102. Quoted *ibid.*

103. Quoted in Herbert Croly, *Willard Straight* (New York: Macmillan, 1925), p. 276.

104. A. Whitney Griswold, *The Far Eastern Policy of the United States* (New Haven: Yale University Press, 1964), p. 157.

105. *Foreign Relations, 1909* (Washington, D.C.: Government Printing Office, 1914), p. 178.

106. Quoted in Croly, *Straight*, pp. 392–393.

107. Quoted in Iriye, *Across the Pacific*, p. 126.

108. James Reed, *The Missionary Mind and American East Asia Policy, 1911–1915* (Cambridge: Harvard University Press, 1983), p. 34.

109. Quoted in Link, *Wilson: New Freedom*, p. 286.

110. *New York Times*, May 5, 1913.

111. Quoted in Roger Daniels, *The Politics of Prejudice* (New York: Atheneum, 1968 [c. 1962]), p. 59.

112. Quoted in David F. Houston, *Eight Years with Wilson's Cabinet* (Garden City, N.Y.: Doubleday, 1926; 2 vols.), I, 66.

113. Quoted in Link, *Wilson: New Freedom*, pp. 300–301.

114. *Foreign Relations, 1915* (Washington, D.C.: Government Printing Office, 1924), p. 146.

115. *Foreign Relations, 1922* (Washington, D.C.: Government Printing Office, 1938; 2 vols.), II, 591.

116. Quoted in Beale, *Theodore Roosevelt*, pp. 81, 152.

117. Morison, *Letters of Roosevelt*, II, 1186–87.

118. Quoted in Beale, *Theodore Roosevelt*, p. 104.

119. Bradford Perkins, *The Great Rapprochement: England and the United States, 1895–1914* (New York: Atheneum, 1968).

120. Quoted in C. S. Campbell, *Anglo-American Understanding, 1898–1903* (Baltimore: The Johns Hopkins Press, 1957), p. 190.

121. Quoted in A. E. Campbell, *Great Britain and the United States* (Westport, Conn.: Greenwood Press, 1974 [c. 1960]), pp. 105–106 and Morison, *Letters of Roosevelt*, III, 66.

122. Quoted in Perkins, *Great Rapprochement*, p. 168.

123. Quoted *ibid.*, p. 169.

124. Morison, *Letters of Roosevelt*, VII, 28.

125. Quoted in Perkins, *Monroe Doctrine*, p. 364.

126. Quoted in Arthur J. Marder, *From the Dreadnought to Scapa Flow: The Royal Navy in the Fisher Era, 1904–1919* (London: Oxford University Press, 1961–1970; 5 vols.), I, 125.

127. Perkins, *Great Rapprochement*, p. 195.

128. Quoted *ibid.*, p. 201.

129. Morison, *Letters of Roosevelt*, IV, 1119.

130. Quoted in Minger, *William Howard Taft*, p. 106.

131. Quoted in Jerry Israel, *Progressivism and the Open Door* (Pittsburgh: University of Pittsburgh Press, 1971), p. 96.

132. Paul A. Varg, *The Making of a Myth* (East Lansing: Michigan State University Press, 1968), p. 36.

133. Quoted in Arturo Morales Carrión, *Puerto Rico: A Political and Cultural History* (New York: W. W. Norton, 1983), p. 163.

134. Quoted in Burton, *Theodore Roosevelt*, p. 190.

135. Glenn A. May, *Social Engineering in the Philippines* (Westport, Conn.: Greenwood Press, 1980).

136. Quoted in Teodoro A. Agoncillo, *A Short History of the Philippines* (New York: New American Library, 1969), p. 120.

Appendix

Makers of American Foreign Policy

Presidents	Secretaries of State	Chairmen of the Senate Foreign Relations Committee
George Washington (1789–1797)	Thomas Jefferson (1790–1794)	
	Edmund Randolph (1794–1795)	
	Timothy Pickering (1795–1800)	
John Adams (1797–1801)	Timothy Pickering (1795–1800)	
	John Marshall (1800–1801)	
Thomas Jefferson (1801–1809)	James Madison (1801–1809)	
James Madison (1809–1817)	Robert Smith (1809–1811)	James Barbour (1816–1818)
	James Monroe (1811–1817)	
James Monroe (1817–1825)	John Quincy Adams (1817–1825)	James Barbour (1816–1818)
		Nathaniel Macon (1818–1819)
		James Brown (1819–1820)
		James Barbour (1820–1821)
		Rufus King (1821–1822)
		James Barbour (1822–1825)
John Quincy Adams (1825–1829)	Henry Clay (1825–1829)	Nathaniel Macon (1825–1826)
		Nathan Sanford (1826–1827)
		Nathaniel Macon (1827–1828)
		Littleton W. Tazewell (1828–1832)
Andrew Jackson (1829–1837)	Martin Van Buren (1829–1831)	Littleton W. Tazewell (1828–1832)
	Edward Livingston (1831–1833)	John Forsyth (1832–1833)
	Louis McLane (1833–1834)	William Wilkins (1833–1834)
	John Forsyth (1834–1841)	Henry Clay (1834–1836)
		James Buchanan (1836–1841)
Martin Van Buren (1837–1841)	John Forsyth (1834–1841)	James Buchanan (1836–1841)
William H. Harrison (1841)	Daniel Webster (1841–1843)	William C. Rives (1841–1842)
John Tyler (1841–1845)	Daniel Webster (1841–1843)	William C. Rives (1841–1842)
	Abel P. Upshur (1843–1844)	William S. Archer (1842–1845)
	John C. Calhoun (1844–1845)	
James K. Polk (1845–1849)	James Buchanan (1845–1849)	William Allen (1845–1846)
		Ambrose H. Sevier (1846–1848)
		Edward A. Hannegan (1848–1849)
		Thomas H. Benton (1849)
Zachary Taylor (1849–1850)	John M. Clayton (1849–1850)	William R. King (1849–1850)
Millard Fillmore (1850–1853)	Daniel Webster (1850–1852)	Henry S. Foote (1850–1851)
	Edward Everett (1852–1853)	James M. Mason (1851–1861)
Franklin Pierce (1853–1857)	William L. Marcy (1853–1857)	James M. Mason (1851–1861)

i

Makers of American Foreign Policy

Presidents	Secretaries of State	Chairmen of the Senate Foreign Relations Committee
James Buchanan (1857–1861)	Lewis Cass (1857–1860)	James M. Mason (1851–1861)
	Jeremiah S. Black (1860–1861)	
Abraham Lincoln (1861–1865)	William H. Seward (1861–1869)	Charles Sumner (1861–1871)
Andrew Johnson (1865–1869)	William H. Seward (1861–1869)	Charles Sumner (1861–1871)
Ulysses S. Grant (1869–1877)	Elihu B. Washburne (1869)	Charles Sumner (1861–1871)
	Hamilton Fish (1869–1877)	Simon Cameron (1871–1877)
Rutherford B. Hayes (1877–1881)	William M. Evarts (1877–1881)	Hannibal Hamlin (1877–1879)
		William W. Eaton (1879–1881)
James A. Garfield (1881)	James G. Blaine (1881)	Ambrose E. Burnside (1881)
		George F. Edmunds (1881)
Chester A. Arthur (1881–1885)	Frederick T. Frelinghuysen (1881–1885)	William Windon (1881–1883)
		John F. Miller (1883–1887)
Grover Cleveland (1885–1889)	Thomas F. Bayard (1885–1889)	John F. Miller (1883–1887)
		John Sherman (1887–1893)
Benjamin Harrison (1889–1893)	James G. Blaine (1889–1892)	John Sherman (1887–1893)
	John W. Foster (1892–1893)	
Grover Cleveland (1893–1897)	Walter Q. Gresham (1893–1895)	John T. Morgan (1893–1895)
	Richard Olney (1895–1897)	John Sherman (1895–1897)
William McKinley (1897–1901)	John Sherman (1897–1898)	William P. Frye (1897)
	William R. Day (1898)	Cushman K. Davis (1897–1901)
	John Hay (1898–1905)	
Theodore Roosevelt (1901–1909)	John Hay (1898–1905)	William P. Frye (1901)
	Elihu Root (1905–1909)	Shelby M. Cullom (1901–1913)
	Robert Bacon (1909)	
William Howard Taft (1909–1913)	Philander C. Knox (1909–1913)	Shelby M. Cullom (1901–1913)
Woodrow Wilson (1913–1921)	William Jennings Bryan (1913–1915)	Augustus O. Bacon (1913–1915)
	Robert Lansing (1915–1920)	William J. Stone (1915–1919)
	Bainbridge Colby (1920–1921)	Henry Cabot Lodge (1919–1924)
Warren G. Harding (1921–1923)	Charles E. Hughes (1921–1925)	Henry Cabot Lodge (1919–1924)
Calvin Coolidge (1923–1929)	Charles E. Hughes (1921–1925)	Henry Cabot Lodge (1919–1924)
	Frank B. Kellogg (1925–1929)	William E. Borah (1925–1933)
Herbert C. Hoover (1929–1933)	Henry L. Stimson (1929–1933)	William E. Borah (1925–1933)
Franklin D. Roosevelt (1933–1945)	Cordell Hull (1933–1944)	Key Pittman (1933–1941)
	Edward R. Stettinius, Jr. (1944–1945)	Walter F. George (1941)
		Tom Connally (1941–1947)

Makers of American Foreign Policy

Presidents	Secretaries of State	Chairmen of the Senate Foreign Relations Committee	Secretaries of Defense	Assistants to the President for National Security Affairs
Harry S Truman (1945–1953)	Edward R. Stettinius, Jr. (1944–1945) James F. Byrnes (1945–1947) George C. Marshall (1947–1949) Dean G. Acheson (1949–1953)	Tom Connally (1941–1947) Arthur H. Vandenberg (1947–1949) Tom Connally (1949–1953)	James V. Forrestal (1947–1949) Louis A. Johnson (1949–1950) George C. Marshall (1950–1951) Robert A. Lovett (1951–1953)	
Dwight D. Eisenhower (1953–1961)	John F. Dulles (1953–1959) Christian A. Herter (1959–1961)	Alexander Wiley (1953–1955) Walter F. George (1955–1957) Theodore F. Green (1957–1959) J. W. Fulbright (1959–1975)	Charles E. Wilson (1953–1957) Neil H. McElroy (1957–1959) Thomas S. Gates, Jr. (1959–1961)	Robert Cutler (1953–1955; 1957–1958) Dillon Anderson (1955–1956) William H. Jackson (1956) Gordon Gray (1958–1961)
John F. Kennedy (1961–1963)	Dean Rusk (1961–1969)	J. W. Fulbright (1959–1975)	Robert S. McNamara (1961–1968)	McGeorge Bundy (1961–1966)
Lyndon B. Johnson (1963–1969)	Dean Rusk (1961–1969)	J. W. Fulbright (1959–1975)	Robert S. McNamara (1961–1968) Clark M. Clifford (1968–1969)	McGeorge Bundy (1961–1966) Walt W. Rostow (1966–1969)
Richard M. Nixon (1969–1974)	William P. Rogers (1969–1973) Henry A. Kissinger (1973–1977)	J. W. Fulbright (1959–1975)	Melvin R. Laird (1969–1973) Elliot L. Richardson (1973) James R. Schlesinger (1973–1976)	Henry A. Kissinger (1969–1975)
Gerald R. Ford (1974–1977)	Henry A. Kissinger (1973–1977)	J. W. Fulbright (1959–1975) John Sparkman (1975–1979)	James R. Schlesinger (1973–1976) Donald Rumsfeld (1976–1977)	Henry A. Kissinger (1969–1975) Brent Scowcroft (1975–1977)
Jimmy Carter (1977–1981)	Cyrus R. Vance (1977–1980) Edmund Muskie (1980–1981)	John Sparkman (1975–1979) Frank Church (1979–1981)	Harold Brown (1977–1981)	Zbigniew Brzezinski (1977–1981)
Ronald Reagan (1981–1989)	Alexander M. Haig, Jr. (1981–1982) George P. Shultz (1982–1989)	Charles Percy (1981–1985) Richard G. Lugar (1985–1987) Claiborne Pell (1987–)	Casper Weinberger (1981–1987) Frank C. Carlucci (1987–1989)	Richard Allen (1981) William P. Clark, Jr. (1981–1983) Robert C. McFarlane (1983–1985) John M. Poindexter (1985–1986) Frank C. Carlucci (1986–1987) Colin L. Powell (1987–1989)
George Bush (1989–)	James A. Baker III (1989–)	Claiborne Pell (1987–)	Richard B. Cheney (1989–)	Brent Scowcroft (1989–)

General Bibliography

Reference Works

Annual Surveys: Amnesty International, *Annual Report* (1961–) (human rights); Barry M. Blechman and Edward N. Luttwak, eds., *The International Security Yearbook* (1984–); Lester R. Brown et al., *State of the World* (1984–); Council on Foreign Relations, *American Foreign Relations, 1971– : A Documentary Record* (1976–) and *The United States in World Affairs, 1931–1970* (1932–1972); H.V. Hodson, ed., *Annual Register* (1758–); Jack W. Hopkins, ed., *Latin America and Caribbean Contemporary Record* (1983–); International Institute for Strategic Studies, *The Military Balance* (1959/60–); Colin Legum, ed., *Africa Contemporary Record* (1968–); Colin Legum et al., eds., *Middle East Contemporary Survey* (1978–); London Institute of World Affairs, *The Yearbook of World Affairs* (1947–); Overseas Development Council, *U.S. Foreign Policy and the Third World* (1973–); Alan F. Pater and Jason R. Pater, eds., *What They Said In . . . : The Yearbook of World Opinion* (1971–); Royal Institute of International Affairs, *Survey of International Affairs, 1920–1963* (1972–1977); Ruth L. Sivard, *World Military and Social Expenditures, 1974–* (1974–); *The Statesman's Year Book: Statistical and Historical Annual of the States of the World* (1864–); Stockholm International Peace Research Institute, *SIPRI Yearbook: International Armaments and Disarmament* (1969–); United Nations, *The United Nations Disarmament Yearbook* (1976–); World Bank, *World Development Report* (1978–).

Atlases: Arthur Banks, *A Military History Atlas of the First World War* (1975) and *A World Atlas of Military History* (1973–1978); Geoffrey Barraclough, *The Times Atlas of World History* (1979); Andrew Boyd, *An Atlas of World Affairs* (1957–1970); Lester J. Cappon, ed., *Atlas of Early American History: The Revolutionary Era, 1760–1790* (1976); Gérard Chaliand and Jean-Pierre Rageau, *Strategic Atlas* (1985); Council on Foreign Relations, *Political Handbook and Atlas of the World* (1963–); Edward W. Fox, *Atlas of American History* (1964); Martin Gilbert, *First World War Atlas* (1970); Simon Goodenough, *War Maps: Great Land Battles of World War II* (1983); *International Geographic Encyclopedia and Atlas* (1976); Kenneth T. Jackson and James T. Adams, *Atlas of American History* (1978); Michael Kidron and Dan Smith, *The State of the World Atlas* (1981) and *The State of War Atlas* (1983); George Kurian, *Atlas of the Third World* (1983); Richard Natkiel et al., eds., *Atlas of the Twentieth Century* (1982); William R. Shepherd, *Shepherd's Historical Atlas* (1976); U.S. Department of the Interior, *The National Atlas of the United States of America* (1970); U.S. Military Academy, *Campaign Atlas to the Second World War* (1980) and *The West Point Atlas of American Wars, 1689–1953* (1959); Andrew Wheatcroft, *The World Atlas of Revolutions* (1983); Peter Young, ed., *Atlas of the Second World War* (1973).

Biographies: Samuel F. Bemis and Robert H. Ferrell, eds., *The American Secretaries of State and Their Diplomacy* (1927–); Paolo E. Coletta et al., eds., *American Secretaries of the Navy* (1980); *Concise Dictionary of American Biography* (1928–); *Current Biography* (1940–); *Dictionary of American Biography* (1946); John A. Garraty, ed., *Encyclopedia of American Biography* (1974); Norman Graebner, ed., *An Uncertain Tradition: American Secretaries of State in the Twentieth Century* (1961); Holger H. Herwig and Neil M. Heyman, *Biographical Dictionary of World War I* (1982); *International Who's Who* (1935–); Harold Josephson, ed., *Biographical Dictionary of Modern Peace Leaders* (1985); Warren F. Kuehl, ed., *Biographical Dictionary of Internationalists* (1983); Frank Merli and Theodore Wilson, eds., *Makers of American Diplomacy* (1974); *National Cyclopedia of American Biography* (1898–); Thomas Parker, *America's Foreign Policy, 1945–1976: Its Creators and Critics* (1982); *Political Profiles, Truman Years to . . .* (1978–); Robert Sobel, ed., *Biographical Dictionary of the United States Executive Branch, 1774–1977* (1977); Roger J. Spiller and Joseph G. Dawson, III, eds., *Dictionary of American Military Biography* (1984); Roger Trask, *The Secretaries of Defense* (1985); U.S. Congress, Senate, *Biographical Directory of the American Congress, 1774–1971* (1971); U.S. Department of State, *The Biographic Register, 1870–* (1870–) and *The Secretaries of State* (1978); Charles Van Doren, ed., *Webster's American Biographies* (1974); *Webster's American Military Biographies* (1978); *Who's Who in America* (1899–); *Who's Who in the World* (1971–).

Chronologies: Lester H. Brune, *Chronological History of United States Foreign Relations* (1985); *Facts on File: A Weekly World News Digest* (1940–); Bernard Grun, *The Timetables of History* (1975); *Keesing's Contemporary Archives* (1931–); Edward Mickolus, *Transnational Terrorism: A Chronology of Events, 1968–1979* (1980); Thomas Parker, *Day by Day: The Sixties* (1983); Jack Sweetman, ed., *American Naval History* (1984).

Encyclopedias and Dictionaries, General: James T. Adams, *Dictionary of American History* (1942–1961); Jerald A. Combs, *American Diplomatic History* (1982); *Concise Dictionary of American History* (1983); Congressional Quarterly, *Congress and the Nation, 1945–1976* (1965–1977); Robert H. Ferrell and John S. Bowman, eds., *The Twentieth Century: An Almanac* (1984); John E. Findling, *Dictionary of American Diplomatic History* (1980); Alexander DeConde, ed., *Encyclopedia of American Foreign Policy* (1978); Otis Graham, Jr. and Meghan R. Wander, eds., *Franklin D. Roosevelt, His Life and Times* (1985); Stanley Hochman, *Yesterday and Today* (1979); *International Encyclopedia of the Social Sciences* (1968–); Howard R. Lamar, ed., *The Reader's Encyclopedia of the American West* (1977); John F. Mack, ed., *The Encyclopedia of American History* (1986); Richard B. Morris, *Encyclopedia of American History* (1982); Richard B. Morris and Graham W. Irwin, eds., *Harper Encyclopedia of the Modern World* (1970); Jack C. Plano and Milton Greenberg, *The American Political Dictionary* (1985); Jack C. Plano and Ray Olton, *The International Relations Dictionary* (1982); Glenn Porter, *Encyclopedia of American Economic History* (1980); Harry Ritter, *Dictionary of Concepts in History* (1986); Arthur M. Schlesinger, Jr., ed., *The Almanac of American History* (1983); Stephen Thernstrom, ed., *Harvard Encyclopedia of American Ethnic Groups* (1980); U.S. Department of State Library, *International Relations Dictionary* (1978); Jack E. Vincent, *A Handbook of International Relations* (1968).

Encyclopedias and Dictionaries, Regions: Simon Collier et al., eds., *The Cambridge Encyclopedia of Latin America and the Caribbean* (1985); George T. Kurian, *Encyclopedia of the Third World* (1981); Barbara P. McCrea et al., *The Soviet and East European Political Dictionary* (1984); Claude S. Phillips, *The African Political Dictionary* (1983); Ernest E. Rossi and Barbara P. McCrea, *The European Political Dictionary* (1985); Ernest E. Rossi and Jack C. Plano, *The Latin American Political Dictionary* (1981); C. L. Thompson et al., eds., *The Current History Encyclopedia of Developing Nations* (1981); Lawrence Ziring, *The Middle East Political Dictionary* (1984); Lawrence Ziring and C.I. Eugene Kim, *The Asian Political Dictionary* (1985).

Encyclopedias and Dictionaries, Wars and Military: Marcel Baudot et al., eds., *The Historical Encyclopedia of World War II* (1980); Mark M. Boatner, III, *Encyclopedia of the American Revolution* (1974); Ernest R. Dupuy and Trevor N. Dupuy, *The Encyclopedia of Military History* (1977); Robert Goralski, *World War II Almanac, 1931–1945* (1981); Wolfram F. Hanrieder and Larry V. Buel, *Words and Arms: A Dictionary of Security and Defense Terms* (1979); John Keegan, ed., *The Rand McNally Encyclopedia of World War II* (1977); Thomas Parrish, ed., *The Simon and Schuster Encyclopedia of World War II* (1978); Louis L. Snyder, *Louis L. Snyder's Historical Guide to World War II* (1982); Harry G. Summers, Jr., *Vietnam War Almanac* (1985); U.S. Department of the Navy, *Dictionary of American Naval Fighting Ships* (1959–); Peter Young, ed., *The World Almanac Book of World War II* (1981).

Statistics: Arthur Banks and William Overstreet, eds., *Political Handbook of the World, 1975–* (1975–); George H. Gallup, *The Gallup Poll: Public Opinion, 1935–1977* (1972–1978); *Handbook of the Nations* (1979–); *International Year Book and Statesmen's Who's Who, 1953–* (1953–); U.S. Agency for Economic Development, *Economic Assistance Programs* (1970); U.S. Agency for International Development, *United States Overseas Loans and Grants and Assistance from International Organizations, July 1, 1945–Sept. 30, 1980* (1981); U.S. Bureau of the Census, *Historical Statistics of the United States: Colonial Times to 1970* (1975) and *Statistical Abstract of the United States* (1879–); U.S. Department of State, *Status of the World's Nations* (1963–).

Documents (Collections and Series)

Yonah Alexander and Allan Nanes, eds., *The United States and Iran* (1980); Robert L. Branyan and Lawrence H. Larsen, eds., *The Eisenhower Administration, 1953–1961* (1971); Council on Foreign Relations, *Documents on American Foreign Relations, 1938/1939–1970* (1939–1973); Francis Deak, ed., *American International Law Cases, 1783–1968* (1971–1978); Leon Friedman, comp., *The Law of War* (1972); G. H. Hackworth, *Digest of International Law* (1940–1944); D. H. Miller, ed., *Treaties and Other International Acts* (1931–1948); Anna K. Nelson, ed., *The State Department Policy Planning Staff Papers, 1947–1949* (1983); Edgar B. Nixon and Donald B. Schewe, eds., *Franklin D. Roosevelt and Foreign Affairs* (1969–); *The Pentagon Papers* (various editions); *Public Papers of the Presidents* (1961–) (Truman to the present); Royal Institute of International Affairs, *Documents on International Affairs, 1928–1963* (1929–1973); A. M. Schlesinger, ed., *The Dynamics of a World Power: A Documentary History of U.S. Foreign Policy, 1945–1973* (1973); *Treaties and Alliances of the World* (1974); U.S. Arms Control and Disarmament Agency, *Documents on Disarmament* (1960–); U.S. Congress, *American State Papers* (1832–1859); U.S. Department of State, *American Foreign Policy: Current Documents, 1956–1967* (1956–1969), *Foreign Relations of the United States, 1861–* (1862–), *Press Conferences of the Secretaries of State, 1922–1974* (no date), and *United States Treaties and Other International Agreements, 1950–* (1952–); *Vital Speeches of the Day* (1934–); Marjorie M. Whiteman, *Digest of International Law* (1963–1970); World Peace Foundation, *Documents on American Foreign Relations* (1939–1952).

Bibliographies

American History: *The American Presidency* (1984); Ray A. Billington, ed., *The American Frontier* (1965); Robert E. Burke and Richard Lowitt, eds., *The New Era and the New Deal, 1920–1940* (1981); Richard D. Burns, *Harry S Truman* (1984); E. D. Cronon and T. D. Rosenof, eds., *The Second World War and the Atomic Age, 1940–1973* (1975); Don E. Fehrenbacher, ed., *Manifest Destiny and the Coming of the Civil War* (1970); E. James Ferguson, ed., *Confederation, Constitution, and Early National Period, 1781–1815* (1975); Frank Freidel, ed., *Harvard Guide to American History* (1974); Robert U. Goehlert and Fenton S. Martin, *The Presidency* (1985); Robert U. Goehlert and John R. Sayre, *The United States Congress* (1981); Rodman W. Paul, ed., *The Frontier and the American West* (1977); Robert V. Remini and Edwin A. Miles, comps., *The Era of Good Feelings and the Age of Jackson, 1816–1841* (1979); U.S. Senate, Senate Historical Office, *The United States Senate: A Historical Bibliography* (1977).

Arms Control, Disarmament, and Peace: Richard Dean Burns, *Arms Control and Disarmament* (1977); Richard Dean Burns and Susan Hoffman, comps., *The SALT Era* (1977); Bernice A. Carroll et al., *Peace and War: A Guide to Bibliographies* (1981); Blanche Wiesen Cook, *Bibliography on Peace Research in History* (1969); United Nations, *Disarmament* (1965–).

Diplomatic History and International Relations:* Samuel Flagg Bemis and Grace Gardner Griffin, *Guide to the Diplomatic History of the United States, 1775–1921* (1935); Joseph L. Black, *Origins, Evolution, and Nature of the Cold War* (1986); John Braeman et al., eds., *Twentieth Century American Foreign Policy* (1971); Richard Dean Burns, ed., *A Guide to American Foreign Relations Since 1700* (1982); Council on Foreign Relations, *Foreign Affairs Bibliography* (1933–); Alexander DeConde, *American Diplomatic History in Transformation* (1976); Byron Dexter, ed., *The Foreign Affairs 50-Year Bibliography* (1972); Justus D. Doenecke, ed., *The Literature of Isolationism* (1972); Wilton B. Fowler, *American Diplomatic History Since 1890* (1975); Robert U. Goehlert and Elizabeth R. Hoffmeister, *The Department of State and American Diplomacy* (1986); Norman A. Graebner, ed., *American Diplomatic History Before 1900* (1978); A. J. R. Groom and C. R. Mitchell, eds., *International Relations Theory* (1978); Gerald K. Haines and J. Samuel Walker, eds., *American Foreign Relations* (1981); Linda Killen and Richard L. Lael, *Versailles and After* (1983); Susan K. Kinnell, ed., *Historiography* (1987); Robert L. Pfaltz-

* For the most recent and comprehensive bibliography in diplomatic history, see the work edited by Richard Dean Burns, *A Guide to American Foreign Relations Since 1700.*

graff, Jr., *The Study of International Relations* (1977); Elmer Plischke, ed., *U.S. Foreign Relations* (1980).

Military, Navy, and Wars: Robert G. Albion, *Naval and Military History* (1972); William M. Arkin, *Research Guide to Current Military and Strategic Affairs* (1981); Benjamin R. Beede, *Intervention and Counter-insurgency* (1984); Richard D. Burns and Milton Leitenberg, *The Wars in Vietnam, Cambodia & Laos* (1984); Paolo E. Coletta, ed., *A Bibliography of American Naval History* (1981); Ronald M. DeVore, *The Arab–Israeli Conflict* (1976); John C. Fredriksen, comp., *Free Trade and Sailors Rights* (1985) (War of 1812); Robert Higham, ed., *A Guide to the Sources of United States Military History* (1975); Robin Higham and Donald J. Mrozek, eds., *A Guide to the Sources of United States Military History: Supplement I* (1981) and *Supplement II* (1986); John E. Jessup and Robert W. Coakley, eds., *A Guide to the Study and Use of Military History* (1979); Jack C. Lane, *America's Military Past* (1980); John R. Lewis, *Uncertain Judgment* (1979) (war crimes trials); Louis A. Peake, ed., *The United States in the Vietnam War* (1985); Myron Smith, Jr., *World War II at Sea* (1976); Dwight L. Smith, *The War of 1812* (1985); Christopher L. Sugnet et al., *Vietnam War Bibliography* (1983); Norman E. Tutorow, ed., *The Mexican–American War* (1981); David R. Woodward and Robert F. Maddox, *America and World War I* (1985); *World War II from an American Perspective* (1982).

Relations with Countries and Regions: Sidney Aster, ed., *British Foreign Policy, 1918–1945* (1984); Jessica S. Brown et al., eds., *The United States in East Asia* (1985); Thomas A. Bryson, *United States–Middle East Diplomatic Relations, 1784–1978* (1979); Alan Cassels, ed., *Italian Foreign Policy, 1918–1945* (1982); Lewis Hanke, ed., *Guide to the Study of United States History Outside the U.S., 1945–1980* (1985); Christoph M. Kimmich, ed., *German Foreign Policy, 1918–1945* (1981); Bruce Kuniholm, *The Persian Gulf and United States Policy* (1984); Thomas M. Leonard, *Central America and United States Policies, 1820s–1980s* (1985); James M. McCutcheon, comp., *China and America* (1973); Michael C. Meyer, ed., *Supplement to a Bibliography of United States–Latin American Relations Since 1810* (1979); *The Middle East in Conflict* (1985); *Sino–Soviet Conflict* (1985); David F. Trask et al., *A Bibliography of United States–Latin American Relations Since 1810* (1968); Robert J. Young, ed., *French Foreign Policy, 1918–1945* (1981).

Miscellaneous International Topics: George W. Baer, ed., *International Organizations, 1918–1945* (1981); Nicole Ball, *World Hunger* (1981); Robert Blackey, ed., *Modern Revolutions and Revolutionists* (1976); Paul W. Blackstock and Frank L. Schaf, eds., *Intelligence, Espionage, Counterespionage, and Covert Operations* (1978); Marjorie W. Cline et al., *Scholar's Guide to Intelligence Literature* (1983); George C. Constantinides, *Intelligence & Espionage* (1983); Ingrid Delupis, ed., *Bibliography of International Law* (1975); Michael Haas, comp., *International Organization* (1971); Peter Janke, *Guerrilla and Terrorist Organizations* (1983); Augustus R. Norton and Martin H. Greenburg, *International Terrorism* (1979); Suzane R. Ontiveros, *Global Terrorism* (1986); Myron J. Smith, Jr., *The Secret Wars* (1980–1981).

Overviews of Relations with Countries and Regions

Afghanistan: Henry S. Bradsher, *Afghanistan and the Soviet Union* (1985); Louis Dupree, *Afghanistan* (1973); Richard S. Newell, *The Politics of Afghanistan* (1972); Nancy P. Newell and Richard S. Newell, *The Struggle for Afghanistan* (1981). See also listing for South Asia.

Africa: Edward W. Chester, *Clash of Titans: Africa and U.S. Foreign Policy* (1974); Philip Curtin, *African History* (1978); Peter Duignan and Lewis H. Gann, *The United States and Africa* (1984); Charles F. Gallagher, *The United States and North Africa: Morocco, Algeria, and Tunisia* (1963); Henry F. Jackson, *From the Congo to Soweto: U.S. Foreign Policy Toward Africa Since 1960* (1982); Michael McCarthy, *Dark Continent: Africa as Seen by Americans* (1983); Thomas J. Noer, *Cold War and Black Liberation: The United States and White Rule in Africa, 1948–1968* (1985); Richard S. Parker, *North Africa* (1984).

Angola: Lawrence W. Henderson, *Angola: Five Centuries of Conflict* (1979); John A. Marcum, *The Angolan Revolution* (1969, 1978).

Argentina: Harold F. Peterson, *Argentina and the United States, 1810–1960* (1964); Arthur P. Whitaker, *The United States and Argentina* (1954) and *The United States and the Southern Cone: Argentina, Chile, and Uruguay* (1976).

Australia: Glen St. John Barclay, *Friends in High Places: The Australian–American Security Relationship Since 1945* (1985); C. H. Grattan, *The United States in the Southwest Pacific* (1961); Werner Levi, *American–Australian Relations* (1947); Trevor R. Reese, *Australia, New Zealand, and the United States: A Survey of International Relations, 1941–1968* (1969).

Austria: William B. Bader, *Austria Between East and West, 1945–1955* (1966); Audrey K. Cronin, *Great Power Politics and the Struggle over Austria, 1945–1955* (1986); Karl S. Stadler, *Austria* (1971).

Bangladesh: See Brown under listing for India.

Belgium: Frank E. Huggett, *Modern Belgium* (1969).

Bolivia: See Pike under listing for Peru.

Brazil: Roger W. Fontaine, *Brazil and the United States* (1974); Lawrence F. Hill, *Diplomatic Relations between the United States and Brazil* (1932); Frank D. McCann, *The Brazilian–American Alliance, 1937–1945* (1973); Robert Wesson, *The United States & Brazil* (1981).

Burma: John F. Cady, *The United States and Burma* (1976).

Cambodia: Prakash C. Pradhan, *Foreign Policy of Kampuchea* (1983); William Shawcross, *The Quality of Mercy: Cambodia, Holocaust, and Modern Conscience* (1984).

Canada: J. B. Brebner, *North Atlantic Triangle* (1966); Gerald M. Craig, *The United States and Canada* (1968); Charles Doran, *Forgotten Partnership* (1985); William T. Fox, *A Continent Apart* (1985); George P. DeT. Glazebrook, *A History of Canadian External Relations* (1950); John Holmes, *Life with Uncle* (1981); H. L. Keenleyside and G. S. Brown, *Canada and the United States* (1952); Lawrence Martin, *The Presidents and the Prime Ministers* (1982); S. F. Wise and Robert C. Brown, *Canada Views the United States* (1967).

Caribbean: Lester D. Langley, *Struggle for the American Mediterranean: United States–European Rivalry and the Caribbean, 1900–1970* (1976) and *The United States and the Caribbean, 1900–1970* (1980); Dexter Perkins, *The United States and the Caribbean* (1966); Whitney T. Perkins, *Constraint of Empire: The United States and Caribbean Intervention* (1981).

Central America: Thomas P. Anderson, *Politics in Central America* (1982); Kenneth M. Coleman and George C. Herring, eds., *The Central American Crisis* (1985); Walter LaFeber, *Inevitable Revolutions* (1983); Ralph L. Woodward, *Central America: A Nation Divided* (1976).

Chile: Michael Monteón, *Chile in the Nitrate Era* (1982); Frederick B. Pike, *Chile and the United States, 1880–1962* (1963); Arthur P. Whitaker, *The United States and the Southern Cone: Argentina, Chile, and Uruguay* (1976).

China (and Taiwan): Jerome Ch'en, *China and the West* (1979); Warren I. Cohen, *America's Response to China* (1980); John K. Fairbank, *China Perceived: Images and Policies in Chinese–American Relations* (1974) and *The United States and China* (1983); John Gittings, *The World and China, 1922–1972* (1974); Michael H. Hunt, *The Making of a Special Relationship: The United States and China to 1914* (1983); Mark Mancall, *China at the Center* (1984); Michael Schaller, *The United States and China in the Twentieth Century* (1979); Robert G. Sutter, *China Watch: Sino–American Reconciliation* (1978).

Colombia: E. Taylor Parks, *Colombia and the United States, 1765–1934* (1935); Stephen J. Randall, *The Diplomacy of Modernization: Colombian–American Relations, 1920–1940* (1977).

Cuba: Philip S. Foner, *A History of Cuba in Its Relations with the United States* (1962–); Lester Langley, *The Cuban Policy of the United States* (1968); Ramon Ruiz, *Cuba: The Making of a Revolution* (1968); Robert F. Smith, *The United States and Cuba* (1960). See also listing for Caribbean.

Dominican Republic: G. Pope Atkins and Larman C. Wilson, *The United States and the Trujillo Regime* (1972); Ian Bell, *The Dominican Republic* (1981); Rayford W. Logan, *Haiti and the Dominican Republic* (1968). See also listing for Caribbean.

East Asia: Warren I. Cohen, ed., *New Frontiers in American–East Asian Relations* (1983); Akira Iriye, *Across the Pacific: An Inner History of American–East Asian Relations* (1967); Ernest R. May and James C. Thomson, Jr., eds., *American–East Asian Relations: A Survey* (1972); James C. Thomson, Jr., Peter W. Stanley, and John C. Perry, *Sentimental Imperialists: The American Experience in East Asia* (1981). See also listings for China and Japan.

Ecuador: See Pike under listing for Peru.

Egypt: William J. Burns, *Economic Aid and American Policy Toward Egypt, 1955–1981* (1985); Gail E. Meyer, *Egypt and the United States: The Formative Years* (1980). See also listing for Middle East.

El Salvador: T. S. Montgomery, *Revolution in El Salvador: Origin and Evolution* (1982); Alastair White, *El Salvador* (1973). See also listing for Central America.

Ethiopia: Harold G. Marcus, *Ethiopia, Britain, and the United States, 1941–1974* (1983).

Finland: Max Jacobson, *Finnish Neutrality* (1969). See also listing for Scandinavia.

France: Henry Blumenthal, *France and the United States: Their Diplomatic Relations, 1789–1914* (1970) and *Illusion and Reality in Franco–American Diplomacy, 1914–1945* (1986); Jean-Baptiste Duroselle, *France and the United States: From the Beginnings to the Present* (1978); David Strauss, *Menace in the West: The Rise of French Anti-Americanism in Modern Times* (1978); Marvin Zahniser, *Uncertain Friendship* (1975).

Germany: Michael Balfour, *West Germany* (1968); Hans W. Gatzke, *Germany and the United States* (1980); Manfred Jonas, *The United States and Germany* (1984); Roger Morgan, *The United States and West Germany, 1945–1973* (1974); Hans L. Trefousse, ed., *Germany and America* (1981); Frank Trommler and Joseph McVeigh, eds., *America and the Germans* (1985).

Great Britain: Harry C. Allen, *Great Britain and the United States* (1955); Kenneth Bourne, *Britain and the Balance of Power in North America, 1815–1908* (1967); Charles S. Campbell, *From Revolution to Rapprochement: The United States and Great Britain, 1783–1900* (1974); William R. Louis and Hedley Bull, eds., *The Special Relationship* (1986); H. G. Nicholas, *The United States and Great Britain* (1975); D. C. Watt, *Succeeding John Bull: America in Britain's Place, 1900–1975* (1984).

Greece: Theodore A. Couloumbis, *Greek Political Reaction to American and NATO Influences* (1966) and *The United States, Greece, and Turkey* (1983); Theodore A. Couloumbis and John O. Iatrides, eds., *Greek–American Relations* (1980); D. George Kousoulas, *Modern Greece* (1974).

Grenada: Gordon K. Lewis, *Grenada: The Jewel Despoiled* (1987); Anthony Payne, Paul Sutton, and Tony Thorndike, *Grenada: Revolution and Invasion* (1984).

Guatemala: Richard Immerman, *The CIA in Guatemala: The Foreign Policy of Intervention* (1982). See also listing for Central America.

Haiti: Robert Heinl and Nancy G. Heinl, *Written in Blood* (1978); Rayford W. Logan, *Diplomatic Relations of the United States with Haiti, 1776–1891* (1941) and *Haiti and the Dominican Republic* (1968); David Nicholls, *From Dessalines to Duvalier* (1979); Robert I. Rotberg, *Haiti* (1971). See also listing for Caribbean.

Honduras: See listing for Central America.

Iceland: Donald E. Neuchterlein, *Iceland: Reluctant Ally* (1975).

India: William J. Barnds, *India, Pakistan, and the Great Powers* (1972); W. Norman Brown, *The United States and India, Pakistan, Bangladesh* (1972); Gary R. Hess, *America Encounters India, 1941–1947* (1971); Harold R. Issacs, *Images of Asia: American Views of China and India* (1958). See also listing for South Asia.

Indonesia: Michael Leifer, *Indonesia's Foreign Policy* (1983); Robert

J. McMahon, *Colonialism and Cold War* (1981); Franklin B. Weinstein, *Indonesian Foreign Policy and the Dilemma of Dependence* (1976). See also listing for Southeast Asia.

Iran: Peter Avery, *Modern Iran* (1965); Alvin J. Cottrell, ed., *The Persian Gulf States* (1980); Nikki R. Keddie, *Roots of Revolution* (1981); George Lenczowski, *Russia and the West in Iran, 1918–1948* (1949); Mark H. Lytle, *The Origins of the Iranian–American Alliance, 1941–1953* (1987); Rouhollah K. Ramazani, *The Foreign Policy of Iran, 1500–1941* (1966), *Iran's Foreign Policy, 1941–1973* (1975), and *Revolutionary Iran: Challenge and Response in the Middle East* (1986); Barry Rubin, *Paved with Good Intentions* (1980). See also listing for Middle East.

Iraq: Alvin J. Cottrell, ed., *The Persian Gulf States* (1980).

Ireland: Donald H. Akenson, *The United States and Ireland* (1973); Thomas N. Brown, *Irish–American Nationalism, 1870–1890* (1966); Francis M. Carroll, *American Opinion and the Irish Question, 1910– 1923* (1978); Alan J. Ward, *Ireland and Anglo–American Relations, 1899–1921* (1969).

Israel: Edward B. Glick, *The Triangular Connection: America, Israel, and American Jews* (1982); Peter Grose, *Israel and the Mind of America* (1983); Bernard Reich, *Quest for Peace: United States–Israel Relations and the Arab–Israeli Conflict* (1979) and *The United States and Israel: Influence in the Special Relationship* (1984); Nadav Safran, *Israel: Embattled Ally* (1978) and *The United States and Israel* (1963).

Italy: Alexander DeConde, *Half-Bitter, Half-Sweet* (1971); H. Stuart Hughes, *The United States and Italy* (1979); Norman Kogan, *The Politics of Italian Foreign Policy* (1963); James E. Miller, *The United States and Italy, 1940–1950* (1986).

Japan: Charles E. Neu, *The Troubled Encounter* (1975); William L. Neumann, *America Encounters Japan* (1963); Edwin E. Reischauer, *The United States and Japan* (1965). See also listing for East Asia.

Korea: Frank Baldwin, ed., *Without Parallel: The American–Korean Relationship Since 1945* (1974); Youngnok Koo and Sung-joo Han, eds., *The Foreign Policy of the Republic of Korea* (1985); Youngnok Koo and Dae-Sook Sun, *Korea and the United States: A Century of Cooperation* (1984); Yun-Bok Lee and Wayne Patterson, eds., *One Hundred Years of Korean–American Relations, 1882–1982* (1986); U.S. Department of State, *Historical Summary of United States–Korean Relations, 1834–1962* (1962).

Laos: Arthur J. Dommen, *Laos: Keystone of Indochina* (1985); Charles A. Stevenson, *The End of Nowhere: American Policy Toward Laos Since 1954* (1972).

Latin America: Samuel Flagg Bemis, *The Latin American Policy of the United States* (1943); Cole Blasier, *The Hovering Giant* (1976); Gordon Connell-Smith, *The United States and Latin America* (1974); Harold E. Davies et al., *Latin American Diplomatic History* (1977) and *Latin American Foreign Policies* (1975); Frederico G. Gil, *Latin American–United States Relations* (1971); J. Lloyd Mecham, *The United States and Inter-American Security, 1889–1960* (1961) and *A Survey of United States–Latin American Relations* (1965); Harold Molineu, *U.S. Policy Toward Latin America: From Regionalism to*

Globalism (1986); John T. Reid, *Spanish–American Images of the U.S., 1790–1960* (1977); Dick Stewart, *Money, Marines, and Mission: Recent U.S.–Latin American Policy* (1980); Graham H. Stuart and James L. Tyner, *Latin America and the United States* (1975). See also listing for Central America.

Lebanon: P. Edward Haley and Lewis W. Snider, eds., *Lebanon in Crisis* (1979); Hamar Rabinovich, *The War for Lebanon, 1970–1985* (1986).

Liberia: D. Elwood Dunn, *The Foreign Policy of Liberia During the Tubman Era, 1944–1971* (1979); Hassan B. Sisay, *Big Powers and Small Nations: A Case Study of United States–Liberian Relations* (1985); Charles M. Wilson, *Liberia* (1985). See also listing for Africa.

Libya: P. Edward Haley, *Qaddafi and the United States Since 1969* (1984).

Malaysia: James W. Gould, *The United States and Malaysia* (1969).

Mexico: Howard F. Cline, *The United States and Mexico* (1963); Karl M. Schmitt, *Mexico and the United States, 1821–1973* (1974); Josefina Vazquez and Lorenzo Meyer, *The United States and Mexico* (1985).

Micronesia: Roger W. Gale, *The Americanization of Micronesia* (1979).

Middle East: Richard Allen, *Imperialism and Nationalism in the Fertile Crescent* (1974); Thomas A. Bryson, *American Diplomatic Relations with the Middle East, 1784–1975* (1977); Uriel Dann, ed., *The Great Powers in the Middle East, 1919–1939* (1987); John A. DeNovo, *American Interests and Policies in the Middle East, 1900–1939* (1963); James A. Field, *America and the Mediterranean World, 1776–1882* (1969); Philip Groisser, *The United States and the Middle East* (1981); George Lenczowski, *The Middle East in World Affairs* (1980); William R. Polk, *The United States and the Arab World* (1975); Benjamin Shwadran, *The Middle East, Oil, and the Great Powers* (1973); Steven L. Spiegel, *The Other Arab–Israeli Conflict* (1985); Robert W. Stookey, *America and the Arab States* (1975).

Morocco: Leon B. Blair, *Western Window in the Arab World* (1970); Luella J. Hall, *The United States and Morocco, 1776–1956* (1961). See also listing for Africa.

The Netherlands: J. W. Schulte Nordholte and Robert P. Swierenga, eds., *A Bilateral Bicentennial: A History of Dutch– American Relations, 1782–1982* (1982).

New Zealand: See Reese under listing for Australia.

Nicaragua: Karl Bermann, *Under the Big Stick: Nicaragua and the U.S. Since 1848* (1986); Craig L. Dozier, *Nicaragua's Mosquito Shore: The Years of British and American Presence* (1985); Richard Millett, *Guardians of the Dynasty* (1977); Thomas W. Walker, *Nicaragua: The Land of Sandino* (1986). See also the listing for Central America.

Norway: Ronald G. Popperwell, *Norway* (1972); Sigmund Skard, *The United States in Norwegian History* (1976). See also listing for Scandinavia.

Pakistan: Shirin Tahir-kheli, *The United States and Pakistan* (1982); M. S. Venkataramani, *The American Role in Pakistan, 1947–1958* (1982). See also Barnds and Brown under listing for India and the listing for South Asia.

Panama: David N. Farnsworth and James W. McKenney, *U.S.–Panama Relations, 1903–1978* (1983); Walter LaFeber, *The Panama Canal* (1978).

Persian Gulf: Alvin J. Cottrell, ed., *The Persian Gulf States* (1980).

Peru: James C. Carey, *Peru and the United States, 1900–1962* (1964); Frederick B. Pike, *The United States and the Andean Republics: Peru, Bolivia, and Ecuador* (1977).

Philippines: Teodoro A. Agoncillo, *A Short History of the Philippines* (1969); Theodore Friend, *Between Two Empires* (1965); Garel A. Grunder and William E. Livezey, *The Philippines and the United States* (1951); Milton W. Meyer, *A Diplomatic History of the Philippine Republic* (1965); Peter W. Stanley, *A Nation in the Making: The Philippines and the United States, 1899–1921* (1974) and ed., *Reappraising an Empire* (1984); George E. Taylor, *The Philippines and the United States* (1964).

Poland: Piotr Wandycz, *The United States and Poland* (1980).

Puerto Rico: Raymond Carr, *Puerto Rico: A Colonial Experiment* (1984); Arturo Morales Carríon, *Puerto Rico* (1984); Truman R. Clark, *Puerto Rico and the United States, 1917–1933* (1975).

Russia (and Soviet Union): John L. Gaddis, *Russia, the Soviet Union, and the United States* (1978); George F. Kennan, *Russia and the West under Lenin and Stalin* (1961); Nikolai Sivachev and Nikolai N. Yakovlev, *Russia and the United States* (1979); Adam B. Ulam, *Expansion and Coexistence* (1973).

Saudi Arabia: Irvine H. Anderson, *Aramco, the United States, and Saudi Arabia* (1981); David E. Long, *The United States and Saudi Arabia: Ambivalent Allies* (1985); Aaron D. Miller, *Search for Security: Saudi Arabian Oil and American Foreign Policy, 1939–1949* (1980); Nadav Safran, *Saudi Arabia: The Ceaseless Quest for Security* (1986).

Scandinavia: Franklin D. Scott, *Scandinavia* (1975) and *The United States and Scandinavia* (1950).

South Africa: Christopher Coker, *The United States and South Africa, 1968–1985* (1986); Richard W. Hall, *Southern Africa* (1981); Thomas J. Noer, *Briton, Boer, and Yankee: The United States and South Africa, 1870–1914* (1978). See also listing for Africa.

South Asia: Stanley Wolpert, *Roots of Confrontation in South Asia: Afghanistan, Pakistan, India & the Superpowers* (1982). See also listings under India, Pakistan, and Afghanistan.

Southeast Asia: Russell H. Fifield, *Americans in Southeast Asia* (1973); Robert Shaplen, *Time Out of Hand* (1970). See also listings for Vietnam and other countries.

Spain: James W. Cortada, *Two Nations over Time: Spain and the United States, 1776–1977* (1978) and ed., *Spain in the Twentieth-Century World* (1980).

Switzerland: Heinz Meier, *Friendship Under Stress: U.S.–Swiss Relations, 1900–1950* (1970) and *The United States and Switzerland in the Nineteenth Century* (1963).

Syria: Tabitha Petran, *Syria* (1972); Patrick Seale, *The Struggle for Syria: A Study in Post-War Arab Politics, 1945–1958* (1965). See also listing for Middle East.

Turkey: George S. Harris, *Troubled Alliance: Turkish–American Problems in Historical Perspective, 1945–1971* (1972); Harry N. Howard, *Turkey, the Straits, and U.S. Policy* (1974); L. V. Thomas and R. N. Frye, *The United States and Turkey and Iran* (1951). See also listing for Greece.

Uruguay: See Whitaker under listing for Argentina.

Venezuela: Sheldon B. Liss, *Diplomacy and Independence* (1978); Stephen G. Rabe, *The Road to OPEC: United States Relations with Venezuela, 1919–1976* (1982).

Vietnam: Frances Fitzgerald, *Fire in the Lake* (1972); William C. Gibbons, *The U.S. Government and the Vietnam War* (1986); George C. Herring, *America's Longest War* (1986); George McT. Kahin and John W. Lewis, *The United States and Vietnam* (1969); Stanley Karnow. *Vietnam* (1983); Gabriel Kolko, *Anatomy of a War* (1985).

Virgin Islands: William W. Boyer, *America's Virgin Islands: A History of Human Rights and Wrongs* (1983).

Western Europe: Michael Smith, *Western Europe and the United States: An Uncertain Alliance* (1984).

Overviews of Subjects

Anti-Americanism: Alvin Z. Rubinstein and Donald E. Smith, eds., *Anti-Americanism in the Third World* (1985); David Strauss, *Menace in the West: The Rise of French Anti-Americanism in Modern Times* (1978).

Arms Sales: Michael T. Klare, *American Arms Supermarket* (1984).

Bureaucracy: Graham Allison, *Essence of Decision* (1971); I. M. Destler, *Presidents, Bureaucrats, and Foreign Policy* (1974); Morton H. Halperin, *Bureaucratic Politics and Foreign Policy* (1974); Morton H. Halperin and Arnold Kanter, eds., *Readings in American Foreign Policy: A Bureaucratic Perspective* (1973); Irving L. Janis, *Victims of Groupthink* (1972); Stephen D. Krasner, "Are Bureaucracies Important?" *Foreign Policy* (1972).

Codes: Ralph E. Weber, *United States Codes and Ciphers, 1775–1938* (1979).

Cold War: Stephen E. Ambrose, *Rise to Globalism* (1985); Louis Halle, *The Cold War as History* (1967); Walter LaFeber, *America, Rus-*

sia, and the Cold War (1985); Thomas G. Paterson, On Every Front (1979); Adam B. Ulam, The Rivals (1971).

Congress: Holbert B. Carroll, The House of Representatives and Foreign Affairs (1966); Robert A. Dahl, Congress and Foreign Policy (1950); David N. Farnsworth, The Senate Committee on Foreign Relations (1961); James A. Robinson, Congress and Foreign Policy-Making (1967); John Rourke, Congress and the Presidency in U.S. Foreign Policymaking (1983); Goran Rystad, ed., Congress and American Foreign Policy (1982); John Spanier and Joseph Nogee, eds., Congress, the Presidency, and Foreign Policy (1980); Francis O. Wilcox, Congress, the Executive and Foreign Policy (1971). See also listing for President.

Constitution: Henry B. Cox, War, Foreign Affairs, and Constitutional Power, 1829–1901 (1984); Louis Henkin, Foreign Affairs and the Constitution (1972); Abraham Sofaer, War, Foreign Affairs, and Constitutional Power: The Origin (1976). See also listing for War Powers.

Containment: Charles Gati, ed., Caging the Bear (1974); Thomas G. Paterson, ed., Containment and the Cold War (1973); John L. Gaddis, Strategies of Containment (1982).

Cultural Relations: Paul J. Braisted, ed., Cultural Affairs and Foreign Relations (1968); Philip H. Coombs, The Fourth Dimension of Foreign Policy: Educational and Cultural Affairs (1964); Morrell Heald and Lawrence S. Kaplan, Culture and Diplomacy: The American Experience (1977); Akira Iriye, "Culture and Power: International Relations as Intercultural Relations," Diplomatic History (1979); Frank A. Ninkovich, The Diplomacy of Ideas: U.S. Foreign Policy and Cultural Relations, 1938–1950 (1981); Charles A. Thomson and Walter H. C. Laves, Cultural Relations and U.S. Foreign Policy (1963).

Department of State and Foreign Service: William Barnes and J. H. Morgan, The Foreign Service of the United States (1961); Homer L. Calkin, Women in the Department of State (1978); Alexander DeConde, The American Secretary of State (1962); Warren F. Ilchman, Professional Diplomacy in the United States, 1779–1939 (1961); Elmer Plischke, United States Diplomats and Their Mission: A Profile of American Diplomatic Emissaries Since 1778 (1979); Robert Schulzinger, The Making of the Diplomatic Mind: The Training, Outlook and Style of United States Foreign Service Officers, 1908–1931 (1975); Zara Steiner, ed., The Times Survey of Foreign Ministries of the World (1982) (chapter by Hugh DeSantis and Waldo Heinrichs); Richard H. Werking, The Master Architects: Building the United States Foreign Service, 1890–1913 (1977).

Deterrence: Alexander L. George and Richard Smoke, Deterrence in American Foreign Policy (1974); Robert Jervis et al., Psychology and Deterrence (1985).

Drug Traffic and Control: Arnold H. Taylor, American Diplomacy and the Narcotics Traffic, 1900–1939 (1969); William O. Walker, III, Drug Control in the Americas (1981).

Economic Relations: William H. Becker and Samuel F. Wells, eds., Economics and World Power (1984); Fred L. Block, The Origins of International Economic Disorder (1977); Alfred E. Eckes, The United States and the Global Struggle for Minerals (1979); Robert A. Pastor,

Congress and the Politics of U.S. Foreign Economic Policy, 1929–1976 (1980); Brian Tew, The Evolution of the International Monetary System, 1945–1977 (1977); Herman Van Der Wee, The Search for Prosperity: The World Economy, 1945–1980 (1986); Mira Wilkins, The Emergence of Multinational Enterprise (1970) and The Maturing of Multinational Enterprise (1975); William Woodruff, America's Impact on the World (1975).

Economic Sanctions: Margaret P. Doxey, Economic Sanctions and International Enforcement (1980); Gary C. Hufbauer and Jeffrey J. Schott, Economic Sanctions Reconsidered (1985); Donald L. Losman, International Economic Sanctions (1979); Sidney Weintraub, ed., Economic Coercion and U.S. Foreign Policy (1982).

Export-Import Bank: Frederick C. Adams, Economic Diplomacy: The Export-Import Bank and American Foreign Policy, 1934–1939 (1976); Richard E. Feinberg, Subsidizing Success: The Export-Import Bank in the United States Economy (1982). See also listing for Economic Relations.

Foreign Aid: David Baldwin, Economic Development and American Foreign Policy, 1943–1962 (1966); Library of Congress, U.S. Foreign Aid (1959); Robert A. Packenham, Liberal America and the Third World (1973).

Human Rights: A. Glenn Mower, The United States, the United Nations, and Human Rights (1979); Lars Schoultz, Human Rights and United States Policy toward Latin America (1981); Kenneth W. Thompson, ed., The Moral Imperatives of Human Rights (1980); Sandy Vogelgesang, American Dream, American Nightmare (1980).

Ideology: Richard J. Barnet, Roots of War (1972); Edward M. Burns, The American Idea of Mission (1957); Arthur A. Ekirch, Jr., Ideas, Ideals, and American Diplomacy (1966); Michael H. Hunt, Ideology and Foreign Policy (1987); Robert E. Osgood, Ideals and Self-Interest in America's Foreign Relations (1953); David M. Potter, People of Plenty (1954); E. L. Tuveson, Redeemer Nation: The Idea of America's Millennial Role (1968); William A. Williams, The Contours of American History (1966) and The Tragedy of American Diplomacy (1962).

Immigration and Ethnic Influence: Marion T. Bennett, American Immigration Policies (1963); Robert A. Divine, American Immigration Policy, 1924–1952 (1957); Louis L. Gerson, The Hyphenate in Recent American Politics and Diplomacy (1964); Gil D. Loescher and John A. Scalan, Calculated Kindness: Refugees and America's Half-Open Door, 1945 to the Present (1986); David M. Reimers, Still the Golden Door: The Third World Comes to America (1985); Stephen Thernstrom, ed., Harvard Encyclopedia of American Ethnic Groups (1980).

Imperialism: Michael B. Brown, The Economics of Imperialism (1974); Benjamin J. Cohen, The Question of Imperialism: The Political Economy of Dominance and Dependence (1973); Gabriel Kolko, The Roots of American Foreign Policy (1969); Harry Magdoff, Imperialism: From the Colonial Age to the Present (1978); Dexter Perkins, The American Approach to Foreign Policy (1968); Richard W. Van Alstyne, The Rising American Empire (1960).

Intelligence and the Central Intelligence Agency: Robert L. Borosage and John Marks, eds., The CIA File (1976); Mark Lowenthal, *U.S. Intelligence* (1984); Ernest R. May, ed., *Knowing One's Enemies: Intelligence Assessment Before the Two World Wars* (1985); John Prados, *Presidents' Secret Wars* (1986); John Ranelagh, *The Agency* (1986); Harry H. Ransom, *The Intelligence Establishment* (1970); Jeffrey T. Richelson, *The United States Intelligence Community* (1985); Harry Rositzke, *The CIA's Secret Operations* (1977); Bradley F. Smith, *The Shadow Warriors: O.S.S. and the Origins of the C.I.A.* (1983); Thomas F. Troy, *Donovan and the CIA* (1981).

Interventionism: Richard J. Barnet, *Intervention and Revolution* (1972); Doris A. Graber, *Crisis Diplomacy* (1959); Robin Higham, ed., *Intervention or Abstention* (1975).

Isolationism: Selig Adler, *The Isolationist Impulse* (1957); Norman A. Graebner, *The New Isolationism* (1956); Manfred Jonas, *Isolationism in America, 1935–1941* (1966); Leroy N. Rieselbach, *The Roots of Isolationism* (1960).

Labor: Ronald Radosh, *American Labor and United States Foreign Policy* (1969).

Law of the Sea: Jack N. Barkenbus, *Deep Seabed Resources* (1979): Ann L. Hollick, *U.S. Foreign Policy and the Law of the Sea* (1981); D. P. O'Connell, *The International Law of the Sea* (1982).

League of Nations: Denna F. Fleming, *The United States and the League of Nations, 1918–1920* (1932); Warren F. Kuehl, *Seeking World Order* (1969); F. S. Northedge, *The League of Nations* (1986); Francis P. Walters, *A History of the League of Nations* (1952).

Manifest Destiny: Norman A. Graebner, ed., *Manifest Destiny* (1968); Thomas R. Hietala, *Manifest Design* (1985); Reginald Horsman, *Race and Manifest Destiny* (1981); Frederick Merk, *Manifest Destiny and Mission in American History* (1963); Albert K. Weinberg, *Manifest Destiny* (1935).

Military: James L. Abrahamson, *American Arms for a New Century* (1981); Edward M. Coffman, *The Old Army: A Portrait of the American Army in Peacetime, 1784–1898* (1986); Kenneth J. Hagan and William R. Roberts, eds., *Against All Enemies: Interpretations of American Military History from Colonial Times to the Present* (1986); Allan R. Millett and Peter Maslowski, *For the Common Defense* (1984); Walter Millis, *Arms and Men* (1958); Michael S. Sherry, *The Rise of American Air Power* (1987); Rusell F. Weigley, *The American Way of War* (1973) and *History of the United States Army* (1984).

Monroe Doctrine: Dexter Perkins, *A History of the Monroe Doctrine* (1963).

NATO: Timothy Ireland, *Creating the Entangling Alliance* (1981); Lawrence S. Kaplan, *The United States and NATO* (1984); Robert Osgood, *NATO: The Entangling Alliance* (1962).

Navy: Edward L. Beach, *The U.S. Navy* (1986); James C. Bradford, ed., *Makers of the American Naval Tradition* (1985–); Kenneth J. Hagan, ed., *In Peace and War: Interpretations of American Naval History, 1775–1984* (1984); Robert E. Johnson, *The Far China Station: The U.S. Navy in Asiatic Waters, 1800–1890* (1979) and *Thence Round Cape Horn: The Story of United States Naval Forces on Pacific Station,*

1818–1923 (1963); Allan R. Millett, *Semper Fidelis: The History of the United States Marine Corps* (1980); Elmer B. Potter, ed., *Sea Power* (1981); Harold and Margaret Sprout, *The Rise of American Naval Power, 1776–1918* (1966); William N. Still, *American Sea Power in the Old World: The United States Navy in European and Near Eastern Waters, 1865–1917* (1980).

Neutral Rights: Philip C. Jessup, ed., *Neutrality* (1935–1936); Carlton Savage, *Policy of the United States Toward Maritime Commerce in War* (1934).

Nuclear Arms Race and Control: Lawrence Freedman, *The Evolution of Nuclear Strategy* (1981); Gregg Herken, *Counsels of War* (1985); Jerome H. Kahan, *Security in the Nuclear Age* (1975); Fred Kaplan, *The Wizards of Armageddon* (1983); Michael Mandelbaum, *The Nuclear Question* (1979); George Quester, *Nuclear Diplomacy* (1970); Stanford Arms Control Group, *International Arms Control* (1984); Paul B. Stares, *The Militarization of Space* (1985).

Oil: Mohammed E. Ahrari, *OPEC: The Failing Giant* (1986); Albert L. Danielson, *The Evolution of OPEC* (1982); Gerald D. Nash, *United States Oil Policy* (1968); David S. Painter, *Oil and the American Century* (1986); Stephen J. Randall, *United States Foreign Oil Policy, 1919–1984* (1985); Michael B. Stoff, *Oil, War, and American Security* (1980). See also Anderson and Miller listed under Saudi Arabia and Rabe listed under Venezuela.

Pan-Americanism: J. Lloyd Mecham, *The United States and Inter-American Security, 1889–1960* (1961); Arthur P. Whitaker, *The Western Hemisphere Idea* (1954).

Peace Movements: Peter Brock, *Pacifism in the United States from the Colonial Era to the First World War* (1968) and *Twentieth-Century Pacifism* (1970); Charles Chatfield, *For Peace and Justice: Pacifism in America, 1914–1941* (1971); Merle Curti, *Peace or War* (1936); Charles DeBenedetti, *The Peace Reform in American History* (1980); Charles F. Howlett and Glen Zeitzer, *The American Peace Movement* (1985); David Patterson, *Toward a Warless World* (1976); Lawrence S. Wittner, *Rebels Against War: The American Peace Movement, 1941–1960* (1969).

Philanthrophy: Edward H. Berman, *The Influence of the Carnegie, Ford, and Rockefeller Foundations on American Foreign Policy* (1983); Merle Curti, *American Philanthropy Abroad* (1963); Robert L. Daniel, *American Philanthropy in the Near East, 1820–1960* (1970).

President: E. S. Corwin, *The President* (1957); Robert A. Divine, *Foreign Policy and U.S. Presidential Elections, 1940–1960* (1974); Erwin C. Hargrove, *The Power of the Modern Presidency* (1974); Manfred Landecker, *The President and Public Opinion* (1968); John E. Mueller, *War, Presidents, and Public Opinion* (1973); Richard E. Neustadt, *Presidential Power* (1980); W. Taylor Revely, *War Powers of the President and Congress* (1981); Arthur M. Schlesinger, Jr., *The Imperial Presidency* (1973). See also listings for Congress and Bureaucracy.

Press: Bernard C. Cohen, *The Press and Foreign Policy* (1963); James Reston, *The Artillery of the Press: Its Influence on American Foreign*

Policy (1967); John Tebbel and Sarah Miles Watts, *The Press and the Presidency* (1985).

Propaganda: Leo Bogart, *Premises for Propaganda: The United States Information Agency's Operating Assumptions in the Cold War* (1976); Robert E. Elder, *The Information Machine* (1968); John W. Henderson, *The United States Information Agency* (1969); Sig Mickelson, *America's Other Voice: The Story of Radio Free Europe and Radio Liberty* (1983); Ronald I. Rubin, *The Objectives of the U.S. Information Agency* (1968); Thomas C. Sorensen, *The World War: The Story of American Propaganda* (1968).

Public Opinion: Gabriel Almond, *The American People and Foreign Policy* (1950); Bernard C. Cohen, *The Public's Impact on Foreign Policy* (1973); H. Schuyler Foster, *Activism Replaces Isolationism: U.S. Public Attitudes, 1940–1975* (1983); Ralph B. Levering, *The Public and American Foreign Policy, 1918–1978* (1978); James Rosenau, *Public Opinion and Foreign Policy* (1961) and ed., *Domestic Sources of Foreign Policy* (1967); Robert D. Schulzinger, *The Wise Men of Foreign Affairs: The History of the Council on Foreign Relations* (1984). See also listing for President.

Race: George W. Shepherd, Jr., ed., *Racial Influence on American Foreign Policy* (1971); Rubin F. Weston, *Racism in U.S. Imperialism: The Influence of Racial Assumptions on American Foreign Policy, 1893–1946* (1972).

Summit Conferences: Keith Eubank, *The Summit Conference, 1919–1960* (1966); Elmer Plischke, *Diplomat in Chief: The President at the Summit* (1986) and *Summit Diplomacy* (1958); Robert D. Putnam and Nicholas Bayne, *Hanging Together: The Seven-Power Summits* (1984); Gordon R. Weihmiller and Dusko Doder, *U.S.–Soviet Summits* (1986).

Tariff: Sidney Ratner, *The Tariff in American History* (1972); Frank W. Taussig, *Tariff History of the United States* (1931); Tom E. Terrill, *The Tariff, Politics, and American Foreign Policy, 1874–1901* (1974).

United Nations: Peter R. Baehr and Leon Gordenker, *The United Nations* (1984); Sydney Bailey, *How Wars End* (1982); Clark M. Eichelberger, *UN: The First Twenty-Five Years* (1970); Seymour M. Finger, *American Ambassadors at the UN* (1987); Thomas M. Frank, *Nation Against Nation* (1985); Evan Luard, *A History of the United Nations, 1945–1955* (1982); John G. Stoessinger, *The United Nations and the Superpowers* (1973).

War Powers: Edward Keynes, *Undeclared War* (1982); John H. Sullivan, *The War Powers Resolution* (1982). See also listing for Constitution.

Index

Abbott, Lyman, 201
Aberdeen, Lord, 102, 104, 107, 116
Adams, Abigail, 14, 56
Adams, Charles Francis, 140–41, 142, 144, 145, 146, 155
Adams, Charles Francis, Jr., 208–9
Adams, Henry, 41, 58, 68, 76, 141, 144, 145, 146
Adams, John, 7, 8, 9, 14, 16, 27–28, 43, 61; as diplomat, 32, 34; presidency of, 51–58; treaty negotiations of, 4–6, 10–12, 15, 17, 21, 22, 23–24; XYZ Affair and, 53–56
Adams, John Quincy, 64, 88, 100, 146; diplomacy of, 18, 55, 73, 116; Florida and, 84–85, 91, 92–93, 94; Great Britain in Latin America and, 96, 98; Mexican-American War and, 83–84; Monroe Doctrine and, 94–99; War of 1812 and, 73, 74–75, 76, 99
Adams–Onís Treaty, 93, 105
Addams, Jane, 206
Adet, Pierre, 45, 50–51
Africa: colonization of, map of, 177; Europeans in, 158, 189, 190; trade with, 175; U.S. in, 175–78
Agreement of 1854, 147
Agriculture, and trade, 44, 91, 159–60
Aguinaldo, Emilio, 204, 207–8, 228, 241
Alabama (ship), 141, 144, 146, 147, 155, 166
Alamo, 106
Alaska, 168; Canadian boundary and, 245–47; Russia and purchase of, 164–65, 166
Albert, Prince, 142
Aldrich, Nelson, 206
Alexander I, Tsar, 18, 73, 84, 95, 97, 98, 145, 164
Algiers, 29, 76
Algonquin Indians, 27
Alien and Sedition Laws, 54
Alverstone, Lord, 247
Ambrister, Robert C., 92, 94

American Asiatic Association, 209, 211
American Board of Commissioners for Foreign Missions, 176
American Colonization Society, 177
American Fur Company, 61
Ames, Fisher, 49
Anderson, Sherwood, 203
Anglo-Russian Treaty of 1825, 245, 247
Anglo-Saxonism, 124, 157, 212, 223, 244
Antietam, battle of, 143, 145
Anti-imperialism, 99, 165–66, 182, 194, 205–6, 208, 224
Anti-Imperialist League, 205
Appomattox, battle of, 146
Arango, José Augustin, 217–18
Arbuthnot, Alexander, 92, 94
Argentina, 180, 236
Arista, Mariano, 81
Arizona, 83
Armed Neutrality League, 17, 18
Armstrong, James, 126
Army, 30, 42, 54, 71, 162, 165, 238
Aroostook War, 101
Arthur, Chester A., 164
Articles of Confederation, 9, 22, 24–30, 31
Ashburton, Lord, 102, 103, 135
Asia, 204; Europeans in, 158, 189, 209–11, 250; maps of, 125, 210; trade with, 47, 91, 175, 201; U.S. in, 121, 124–26, 148, 159, 163, 212, 239, 241, 250. *See also specific countries*
Astor, John Jacob, 61
Atlanta (ship), 163
Austin, Moses, 105
Austin, Stephen, 105
Australia, 173
Austria, 16, 17, 18, 95, 127

Babcock, Orville, 154, 155
Babe, Jerome L., 176–77
Bacon, Robert, 224
Baez, Buenaventura, 153, 154

Bahama Islands, 166
Baker, Newton D., 238
Balfour, Arthur, 230, 247
Balkans, 250
Baltic States, 17
Baltimore (ship), 180–81
Bancroft, George, 82, 127–28
Barbary pirates, 29–30, 62, 76
Barron, James, 39–41
Bayard, James, 73, 74
Bayard, Thomas F., 164, 174, 190, 191
Bay Islands, 136, 138
Beach, Moses Y., 109
Beaumarchais, Pierre Augustin Caron de, 12, 13, 14
Beaupré, Arthur N., 221
Beauregard, Pierre G. T., 138
Beijing, 168, 170, 171
Beisner, Robert L., 202–3
Belgium, 176
Bell, Alexander Graham, 160
Belmont, August, 134
Bemis, Samuel Flagg, 5, 19, 24, 47, 50, 168
Benchley, Robert, 100
Benton, Thomas Hart, 86, 88, 89, 104, 105, 108
Bering Sea, 167–68
Berkhofer, Robert, 87
Berlin Conference of 1889, 175, 176, 178
Berlin Decree, 63, 65, 68, 71
Bermuda (ship), 141
Bernstorff, Johann von, 238
Beveridge, Albert, 201
Biddle, James, 122
Bismarck, Otto von, 174–75
Black Americans, 87, 157, 206, 244; in Africa, 177; in Spanish-American War, 203, 204
Black, Jeremiah, S., 128
Black Hawk War of 1832, 115
Black Warrior (ship), 133–34
Blaine, James D., 156, 164, 172, 179, 180

Index

Blount, James H., 173
Boer Republic, 212, 245, 246
Bolívar, Simon, 94
Bolivia, 180
Boston, 24
Boston (ship), 163, 173
Boston Tea Party, 7
Bourbon Family Compact, 12, 18
Bourne, Kenneth E., 136, 138
Bowie, James, 106
Boxer Rebellion, 211, 239, 241, 243
Boyd, Julian P., 27
Brack, Gene M., 105
Brazil, 98, 126, 128, 159, 179, 182, 236
British Columbia, 166
British East Indies, 47
British Empire. *See* Great Britain
British Guiana, 187
British West Indies, 9, 11, 26, 27, 44, 47, 48, 77, 85, 99–100
Broadsides, 67
Brown, John, 127
Bryan, William Jennings, 196, 197, 250; as anti-imperialist, 205, 207; China and, 242–43; dollar diplomacy and, 231, 233; Mexico and, 234; Philippines and, 205, 207; as secretary of state, 224, 225
Bryan-Chamorro Treaty, 233
Bryant & Sturgis Co., 90
Buchanan, James, 87, 88, 104, 128, 133, 134–35, 137
Bulloch, James D., 141, 144, 145.
Bull Run, battle of, 144
Bulwer, Henry, 136
Bunau-Varilla, Philippe, 218, 221, 222
Burgoyne, John, 14, 20
Burlingame, Anson, 170
Burlingame Treaty, 170
Burr, Aaron, 38, 55, 61, 109
Butler, Anthony, 105

Calhoun, John C., 70, 83, 88, 92, 96, 103, 107, 112
California, 83, 85, 88, 90, 103, 104; acquisition of, 82, 113, 116–17, 129; gold rush in, 124, 136; Great Britain in, 84, 88, 108, 116–17; Mexico and, 108–9; racism in, 169, 240, 243–44; U.S. in, 115, 147
Campbell, Charles S., 136
Canada, 46, 99, 100–101, 126, 160, 191; American attacks on, 9–10, 166; boundaries of, 7, 100, 101, 102–3; Civil War and, 142, 143; commerce and, 27; control of, 20, 21, 42, 69–

76; France and, 6–7, 11, 12, 16; nationalism in, 166; reciprocity with, 136, 137, 147–48; U.S. and, 100, 137, 159, 163, 166–67, 226; War of 1812 and, 69, 71–76
Canal Zone. *See* Panama Canal
Canary Islands, 28
Canning, George, 42, 68, 95–96, 98, 100
Cannon, Joe, 200
Canton, China, 24, 62, 89, 124
Cape Breton Island, 7
Caribbean, 114, 115, 153, 156; France in, 15, 64; Great Britain in, 21, 147, 247; U.S. in, 128, 133, 135, 147, 164, 192, 193, 226, 250; U.S. interventions in, map of, 232. *See also* Latin America *and specific countries*
Carnegie, Andrew, 158, 180, 205, 206
Caroline (ship), 101–3
Carranza, Venustiano, 234, 235, 236–38
Cartagena (ship), 218
Cass, Lewis, 112, 128
Castlereagh, Lord, 69, 73, 74, 95, 99, 100, 116
Castro, Cipriano, 229
Catherine the Great, of Russia, 17, 18
Catholics, 106, 157, 165
Cazneau, William, 154, 155
Central America, 130, 233; canal across, 124, 163, 178, 179, 218, 245; Great Britain in, 128, 135–38, 147, 245, 246; U.S. in, 135, 147, 191, 226, 245, 250. *See also* Latin America *and specific countries*
Central and South American Telegraph Company, 180
Charles III, King of Spain, 14, 18
Charles, Joseph, 48
Charleston, S.C., 19, 140
Chemulpo, Treaty of, 172
Chesapeake (ship), 38, 39–42, 64, 65–66, 70, 71
Chicago (ship), 163
Chile, 94, 159, 180–81, 236
China, 128, 171, 172, 244; Japan and, 170, 195, 209, 211, 244; nationalism of, 240–41; Open Door policy in, 239, 240, 243, 244; Russia and, 209, 211, 248; trade with, 24, 25, 89, 91, 124–26, 128, 168, 169, 204, 206, 209, 211, 226, 250; U.S. and, 168–70, 193, 209–12, 239, 240–42, 248
Choiseul, Duc de, 12
Civil War, 127, 128, 138–48, 162, 163, 203; blockade in, 143–44, 148; economic factors in, 139–40; expansion

after, 156, 157; Great Britain in, 138–48, 166–67; legacy of, 148, 183
Clark, George Rogers, 45, 61
Clay, Henry, 88, 94, 99, 107; Florida and, 92, 94; War of 1812 and, 69, 72, 73, 74, 75
Clay, Matthew, 70
Clayton, John M., 128, 136
Clayton-Bulwer Treaty, 136, 179, 218–19, 245
Cleveland, Grover, 164, 167, 176, 179, 194, 195, 213; Cuba and, 196–98; Hawaii and, 173, 195; Venezuela and, 186, 187–92, 195
Clinton, George, 41, 46
Coercive Acts, 7
Colombia, 94, 98, 135, 217–18, 219, 221–23, 247, 250
Cólon, 217, 218
Colonial Dames of America, 157
Columbia (ship), 24, 25
Columbia River Basin, 25, 89, 90, 93, 100, 103–5
Commerce. *See* Trade
Common Sense (Paine), 9, 10, 26, 85
Communications, improvements in, 158, 159
Compromise of 1850, 127, 129, 131
Concert of Europe, 95
Concord, battle of, 7
Condorcet, Maria Jean, Marquis de, 8
Confederacy, 138, 140, 143–48, 166–67
Congo, 176, 178
Congress, 28–29, 54, 92, 94, 175, 176, 240, 251; Alaska and, 165; Continental, 3, 4, 6, 9; Cuba and, 134–35, 196, 197, 200–202; Dominican Republic and, 154–55, 231; foreign policy and, 26, 213; Hawaii and, 204–5; immigration and, 170, 241; Japan and, 122, 124; Jay's Treaty and, 48–49; Mexico and, 83, 112–13; military and, 42; Model Treaty and, 10–12; Navy and, 160, 162, 163; Oregon and, 103, 104, 105; Panama Canal and, 221, 222; power of, 30–31, 250; Spanish-American War and, 198, 200–201, 202, 206–7; struggle for independence and, 16, 19; Texas and, 107–8; trade and, 18; Treaty of Paris and, 21, 22, 26; Venezuela and, 195; War of 1812 and, 66, 69–70, 71, 73
Congress of Troppau, 95
Congress of Verona, 95
Congress of Vienna, 95
Constitution, 29, 30–34, 61

Constitution (ship), 39, 54, 62
Continental Army, 26
Continental Congress, 3, 4, 6, 9
Continental System, 64, 72
Convention of 1800, 56
Convention of 1818, 93, 100, 137
Convention of 1866, 171
Copyright laws, 102
Corn Laws, 99, 116
Cornwallis, Lord, 20, 33
Corregidor, 204
Corwin, Thomas, 128
Costa Rica, 131–32
Cotton, 84, 91, 107, 139, 143–44, 145,
   146, 159
Creek Indians, 27, 28, 115
Creole (ship), 102, 103
Crimea, 18
Crimean War, 137
Crittenden, William, 131
Crockett, Davy, 106
Cromwell, William Nelson, 220–21
Crook, David P., 143, 167
Cuba, 114, 141, 159, 211; attempted
   annexation of, 98, 165, 198, 226;
   McKinley and, 195–203; *Maine* inci-
   dent and, 198–200; revolution in,
   155, 164, 178–79, 195–205; Spanish-
   American War and, 201–5; trade
   with, 160; U.S. in, 126, 128, 130–35,
   165, 179, 192, 193, 207, 212, 226–29,
   231, 240, 250
Cumberland, Richard, 19
Currier, N., 85
Cushing, Caleb, 89, 124, 126
Cyane (ship), 137

Dana, Francis, 19
Dana, Richard Henry, 90
Dangerfield, George, 93
Daniels, Josephus, 236
Danish West Indies. *See* Virgin Islands
Darwinism, Social, 157, 206, 223
Daughters of the American Revolu-
   tion, 157
Davie, William R., 56
Davis, Jefferson, 138–41
Day, William R., 194, 205
DeBow, James D. E. B., 130, 131
Decatur, Stephen, 40, 62, 76
Declaration of Independence, 10, 206
Declaration of Paris, 138, 141
De Lesseps, Ferdinand, 179, 220, 221
De Lôme, Enrique Dupuy, 198–99,
   200, 201, 206
Democratic party, 82, 112, 196, 207,

222, 225, 243, 251; expansionism
   and, 103, 104, 107, 127, 133; Vene-
   zuela and, 188, 191
Denmark, 18, 47, 164, 251
Denver (ship), 228
Department of Foreign Affairs, 26
Depressions, Economic, 69, 70, 71, 88,
   158, 182, 188, 192, 194
Dewey, George, 163, 181, 204, 207, 218
Díaz, Adolfo, 233
Díaz, Porfirio, 115, 179, 233
Dickens, Charles, 102
Dobbin, James C., 124
Dollar diplomacy, 225, 229, 233, 242,
   248, 251
Dominican Republic (Santo Domingo),
   152, 232; Grant's attempt to annex,
   153–56, 175; U.S. and, 147, 164,
   165, 230–31
Donelson, Fort, 143
Dorchester, Lord, 46
Douglas, Stephen, 91, 127
Douglass, Frederick, 130
Dred Scott decision, 127
Dull, Jonathan, 13, 24
Dunne, Finley Peter, 201
Durfee, Amos, 101

East Indies, 126
Edison, Thomas, 158, 160, 172
Egypt, 54, 144, 177, 178, 249, 251
Elgin, Lord, 137
Eliot, Charles W., 205
Elliott, Matthew, 42
Ellsworth, Oliver, 48, 56
El Salvador, 180
Emancipation Proclamation, 145
Embargo Act, 66, 70
Emerson, Ralph Waldo, 113–14
Empress of China (ship), 24
England. *See* Great Britain
Erskine, David M., 68
Essex (ship), 63
Estrada Palma, Tomás, 228
Evans, Robley D., 181
Evarts, William M., 159, 164
Everett, Edward, 128, 133
Expansionism, 84–86, 87, 94, 104, 182,
   197; in Asia, 121, 124, 126; conse-
   quences of, 113–15; Dominican Re-
   public and, 153–56; Great Britain
   and, 99–103; Indians and, 69, 114–
   15; in Latin America, 128, 135, 179;
   map of, 111; in Pacific, 89–91; phi-
   losophy of, 116, 156–58; revival of,
   146–48; Seward and, 163–66; slav-

ery and, 128–32; War of 1812 and,
   70, 77. *See also* Manifest Destiny
Extraterritoriality, 168

Fabens, Joseph, 154, 155
Fairbank, John K., 124
Falkland Islands, 115
Fallen Timbers, battle of, 47
Far East, 84, 193, 248. *See also* Asia *and
   specific countries*
Farragut, David G., 143
Fauchet, Joseph, 46, 48–49, 50
Federal Convention of 1787, 27, 30
Federalist Papers, 31
Federalist party, 47, 48, 49, 66, 68, 71,
   74, 75, 76, 83; as first U.S. party,
   43, 44–45, 57, 58; Louisiana Pur-
   chase and, 59, 60–61; XYZ Affair
   and, 52, 54, 56
Fenian Brotherhood, 166
Ferdinand VII, King of Spain, 95
Ferdinand Maximilian, Archduke, 143,
   178
Field, Cyrus, 159
Filibusters, 130–33
Fillmore, Millard, 122, 128, 133, 137
Fish, Hamilton, 154, 164, 167, 178–79
Fisher, John, 247–48
Fisheries, 4, 5, 11, 12, 21–22, 74, 100,
   137, 167, 247
Florida: acquisition of, 84, 85, 91, 93;
   boundary of, 19, 21, 28, 50, 60;
   Spain and, 3, 6, 16, 19, 24, 43, 54,
   58, 59, 60, 61, 85, 91–93
Florida (ship), 141, 144
Floridablanca, Count, 18, 19
Foraker, Joseph B., 227
Foreign trade. *See* Trade
Formosa, 211
Forsyth, John, 88, 101
Ft. Stanwix, Treaty of, 7
Fort Sumter, 138
Foster, Augustus, 71
Foster, John W., 164
France, 137, 175; Africa and, 128, 178,
   249–50; Canada and, 6–7; China
   and, 126, 209–11, 242, 244; Civil
   War and, 138, 142; Egypt and, 249;
   Europe and, 16–17, 95, 143; Great
   Britain and, 6–7, 47, 48, 50–51;
   Haiti and, 231; Indochina and, 209;
   Jay's Treaty and, 50–51; Latin
   America and, 58, 96, 133, 164, 178;
   Louisiana Purchase and, 56, 58–61;
   Manchuria and, 242, 244; Mexico
   and, 107, 115, 143, 146, 147, 178,

France (*continued*)
188–89; Model Treaty and, 10–12; Morocco and, 249–50; Revolutionary War peace negotiations and, 3–6, 20–24; Spain and, 18–20, 96, 97; struggle for independence and, 12–17; trade with, 24, 29, 33, 50–51, 62–64, 66, 68–69, 70, 85–86, 144; U.S. and, 8, 29, 34, 43–47, 48, 52–58, 93; War of 1812 and, 66, 67, 71–72; XYZ Affair and, 53–56

Franklin, Benjamin, 2, 8–10, 16, 103; France and, 7, 10, 12, 14, 15, 20, 21, 23, 29, 33; Revolutionary War peace negotiations and, 3–6; treaties and, 12, 17, 30

Franklin, William, 22

Frederick the Great, 16, 17

Free Soil party, 107, 134

Frémont, John C., 108, 127

French and Indian Wars, 6–7

French Revolution, 34, 44–46, 53, 95

French West Indies, 29, 46, 52, 63

Freylinghuysen, Frederick T., 164

Fugitive Slave Act, 127

Fur trade, 24, 27, 61, 167–68

Gadsden Purchase, 126

Gallatin, Albert, 42, 66, 68, 73–75, 99, 100, 107, 113

Gamboa, Frederico, 234

Gardoqui, Diego de, 28–30

Garfield, James A., 164

Garibaldi, Giuseppe, 127

Gast, Thomas, 86

General Sherman (ship), 171–72

Genêt, Edmond Charles, 45, 46, 50

George III, King of England, 16, 19, 30, 71; American independence and, 6, 9, 16, 17, 20, 22, 27

Germany, 8, 159, 176, 191; Africa and, 178, 192, 249–50; Asia and, 209, 211, 229, 242, 244, 248; Great Britain and, 223, 249–50; Latin America and, 231–32, 235, 236, 247, 251; power of, 193, 206; Samoa and, 173–75; trade with, 160; U.S. and, 157, 212, 229, 237; Venezuela and, 229–30, 247; World War I and, 238–39, 244, 248

Geronimo, 227

Gerry, Elbridge, 30, 52, 53, 55

Gettysburg, battle of, 145

Ghent, Peace of, 74–75, 99–100

Gibralter, 18–19, 21, 23

Gilbert, Felix, 9

Girondins, 46

Godkin, E. L., 155, 165, 191

Godoy, Manuel de, 50

Goetzmann, William H., 132

Gold rush of 1849, 124, 136

Gómez, Máximo, 195

Gompers, Samuel, 205

Grant, Ulysses S., 154, 164, 178; Civil War and, 143, 145, 146; Dominican Republic and, 153–55, 175

Great Britain, 30, 159, 164, 168; Africa and, 178, 245; American expansionism and, 77, 99–103; Asia and, 124–26, 128, 250; California and, 88, 108, 116–17; Canadian boundary and, 16, 74, 137, 245–47; Central America and, 135–38, 147, 179; *Chesapeake* affair and, 39–42, 64; China and, 89, 168, 211, 242, 244; Civil War and, 138–48, 166–67; colonial wars and, 7–8; commerce and, 24–25, 26–28, 44, 46–49, 52, 64–69, 95, 99–100, 147, 160, 166–67, 193, 248; Egypt and, 177, 178, 249; France and, 6–7, 11–12, 14, 16, 17, 19, 43–45, 50–51, 54–55, 62, 72, 249–50; Germany and, 247; Hawaii and, 172; Japan and, 239, 250; Latin America and, 85, 95–96, 98, 115, 128, 133, 142–43, 147, 178, 180, 188, 223, 229, 235; maritime power of, 60, 62–64; Model Treaty and, 11–12; Oregon and, 88, 103–5, 113; Pacific Northwest and, 74, 84; Panama Canal and, 218–19, 223, 245; Revolutionary War peace negotiations and, 3–6, 20–24; Samoa and, 173–75; Spain and, 18, 19; struggle for independence and, 12, 14, 15, 16; Texas and, 107; U.S. and, 34, 35, 61, 65, 69, 92, 94, 142, 157, 212, 225, 244, 246, 250, 251; Venezuela and, 187–92, 212; War of 1812 and, 66–77, 91; World War I and, 238

Great Lakes, 21, 27, 100

Great Northern Railroad, 160

Greece, 95, 96

Greenland, 164

Greenville, Treaty of, 47

Grenville, Lord, 49, 55

Gresham, Walter Q., 164, 173, 194

Grey, Edward, 248

Greytown, Nicaragua, 135–36, 137

Griswold, A. Whitney, 242

Grosvenor, Edwin A., 212

Guadalupe Hidalgo, Treaty of, 112

Guam, 205

Guantánamo Bay, Cuba, 228

Guatemala, 131, 179, 180

Hague Conferences, 249

Hague Court, 100, 230, 247, 250

Haiti, 153, 154, 164, 231–32

Hamilton, Alexander, 51, 54, 55; Constitution and, 31–34; diplomacy of, 43–44, 45; Jay's Treaty and, 47, 48; Louisiana Purchase and, 59, 61

Hamilton, Grant, 202

Hammond, George, 44, 45, 47, 49

Hanna, Mark, 221

Harbaugh, William, 223, 230

Harriman, E. H., 241

Harrison, Benjamin, 164, 167, 168, 173, 180, 181

Harrison, William H., 69, 88

Hartford Convention, 75

Hartley, David, 26

Hatzenbuehler, Ronald L., 64

Hawaii, 31, 114, 115; annexation of, 163, 173, 188, 195, 204–5, 206; trade with, 25, 90; U.S. in, 161, 164, 172–73, 198, 207, 212, 240

Hay, John, 194, 203, 211, 223–24; China and, 239, 243; Panama Canal and, 218, 219, 221, 245

Hay-Bunau-Varilla Treaty, 218, 222, 247, 250

Hayes, Rutherford B., 164, 170, 179

Hay-Herrán Treaty, 221, 247

Hay-Pauncefote Treaty, 219, 223, 229, 245

Healy, David, 232

Hearst, William Randolph, 198, 201

Henderson, John, 130

Henry, Patrick, 7, 10

Hepburn Bill, 220

Hebert, Michael, 247

Herrán, Tomás, 221

Hietala, Thomas, 86, 87

Hill, James J., 160

Hippisley, Alfred, 211

Hispaniola, 153

Hoar, George, 201, 205, 206

Holland. *See* Netherlands

Holy Alliance, 95, 96, 98

Homestead Act, 147

Honduras, 131, 132, 136, 138, 164

Honolulu, 90

House of Representatives. *See* Congress

Houston, Sam, 106

Hubbard, John, 218

Hudson's Bay Company, 104, 105

Huerta, Victoriano, 233–36, 248

Humphreys, S. P., 40, 41

Index

Hunt, Michael, 89
Hutson, James H., 8
Huxley, Thomas, 183

Iceland, 164
Illinois, 31
Immigration, 170, 211, 212–13; from China, 169–70, 241; from Japan, 240, 243–44
Imperialism, 193, 197–98, 201, 205; defined, 156; European, 188; in 19th century, 157–58, 163; Philippines and, 206–7, 208
Impressment of seamen, 42, 64–65, 70, 71, 73, 76, 100, 102
India, 7, 126, 144, 251
Indiana, 31
Indiana (ship), 163
Indians (Native Americans), 7, 27, 92, 203; battles with, 47; Great Britain and, 42, 49, 69, 71; removal of, 87, 114–15; U.S. expansionism and, 73, 84, 87, 99, 114. *See also specific tribes*
Indo-China, 209
Indonesia, 209
Industrialization, 158
Industrial revolution, 147
Insurgente (ship), 54
International Bureau of American Republics, 180
International Harvester Company, 160
Iowa (ship), 163
Ireland, 27, 166
Irish-Americans, 166, 191
Iriye, Akira, 239
Iroquois Indians, 27
Irving, John Beaufain, 123
Ishii, Kikujiro, 244
Isolationism, 97, 213
Israel, Jerry, 226
Italy, 144–45, 211, 212
Ivie, Robert L., 64

Jackson, Andrew, 42, 80, 85–86, 88, 110; Florida and, 91–92, 94; at New Orleans, 75–76; Texas and, 105, 106, 107
Jackson, Francis James, 68
Jacobins, 44, 46
James, Marquis, 105
James, William, 208
Japan, 158, 168; China and, 170, 195, 209, 211, 244; discrimination against immigrants from, 240, 243–44; early American views of, 122; expansion-

ism and, 206, 239; Great Britain and, 239, 250; Korea and, 170–72, 239–40; Manchuria and, 242–44; opening of, 121–24, 128; Russia and, 239–40, 248; trade with, 171; U.S. and, 170–72, 238, 239–41, 243, 248, 250
Jay, John, 24, 31, 33, 43, 103; diplomacy of, 26, 29, 30, 32; Great Britain and, 28, 47; Revolutionary War peace negotiations and, 3–6; Spain and, 19–20, 28–29; treaty of, 48–51, 56, 58, 99; Treaty of Paris and, 21, 22, 23, 24
Jay, Sarah, 19, 28
Jefferson, Thomas, 10, 12, 43, 46, 48, 52, 58–61, 73, 93, 96, 110; *Chesapeake* affair and, 38, 41–42; diplomacy of, 29–30, 32, 42–44, 45, 46, 64, 248–49; expansionism and, 62, 86, 133; France and, 34, 45, 54; Great Britain and, 54, 65–66, 67, 71; Lewis and Clark Expedition, and, 61; Louisiana Purchase and, 58–60; presidency of, 51, 57, 58
Jeffersonians, 44, 54
Jim Crow laws, 203
Jingoism, 192, 194, 195, 244
Johnson, Andrew, 164, 165, 178
Johnson, Hiram, 243
Jones, Anson, 108
Jones, Thomas ap Catesby, 108–9
Jones Act, 251
Jordan, David Starr, 206
Joseph II, King of Austria, 16–17
Juárez, Benito, 178

Kanagawa, Treaty of, 123–24
Kaplan, Lawrence, 20, 23
Kansas, 127
Katsura, Taro, 240, 248
Kearney, Dennis, 169
Kearsarge (ship), 146
Kentucky, 24
King, Rufus, 32, 55, 61
Knights of the Golden Circle, 130
Knox, Philander C., 224, 225, 231, 233, 240, 242, 248, 250
Korea, 170, 171–72, 182, 209, 211, 239, 240
Kossuth, Lajos, 127

Labrador, 100
Lafayette, Marquis de, 20, 44
LaFeber, Walter, 12, 163, 203

LaFollette, Robert M., 224
Langley, Lester, 198
Lansdowne, Lord, 246
Lansing, Robert, 225, 232, 238, 244
Larkin, Thomas O., 90, 108
Latin America, 66, 128; American expansionism in, 128, 135, 179; Europe and, 54, 96, 97, 98, 143, 158, 188, 189; independent governments in, 94, 96, 99, 231; revolution in, 94; trade with, 84, 85, 94–95, 179, 197, 201, 226, 248; Theodore Roosevelt and, 229–31; U.S. and, 126, 127, 147, 158, 159, 163, 178–82, 192, 197, 223, 225, 251. *See also specific countries*
League of Armed Neutrality, 17, 18
Leander (ship), 41
Leclerc, Victor Emmanuel, 58
Lee, Fitzhugh, 196, 198
Lee, Richard Henry, 10
Lee, Robert E., 143, 145, 196
Lee, William, 17
Leopard (ship), 38, 39–41
Leopold II, King of Belgium, 176
Lewis and Clark Expedition, 61, 86
Lexington, battle of, 7
Liberia, 176, 177–78
Liliuokalani, Queen of Hawaii, 173, 204
Lincoln, Abraham, 113, 128, 146, 211, 225; Civil War and, 138–46, 148; slavery and, 127, 135, 145
Lind, John, 234
Lindneux, Robert, 114
Little Sarah (ship), 45
Liverpool, Lord, 73, 74
Livingston, David, 176
Livingston, Edward, 88
Livingston, Robert, 9, 22, 58, 60
Lodge, Henry Cabot, 163, 191, 206, 245, 247
London *Times*, 104, 136, 178
Loomis, Francis B., 217
López, Narciso, 130–31, 133
Louis XVI, King of France, 4, 12, 44, 45, 46
Louisbourg, Cape Breton Island, 7
Louisiana: France and, 59–60; Spain and, 6, 45, 54, 56–57; U.S. expansionism and, 147, 206
Louisiana Purchase, 31, 58, 85, 91, 100
L'Ouverture, Toussaint, 58
Loyalists, 22, 27
Luce, Stephen B., 162
Lusitania (ship), 237, 244
Lyons, Richard, 138, 140, 142

Macao, 126
McClellan, George B., 143
McCormick, Cyrus, 160, 182
Macdonald, John A., 166, 167
Mackenzie, William Lyon, 101
McKinley, William, 197–206, 209, 213, 225, 227; canal and, 218, 245; Cuba and, 197–206, 226; imperialism and, 206, 208; *Maine* incident and, 198–200; Philippines and, 208; Spanish-American War and, 194–95, 200–206
McKinley Tariff of 1890, 160
McLane, Louis, 88
McLeod, Alexander, 101–2
Macon's Bill Number Two, 68–69
Madero, Francisco I., 233
Madison, James, 21, 43, 58, 61, 85, 88, 91; commercial policy of, 43–44; Constitution and, 30, 31, 32; diplomacy of, 32, 74, 76; embargo and, 67–69; Great Britain and, 41, 45, 65, 67, 77, 96; War of 1812 and, 70–75, 76
Magoon, Charles E., 228
Mahan, Alfred T., 162–63, 180, 181, 218, 223, 225
Maine, 27, 74, 101, 102–3, 135
Maine (ship),163, 198–202
Malay Peninsula, 209
Manassas Junction, battle of, 141
Manchu dynasty, 211, 240
Manchuria, 239–40, 241–42, 244
Manifest Destiny, 70, 84–88, 93, 114, 117, 131, 147; Mexican War and, 109, 112; origin of term, 87; rhetoric of, 88, 116, 130, 132, 156; slavery and, 127–28
Manila, 163, 204, 207, 208
Marcy, William, 127, 128, 133–34, 137
Marie Antoinette, Queen of France, 14
Marines, 229, 231, 232, 233, 236, 251
Marks, Frederick W., 46, 216, 219
Marshall, John, 42, 52–53, 136
Martí, José, 195
Maryland, 24
Mason, George, 30, 33
Mason, James M., 141–42
Mason, John Y., 133–34
Massachusetts, 26, 103, 137, 247
Massachusetts (ship), 163
Matamoros, Mexico, 81, 109
Maury, Matthew, 89, 126
Maximilian, Archduke, 146, 147
May, Glenn, 251
May, Robert E., 132
Mayo, Henry T., 236
Mazzini, Giuseppe, 127

Meade, John, 40
Melampus (ship), 39, 41
Melville, Herman, 122
Mercantilists, 26–27
Merk, Frederick, 89, 112
Merry, Anthony, 64
Metternich, Klemens von, 95, 98
Mexican Cession, 84, 114, 129, 132
Mexican War, 81–84, 109–13, 115, 116–17, 124, 126, 127; beginnings of, 81–84, 104, 105; consequences of, 113–15; map of, 82
Mexico, 94, 142–43; American expansionism and, 87, 107–9, 126, 128, 129; France and, 143, 146, 147, 178, 188–89; revolution in, 233; Seward and, 163, 178; trade with, 160, 163, 179, 206; U.S. and, 103, 115, 161, 233–39, 244, 248, 250
Mexico City, 87, 90, 110, 117, 159
Michigan, 31
Middle East, 235, 250
Midway Islands, 164
Milan Decree, 63, 68, 71
Miranda, Francisco de, 54
Missionaries, 169, 170, 176, 241
Mississippi (ship), 120, 137
Mississippi River, 28–29, 32–33, 50, 58–59, 89, 91; Civil War and, 143, 145; disputes over, 43, 74–75; Revolutionary War peace negotiations and, 3, 4, 5, 19, 21
Missouri, 115
Missouri Compromise, 129
Model Treaty, 10–12, 15, 28, 32, 35, 56, 65
Môle Saint Nicholas, Haiti, 231, 232, 238
Monaghan, Jay, 140
Mongolia, 244
Monroe, James, 33, 43, 88, 97; Florida and, 91–94; France and, 46, 50, 52; Great Britain and, 42, 65, 69, 72, 73, 94, 96–99, 100; Louisiana Purchase and, 58, 59, 60
Monroe Doctrine, 85, 94–99, 104, 143; Cuba and, 196, 229; essential points of, 97–98; Europe and, 192; formulation of, 97; Great Britain and, 100, 143; Latin America and, 155, 178, 229; Panama Canal and, 245; response to, 98–99; Roosevelt Corollary to, 230–31; Venezuela and, 187, 188, 189, 190
Monroe-Pinkney Treaty, 65
Montesquieu, Baron de La Brède, et, 31

Moore, John Bassett, 191
Morgan, J. P., 159, 241, 242
Morison, Samuel Eliot, 90
Morocco, 28, 29, 249–50
Morrill, Justin, 165
Morrill Act, 147
Morris, Gouverneur, 32, 45–46, 52
Morse, Jedidiah, 33
Morse, Samuel, 87
Mortefontaine, Treaty of, 56–58
Mosquito Coast, 135, 136, 138
Mukden incident, 239
Murray, William Vans, 55–57
Muskogean Indians, 27

Nagasaki, 122
Nanjing, Treaty of, 89
Nankivell, Frank, 219
Napoleon Bonaparte, 52, 58, 71, 73; American Shipping and, 63–64, 65, 66, 68–69, 71–72; defeat of, 76, 95; Louisiana Purchase and, 56–57, 58, 60, 61
Napoleon III, 143, 144, 146, 178
Nashville (ship), 217, 218, 222
National Association of Manufacturers, 188
National Cash Register Co., 160
Nationalism, 161, 229, 250–51; China and, 240–41; U.S. and, 157–58, 182, 202
Native Americans. *See* Indians (Native Americans)
Naval War College, 162, 163, 223
Navy, 26, 54, 89, 165, 171, 181, 193; battles, map of, 57; beginning of, 9, 30; Congress and, 162; Dominican Republic and, 153, 154–55; expansionism and, 89; Latin America and, 123, 130, 223, 228, 231, 236; pirates and, 62; strength of, 42, 89, 181, 198, 201, 204, 212, 240, 249; trade and, 160, 161–63; War of 1812 and, 71, 73
Navy Act of 1896, 192
Nelson, Horatio, 63
Netherlands, 16, 23, 103, 126; Revolutionary War and, 5; trade and, 4, 21, 24, 33; U.S. and, 17–18, 34
Neu, Charles E., 126
Neutrality Act, 130, 131
Neutrality of U.S., 33–34, 56, 62–65, 149
Nevada, 83
Nevins, Allan, 128, 132
New Brunswick, 27, 101, 102

Newfoundland, 4, 5, 11, 12, 21–22, 100, 247
New Mexico, 82, 83, 84, 112, 116
New Orleans, 19, 50, 59, 60, 75–76, 85, 130
New Panama Canal Company, 219–21
Newspapers, 87
New York Chamber of Commerce, 124
New York Herald, 176
New York Journal, 198, 201
New York Life Insurance Company, 160
New York World, 177, 201, 221
Nicaragua, 136; American expansion-ism and, 128, 131–32; as canal site, 179, 198, 219, 220–21, 233; Great Britain in, 138, 188
Nicholas II, Tsar, 239
Nobel Peace Prize, 224
Noer, Thomas, 246
Non-Intercourse Act, 66–70
North, Lord, 20
North (U.S.), and expansionism, 87, 130, 132, 213
Northwest (U.S.), 27, 28, 47, 49, 50, 74, 114, 116
Northwest Ordinance, 31

O'Higgins, Bernardo, 94
Ohio, 31
Ohio (ship), 222
Ohio Valley, 6–7, 27, 28, 42
Oil, 160
Oklahoma, 115
Olney, Richard, 164, 187–92, 194, 196–98, 206
Olympia (ship), 163, 204
Onís, Don Luis de, 91–93
Open Door policy and notes, 170, 193, 211–12, 225, 250; China and, 239, 240, 243, 244; Japan and, 240, 244, 250
Opium War, 89, 126
Oregon, 86, 88, 116; American claims to, 25, 103–5, 107, 115, 137; Great Britain in, 88, 100, 102, 105, 113; Polk and, 84, 132, 135; settlement of, 89, 91, 103, 104, 113, 114, 124
Oregon (ship), 163, 218, 223
Orinoco River, 187, 188, 190, 191, 192
Ostend Manifesto, 134
O'Sullivan, John L., 87, 130
Oswald, Richard, 20, 21

Pacific, 147, 156, 158, 163, 193. *See also specific countries and islands*

Paine, Thomas, 9–10, 16, 26, 44, 51, 85
Pakenham, Richard, 104
Palmerston, Lord, 101, 102, 103, 116, 133, 135, 136, 137–38; *Caroline* affair and, 101, 102, 103; Civil War and, 142–46
Panama, 135–37, 217–23, 247, 250; as possible canal site, 135, 136, 179; U.S. in, 179, 182
Panama Canal: building of, 222–23; map of, 220; security of, 230–31; site selection for, 219–21; U.S. and, 218–21, 248, 250
Pan American Conference, 180
Pan Americanism, 178, 180, 181, 237
Pan American Union, 180
Panic of 1819, 88
Panic of 1857, 127
Paris, Declaration of (1856), 138, 141
Paris, Treaties of: 1763, 6; 1783, 20–24, 27, 28; 1815, 95; 1899, 207, 208; map of U.S. after 1783, 25
Pauncefote, Julian, 191, 219, 245, 246
Pearl Harbor, 172
Peking. *See* Beijing
Peninsular War, 95
Percival, Spencer, 71
Perkins, Bradford, 42, 55, 248
Perkins, Dexter, 251
Perry, Matthew C., 89, 120, 121–24, 126, 137, 170, 172
Perry, Oliver Hazard, 73, 121
Pershing, John J., 238
Peru, 94, 180
Peterhoff (ship), 148
Peterson, Merrill, 33
Philadelphia, 24
Philadelphia (ship), 62, 72
Philippine Islands, 226, 250; Japan and, 240; Taft and, 224, 228; U.S. and, 163, 204, 206–9, 211, 213, 218, 240, 241, 251
Philosophes, 8
Pickering, Timothy, 43, 49, 54, 56
Pierce, Franklin, 126, 128, 131, 133–34, 137
Pike, Zebulon M., 61
Pinckney, Charles C., 52–54
Pinckney, Thomas, 44, 49, 50
Pinckney's Treaty, 49–50, 58, 59, 91
Pinkney, William, 65, 71
Pitt, William, 8, 26
Plan of 1776, 10, 17, 18
Platt, Orville, 183, 204, 227
Platt Amendment, 225, 227–28, 229
Pletcher, David, 116
Poinsett, Joel, 105

Poland, 146
Polignac Memorandum, 96, 98
Polk, James K., 80, 88, 115–16, 128, 132–33, 135; Mexican War and, 82–87, 109–13, 117; Oregon and, 103–5; Texas and, 107, 108–9
Polly (ship), 63
Port Arthur, China, 209, 239
Portsmouth Conference, 224, 239
Portugal, 16, 18, 126
Potato War, 16
Preble, Edward, 62
Printing press, 87
Privateering, 138
Proctor, Redfield, 200
Prophet, the (Native American), 42, 69
Progressives, 243
Prussia, 16–18, 33, 74, 95
Public opinion, 194–95, 229
Puerto Rico, 204, 206, 231, 251
Pulitzer, Joseph, 201

Quadruple Alliance, 95
Quebec act of 1774, 7
Quintuple Alliance, 95
Quitman, John A., 115, 130, 131

Racism, 213; expansionism and, 114, 160, 206, 208; foreign policy and, 223–24; immigration and, 240, 241, 244; Spanish-American War and, 203
Railroads, 87, 91, 124, 135–36, 147, 158, 159, 164, 165, 241, 242
Randolph, Edmund, 30, 32, 43, 47, 48–49
Randolph, John, 66, 70
Ratford, Jenkin, 41
Rayneval, Gerard de, 3, 4
Reconstruction, 164, 165–66
Reed, James, 242
Reid, Whitelaw, 191
Remington Company, 160
Republican party, 49, 54, 58, 127, 165, 207; France and, 44, 47, 48; Latin America and, 155, 196, 197–98, 201; treaties and, 50; Venezuela and, 188, 191; War of 1812 and, 70, 71
Ricarte, Artemio, 251
Rickover, Hyman G., 199
Rio Grande: as boundary, 91, 106, 108, 109, 112, 116; Mexican War and, 81, 83, 84, 87
Risjord, Norman, 70
Roberts, Grace, 241

Rochambeau, Comte de, 33
Rockefeller, John D., 158, 160
Rockhill, William W., 211, 242
Rockingham, Marquess of, 20
Rocky Mountains, 86, 93
Rodgers, John, 124, 126
Rodrigue Hortalez and Company, 12, 14
Roosevelt, Theodore, 116, 194, 197, 216, 219, 243, 251; Alaska and, 246, 247; China and, 239, 240, 243; Cuba and, 228; Germany and, 174–75, 230; Great Britain and, 244–47, 249–50, 251; imperialism and, 163, 194, 212, 231, 251; Japan and, 239–40, 241; Latin America and, 191, 223, 224, 229–31, 233; Panama Canal and, 216, 218–23; Spanish-American War and, 203, 204, 206; trade and, 225–26; views of, 223–24
Roosevelt Corollary, 230–31, 247
Root, Elihu, 224, 225, 243, 247, 250; Cuba and, 226, 227, 229; Japan and, 240; Panama Canal and, 230, 233
Rough Riders, 203, 204, 227
Ruíz, Ramón E., 236
Rule of 1756, 63, 68
Rush, Benjamin, 30
Rush, Richard, 95–96, 100
Rush-Bagot Agreement, 100
Russell, Jonathan, 71–75
Russell, John, 140–41, 142–43, 144, 145, 146
Russia, 17, 18, 47, 89, 95, 137, 168, 250; Alaska and, 164–65; China and, 209, 211, 239, 248; France and, 72, 73; Great Britain and, 64, 72–73, 137; Japan and, 239–40, 242; U.S. and, 17, 97–98, 145, 160, 239
Rutland, Robert, 65

Sackville-West, Lionel, 167
St. Eustatius, West Indies, 17
St. Lawrence River, 7, 21, 101, 137
St. Louis, 89
Salisbury, Lord, 167, 190, 191, 192
Sam, Guillaume, 232
Samaná Bay, 153, 154, 164
Samoa, 173–75
San Diego, 124
Sanford, Henry S., 176
San Francisco, 89, 90, 124, 136, 169, 240
San Jacinto (ship), 141, 142
San Juan Islands, 167
San Lorenzo, Treaty of, 49–50

San Martin, José, 94
San Salvador, 131
Santa Anna, Antonio Lopez de, 106, 108, 109, 117
Santo Domingo. *See* Dominican Republic (Santo Domingo)
Santo Zelaya, José, 234
Saratoga, battle of, 14
Schley, Winfield S., 181
Schmitt, Karl M., 179
Schomburgk, Robert, 187, 191
Scott, Winfield, 87, 101, 109, 110, 112, 115
Scruggs, William L., 188, 192
Scrymser, James A., 159, 180
Seal hunting, 167–68
Sedition Act of 1901, 251
Seminole Indians, 92, 94, 115
Semmes, Raphael, 144
Senate. *See* Congress
Seward, William H., 126, 128, 164, 170, 171; Alaska and, 164–65, 166; Civil War and, 138–40, 142, 143, 148; expansionism and, 147–48, 163–66; imperialism and, 193, 197–98; Mexico and, 146, 178
Shandong Peninsula, 244, 248
Shawnee Indians, 27, 42, 69
Shays' Rebellion, 27, 30
Sheffield, Earl F., 26, 27
Shelburne, Lord, 6, 16, 20, 21, 26
Sheridan, Philip H., 162, 178
Sherman, John, 194, 198
Sherman, Roger, 33
Sherman, William, 146
Shimoda, Japan, 124, 126
Shoup, George, 181
Shufeldt, Robert W., 161, 171–72, 175
Sigur, Laurence, 130
Singer Sewing Company, 160, 169, 182, 226
Sino-Japanese War, 170, 171, 195, 209
Sioux Indians, 166
Slavery, 48, 91, 99, 102; Cuba and, 132, 165, 178, 179; Emancipation Proclamation and, 145; extension of, 80, 87; Latin America and, 127, 128–32, 137; Mexican Cession and, 112–14; Texas and, 106, 107
Slidell, John, 108, 109, 112, 116, 141–42
Sloat, John D., 108
Smelser, Marshall, 59–60, 71–72
Smith, Adam, 21
Smith, Geoffrey, 89, 123
Smith, Hamilton, 177
Smith, Justin A., 116
Smith, Robert, 43

Smith, Samuel, 41
Social Darwinism, 157, 206, 223
Society of Colonial Wars, 157
Soulé, Pierre, 131, 133, 134
South (U.S.), 213; Europe in Civil War and, 143, 147, 170; expansionism and, 87, 127, 128–30, 133, 135, 166, 213; perspective on expansion, map of, 129; trade and, 44, 91, 107; War of 1812 and, 70. *See also* Confederacy
South Africa, 176–77, 191, 212, 245
South America, 226, 229; Spain and, 91; trade with, 63, 191. *See also* Latin America *and specific countries*
Southern Democrats, 104, 173
Southgate, Donald, 136
Southwest (U.S.), 28, 114
Southwest Africa, 178
Spain, 43, 99, 143, 250; Cuba and, 98, 130, 131, 132–35, 178–79, 195, 196–97, 198–200, 201, 202, 226; Dominican Republic and, 138, 147; Florida and, 3, 6, 16, 19, 24, 43, 54, 58, 59, 60, 61, 85, 91–93; France and, 43, 44, 96, 97; Great Britain and, 64, 66, 72; Latin America and, 54–55, 164; Louisiana and, 45, 56, 58–60, 61; Monroe Doctrine and, 94–95; Philippines and, 163, 204, 205, 206, 207, 218; Pinckney's Treaty and, 49–50; Revolutionary War peace negotiations and, 3, 4, 5, 23, 24; struggle for independence and, 12, 14, 17, 18–20; Texas and, 105; U.S. and, 28–29, 33, 34, 84–87, 94, 128, 201–5, 212, 213
Spanish-American War, 175, 193, 201–5, 212, 213, 223
Sparks, Jared, 103
Speck von Sternberg, Hermann, 230
Spivak, Burton, 67
Spooner, John C., 221
Spooner Act, 221
Stagg, J. C. A., 71
Standard Oil Company, 160, 168, 226
Stanley, Henry M., 176
Stevens, John L., 173
Stevenson, Robert Louis, 175
Stinchcombe, William, 33
Stoeckl, Edouard de, 165
Stormont, Lord, 14
Storms, Jane McManus, 109
Straight, Willard, 241–42, 250
Strait of Juan de Fuca, 89, 90, 104, 105, 167
Strong, Josiah, 157

Student Volunteer Movement, 157
Suez Canal, 159, 179
Sugar, 172–73, 179, 182, 195, 226, 229
Sumner, Charles, 141, 142, 165; Dominican Republic and, 153, 154, 155; Great Britain and, 166–67
Sumter, Fort, 138
Susquehanna (ship), 120, 122
Sweden, 18, 33, 47, 64, 164

Taft, William Howard, 208, 224; China and, 226, 244; Cuba and, 228; dollar diplomacy and, 233, 248, 251; Japan and, 240–42, 244; Latin America and, 231, 250; Manchuria and, 242–43; Mexico and, 233–34
Takahira, Kogoro, 239, 240, 242, 248
Talleyrand-Périgord, Charles Maurice de, 52–53, 55–56, 58, 59, 60
Tariffs, 26, 147, 160, 163, 166, 171, 172–73, 180, 195, 197, 198
Taylor, James, 152
Taylor, Zachary, 81–82, 83, 109, 112, 115, 116, 128, 136
Tea Act of 1773, 7
Tecumseh, 42, 69, 73
Telegraph, 87, 158, 159, 160
Telephone, 158, 160
Teller Amendment, 201, 226, 228, 229
Tennessee, 24
Texas, 104, 114, 143; annexation of, 82, 83, 84, 105–9, 113; claims for, 93; Great Britain and, 84, 88, 102, independence of, 101, 106, 107; Mexican War and, 105, 108, 110; Spain and, 60, 61; U.S. and, 115, 147
Third World, 162
Thorne, Christopher, 211
Thornton, Seth B., 81–82
Tianjin, Treaty of, 126
Ticonderoga (ship), 172, 175
Tigre Island, 164
Tillman, Benjamin, 213
Tobacco, 24, 91
Tories, 22
Tracy, Benjamin F., 163, 181
Trade: Africa and, 175; balance of, 11, 24, 122, 123, 158–61; China and, 24, 25, 89, 91, 124–26, 128, 168, 169, 204, 206, 209, 211, 226, 250; Civil War blockade of, 143–44, 148; in colonial period, 7, 9–10, 18; Cuba and, 132, 229; economic growth and, 158–61; France and, 24, 29, 33, 44–46, 50–51, 52, 62–64, 66, 68–69, 70, 85–86, 144; Great Britain and,

9–10, 24–25, 26–28, 44–45, 46–49, 52, 64–69, 76–77, 95, 99–100, 135, 147, 167–68, 193, 248; impressment of seamen and, 64–65; Japan and, 122, 123–24, 171; Jay's Treaty and, 46–49; Jefferson and, 61–62; Korea and, 172; Latin America and, 84, 85, 94–95, 179–80, 188, 197, 201, 226, 248; Lewis and Clark Expedition and, 61; Madison and, 43–44; Model Treaty and, 11; Navy and, 160, 161–63; neutrality and, 62–65; Pacific and, 89–91; after Revolutionary War, 24–25; Theodore Roosevelt and, 225–26; Venezuela and, 193
Transcontinental Treaty of 1819, 93, 94
Treaty of 1844, 124
Treaty of 1846, 167
Trent (ship), 141–42
Trist, Nicholas, 110–12, 117
Tunisia, 29, 76, 178
Turkey, 18, 95
Turner, Frederick Jackson, 157–58
Turner, Henry, 176
Twain, Mark, 165, 205, 206
Twenty-One Demands, 244
Tyler, John, 88, 89, 106–8, 115

United Fruit Company, 226
Upshur, Abel P., 88
Urbanization, 158
Utah, 83

Van Alstyne, Richard, 94
Van Buren, Martin, 88, 101, 106
Vanderbilt, Cornelius, 131, 136
Vanderlip, Frank, 209
Van Rensselaer, Rensselaer, 101
Varg, Paul A., 65, 150
Venezuela, 180, 244; Germany and, 229–30, 247; trade with, 193; U.S. and, 186, 187–92, 195, 196, 212
Veracruz, Mexico, 142–43, 235, 236
Vergennes, Charles Gravier, 3–5, 8, 12–17, 20–23, 29, 33
Vermont, 27
Verona, Congress of, 95
Victoria, Queen of England, 142
Vienna, Congress of, 74, 95
Villa, Francisco (Pancho), 237–38
Virginia, 24
Virginia Plan, 30
Virgin Islands, 164, 198, 251

Virginius (ship), 178–79

Walker, William, 130, 131–32
Walker Isthmian Canal Commission, 219—21
Wangxia, Treaty of, 89, 126
War of Bavarian Succession, 16–17
War of 1812, 62, 65–77, 91; background to, 65–69; causes of, 69–70; France and, 71–72; legacy of, 95–97, 99; Peace of Ghent and, 72–75
War of the Pacific, 180
Warren, Gordon H., 142
Washburne, Elihu B., 164
Washington, George, 26, 28, 54, 55; administration of, 31–32, 34, 43, 45, 57–58; Farewell Address of, 51–52, 85, 98, 133, 206, 248; Jay's Treaty and, 47, 48, 49, 50; Revolutionary War and, 20, 33
Washington, Treaty of, 100, 167, 174, 178
Wayne, Anthony, 47
Webster, Daniel, 88–90, 102–4, 127, 128, 131, 135
Webster, Noah, 24
Webster-Ashburton Treaty, 102–3, 137
Welles, Gideon, 139, 146
Wellington, Duke of, 74, 76
Wells, David A., 159
West (U.S.), 60, 69, 70
West Indies, 133; 154; France in, 11, 15, 45, 46; trade with, 17, 63, 99; U.S. in, 52, 206, 212
Westinghouse, George, 158
Weyler, Valeriano y Nicolau, 195–96, 198, 202
Whaling, 122
Wheat, 159
Wheeler, John Hill, 131
Whigs, 8, 9, 83, 104, 107, 112, 115–16
Whiskey Rebellion, 49
Whitaker, Arthur P., 50
Whitney, Asa, 91
Wilhelm II, Kaiser of Germany, 229–30, 249, 250
Wilkes, Charles, 89, 141–42, 173
Wilmot, David, 112
Wilmot Proviso, 112, 113, 127
Wilson, Henry Lane, 233, 234
Wilson, Woodrow, 224, 225, 251; China and, 242–44; Cuba and, 228–29; foreign policy of, 213, 225, 231, 248; Haiti and, 231–32; Japan and, 250; Latin America and, 213, 226, 233, 248; Mexico and, 234–39

Index

Wilz, John, 240
Winthrop, John 8
Wisconsin, 31
Wolcott, Oliver, 54
Wolff, H. Drummond, 197
Wood, Leonard, 203, 226–27, 228
Woodford, Stewart L., 198, 200
Workingmen's party, 169
World War I, 148, 225, 244; beginning of, 231, 238–39, 248, 249, 251

Wright, Esmond, 19

XYZ Affair, 53–56

Yale University-in-China, 226
Yellow journalism, 194, 201–2, 240
Yihequan (society), 211
Yorktown, battle of, 5, 20
Yorktown (ship), 181

Young, Marilyn Blatt, 211–12
Young America Movement, 127
Young Men's Christian Association (YMCA), 226
Ypiranga (ship), 236
Yüan Shihkai, 242

Zanzibar, 175, 176
Zimmermann Telegram, 238